Armies and Insurgencies
in the Arab Spring

ARMIES AND INSURGENCIES IN THE ARAB SPRING

Edited by
Holger Albrecht, Aurel Croissant,
and Fred H. Lawson

UNIVERSITY OF PENNSYLVANIA PRESS

PHILADELPHIA

Published by
University of Pennsylvania Press
Philadelphia, Pennsylvania 19104-4112
www.upenn.edu/pennpress

Printed in the United States of America on acid-free paper
10 9 8 7 6 5 4 3 2

Library of Congress Cataloging-in-Publication Data
ISBN 978-0-8122-4854-8

CONTENTS

Armies and Insurgencies
in the Arab Spring

Military Engagement in Mobilizing Societies: The Research Agenda

Holger Albrecht, Aurel Croissant, and Fred H. Lawson

Politics in any society involves the management of coercive power. Therefore, the interactions between the armed forces and other actors, organizations, and institutions of the political system have important consequences for the stability and survival of all forms of political regimes (Croissant and Kuehn 2015). In authoritarian regimes, the "civil-military problematique" (Feaver 1996) is particularly pertinent: autocracies tend to maintain a much larger coercive apparatus than democracies do, of which the military is the largest and most powerful. While most dictators rely on the police and specialized internal security agencies for everyday repression, the military is the final guarantor of regime security against vertical threats that arise from the citizenry (Svolik 2012). However, a strong military is a double-edged sword for authoritarian leaders. A more powerful military is more effective in repressing political conflicts between the ruling elite and the masses but at the same time may create threats to regime survival that emerge from within the regime coalition, as is demonstrated by the high frequency of coups in autocratic regimes (Frantz and Ezrow 2011; Croissant 2013a). Moreover, a strong military is in a better position to demand substantial political and economic concessions in exchange for its role in maintaining the regime (Acemoglu and Robinson 2006:219; Bhave and Kingston 2010).

Therefore, no authoritarian government can hold on to the reins of power without the expressed consent of military leaders. This is especially

evident in times of political contention, when opposition mobilizes against
the authorities (Skocpol 1979; Chenoweth and Stephan 2011). Whether the
military chooses to stand firm and protect the established order or instead
opts to defect and take sides with the opposition attracted the interest of
observers of politics in the Middle East and North Africa (MENA) from the
moment large-scale insurgencies broke out across the region in the winter
of 2010–2011.

Middle East studies and political science were ill-equipped to analyze the
Arab militaries' role in these events. Over the past two decades, scholarship
on the "new authoritarianism" (King 2009) had paid relatively little systematic attention to the armed forces in the region. In fact, as a consequence of
the decreasing number of direct military regimes and military coups d'état in
the Arab world since the late 1970s, scholarship on governance in the MENA
had focused mostly on trends in the local political economy and the reemergence of nominally democratic institutions, such as elections, political parties, and legislatures (Lust-Okar 2005; Brownlee 2007; Blaydes 2010). Even
though the new scholarship on Arab authoritarianism did not (at least, not
explicitly) argue that armed forces and security apparatuses played no role as
custodians of the authoritarian order, with few exceptions (Cook 2007; Barak
and David 2010) researchers had lost interest in the military.

And there were good intuitive grounds for looking beyond the armed
forces in order to explain politics in Middle Eastern countries. Authoritarian
regimes in the MENA region consolidated their power while escaping coup
cascades—the rapid sequences of military intervention that had characterized politics across the region in previous decades—and military juntas were
steadily supplanted by civilian institutions, including presidents in civilian
clothing, formal constitutions, well-articulated bureaucratic apparatuses, and
electoral politics at the local and national levels. Furthermore, since the early
1980s, in a number of countries the increasing economic and developmental
activities of officers and military apparatuses appeared to demonstrate that
officers could be convinced to keep themselves busy making money rather
than engaging in politics.

With the onset of the popular insurgencies that came to be known as the
Arab Spring, the premise that militaries had returned to the barracks was put
in question, as it became clear from the outset of the revolts that the armed
forces and internal security services would play a decisive part in determining
the course and outcome of events (Barany 2011; Bellin 2012; Croissant 2013b;
Droz-Vincent 2014a; Albrecht 2015). The politics of transition precipitated

by these rebellions soon presented scholars with an analytical laboratory of sorts in which to study the most important puzzle of civil-military relations— the question of loyalty versus insubordination.

The events of 2010–2011 have triggered a renaissance of scholarship on political-military relations in the MENA region. The first wave of academic literature consists of studies that are more descriptive than explanatory in nature (Lutterbeck 2013; Nepstad 2013; Makara 2013), and the analytical problem is compounded by the small number of empirical cases at our disposal, which exhibit sharply divergent characteristics. It is nevertheless clear that initial attempts to account for recent events fail to provide convincing answers to the most important analytical questions:

- How and why do military apparatuses actively intervene in politics, especially under conditions of mobilized opposition against authoritarian leadership?
- What explains the fact that in some countries during a regime crisis triggered by mass mobilization, military officers and organizations take steps to defend the incumbent, whereas in other countries they defect and refrain from suppressing popular protest?
- Which units or individuals within a military apparatus remain loyal to embattled incumbents, and which ones do not?
- Are the most significant institutional legacies of the military's engagement during mass uprisings, since almost all MENA armies captured a more active and visible position in political affairs in the immediate aftermath of the uprisings?

While research into the causes of coups d'état was primarily driven by large-N analyses—using global data or focusing on African politics (Roessler 2011; Powell 2012b; Singh 2014)—scholarship on military sociology and the internal dynamics of political-military relations in authoritarian regimes has long been dominated by single-country case studies, along with the occasional small-N comparative analysis, and has concentrated primarily on examples drawn from Latin America (Stepan 1971; Rouquie 1987; Remmer 1985; Arceneaux 2001). Systematic, cross-regional comparisons of political-military relations are especially rare, and the experience of Middle Eastern countries with regard to the political role of the armed forces is conspicuously absent from the broader literature in political science (Kuehn and Lorenz 2011; Pion-Berlin 2011).

Moreover, existing theories concerning the politics of the armed forces pay relatively little systematic attention to the response of the military and security apparatuses to mass protest. Structuralist explanations can account for the broad propensity of militaries to stage coups d'état (Croissant et al. 2011, 2013) but fail to adequately explain the military's involvement in particular popular uprisings (Pion-Berlin and Trinkunas 2010). Agency-centered approaches fare no better. While Barbara Geddes's explanation for why militaries decide to return to the barracks during regime crises in terms of military officers' rational perceptions of institutional and personal interest is admirably parsimonious, Terence Lee (2009) offers a game-theoretical model that posits that fissures inside the armed forces constitute the decisive factor in explaining military intervention. Lee's major hypothesis—that militaries accept regime change whenever they are confronted by a significant degree of internal conflict—is brought into question, however, by the cases of Tunisia and Egypt, where relatively unified and homogeneous militaries ended up turning against their respective political leadership.

In light of fundamental shortcomings in the existing literature, this volume contributes to our understanding of the politics of the armed forces in authoritarian regimes in the MENA region and beyond in three distinct ways. The chapters offer empirically rich reappraisals of the political role of military establishments in a broad range of MENA cases, shed new light on the part that the armed forces played in determining the course and outcome of the insurgencies that have swept across the region beginning in 2010–2011, and explicitly aim to advance theoretical propositions that can account for the corporate behavior of the military before, during, and after large-scale popular uprisings not only in the MENA but in other regions of the world as well. The editors and authors hope that the eleven substantive chapters collected in this book will contribute to a better understanding of the peculiar history of military engagement that one sees in the Arab Spring and also explain significant aspects of the transformation of political-military relations in other regions of the contemporary world.

Early versions of the papers in this volume were presented at a workshop in Heidelberg in November 2013, sponsored by the Fritz Thyssen Stiftung, Cologne, Germany. The editors are most grateful for the Fritz Thyssen Stiftung's generous financial support for the workshop and manuscript preparation.

PART I

Military Politics
and Regime Dynamics

CHAPTER 1

Military Relations in Comparative Perspective

David Pion-Berlin

As a thoroughly captivated international audience watched hundreds of thousands of Egyptians pouring into Tahrir Square in January and February 2011 demanding the ouster of longtime dictator Hosni Mubarak, the event was also significant for those outside the spotlight: soldiers. While some tanks were visible, parked along the edges of the square, not a single shot was fired by the Egyptian armed forces in order to put an end to the uprising. Egypt was not unique. In Tunisia, soldiers also refused to rescue President Zine El Abidine Ben Ali's regime in the face of massive civilian protests. And the Arab Spring itself is not the exception. Militaries from Asia, Eastern Europe, the former Soviet Union (FSU) republics, and Latin America have remained garrisoned (or quartered, confined to their barracks) or sidelined, refusing to follow presidential orders to suppress civilian uprisings. This was evident during the People Power Revolution in the Philippines in 1986, the Indonesian uprising that toppled longtime military president General Suharto (1998), the "Color Revolutions" in the first decade of the twenty-first century, and the constitutional crises witnessed in several countries of Latin America during the same period.

These forms of military disobedience are not common, but neither are they unique to a specific region, regime, or political culture. They occur most frequently during moments of upheaval, when civilian opposition forces decide that merely changing government policy is not enough, that what is required is a change in government—and at times the regime itself. Civilian opponents have taken to the streets in largely nonviolent acts of protest. If these uprisings reach a critical mass—when so many have joined that the movement seems irreversible and its political force unstoppable—they have the potential to bring down heads of state, governments, and regimes. While the principal protagonists in this drama are the civilian protesters themselves, the security agencies of state—and particularly the armed forces—play a critical role.

Unfortunately, the military has often escaped the notice of scholars who study social movements and political protests.[1] Movement attributes and state-centered political opportunity structures are the twin preoccupations in this literature. Scholars repeatedly fail to acknowledge that the military itself affords protest movements a huge opportunity, both by allowing demonstrations to unfold and by pulling the rug out from under detested political leaders. In every case where a president (and his government) has fallen from power as a consequence of a civilian uprising, the armed forces had refused his pleas for assistance by remaining quartered or on the sidelines. In each instance, police forces were overwhelmed and overrun by the sheer size and persistence of the demonstrations. They retreated, compelling presidents to call on their armed forces to quell the uprising, only to find them unwilling to do so. Military insubordination has helped to bring down authoritarian, hybrid, and democratic leaders and has done so in countries both with and without traditions of military intervention. Conversely, presidents have frequently survived the ordeal when armies chose to defend them.[2] The parallels are striking, despite the fact that these events occurred in such vastly different corners of the globe.

Why would these armies choose to defy civilian orders to repress and instead remain quartered? Rather than search for region-specific or country-specific explanations, study should search for clues inside the military institution itself, examining motivations stemming from its strategic calculations and professional interests. Certainly, militaries differ by size, resources, political clout, doctrines, and customary roles. However, they all share some core attributes that could serve as a starting point for analysis. The military is goal oriented, weighing the costs and benefits of alternative courses of action in order to maximize its well-being. In the midst of crisis, it makes on-the-spot decisions based on calculations about the president's chances for survival versus the demonstrators' determination to bring him down. It wants to bet on the winning side to secure its own position in the future.

Yet the military is not a disinterested bystander wagering on one side or the other. It is a formidable actor whose decisions alter the course of events that unfold in crisis. Those decisions are also guided by core institutional interests that predate the crisis period. The military's view of the regime will be shaded by its treatment at the hands of political elites in the past. Staying garrisoned can be a means of registering displeasure over resources denied to it. Its view of the demonstrating public will be molded by its connectedness to them and whether coming to their defense is vital to its own professional reputation or whether attachments to the regime override sensitivities to public attitudes. Furthermore, militaries are comprised of individual soldiers who have career aspirations themselves. Officers want to avoid behaviors that could harm their careers by subjecting them to investigation or prosecution.

A brief review of regionally based scholarship suggests no convincing explanations for military defiance of orders to suppress mass civilian uprisings. To the contrary, widely accepted interpretations of civil-military relations in the former Soviet bloc, the Middle East, and Latin America raise more questions instead of providing answers. That leads us to consider a more comparative approach, one that is centered on the military institution itself. By identifying motivational interests shared by all militaries, we can then assess to what extent military decisions to either obey or disobey orders to repress in each of the countries derive from a common set of concerns. Those concerns are twofold. The first refers to making strategic decisions in the midst of crisis that will allow the military to emerge relatively unscathed. The second amounts to institutional motivators for behavior that predate the crisis and revolve around core institutional needs that include organizational survival, protection of material well-being, and enhancement of reputations and avoidance of risks to career advancement. If these motivators can be identified in each of the cases under review, we will have a basis for making more general observations about military dissent that cut across countries and regions. This means that in contrast to the approach chosen by Croissant and Selge in their contribution to this volume, this chapter excludes so-called coup-proofing strategies employed by governments in order to protect their rule against the threat of a military coup d'état.

Regional Realities and Unexpected Military Defiance

The common complaint about comparing cross regionally is that contexts are so unique that they must shape political outcomes in ways that are not comparable or that merely accentuate the differences. If, in fact, comparisons between for example Latin America and the Middle East only result in affirmations about how results differ greatly due to contextual contrasts, then what is the added value of the exercise?

It would be tempting to fall back on idiosyncratic accounts that hinge on the peculiarities of each context to derive a "Middle Eastern" or "Latin American" or "East European" explanation for each set of cases here and settle with that. For example, one could easily see that the Middle East and the FSU, in contrast to Latin America, are two regions practically devoid of a democratic past. Strong traditions of autocratic, sultanistic, and monarchical rule in the Middle East and a long history of Soviet party-styled domination in the FSU followed by electoral authoritarian regimes in the postcommunist era might suggest that the dynamic between the regime, the military, and the protesters would be sizably different from that in Latin America.[3] We might hypothesize that political leaders in the first two regions would have an easier time demanding compliance from their armed forces because of traditions of obedience to authoritarian leaders (more so in the FSU, less so in parts of the Middle East). Second, since authoritarian regimes are less accountable to the public, they should be able to resort to coercion against civilian protesters more easily than democratic regimes. Without established democratic cultures, laws, and norms in the Middle East and the FSU, we would expect there to be fewer restraints on the use of force against unarmed protesters, and military repression should be a first resort. Generally speaking, authoritarian regimes *are* less restrained in their ability to use force, and when force is unleashed on unarmed protesters, as it was against the Egyptian Muslim Brotherhood in 2013, the scale of repression can easily surpass what is observable in democratic countries. This depends, however, on those autocratic regimes having the full cooperation of their armed forces—something that cannot be taken for granted.

The fact is that regional differences pose comparable puzzles more than they expose suitable explanations. Military dissent does not make sense if we consider some of the regional and country-specific traits we know to be true. East European and FSU republics had long legacies of military compliance with the power holder. Scholars concur that the communist parties held enormous power over their militaries, even as they disagreed about how that influence was to be wielded.[4] A particularly persuasive theory centers on organizational culture perspectives, suggesting that military allegiances to the Communist Party had become deeply ingrained and that those allegiances would be transferred to the new political authorities in the postcommunist era. This is because of a deeply embedded belief that it is not for soldiers to question the commands of legitimate governments—regardless of their ideology or the nature of the party in power.[5]

Whether forced on them or ingrained in their beliefs, soldiers grew accustomed to falling in line with the political authorities over the course of several decades. All of these explanations predict—albeit for different reasons—the military compliance with civilian rule in the postcommunist era in Russia, Eastern Europe, and the FSU states. Ukraine, as a former Soviet state, certainly inherited the traditions of unflinching military subordination to civilian control. An absence of any real military autonomy meant that even after the transition to postcommunist rule, this military did not have the requisite authority to challenge the policies it disagreed with and tended to transfer allegiance to the new rulers. In turn, that mentality should have inhibited the military from defying orders to repress during the Orange Revolution in 2004. The same could be said for the Georgian Rose Revolution the year before and the Serbian Bulldozer Revolution of 2000. But defiance is exactly what these militaries practiced, as they allowed mass protests to triumph against sitting presidents. Why?

The Middle East featured what Eva Bellin (2004) described as robust authoritarian regimes. While other regions were experiencing democratic transitions, or at the very least departures from authoritarian rule, the Middle East seemed relatively immune to such changes—that is, up until the Arab Spring. Scholarship suggested that militaries would choose to defend autocratic regimes against civilian uprisings where they are organized along patrimonial lines. This refers to a military in which career advances are dictated by cronyism rather than merit and where ascriptive ties to regime leaders, based on ethnic, religious, tribal, or familial bonds, are powerful enough to override other imperatives, including defense of the nation and its people (Barany 2011; Bellin 2012; Lutterbeck 2013). Regime survival is of critical importance for the armed forces, not only because soldiers have strong ties to political leaders but because of the material benefits that have accrued to them and the sizable material loss should the regime fall into the wrong hands. Others allege that the armed forces conspire with political officeholders to design systems that are stable and have the veneer of democratic pluralism but are deeply authoritarian. Militaries dominate these systems without governing on a day-to-day basis (Cook 2007). Others contend that the military has been politically marginalized from the centers of governance but cooperate with the regime nonetheless so long as its economic interests are protected.[6]

These views about military support for entrenched authoritarianism are long held, and the surprise with which the Arab Spring struck Middle East scholars as well as many other scholars working on other parts of the world is proof enough that durable autocratic rule was the conventional wisdom. Why, then, did militaries refuse to come to the aid of besieged autocratic leaders in Tunisia and Egypt? Why, in particular, would the Egyptian military abandon Mubarak if it had been the beneficiary of an extensive and elaborate system of patronage and profit-making schemes? The members of the military became huge landowners, had overseen state-owned holding companies, and had won controlling shares in public-private ventures, benefits that expanded greatly under Mubarak (1981–2011) (Harb 2003). They should have been content, willing to stand shoulder to shoulder with their president until the bitter end.[7] Why didn't they?

Latin America did have a long history of military praetorianism beginning in the 1930s. The coup d'état was a familiar political event in that region, and few elected governments could serve out their full terms over the course of decades, having fallen prey to military intervention (Lowenthal and Fitch 1986; Loveman 1999). Armies were motivated to unseat political leaders by security concerns, ideologies, class alliances, and professional norms. By contrast, it was uncommon for the military to sit out political conflicts between civilian protesters and regimes by remaining confined to the barracks. Having become political, officers were much more prone to enter the fray either by arbitrating disputes or putting an end to them entirely by seizing power and silencing all those parties and organizations responsible for the conflicts.

However, with the end of the Cold War, the defeat of revolutionary insurgents, and the transitions to democratic rule in the last three decades, the political landscape there has changed dramatically. Significant gains have been made both in progress toward democratic consolidation and civilian control after decades of praetorian intervention. The United States has withdrawn its support for dictatorship, and regional organizations are committed to democratic endurance. Militaries do wield some political influence but mostly within official corridors (Pion-Berlin 1997). Latin American armies have harnessed their energies on behalf of their governments' domestic and foreign policy objectives: to aid in disaster relief and development projects at home and to join international peacekeeping operations abroad. One country that stands out in particular for having subordinated its armed forces to civilian control is Argentina. Why, then, did its military refuse the urgent pleas of the president in December 2001 to put down a civilian uprising and instead sat on the sidelines and watched as mass demonstrations brought down their commander in chief?

The Case for Cross-Regional, Cross-National Study

Neither the regional authoritarian legacies nor prior military support for regimes or former levels of civilian control will sufficiently account for military dissent from orders to repress in these regions. In fact, the Middle East and FSU countries could be considered least likely cases for military dissent, given how powerful the conditions there were to favor military subordination to or cooperation with incumbent leaders. Naturally, there are other effects that could be considered, and this brief treatment of regime characteristics cannot and should not discount the regional influence. But it does force us to search for other causes that may or may not be entirely unique to one region or another.

It is my view that an analysis focusing only on Middle Eastern, Latin American, or FSU explanations for military dissent is less than desirable. In the end, these accounts may be suitable for one or more locales but will not travel to other regions. As a result, we will never get to a more general account for military dissent that can cross over national and regional boundaries. A better approach is to begin with the military institution and the common core military attributes found nearly everywhere. There is a basic set of concerns shared by all militaries. If we take these into consideration, they give us a single menu of appropriate, comparable motivators from which we can choose. By establishing a baseline with which to evaluate military motives, one can analyze actual military conduct within and across these regions with core attributes in mind. Finally, we may gain some leverage in understanding why some armies supported their presidents while others refused to.

While institutional concerns should remain relatively constant, specific cost-benefit calculations and resulting courses of action will vary because military core interests are affected differently. Another way of putting it is that the dimensions are the same, but the values they take on differ. The advantage of pursuing the research this way is that we can tie all the cases together in a comparable framework. We ask the same set of questions of each, based on the same set of variables. The answers we get will differ, but they will fall out in predictable patterns. This approach makes the assumption that cross-national and cross-regional comparisons are doable, because militaries share common internal structures, institutional interests, and values. This does not mean, however, that militaries are identical; they are not. It simply means that they are sufficiently similar in some core dimensions to allow for meaningful comparisons. In addition, each of the militaries studied here was thrust into crisis scenarios that had very similar features. This further justifies comparative research, because those crisis conditions established comparable opportunities and constraints for the armed forces.

Common Endgame Scenarios and Case Selection

What is the comparable crisis scenario? These are countries that experienced massive civilian protests and presidential crises where the survival of a head of state was at stake. In all instances, presidents were met with sizable popular uprisings that took the form of organized street demonstrations that peaked at hundreds of thousands of civilians or more. Protesters were primarily nonviolent, with a few instances of violent resistance. These protests were mostly triggered by grievances over democratic irregularities and curtailments as well as economic difficulties.

A government's options quickly dwindled to a few because of a lack of negotiating skills, the presence of conciliatory predilections, and a hardening of positions on either side. Protesters escalated their demands, moving from pleas for reform to calls for the removal of those holding executive office or even for regime overthrow. In no instance did presidents make major strategic adjustments midstream in order to mollify the opposition, offering to redo elections, clean up corrupt practices, or announce significant new economic policies. Nearly all offered up last-minute concessions, but these were always too little and too late. Hence, what is under review here is a set of endgame scenarios where the negotiated options had disappeared and both sides were digging in their heels. The authorities desperately tried to cling to power by dispersing the crowds. Police either remained in the background or were called out but overwhelmed as the demonstrations swelled. Governments then fell back on military forces to subdue the uprisings.[8]

These cases can then be divided into two groups. In the first, labeled positive cases, militaries defied presidential orders to repress. In every instance, the result is the same: the president's exit from office and at times even the demise of the regime itself. The countries that we consider are Serbia (2000) during the Bulldozer Revolution, which toppled President Slobodan Milosevic; the Rose Revolution in Georgia (2003), which brought down Eduard Shevardnadze; the Orange Revolution in Ukraine (2004), which ended the government of Leonid Kuchma and defeated incumbent party candidate Viktor Yanukovych; the economically motivated riots and protests in Argentina

(2001), which threw President Fernando De la Rúa out of office; presidential corruption that fueled successful demonstrations against Ecuadorian president Lucio Gutiérrez (2005); and finally, the Arab Spring revolts in Tunisia (2010–2011) and Egypt (2011). In the second and smaller set of negative cases, militaries obeyed orders to repress the civilian uprising. These countries are Bolivia during the so-called gas protests of 2003, Iran's crackdown on the Green Revolution (2009), and Bahrain's Arab Spring repression (2011). Only in Bolivia did the president fail to survive in office. We also mention the Syrian case (2011–present), even though it does not conform to all of the endgame scenario requirements.

What Calculations Would Militaries Likely Make in the Midst of Crises?

Within the endgame scenario, there is a set of calculations that all militaries had to make concerning their assessment of the president's strength and legitimacy and how long he could reasonably hold on to the reins of power in the face of massive civilian resistance and what might befall the military in the postcrisis period.

Under normal circumstances, with principles of civilian control in mind, the military's decision would be a simple one: stay in the barracks if ordered and suppress dissent if mandated but do what the government demands. However, these are special circumstances where a military's professional well-being may be at great risk for blindly going along with a government that has lost its way. Additionally, a military under civilian control may be asked to conduct missions that have dreadful consequences for society. Hence, the military must question whether it is worth the risk of supporting a government if this entails being drawn into violent clashes with rebellious citizens, potentially causing a loss of life. Should it therefore stay above the political fray by remaining quartered and joining neither the government nor the opposition? Or should it remain loyal to the regime?

To answer these questions, the military calculates just how tenable the current government is. It has a keen interest in "betting on the right horse." If the military believes that the president will prevail, staying loyal will have its payoffs, though acts of repression will undoubtedly tarnish its reputation. If, on the other hand, it gambles on the current government and loses, it will be viewed as an agent of repression in the service of a discredited administration.

In that scenario, the new leaders will demand reprisals by, for example, reducing the defense budget, downsizing the forces, cashiering officers, or recommending prosecution for those complicit in state violence. If the military reasons that the government is on its last legs, it might want to wager its fortunes on the civilian opposition by letting events take their own course (i.e., remaining quartered). That way, it will have deflected criticism from a successor government that is ushered to power by the force of the opposition.

Nevertheless, no military contemplates insubordination lightly. The fact that military defiance of presidential orders is exceedingly uncommon is proof enough. Conditioned by principles of civilian control and mindful of the costs of cutting ties with the regime, military leaders will not make a decision to defy their commander in chief blatantly. They are bound to carefully gauge the president's power, support, and legitimacy before dissenting. They want to be sure not to underestimate the president's clout within the ruling coalition, the security services, and the public at large. Too hasty a dissent could leave military plotters in a weakened position should the president still retain formidable political allies who could defend him against his detractors. Where allies remain within the security services as well, they could trigger serious rifts within the military and even come to blows with the dissenting factions, placing in peril organizational cohesion.[9] Should a significant fraction of the public still be backing the president, a premature military move against him could cause intraregime feuds to widen into societal conflicts that would soon enough rebound to the military itself, with dreadful, divisive results.

To avoid all of these costs of defection, most militaries, most of the time, choose loyalty over disobedience. For those armies that do contemplate disobedience, it is in their interest to allow the president to "run out the string"—to have exhausted all his options before making the fateful decision to defect. It is easier for the security forces to defect from a weakened leader than from a strengthened one. Once protests expand geometrically in size, police appear to be overwhelmed, and presidents seem to be on their last legs, then militaries can better contemplate defiance of orders to repress.

At that juncture, it makes sense for the armed forces to wager their fortunes on the civilian opposition by remaining on the sidelines.[10] A military without crowd control training—forced to clash with throngs of unarmed citizens—would only spell disaster in the form of bloodshed on a massive scale that would haunt them later on. That is, by remaining confined to the barracks, soldiers avoided carrying out actions that could invite widespread

public scorn and eventually redound in the form of internal schisms, demo-
tions, and legal recriminations. Rather than being viewed as agents of repression in the service of a discredited administration, they may instead earn
themselves esteem from the next government and the public for having facilitated popular political change.[11]

What Institutional Interests Would Influence
the Military Calculations Made?

The president's survival in times of endgame crisis hinges on the military's
inclination whether to come to his defense or not. So, when the military
makes its wager, it is not a disinterested bystander but a chief protagonist.
Its decisions will alter the course of the public protests and ultimately seal
the president's fate. Militaries assess the entire situation based not just on the
chances of presidential survival but also on their core institutional interests.
These concerns predate the endgame scenario and center on key facets of the
profession. Samuel Finer (1988) wrote of dispositions to intervene to convey
the idea that the military must have the motive and will to act. Similarly,
a military predisposed to either defend the president and his regime or to
defect has to be properly motivated, driven by issues that are paramount to
the institution.[12] What are these issues?

The armed forces have common institutional imperatives. First and
foremost, they want to safeguard their institutional well-being, specifically
their survival, material interests, institutional reputation, and careerist aspirations.[13] Survival instincts dictate that they contain or eliminate forces in
their environment that pose threats of an existential nature. Materially, they
want to obtain sufficient budget shares for personnel, equipment, training,
and pensions—now and in the future—and guard against significant losses.
They care about their image; they want to salvage their standing with the
government, the public, and the nation as a whole. Finally, promoting careers
means that militaries wish to retain a system that rewards officers for their
service but also protects them from judicial reproach that could threaten
their careers.

These interests are paramount when contemplating strategic responses
to presidential commands in a context of mass civilian uprisings. Yet none
of these interests alone predicts what course of action the military will take.

That hinges on the particular circumstances surrounding the defense of those valued assets. In some cases survival is at risk, and in others it is not. Material resources may be plentiful in some countries and depleted in others. Reputations are earned in different ways, and careers may either be threatened or secured. Identifying those conditions is what helps us determine the military response. Each institutional dimension will be explained, followed by an account of its influence in specific countries. For each dimension, where possible, we illustrate positive cases where militaries refused orders, followed by negative cases, where militaries complied with them.

Organizational Survival

Militaries that face the gravest crises are those that believe their very survival may be at stake. Only a few militaries face this dreadful prospect, though many more move to a kind of survival mode or mentality when they are put on the defensive (Campbell 1998). The armed forces quickly adapt to a hostile environment by closing ranks and forging internal unity; they prepare for the worst. In a classic interstate war, the vanquished army may still live to see another day once a cease-fire is declared and the terms of surrender are spelled out. The kinds of conflict that are pertinent to this study are ones that take place within national borders, where the two sides have irreconcilable differences, and view each other as implacable foes. As citizens of the same nation-state, the military and its adversary have nowhere to go (except for mass exile). Nothing less than the dismantling of the vanquished party will suffice. Such views may arise out of religious, ethnic, or ideological convictions and antagonisms.

Survival instincts could steer the military in more than one direction. During the Cold War, armies in Latin America viewed themselves at war with the "communist menace," which in their eyes posed an existential threat. Having witnessed the complete destruction of President Fulgencio Batista's armed forces in Cuba at the hands of Fidel Castro's revolutionaries in 1959, militaries from that point forward understood the gravity of the threat. Should, in their view, elected regimes demonstrate an inability to effectively encourage communism, the militaries in the region did not hesitate to overturn those governments and assume power for themselves. In the Middle Eastern cases under review here, survival instinct dictated a different course of action: a fierce defense of the regime in power.

Positive Case Exemplars

None of the militaries that chose to refuse orders to repress faced existential crises. In Egypt, Tunisia, Serbia, the Ukraine, Georgia, Argentina, and Ecuador, dissenting militaries would have survived, regardless of what choice they had made. Nonetheless, they had to contemplate professional concerns of other sorts, which will be discussed below.

Negative Case Exemplars: Bahrain and Syria

Organizational survival may apply in Bahrain (for more detail, see Ohl in this volume). The Bahraini military was closely aligned with the Al-Khalifa regime, which always had been due to the demographics of the country. The military followed orders from the regime because of its shared Sunni identity in a country whose Islamic population is 66–70 percent Shiite (Barany 2011). There is an "us against them" mentality that manifested itself in the bloody crackdown of protesters in 2011 and before that during the mid-1990s, when the Bahrain Defense Forces (BDF) was actively involved in the killing of protestors (Waldman 1995). The separation between these religious groups is reinforced by the fact that the military is nonconscripted. Maintaining itself as an all-volunteer force is another means to prevent Shiite insertion into and eventual domination of the military (Barany 2011:35).

In Syria, attachments to the Bashar al-Assad regime are forged out of fierce instincts for survival. Like the Assad family itself, officers from the Republican Guard and the Fourth Armored Division, responsible for most of the repression, are predominantly Alawites, a small minority (11 percent) Shiite faction that rules over a mostly Sunni society. To concede to the protesters would be, in their eyes, to set the stage for unyielding reprisals against all Alawites (Jamestown Foundation 2011). In addition to that, bloodlines forge tremendous unity as well, since close members of the Assad family have key positions of leadership in the military and intelligence services (Kandil 2012; Droz-Vincent in this volume). Defeat in this civil war, or betrayal of the regime, would mean collective suicide for the Alawites and for the president's family. One important caveat should be made: Syria is something of an outlier, because it violates one condition of inclusion on our commonest of cases, that the opposition to the regime must be mostly nonviolent. This was true during approximately the first three months of the uprising, but not thereafter, when the repression-protest dynamic transformed into a bloody civil war, pitting several well-armed adversaries against each other and exhibiting devastating consequences for the society, the economy, and the military itself (Droz-Vincent in this volume).

Military Material Interests

Material interests are central to military organizations (Abrahammson 1972; Nordlinger 1977; Finer 1988). Soldiers are protective of their budgets, wanting to ensure an adequate flow of resources to enhance salaries, pensions, training regiments, equipment, procurement, and repairs. Where soldiers are well taken care of, gratitude is often expressed in terms of greater support for the authorities, which in turn could transfer to a readiness to accept difficult assignments. Obviously, when military budget shares decline, this can be the source of disgruntlement. Losses in the defense share of the budget often translate into a decline in influence, prestige, and political clout. Losses may be absolute or relative in nature. A military is troubled by either real declines in salaries, hardware, and living conditions or by a loss of position vis-à-vis other organized interests or its former self. Militaries that are denied resources can grow increasingly frustrated and disenchanted with the regime. Studies have also shown that soldiers who are deprived of resources suffer morale problems, which can lead to indiscipline (Mantle 2006). It is unlikely, however, that any incremental decrease in military budgets would *precipitate* so drastic a decision as to refuse presidential orders quartered in the face of orders to repress. It is more likely that a steady accumulation of pent-up grievances could *predispose* the military to be less than cooperative in the face of an onerous mission. A sudden, significant change in material fortunes could have the same effect.

Positive Case Exemplar: Ukraine

Economic hardship plagued the Ukrainian services practically from the outset.[14] A year after independence from the Soviet Union, Ukraine's defense budget could meet only 34 percent of its forces' financial needs; by 1995, it was down to 17 percent. Some 73,000 officers had no housing, and there was practically no money for spare parts or fuel. As a result, maintenance could not be performed on military vehicles and armaments, and air force pilots could not log even a minimum number of flight hours necessary for basic training. By 1999 things had gotten worse, and the decline persisted until 2004, the year of the Orange Revolution. In Ukraine, budget cuts were so severe that overall combat readiness of the military was in serious peril, and morale was at an all-time low.[15] The economic despair within the military turned into defiance, as 80 percent of families supported their children's decision to evade service. Demoralization also led to a deepening distrust of political leaders and an expressed willingness among some to take "extreme measures" (including physical attacks on high-ranking officers) if social problems (housing, diet, living standards) were not addressed (Kuzio 1995; Copsey 2010). The plight of these soldiers allowed them to more readily identify with ordinary citizens who were also living under difficult economic circumstances. It stands to reason that when ordered to assault those very citizens, disgruntled troops might question their loyalty to those in power.

Other Positive Cases

In nearly all the cases of military dissent reviewed, material conditions (budgets, salaries, housing, equipment, and training) were poor, had deteriorated in the lead-up to the crises, or had placed militaries in a relative disadvantage. Soldiers complained about the downsizing of military units and facilities without adequate structural adjustments to compensate for the losses (Argentina). Others reluctantly took on secondary employment to supplement inadequate salaries (Georgia). There were persistent complaints about food, clothing, living conditions, the state of disrepair of equipment, and lack of funds for territorial defense (Argentina, Georgia, and Ecuador). In Ecuador, grievances about insufficient funds for border defense were common (Jaskoski 2012). Enormous sustained budget reductions in the fifteen years preceding the constitutional crisis in Argentina in 2001 prompted Defense Minister Ricardo Murphy to comment just a year before the crisis that if one compared the shrunken size of his nation's military in terms of the territory, budget, or gross domestic product (GDP), the military had become the smallest in the world (*La Nación* 2000). Almost half of the units, command centers, and administrative services in that nation's army had been scrapped.

In Tunisia, President Ben Ali's family amassed a fortune, as did his cronies who were tied into a lucrative, corrupt patronage network. But the armed forces—while not "apolitical"—were entirely excluded from this network (Brooks in this volume). In other countries, relative losses were sometimes as compelling as absolute losses (Binnendijk and Marovic 2006). For instance, in Serbia, soldiers took umbrage over the fact that the regime had increasingly invested in internal police forces to their detriment. And in Egypt, many officers have benefited from military ownership of agricultural real estate and a wide range of industries (Springborg in this volume; Harb 2003). At the same time, officers resented more recent efforts by Mubarak's son Gamal to build patronage networks in which midlevel officers were increasingly replaced by businessmen (Kandil 2012; Springborg 1989). Here, Egyptian officers compared their present fortunes to those in the past.

Negative Case Exemplars: Iran and Bahrain

Material conditions were excellent and had improved over time in those countries where armies professed loyalty to the regime. In Iran, the Iranian Republican Guard Corps (IRGC) controls a huge military industrial complex, with ties to over a hundred companies that bring in an estimated annual revenue of more than US$12 billion (*Economist* 2009). Expansion took off in the late 1990s, with the Ahmadinejad presidency offering the IRGC no-bid contracts in oil, natural gas extraction, and infrastructure development (Rand Corporation 2009:56). The IRGC became the state's principal business partner, with one of its affiliated companies alone having been awarded 750 contracts through the Ministry of Oil, Transport, and Energy to construct dams, highways, tunnels, and water supply systems (Rand Corporation 2009:60). The IRGC is now the sole contractor for the nation's gas industry. Profits from all of these ventures are used to finance military activities, while soldiers and their families have economic privileges not awarded to other Iranians, including university admission and subsidized commodities (*New York Times* 2009a).

The material resources available to the Bahraini military are substantial and have been for some time. The military receives good pay, the latest training, and weapons. Military expenditures as a percent of GDP placed Bahrain nineteenth in the world as of 2012, and the country receives the latest in training and weapons with help from the United States and the Gulf Cooperation Council (Central Intelligence Agency 2013). Furthermore, there is another material interest at work in this case. An increasing number of Bahraini troops are recruited from abroad where unemployment levels are high (see Ohl in this volume). The Al-Khalifa government posted advertisements in Pakistani newspapers to enlist soldiers from that country into its antiriot units. Some foreign recruits have been granted Bahraini citizenship as a reward. But whether they are rewarded with it or not, all foreign troops depend on the BDF for employment and have a material incentive to fully comply with the authorities or risk being sent home (International Crisis Group 2011b).

Reputation

Militaries are normally concerned with their image. How are they viewed by the government, the public at large, regionally, and internationally?[16] A tarnished reputation can reflect on the detriment of the organization, bruising its self-image and confidence, and lead to dissatisfaction and dissension within the ranks. An enhanced reputation could translate into greater self-esteem, professional pride, organizational cohesion, and political influence. Reputations can be earned in numerous ways: through revolutionary heroics during struggles for independence, mission performance in war, civic action projects, rescue operations during national emergencies, etc.

Not all militaries are equally sensitive to the same reference groups or to the same criteria. Some are tightly moored to the political authorities, having come to believe that the regime is the embodiment of national interest, revolutionary ambitions, or public will. If this is the case, then military behavior is singularly oriented toward satisfying the goals set out by the regime, and its self-image is tethered to the regime's assessment of its performance. Reputation springs from loyalty, and fulfilling an order to repress could be legitimizing for a military whose fate is intertwined with the political ruling elite. This is in contrast to armies that may associate more directly with public aspirations that are in conflict with regime goals. Convinced that leaders have lost touch with the public, harmed national interest, and lost a strong measure of credibility, some militaries will legitimate themselves as trusted public servants by distancing themselves from the regime and refusing orders to repress. Their reputations would rest on avoiding harm to the protesters and emerging from the crisis as public heroes who stood up against a discredited regime. When there are greater personal connections between civilians and those enlisted across a broad swath of society, then militaries may associate reputational enhancement with public endorsement (Feaver and Kohn 2001).[17]

Positive Case Exemplar: Egypt

Egyptians took to the streets on January 25, 2011, to protest peacefully against President Hosni Mubarak's thirty-year rule, calling for social justice, democracy, and an end to police brutality. Hundreds were killed or wounded by the regime's police forces, but a tipping point was reached when public fear turned into outrage, and the police were forced into retreat. President Mubarak had no recourse but to call on his armed forces to suppress the uprising and rescue his government. But the military would remain on the sidelines, refusing to come to his defense. And with that, Mubarak was forced to step down on February 11.

The Egyptian military staked its reputation on defense of popular sentiments. According to Article 180 of the Egyptian Constitution, the armed forces "owe their allegiance to the people." The Egyptian high command took that commitment seriously, stating on February of 2011: "To the great people of Egypt, your armed forces, acknowledging the legitimate rights of the people . . . have not and will not use force against the Egyptian people" (Doucet 2011). The armed forces remained on the sidelines, waiting until public opinion had turned overwhelmingly against Mubarak and the uprising had reached a kind of critical mass. Only then did they insist that the president leave office, confident that their actions would meet with enthusiastic popular support and that their reputations would be enhanced. They were proven correct (see Chams El-Dine in this volume).

This naturally raises the question as to why the military resorted to brute force to quell Muslim Brotherhood protests following the removal of President Muhammad Mursi on July 3, 2013 (Fleishman 2013). Ironically, the crackdown, which left hundreds dead, may have been motivated for the same reasons that caused the military to pull the rug out from under Mubarak. The military reacted with force only after vast portions of the public had turned against President Mursi and his government. The opposition had galvanized against a government that seemed intent on ruling autocratically via decree, suspending the authority of the courts while they pushed through an Islamic constitution. With no regard for democratic processes or inclusion, and having left the economy teetering on the verge of collapse, the Muslim Brotherhood had worn out its welcome. Public anger swelled as some 15 million Egyptians signed a petition calling for Mursi's resignation, followed by a demonstration at Tahrir Square on June 30, 2013, that appeared to have exceeded in scale the initial protest that brought down Mubarak.

The military could rationalize its coup and crackdown as a response to an overwhelming public sentiment for change. It is, of course, convenient for an army to do so, especially when it ignores other portions of the public. However self-serving and disingenuous their claims may have been, they sat well with the armed forces themselves, who said, "The military acts only with the will of the great Egyptian people and their ambitions towards change and reform" (Hauslohner 2013). No doubt, the armed forces were pleased by the public's affirmation of them and continued to stake their reputation on popular appeal. A poll conducted in January 2012, nearly a year after the military had taken over as the country's interim government, found that some 90 percent of Egyptians still had confidence in the military and its Supreme Council (Collard 2013). A year and a half later, following the attacks on the Muslim Brotherhood, a survey found that 93 percent of adults still had confidence in the Egyptian armed forces (Arab American Institute 2013). But with the military's more recent resort to heavy-handed tactics against all opponents, it remains to be seen whether this kind of popularity can be sustained.

Other Positive Cases

In Ukraine, the army and national intelligence forces made public statements that they were on the side of the people and would not take part in a violent crackdown. Some approached police, who were on the street awaiting orders to suppress the demonstrators, and said, "Don't forget you are called to serve the people" (York 2007). In Georgia, the military was troubled by the president's failure to meet the basic needs of average Georgians and could no longer support him (Darchiashvili 2005:145). In Ecuador, officers did not consider repression of unarmed citizens to be part of their mandate. To the contrary, there has been a long tradition of the military sympathizing with popular causes and indigenous groups, and even while in power, the armed forces earned a reputation for showing great tolerance toward the opposition.[18] In all of these cases, reputations hinged on earning public respect and, at the very least, not harming protesters.

Negative Case Exemplar: Iran

The IRGC is a professionalized force numbering 125,000, but it is also highly politicized by virtue of its insertion into the Islamic regime[19] and its role in defending the revolution against its internal "enemies." Article 150 of the constitution defines the IRGC as the "guardian of the revolution and its achievements."[20] Its very existence dates back to May 1979, just months after the revolution's triumph, when Ayatollah Khomeini ordered the creation of the IRGC, also known as the Pasradan, to battle counterrevolutionaries inside the country in defense of the new regime (Rand Corporation 2009). Along with its people's militia known as the Basij, the IRGC role has always been to protect the regime. Soldiers and officers were indoctrinated to support regime institutions to fulfill revolutionary goals. The IRGC and the Basij are specifically trained to avert "soft coups," meaning Western-inspired liberal revolts against a revolution similar to the colored revolutions in 2003–2005 (Rand Corporation 2009:47). IRGC officers were taught that defying the supreme leader was tantamount to defying the will of God. In fact, as commander in chief, the supreme leader wields direct authority over the IRGC, bypassing the president and Defense Ministry.

The reputation of the IRGC hinges on its effectiveness in silencing opponents to the Islamic regime. In fact in the early goings on, the IRGC competed with other groups to win the regime's approval via superior enforcement of the mullahs' edicts (Rand Corporation 2009:23). Ali Jafari, who took over command of the IRGC in September 2007, said that "The main mission of the IRG is to deal with the internal enemies" (*Christian Science Monitor* 2009). He added, "The Guards will firmly confront in a revolutionary manner rioters and all those who violate the law" (*New York Times* 2009b). He was true to his word. The IRGC and its paramilitary arm, the Basij, showed no hesitation in crushing the Green Revolution of June 2009. The opposition put the figure of those killed by security forces in the streets at 70, and upwards of 4,000 arrested in the postelection unrest. Hundreds of those were held incommunicado without charge, and 112 of those were executed in July and August of the same year (Amnesty International 2009a:10–11).

Careerism

The pursuit of individual career ambition is part and parcel of the military (Moskos and Wood 1988).[21] Officers contemplate what must be done to advance their careers within the military profession and avoid behaviors that could jeopardize their promotions. While most studies of careerism focus on inside conditions, ranging from performance metrics to pay and benefits to work conditions,[22] another aspect focuses on the external dimension. Threats to career advancement could arise from actions taken against soldiers outside of the military organization itself (Pion-Berlin and Trinkunas 2010). Where repression of mass protests would result in considerable bloodshed, an assessment is made about the likelihood of recriminations in the future. Even if repression is successful in the short term and the holder of power survives, soldiers may worry about the future, when a new administration is in place with no loyalties to its predecessor and when families of those victimized are seeking justice. Those soldiers may find themselves as targets for prosecution in countries where civilian courts claim jurisdiction over human rights cases and where officers are not immunized by military tribunals or amnesties. When a soldier reasonably concludes that there is a chance he could be indicted and convicted for human rights crimes—a career-ending fate—he will be more reluctant to follow orders to repress.

Positive Case Exemplar: Argentina

Argentine president Fernando De la Rúa (1999–2001) was forced to step down only halfway through his term on December 20, 2001, amid widespread demonstrations, uncontrolled rioting, and looting. Protests were triggered by public wrath over the government's handling of an economic crisis, and the demonstrators' aim was nothing less than the removal of De la Rúa from office (La Nación 2001b). After the police failed to stem the uprising, the president requested the military's assistance, only to be rebuffed. Why was that the case?

Career jeopardy played an important role here. The military perceived the costs of repression to be unusually high. During the 1980s, Argentina had become the first Latin American country to successfully prosecute its own generals for human rights abuses committed during the Dirty War in the prior decade. Though trials were halted by the early 1990s through legislative annulments and presidential pardons, the fear that they could resume was genuine. Indeed, by 1998 cases involving the kidnapping of children of political prisoners held by the military regime had opened against the former junta leaders. By the summer of 2001, there were many new cases and indictments, with courts ordering the preventive arrests of dozens of military suspects (La Nación 2001a). If the military had resorted to force against unarmed civilians, there was a strong likelihood of bloodshed, since the army in particular was not trained in public order maintenance. Soldiers and their commanders could have been on the hook for injuries and fatalities, and their cases would have been sent to civilian courts for processing. The prospect of conviction and imprisonment for human rights abuses should have been sufficient to dissuade the military from chancing encounters with determined protesters.

Negative Case Exemplar: Bolivia

In Bolivia, tensions that had been simmering beneath the surface for some time broke into open conflict over how to best harness and control the country's vast reserves of natural gas and petroleum. In September 2003, protests occurred when the government announced plans to export unprocessed natural gas through Chilean ports. Aside from Bolivian aversions to dependence on the port facilities of its historic adversary, critics also argued that the nation would get the short end of the gas pipeline deal because it would receive less revenue for exporting unrefined gas. The president, Gonzalo Sánchez de Lozada, refused to reconsider his policy. Protests took the form of marches, demonstrations, strikes, and, most important, road blockades. Police and then military units responded violently, and when all was said and done, some eighty civilians had been killed and hundreds were wounded (*El Deber* 2015).

The risks to repression, let alone the use of deadly force, are fewer where the armed forces have gotten away with similar actions in the past and anticipate the same in the present. The Bolivian armed forces calculated that it was unlikely they would be prosecuted in civilian courts for human rights offenses. For decades, human rights cases involving officers had been handled by military tribunals that were notorious for dropping charges prematurely and closing files (Human Rights Watch 2003). If, per chance, a case were to wind its way to a civilian tribunal, the military had little to worry about. Civilian judges and prosecutors were weak, corrupt, and subject to political pressures. Political party elites with long-standing, informal relations with military commanders hindered the judicial process on the military's behalf by applying pressure to prosecutors who were appointed provisionally or by underfunding the attorney general's office charged with investigating these cases (Quintana 2004). The combination of military judicial strength and civilian weakness is telling. Between 1985 and 2003, three hundred deaths were reported from protests or social conflicts at the hands of security forces. Not one officer or soldier was ever convicted for these incidents (Human

Rights Watch 2003). Given that history, individual soldiers involved in repression during the fall of 2003 must have reasoned that the judicial risks of following orders to repress were low.

Other Negative Cases

In Bahrain repression had become customary, and soldiers were immune from prosecution. Throughout the protests of the mid-1990s, the BDF was actively involved in repression, including in the killing of protestors (Waldman 1995). To address the growing internal violence, the Bahrain National Guard was created and integrated into the regular armed forces. Bahraini security personnel and military personnel were effectively pardoned under Decree Law No. 56 (2002), issued by King Hamad, for human rights violations during the protests of the mid-1990s (Bassiouni et al. 2011). That decree was in force when the military violently cracked down on protests in 2011.

Conclusion

The findings are summarized in Table 1.1. Check marks indicate the presence of a dimension that has been substantiated. Empty cells indicate that information has not as yet been gathered for those countries.

The author is fairly confident that when found, the data will substantiate the relevance of those dimensions for many of the remaining countries.

Across vastly different regions, nations, and regime types, seven militaries chose to defy the political orders to suppress nonviolent civilian uprisings. Authoritarian leaders from the Middle East lost control over their militaries as easily as did democratic leaders from Latin America. Those who presided over hybrid competitive-authoritarian regimes in Eastern Europe and the FSU fared no better. Four other militaries complied with orders, and they too came from different regions and societies, ruled by different kinds of regimes. Whether they disobeyed or obeyed orders, all of the militaries under review here appear to have been motivated by institutional self-preservation and well-being. They, like so many militaries, covet resources and react defensively to their loss, have the desire to preserve their reputational standing, and worry about career advancement. In a few cases, the organization's very survival seemed to be at stake, which naturally took precedence over other concerns.

Table 1.1. Military Core Interests and Cases

	Survival	Material Interests	Reputation	Career Issues
Military Dissent Cases				
Ukraine	n/a	√	√	
Georgia	n/a	√	√	
Serbia	n/a	√		
Argentina	n/a	√	√	√
Ecuador	n/a	√	√	
Egypt	n/a	√	√	
Tunisia	n/a	√		
Military Compliance Cases				
Bahrain	√	√		√
Iran	√	√	√	
Bolivia	n/a	√		√
Syria	√			

Which of the two courses of action they chose (disobey or obey) depended on whether and how those institutional assets were secured. Material declines drove one group of militaries to dissent, while material enrichment drove the other group to comply. Where militaries tied their reputations to standing with the public, they refused to crack down on demonstrators; where reputations hinged on regime approval, they came to the defense of besieged leaders. Finally, where careers could have been jeopardized by legal recriminations, soldiers preferred to avoid confrontation and instead remain in the barracks. Where soldiers were effectively immunized from prosecution, they could repress without fear of consequences.

What the study indicates is that contextual differences notwithstanding, cases of military dissent are comparable, as are cases of military compliance. The Arab Spring is not unique; it can be put into a larger set of parameters that are defined by the dynamic interactions between oppositions, regimes, and armies. When confrontations between political elites and masses descend into zero-sum endgame scenarios, militaries take center stage, making decisions—driven by common institutional needs—that are pivotal to the fate of either side of the conflict. The decisions made by the Egyptian military in February 2011 are comparable to those made in Tunisia, Argentina, and Ukraine.

This is not to suggest that the cases are identical; far from it. Each country has its own narrative, a complex sequence of events that predate and postdate the crises. Those narratives are shaped by distinct historical trajectories, actors, and interactions. The benefit of doing cross-national, cross-regional work is that we can pull some common threads from those narratives and begin to see broader patterns of behavior, which then make identification of common causes possible.[23]

Notes

1. Fortunately, this trend is beginning to turn around with recent publications on the Arab Spring, such as this volume. However, see also Barany (2011), Bellin (2012), Lutterbeck (2013), and, for a treatment of military defection or loyalty during episodes of civic resistance, Lee (2015) as well as Croissant and Selge in this volume.

2. This was so in China (1989), Iran (2009), and Bahrain (2011).

3. For conceptual and empirical research on electoral authoritarianism and the differences between competitive and hegemonic variants of such regimes, see Levitsky and Way (2010) and Schedler (2006, 2013).

4. Three of the top scholars on civil-military relations in the Soviet Union agreed that the military had been subordinate but disagreed on the causes of that subordination. See Kolkowicz (1967), Colton (1979), and Odom (1998).

5. An example of insightful scholarship on the organizational and cultural roots of compliance can be found in Taylor (2003).

6. Imad Harb (2003:270) says that the Egyptian military withdrew from participation in politics under President Anwar al-Sadat, and "since the 1980s, this non-participation has led to the military's complete subordination to the civilianized authority of President Hosni Mubarak." Kandil (2012) argues that the military had become politically marginalized even before Mubarak stepped in. See also Bellin (2004).

7. According to Robert Springborg (1989:95), there were strong material incentives for officers to be loyal to the regime (i.e., the various businesses owned by the Egyptian military). See also Mullins (2011).

8. This understanding, developed in Pion-Berlin and Trinkunas (2010) and in Pion-Berlin, Grisham, and Esparza (2014), is broader than, for instance, the concept of "dictator's endgame" that Croissant and Selge present in their contribution to this volume. The most important difference is that our definition includes episodes of anti-incumbent contention in democracies as well as in authoritarian regimes.

9. On the importance of organizational cohesion to the military, see Lee (2015). For a critical discussion of conceptual and measurement problems, see Ohl's contribution in this volume.

10. Alternatively, the military could take the more perilous path of rebellion, defying the regime by siding with the civilian uprising. With rare exceptions, armies opt not to. Rebellion is a profoundly subversive act that contravenes the constitution and seeks

to overthrow the elected incumbent. It commonly induces ideological splits; divides conspirators, fence sitters, and loyalists against each other; breaks the chain of command; and does great damage to the institution's integrity in the process.

11. For a similar argument, see Pion-Berlin and Trinkunas (2010).

12. This in turn presumes that all militaries are capable of making some separation—however small—between themselves and the regimes they serve. They must visualize themselves as organizations with their own set of needs as distinct from those of the political elites, where their interests may occasionally collide with those of the regime. Hence, they have some measure of autonomy from the regime. This seems reasonable when we consider that armies have demonstrated some independence of mind in the least likely places. For instance, in the lead-up to the Tiananmen Square massacre in China on June 4, 1989, there was ample evidence of widespread dissent within the military to the prospect of violently assaulting the prodemocracy demonstrators. This was especially true of units from the Beijing Military Region, within which some 110 officers and 1,400 soldiers actually refused Communist Party orders and led the regime to rely heavily on soldiers from outlying provinces to do the dirty work. If some measure of autonomous defiance can be expressed in the confines of a powerful Communist Party-dominated regime, then presumably it can be found elsewhere.

13. Maintaining organizational unity or cohesion is another central goal but one that is not explored in this study. On organizational cohesion, see Pion-Berlin, Grisham, and Esparza (2014).

14. On the military's economic problems, see Parchomenko (2000).

15. A sobering fact is that by 1996, half the suicides in Ukraine were occurring in the armed forces (D'Anieri, Kravchuk, and Kuzio 1999:246; Fesiak 2002:165).

16. The U.S. military is very concerned with its reputation and devotes hundreds of millions of dollars annually to touting its brand through advertisements, VIP tours, etc. (Belkin 2008). Militaries have engaged in peacekeeping operations as a means of overcoming tarnished reputations. This is true in the case of Argentina (Worboys 2007).

17. Conscription, in my view, is not the cause of military reluctance to repress. Historically, conscripted armies in Latin America showed little remorse in shooting political leftists. The Iranian Republican Guard Corps is largely conscripted, but it too was willing to use the harshest measures against its own citizens. Conversely, Argentina and Ecuador had volunteer forces, yet they refused to crack down on protesters. Reactions depend on how soldiers are indoctrinated, believing that they are either servants of the people first or servants of the regime.

18. Under Ecuadorian military rule, "human rights abuses were virtually non-existent" (Fitch 1998:72).

19. The IRGC is woven into the fabric of the Islamic regime. Many well-placed cabinet officials, heads of the Supreme National Security Council, dozens of parliamentarians, and a past president are or were at one time IRGC members.

20. Islamic Republic of Iran Constitution, http://www.iranonline.com/iran/iran -info/government/constitution-9-3.html.

21. When more career-minded officers enter the force, this can influence the entire military ethos, creating a divergence from average civilian values (Bachman and Blair 1975).

22. Discontent with employment, related to pay, service, or work conditions, can cause institutional disunity (Heinecken 2009).

23. This research model fits within what is well known as structured, focused comparative inquiries (see George and Bennett 2005).

CHAPTER 2

Officers and Regimes:
The Historical Origins of Political-Military
Relations in Middle Eastern Republics

Kevin Koehler

> It is not reasonable to assume that he who is armed
> should willingly obey him who is unarmed, or that the
> unarmed should be secure among armed servants.
> —Niccolò Machiavelli, *Il Principe*, Chapter 14

Had he written *Il Principe* in the early twenty-first century rather than the early sixteenth century, Machiavelli could have well given similar advice to authoritarian incumbents. Throughout the second half of the twentieth century, authoritarian leaders were more likely to lose office as a result of some form of military intervention than by any other type of exit (Goemans, Gleditsch, and Chiozza 2009). According to Milan Svolik's (2012) data on leadership change in authoritarian regimes, the armed forces were involved in ousting the incumbent leader in 82.5 percent of cases in which an authoritarian ruler lost power to elite competitors between 1945 and 2008. It is thus not surprising that authoritarian rulers feel the need to protect themselves against those who specialize in the application of violence.

While the challenge is universal, however, the strategies aimed at securing the loyalty of the military are not (Brooks 1998; Quinlivan 1999). In fact, although the military has played a central role in the foundation of almost all authoritarian republics in the Middle East and North Africa (MENA)—the exception being Tunisia—and although authoritarian consolidation and coup-proofing have successfully reduced the overt role of military officers in most cases, the MENA before the Arab Spring was still home to a variety of different forms of political-military relations.

This variation took center stage in scholarly debates following the Arab Spring. Several authors have argued that variation in political-military relations can explain the behavior of Middle Eastern militaries during the mass uprisings. Eva Bellin (2012:133), for example, argued that "patrimonial" political-military relations can account for military loyalty. Where military career patterns were characterized by favoritism and officers were "linked to regime elites through bonds of blood or sect or ethnicity," Bellin maintained, the armed forces were likely to remain loyal in the face of popular mass uprisings. Building on Bellin's analysis, Derek Lutterbeck (2013) has suggested that the relationship between the armed forces and society at large should be taken into account alongside the degree of patrimonialism. Where the armed forces have strong links with society, Lutterbeck suggested, defections might occur even if military organization is characterized by patrimonialism. Similarly, Michael Makara (2013) and Hicham Bou Nassif (2013) have differentiated between types of coup-proofing that have varying implications for the question of loyalty or defection during mass uprisings. There is thus strong evidence that political-military relations were crucial in shaping military behavior in the Arab Spring (Brownlee, Masoud, and Reynolds 2015).

Rather than adding yet another account of military behavior in the Arab Spring to this growing list, in this chapter I take a step back and ask why we see different forms of political-military relations in the first place. In particular, I focus on the question of why and how in some MENA republics a separation between the political and military elite segments of the regime coalition developed, while in others the two elite segments remained tightly intertwined.

Differences in the way in which political and military elites relate to each other in the MENA have not been in the center of scholarly attention thus far. Early studies focused primarily on structural determinants of military intervention and thus described the interventionist militaries of the region as the vanguard of the "new middle class" (Halpern 1963) or as products of praetorian societies (Perlmutter 1974). However, they paid little attention to variation in the relation between political and military elites that followed such interventions. Following an initial wave of studies on Arab militaries in the 1950s and 1960s, moreover, interest in the military in politics largely subsided. There were a number of works that endeavored to explain the demilitarization of politics in several Middle Eastern countries (Beeri 1982; Picard 1990); on the whole, however, it is fair to say that interest in the political role of the military in the Arab world diminished with the decreasing visibility of military actors. As Beeri (1982:74) remarks, "with the coups becoming less frequent and less spectacular and the performance of the ruling officers less brilliant, books about them became more sparse and theorizing about them more modest." A partial exception is the fact that the Middle East figured prominently in debates on coup-proofing even before the Arab Spring. Beyond the pioneering efforts of Risa Brooks (1998), James Quinlivan (1999), and Steven Cook (2007), however, systematic comparisons of and explanations for the different political roles of Arab militaries remained scarce.

Consequently, we have very little in the way of comparative typologies of political-military relations in the MENA. Mehran Kamrava's (2000) study attempts such a typology, but since his focus is on the Middle East as a whole—including not only the monarchies of the Persian Gulf region, Jordan, and Morocco but also the democracies of Israel and Turkey—his categories do not help us in identifying dimensions of variation in political-military relations among Middle Eastern republics. Indeed, Egypt, Syria, and Tunisia all fall into Kamrava's category of "*mukhabarat* states" despite the significant differences between these countries, which I will describe below.

This chapter offers a comparative historical perspective on the political role of the military in authoritarian Arab republics. The aim is to address the issue of variation in political-military relations from a systematic perspective. In particular, I focus on whether military elites are separated from or incorporated into the ruling coalition as a major dimension of variation. I develop a theoretical narrative that traces the form of political-military relations back to the role of the military in early conflicts surrounding regime foundation.

In developing this model, I draw on the experiences of Egypt, Syria, and Tunisia. This case selection is of course not random. Rather, I chose these three cases to represent a range of outcomes. Tunisia, to begin with, is an outlier among the authoritarian MENA republics in that the military did not play a major role in regime foundation. Since this is the case, Tunisian military officers were never incorporated into the regime coalition. This makes Tunisia a crucial case for my argument about the importance of regime foundation in laying the basis of political-military relations.

The Egyptian and Syrian regimes, on the other hand, both originated in military coups, the armed forces developed into powerful institutions, and military officers originally were central pillars of the ruling coalitions. At one point, however, the paths of the two countries started to diverge. While Egypt experienced a process of demilitarization of politics, in Syria no similar dynamic materialized. The result was that the Egyptian military elite developed a great deal of autonomy from the regime coalition, while Syrian military leaders remained tied to the regime.

The chapter proceeds as follows. In the next section, I briefly discuss the conceptual framework that will structure the comparison, focusing on the path-dependent nature of political-military relations and the dynamics of authoritarian consolidation and coup-proofing. The remainder of this chapter is devoted to a comparative historical analysis of the emergence and development of different forms of political-military relations in Egypt, Syria, and Tunisia. I first examine the period of regime foundation, explaining why the Tunisian military was rather inconsequential compared to its Egyptian and Syrian counterparts and how this shaped the fundamental contours of political-military relations. I then turn to a period of reform in political-military relations following the 1967 war against Israel that led to divergence between Egypt and Syria. The conclusion recapitulates the argument and argues that the historical typology developed in this chapter offers an alternative explanation to voluntarist notions of coup-proofing.

Officers and Regimes in the MENA: Incorporation Versus Exclusion

In one of the few recent studies of the political role of Middle Eastern armies, Risa Brooks (1998:11) argues that what she calls "the political-military balance" is a core feature of Arab regimes. Going beyond the question of regime types and direct military rule, this perspective recognizes that the military plays an important role in most authoritarian coalitions—even where this role is less visible. As Geddes et al. (2014:149) remind us, "Even where they do not rule, the military is an important faction in authoritarian ruling alliances," although "most theories of autocracy ignore this gorilla in the room." The political role of the military under different authoritarian regimes is the core interest of this chapter.

At the same time, this concern is narrower than what is usually covered under the rubric of civil-military relations (Feaver 1999). While the latter term encompasses all relations between the military and society at large, my interest more narrowly concerns the extent to which the military does or does not play a political role. I find that Brooks's (1998) term "political-military relations" best describes this interest.

Variation in political-military relations among the three countries is considerable. As can be gleaned from Table 2.1, the three armed forces have very different histories of military intervention and differ widely in terms of their resource base. Syria boasts the largest force levels, experienced the most coups or coup attempts, and leads the field in terms of official military spending in relation to gross domestic product (GDP). Egypt's armed forces, in turn, intervened less frequently, receive a smaller share of GDP from the official state budget, and are smaller in relation to the overall population. And in Tunisia there was only one coup, military expenditure as a percentage of GDP is very low, and the military is small even in relation to the country's small population. Although these indicators should not be taken as direct measures of political-military relations, the differences they reveal nevertheless tell us something about political-military relations in the three cases.

Beyond such quantitative indicators, military officers dominated the Egyptian cabinet up to the early 1970s (Cooper 1982), they continue to play an important role in the Syrian Ba'th party (Hinnebusch 2001), but were legally prohibited from joining political parties in Tunisia—including the successive regime parties, the Neo-Destour and the Rassemblement Constitutionnel Démocratique (Willis 2012). Moreover, all chief executives in Egypt and Syria up to the Arab Spring hailed from the armed forces. In Tunisia, however, only Ben Ali could be said to have such a profile, although he was socialized more in the country's internal security than in the military proper. In short, variation among the three cases is considerable and in need of explanation.

Table 2.1. Variation in Political-Military Relations

	Egypt	Syria	Tunisia
Coups since 1950[a]	4	11	1
Military expenditure (% of GDP)[b]	2.7	4.7	1.4
Military personnel (per 1,000 population)[c]	7.7	24.2	4.1

[a] Coups and coup attempts, data from the Powell/Thyne coup dataset, available at http://www .uky.edu/~clthyn2/coup_data/home.htm.

[b] Average for the 2000s, from World Development Indicators (includes only official military spending).

[c] Averages since regime foundation (Egypt 1952, Syria 1963, Tunisia 1956), from Correlates of War Material Capabilities Dataset (v.4.0); see Singer, Bremer, and Stuckey (1972).

Shaping Political-Military Relations in the MENA

Theories of coups d'état have long argued that military intervention in civilian politics is connected to the extent of social mobilization and to the strength or weakness of civilian institutions (Finer 1962; Huntington 1968). Such theories are immediately relevant for the comparison of regime foundation in MENA republics and the role of the armed forces in this process. Regime foundation in the post-World War II MENA took place against the backdrop of significant mobilization and in the context of rather inefficient institutional systems. Military coups were the rule rather than the exception. Political regimes in Libya, Egypt, Iraq, Syria, and Yemen were founded by coups. In brief, the "quasi-ordinary form of change of a regime or of a government in the Arab states had become the military coup" (Beeri 1982:69).

Seen from this perspective, what is in need of explanation is not so much military intervention as such but rather that it did not occur everywhere in the Middle East. Tunisia is the only authoritarian Arab republic[1] to attain independence and to form a postindependence regime without major military involvement. This set political-military relations in that country on a path that differed significantly from the one traveled by its regional neighbors. In a nutshell, the Tunisian military, compared to the militaries of the country's regional neighbors, remained a small and poorly funded organization. Military officers in Tunisia did not serve in cabinet positions—not even as ministers of defense—and even Ben Ali's "constitutional coup" of 1987 did not lead to a stronger role for the armed forces. In brief, in Tunisia—in contrast to all other authoritarian Arab republics—the pattern of political-military relations emerging from regime foundation was one in which military officers were excluded from political power. Thus, as Brooks (2013:5) argues, "Understanding the structure of civil-military relations under the Ben Ali regime requires first assessing the historical role of the military. . . . The character of civil-military relations in Tunisia exhibits some degree of path dependence, with Ben Ali inheriting a particular set of informal norms and institutions and then elaborating in their structure." As the next section indicates, regime foundation is the "critical juncture" (Collier and Collier 1991) that set Tunisia on this specific path.

While the role of the armed forces in regime foundation shaped the fundamental contours of political-military relations, it did not completely determine the subsequent evolution of the military's political role. Rather, the political-military balance was subject to reconfiguration, in particular following major political junctures such as changes in leadership or political crises. In such situations the choices open to political actors remained constrained by existing patterns of political-military relations, however. In other words, the development of political-military relations in the Middle East was path-dependent, and major changes were difficult to implement given that powerful vested interests were associated with the status quo.

Empirically, Middle Eastern republics founded by the military developed two main patterns of political-military relations. In some cases, the military faded to the background and became less prominent as a political actor. In such cases, officers were "ruling but not governing" and presided over large military enclaves; at the same time, however, military officers were separated from active politics (Cook 2007). Political-military relations in Egypt and Algeria illustrate this pattern. In other cases, by contrast, no such separation developed, and military officers continued to play important roles as political elites. The presidents of Iraq, Libya, Syria, and Yemen all had their sons (and supposed successors) rise through the military, an indication that the armed forces were perceived as an imminently political institution. In these cases, high-ranking military officers remained eminently incorporated into the regime coalition. Figure 2.1 summarizes these different historical paths.

Comparing the trajectories of Egypt and Syria thus provides analytical leverage over the determinants of such periods of reconfiguration. Both countries had large and powerful military institutions, both fought in and lost the 1967 war against Israel, and in both countries the post-1967 period coincided with leadership change, in Egypt from Nasser to Sadat and in Syria from Jadid to Hafiz al-Assad. Yet while in Egypt the armed forces were separated from active politics from the 1970s onward, in Syria the power consolidation of Assad led to an even closer incorporation of military elites into the ruling coalition.

In other words, after 1967 Egypt and Syria followed diametrically opposed strategies of reform in political-military relations. While both strategies were aimed at coup-proofing the respective regime and at consolidating the position of the new chief executive, the comparison between Egypt and Syria points to two fundamentally different sets of coup-proofing strategies: strategies aimed at separating military from political elites and strategies aimed at incorporating military leaders into the ruling coalition (Albrecht 2015).

In *The Soldier and the State*, Samuel Huntington (1957) famously argued that civilian control over the military presupposed a strict separation of the

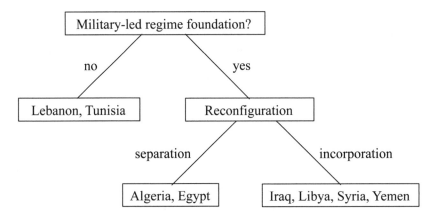

Figure 2.1 Political-Military Relations in Middle Eastern Republics

civilian and military spheres. Coup-proofing strategies aimed at separating military officers from active politics seem to be predicated on such an under-standing of civil-military relations. It is important to see, however, that the separation of the military and political spheres does not imply civilian control of the military. Rather, a strong and autonomous military might not actively interfere in politics; nevertheless, at the same time such an arrangement also prevents political control over military matters. In the MENA, the return to the barracks of officers in formerly military-dominated regimes was bought with the emergence of such "military enclaves" (Cook 2007:14), in which officers and the military as an institution enjoyed wide-ranging autonomy. The existence of military enclaves protects the regime coalition from mili-tary intervention to the extent to which military autonomy lowers the stakes of the political game for officers. Since this system guarantees the military a privileged position and allows officers to run the military as a state in the state, they have little reason to intervene in politics as long as this balance is not upset (Harb 2003; Sayigh 2012).

On the other hand, military acquiescence can also be achieved by including officers into the regime coalition. Geddes et al. (2014:153) have described this process in terms of credible commitments of power sharing. In the course of regime consolidation, they argue, an aspiring incumbent "must make credible commitments to share spoils and policy influence with other officers in return for their commitment to refrain from overthrowing him." Strategies that bind military elites to the regime or to the incumbent by exploiting personal, ethnic, or sectarian loyalties are such mechanisms of incorporation (Bellin 2012; Quinlivan 1999). However, credible commitments of power sharing can also be set up through the establishment of military juntas or through other forms of consultation within the military (Geddes et al. 2014).

Historically, the second form of political-military relations, namely the incorporation of military elites into regime coalitions, was the norm rather than the exception in the MENA. There are two different historical paths, however, that led to a separation of political and military elites. The Tunisian path starts from the historical marginalization of the Tunisian military that has its roots in the political conflicts of the preindependence era. In contrast to all other authoritarian Arab republics, the Tunisian military did not play a major role in regime foundation, which explains the Tunisian exception whereby the military never acquired much political clout. The Egyptian path, on the other hand, starts from a strong military that played a crucial role in regime foundation and developed into the main institutional pillar of the regime. Only later, and in reaction to the exogenous shock of military defeat, did political-military relations in Egypt undergo major reforms.

To understand these two historical paths requires a focus on two distinct periods. The crucial period for the Tunisian path is the first half of the 20th century and the establishment of regime coalitions in the context of political conflict. The challenge here is to explain why Tunisia was the only authoritarian Arab republic not to come into being through a military coup. The crucial period for the Egyptian path, on the other hand, is the aftermath of the 1967 Six-Day War. In reaction to their military defeat in this war, the Egyptian armed forces underwent major restructuring that ultimately set them on a path of depoliticization. Here, the comparison between Egypt and Syria is pertinent: while both Egypt and Syria suffered defeat in the 1967 war, only in Egypt did the reforms introduced in the aftermath of defeat lead to the depoliticization of the military and to the emergence of a split between the military and civilian elite sectors.

The "Tunisian Path": Regime Foundation

Military officers played a major role in the political histories of most authoritarian Arab republics but were rather marginal in Tunisia. All presidents in Egypt and Syria since the foundation of the respective regimes and up to the

Arab Spring, for example, were military officers; in Tunisia, by contrast, active members of the armed forces were prohibited from becoming members of the ruling party, and even the post of minister of defense was always held by a civilian. In short, the Egyptian and Syrian armed forces were major players in their respective regimes (Kandil 2012; Hinnebusch 2001), while the Tunisian military remained at the margins of political processes and under the control of civilian elites (Brooks 2013; Willis 2012).

What accounts for these differences? The crucial factor is the role played by the armed forces during regime foundation. In all three cases, the first half of the twentieth century saw the emergence of conflicts between the political authorities of the day—monarchies backed by colonial powers in Egypt and Tunisia and an oligarchical republic in Syria—and aspiring new elites. Such rising actors, aptly termed "second generation elites" by Michelle Penner Angrist (2006), had experienced limited upward social mobility under the old order but found their further advancement blocked by the political and economic power of traditional elites. In the ensuing conflicts, second generation elites chose different routes to power based on different coalitions that shaped the nature of the emerging regimes. The relatively marginal role of the Tunisian military is due to the fact that in contrast to all other authoritarian Arab republics, the military was kept out of regime foundation. Instead, Tunisian second generation elites took power in the wake of a campaign for independence supported by a mass-mobilizing party.

These differences, in turn, are the result of the strategic situation in which second generation elites found themselves. In both Egypt and Syria, second generation elites were blocked from rising to power through formal political competition by traditional elites who controlled major parts of the political scene. In Egypt in the late 1930s and 1940s, traditional elites tightened their grip on the Delegation (Wafd) Party, the main expression of the nationalist movement, and thus prevented the Wafd from turning into a channel of advancement for second generation elites. Meanwhile, in the mid-1950s collusion between the National Party and the People's Party, both led by different factions of the traditional elite, marginalized the second generation challenge in Syria. As a result, second generation elites in both countries focused their efforts on a military route to power.

In Tunisia, by contrast, second generation elites managed to secure the leadership of the nationalist movement for themselves, entered into a strategic alliance with progressive factions of the traditional elite, and wrested control from the French through a largely nonviolent political process. As a result, the Neo-Destour Party, built on a corporatist alliance with trade unions and employer associations, developed into the main institutional pillar of the regime while the military was marginalized.

By and large, the historical cases of Egypt, Syria, and Tunisia thus support arguments that see the degree of social mobilization and conflict as a major structural determinant of military coups (Johnson, Slater, and McGowan 1984): where social conflict was intense, a high degree of polarization between traditional and second generation elites precluded regime-founding processes based on compromise and institutionalized politics. In such cases, second generation elites ultimately took power through military coups. Where, on the other hand, social conflict was more muted, military intervention could be averted.

These claims hold for MENA republics beyond the three cases examined here. In cases of high polarization, conflicts at times escalated into open violence, as with the anticolonial struggle in Algeria (1954–1962) and the North Yemen Civil War (1962–1970). The common denominator, however, is that regime foundation was achieved through the military. Tunisia is unique among authoritarian Middle Eastern republics in having experienced a non-military form of regime formation. In the only other republican case, Lebanon, power-sharing arrangements between the country's different sectarian groups prevented the emergence of a strong authoritarian regime. In the following pages, I illustrate these dynamics by drawing on the cases of Egypt, Syria, and Tunisia. The actual historical sequence of events was of course different in other cases; the development of political-military relations in these three cases nevertheless illustrates broad patterns.

Egypt was ruled as a de facto British protectorate after 1882, a status that was formalized in 1914. Although the country gained formal independence in 1922 and a constitution was promulgated the following year, Egyptian politics during the so-called liberal age (1923–1952) was dominated by the British and the palace, both of which routinely interfered in formal electoral politics (Botman 1991; Deeb 1979; al-Sayyid-Marsot 1977). Socially, the political elite in early twentieth-century Egypt was dominated by large landholders who, by virtue of their control of the countryside, exerted considerable control over national politics. Thus, in the fifty different cabinets formed between 1914 and 1952, large landowners were represented with 58 percent of the posts (Botman 1991:79). The main nationalist party, the Wafd, had originated in the 1919 revolution and represented a coalition of progressive elements drawn from the urban professional middle classes, a small group of emerging capitalists, and traditional elite landholders (Deeb 1979). Polarization between traditional and second generation elites was intense, however, and representatives of Egypt's traditional landholding elite worked to marginalize their second generation competitors within the Wafd. This led to the dissolution of the original coalition. Second generation nationalists increasingly turned to extraparliamentary groups for two reasons: first, the increasing influence of traditional elites on the course of the party under the leadership of Secretary-General Fuad Serageddin after 1936 (Gordon 1989), and second, the related loss in the party's appeal among nationalist urban strata, especially after the Abdeen Palace Incident of 1942 in which British tanks forced a Wafd government on King Faruq (Smith 1979). Despite this, however, the Wafd continued to dominate electoral politics, creating a situation in which a military coup appeared as the only way to realize full Egyptian independence for second generation elites.

In Syria, a different setting led to similar results. Under the French mandate (1920–1947), Syria developed into an oligarchic republic. Big landholding interests found their political expression in the National Bloc (al-Kutla al-Wataniyya). The socioeconomic conflict between absentee landlords and the peasantry was reinforced in Syria by an additional cultural center-periphery conflict as well as by ethnic and religious differences. The traditional Syrian elite was mainly composed of urban Sunni Arabs, while religious and ethnic minorities were concentrated in the rural periphery (van Dam 2011:1–14). This landholder-peasant conflict was the "root cause of the eventual fall of the ancien régime" (Hinnebusch 2001:22). Syria gained independence from France with relative ease in 1946, and the National Bloc subsequently split into the National Party (al-Hizb al-Watani), representing landholding interests, and the People's Party (Hizb al-Sha'b), representing emerging business interests (Heydemann 1999:37–52). Second generation challengers, on the other hand, were represented by the Ba'th Party as well as a number of leftist and communist groups. In the first postindependence elections in 1947, the People's Party joined the Ba'th Party in a tactical alliance and alienated its former allies in the National Party by advocating land reform. In these elections, the opposition against the National Party won the relative majority, but traditional elite interests continued to dominate with the help of independent deputies. The resulting political deadlock was broken by military intervention in 1949, an event that initiated a series of coups and countercoups. With their electoral fortunes on the rise in the mid-1950s, the Ba'th Party campaigned for radical reforms alongside the communists, prompting the business interests represented by the People's Party to reconsider their reformist stance and rejoin traditional landholders in their resistance against reform. Thus, given the high levels of political polarization between traditional and second generation elites in Syria in the mid-1950s, "Land and capital joined to defeat an increasingly militant force of workers and peasants" (Heydemann 1999:51–52). In reaction, second generation elites sought salvation first in alliance with Nasser, leading Syria into its ill-conceived union with Egypt as the United Arab Republic (1958–1961) and then in the military route to power. Despite the fact that the union was rather short-lived, falling prey to a military coup backed by traditional elites in 1961, it transformed the Syrian political scene in important ways. Crucially, the Ba'th Party, having voluntarily dissolved under the union, was revived in opposition to Nasser in the form of the Military Committee that was composed of officers, many of whom came from a rural-minority background (Devlin 1976). This Military Committee staged the coup that brought the Ba'th Party to power in 1963.

In Tunisia, the situation was markedly different. Tunisia was ruled as a French colony between 1881 and 1956, but in contrast to Egypt and Syria, French policy in Tunisia included an element of direct colonization by French settlers. As a result, the impact of colonialism on traditional social structures was much more pronounced. Land acquisitions by French *colons* under the policy of "official colonization" transferred most large landholdings into French ownership (King 2009:47). This crucially weakened traditional elites and their political stature and loosened their grip on the nationalist movement (Anderson 1986:153–54). As a result, polarization between traditional and second generation elites in the Tunisian nationalist movement was much weaker than in Egypt or Syria, and second generation elites ultimately remained in control of the movement. Organizationally, the Tunisian independence movement went through several stages. Whereas the original Destour Party (from the Arabic *dustur*, meaning "constitution") was dominated by urban elites and thus failed to develop a social appeal and reach out to the emerging labor movement, the Neo-Destour, emerging from a split in 1934, explicitly took up social concerns and aimed at mobilizing the rural hinterlands (Moore 1964). With traditional elites weakened by colonial policies and the Neo-Destour developing an effective alliance with the labor movement represented by the Union Générale des Travailleurs Tunisiens, more traditionally inclined nationalists had little choice but to join the movement under the leadership of the Neo-Destour. As Clement Henry Moore (1964:81) observed, the Neo-Destour "appealed mainly to the new middle classes rather than to the Old Destour's broad-based but entirely traditional elite. This difference helps to explain the success of the Neo-Destour, for socially and politically the newer classes, created but not compromised by the colonial situation, were more prepared to spearhead political change." In other words, the emergence of the Neo-Destour as the leading force in the Tunisian nationalist movement signaled the passing of the mantle to second generation elites. Having gained independence for Tunisia in 1956, the Neo-Destour under the leadership of Habib Bourguiba proceeded to institutionalize a party-based regime. The fact that the military had not played a special role in the foundation of this regime meant that the armed forces could be kept out of politics.

The long-term influence of the role played by the armed forces during the period of regime foundation was crucial. Throughout postindependence Tunisian history, the military remained small and depoliticized, while the armed forces played key political roles in Egypt and Syria. In the next section, I illustrate how the fundamentals of political-military relations, created during regime foundation, constrained the later processes of reconfiguration.

The "Egyptian Path": Military Reform

In all three countries, the years following regime foundation saw the consolidation of institutional systems that were strongly shaped by the coalition of actors that had backed regime foundation. In both Egypt and Syria, this meant that the armed forces grew in size and importance, while in Tunisia the military was kept small and poorly funded and the Neo-Destour Party developed into the main institutional pillar of the regime.

Before long, however, all three regimes experienced major crises, and all three reacted with a partial remodeling of their institutional systems. The regime crises hit on several levels. On the economic level, all three countries initiated major reform programs, all except the Syrian one under the auspices of the international financial institutions. Politically, there were steps of political liberalization that went along with the reintroduction of multiparty politics in Egypt and Tunisia and with a more limited liberalization of electoral politics in Syria (Baaklini, Denoeux, and Springborg 1999). Also, in all three cases there were changes in the top executive position, with the transitions from Nasser to Sadat in Egypt, from Jadid to Assad in Syria, and from Bourguiba to Ben Ali in Tunisia.

The armed forces, however, were unequally affected by these reforms. In Tunisia, the political-military balance remained largely unchanged. Even though Ben Ali had come to power through a palace coup in 1987, the military remained a small and poorly funded force, and military officers did not assume active roles in politics under Ben Ali. By contrast, in both Egypt and Syria, another exogenous shock meant that the armed forces could not evade reform: the defeat of both the Egyptian and the Syrian armed forces in the 1967 war against Israel. While both Egypt and Syria suffered military defeat in 1967 and in both cases the battlefield ineffectiveness of the respective armed forces was blamed on political reasons (Hinnebusch 1990:158; Kandil 2012), different political contexts drove Anwar al-Sadat in Egypt and Hafiz al-Assad in Syria to adopt approaches that were diametrically opposed.

While Sadat removed the "centers of power" in the military and the party and pushed the military out of active politics (Harb 2003), in Syria, Assad dissolved the "army-party symbiosis" (Rabinovich 1972) that had characterized political-military relations before his 1970 coup by appointing military commanders personally loyal to him. This set political-military relations in the two countries on different courses.

In Egypt, the armed forces had seen significant growth. By 1970, force levels had increased to 255,000—an increase of more than 100,000 within a decade—and military expenditure rose by about 10 percent during that period (Koehler 2013:147). At the same time, military officers played important roles in other state institutions as well, leading to the emergence of what the Egyptian sociologist Anouar Abdel-Malek (1968) described as a "military society." In brief, the armed forces were one of the main beneficiaries of the growth of the Egyptian state under Nasser.

This crucial period in the history of the Egyptian armed forces was overseen by the powerful figure of Field Marshall 'Abd al-Hakim 'Amir, who served as chief of staff and minister of defense between 1956 and 1967. During his tenure, 'Amir built patronage networks within the armed forces that firmly entrenched him in his position and even prevented Nasser from removing him from his command after the failure of the union with Syria in 1961 (Kandil 2012:53). Thus, the "years between 1955 and 1966 constituted the zenith of the military's political centrality and power. This coincides with the period when the Egyptian armed forces were at their worst in terms of military effectiveness" (Hashim 2011:69).

The lack of military effectiveness became painfully obvious in Israel's victory over Egypt in 1967. The immediate result was 'Amir's removal from the military in 1967, but this was only a first and highly visible step in a process that transformed the position of the Egyptian armed forces in the wider system of regime institutions (Brooks 2006; Kandil 2012). In his 1971 "Corrective Revolution," Sadat moved against his opponents in the party and the military, purging ninety-one officials on a single day, about half of whom were military officers (Kandil 2012:107). This set the stage for a new approach in political-military relations: while 'Amir served as minister of defense for eleven years during the sixteen years of the Nasser era, six different individuals occupied this position during the eleven years of Sadat's presidency (Koehler 2013:182). Similarly, while 35 percent of the 131 ministers under Nasser had come from a military background, only 19 percent of Sadat's 163 ministers had such a career path, and the proportion declined further to 10 percent of the 120 ministers serving under Hosni Mubarak up to 2005 (Hilal 2006:156, 162–63, 189; Stacher 2012:62). In brief, the direct political influence of the military declined, and recruitment and promotion patterns became significantly more institutionalized.

At the same time, however, the military expanded horizontally into the economic sphere, and the practice of appointing retired officers to administrative positions in the state or public sector continued unabated (Bou Nassif 2013; Sayigh 2012; Springborg 1989). This process experienced another boost under the tenure of Muhammad 'Abd al-Halim Abu Ghazala as minister of defense (1981–1989) and led to the emergence of what Yezid Sayigh (2012) has aptly termed an "officers' republic." These developments notwithstanding, the reform of political-military relations in Egypt in the wake of the 1967 defeat led to the depoliticization of the Egyptian military and to the emergence of a powerful yet separate "military enclave" (Cook 2007).

Just as in Egypt, the Syrian armed forces also experienced significant and sustained growth. While the armed forces had only about 80,000 troops in the 1960s, force levels grew to 400,000 by the end of the 1980s (Zisser 2002:122). Defense expenditures also experienced an upward trend, especially after the 1967 war (Koehler 2013:151). In contrast to Egypt, however, the Syrian armed forces were strongly politicized. Between independence in 1946 and 1970, Syria experienced more than ten successful military coups.

What is more, attempts to politically control the army by appointing loyal officers after the 1963 Ba'thist takeover had infected the military with the factionalism of the party (Hinnebusch 1990:158).

As it happened, however, the 1967 defeat against Israel coincided with a struggle for power between Hafiz al-Assad, who had taken the position as minister of defense in 1966, and Salah Jadid, the Ba'th secretary general (van Dam 2011). From his position in the Ministry of Defense, Assad used the 1967 defeat to introduce limited reforms in political-military relations. These reforms, however, aimed at weakening the influence of the party within the military and strengthening the position of officers personally loyal to Assad in preparation for his assumption of power. Thus, in February 1968, Chief of Staff Ahmad al-Suwaidani was replaced with Assad's close friend Mustafa Tlass, who was to serve in high military positions (first as chief of staff and then as minister of defense) until 2004; similarly, the crisis of the late 1960s saw the rise of Rif'at al-Assad, Hafiz's younger brother, who was instrumental in the fall of the intelligence chief and Jadid-loyalist 'Abd al-Karim al-Jundi (Seale 1988:148–53). These tactics significantly strengthened Hafiz al-Assad's hand in the 1970 confrontation with the party in which Jadid was finally overthrown.

In the wake of the "Corrective Movement," as Assad's 1970 military take-over became known, the new strongman continued to consolidate his grip on the military, relying on strategies of personal control that had served him well in the struggle against Jadid. In addition to Tlass, Assad's cronies included such men as Hikmat al-Shihabi, chief of staff between 1974 and 1998; 'Ali Duba, head of Military Intelligence (Shu'ba al-Mukhabarat al-'Askariyya) from 1974 up to 2000; and his brother Rif'at, commander of the praetorian Defense Companies (Siraya al-Difa') (Koehler 2013:153). In sharp contrast to Egypt, the changes introduced to political-military relations in Syria in the wake of the 1967 defeat shaped patterns of military integration into the regime coalition that not only endured for the better part of four decades but also survived the transition from Hafiz to his son Bashar in 2000.

Bashar al-Assad's succession was carefully prepared through the reshuffling of Syria's military and security elite in the late 1990s (Gambill 2002), as officers loyal to Bashar replaced his father's cronies. This led to the rise of figures such as Bashar's brother-in-law General 'Asif Shawkat as head of Military Intelligence after 2005 and Bashar's brother Basil as commander of the Fourth Armored Division, which included major parts of the Defense Companies formed by their uncle Rif'at. Thus, while the personnel changed in the transition to Bashar, the pattern of military incorporation introduced by Hafiz after 1967 continued. This was to prove crucial for the behavior of the Syrian armed forces in the crisis of 2011.

Preexisting patterns of political-military relations thus shaped these processes in two different ways. To begin with, the fact that both the Egyptian and Syrian militaries had played important political roles and had consequently grown into powerful institutions precluded their full submission to civilian control. Although the post-1967 crisis represented an opportunity for change in political-military relations, the Tunisian-style marginalization of the armed forces from the political process was not an option in either Egypt or Syria. In brief, officers in Egypt and Syria needed to be enticed into accepting a reformed political-military balance.

The difference between Egypt and Syria stems from this context as well, and this is the second way in which existing patterns constrained reform options. In Egypt, Sadat took power as the designated successor to Nasser during a period in which the military's reputation was at an all-time low. Drawing on an initial elite consensus in his favor, Sadat then moved to eliminate the "centers of power" in several state institutions, including the party and the army. Resistance against Sadat, however, was not concentrated in any particular institution, and the new president built up support in different quarters. By contrast, Hafiz al-Assad took power in a military coup directed against the party. Therefore, in the power struggles surrounding his rise to the presidency, the camps were rather clear-cut. While Assad could count on support from within the military, which he had cultivated as an original member of the Ba'th Military Committee and strengthened during his time as defense minister, resistance was concentrated in the party. Consequently, Assad moved to consolidate his support in the army and to weaken the influence of party representatives over the armed forces. The result was a pattern of political-military relations in which the political and military elite sectors became tightly intertwined.

Conclusion

In this chapter, I have sketched a historical typology of political-military relations in authoritarian MENA republics and have stressed that the political-military balance is historically determined and changes only incrementally absent fundamental ruptures. In Tunisia, for example, the armed forces did not assume a more central position, despite Ben Ali having come to power through a soft coup; similarly, while the military took on an important role in the last days of the Ben Ali regime, it withdrew to the barracks immediately afterward and handed power to civilian elites. This is evidence that political-military relations constitute ingrained patterns of behavior, which continue to shape actors' strategies even in response to crisis situations.

On the other hand, I have also argued that the evolution of political-military relations is part and parcel of larger dynamics of regime development. In both Egypt and Syria, the political-military balance was reconfigured during phases of regime consolidation that followed major domestic crises. While in these two cases reform occurred against the backdrop of political succession in a context in which the military had been weakened by a defeat, in other MENA republics other triggers prompted reform. In Libya, for example, a failed 1976 coup attempt against Qaddafi triggered change in the political-military balance (Gaub 2013), while in Yemen, attempts to secure the dynastic succession of President Salih's son upset political-military relations (Fattah 2010; Albrecht in this volume).

On a more general level, I argue that a historical model such as the one described in the preceding pages offers an alternative to overly voluntarist notions of coup-proofing. Authoritarian incumbents do not choose coup-proofing strategies. Rather, the management of political-military relations is intimately linked to larger dynamics of regime development. A Tunisian scenario of military marginalization, for example, was not an option for either Egypt or Syria or, for that matter, for any other authoritarian republic in the MENA. The marginalization of the Tunisian military was not so much a policy choice that can be replicated in other cases and that was adopted by Bourguiba and Ben Ali as the result of a rational choice between different options as it was the outcome of a complex historical process. In the same vein, a strategy of military incorporation cannot easily be transformed into the separation of military and political elites. Such strategies create vested interests, and absent a major shock such as defeat in war, leadership change, or the mass uprisings of 2011, changing course would upset the political-military balance and thus achieve exactly the opposite of what coup-proofing strategies are meant to achieve.

This does not mean that political-military relations in the MENA cannot be reformed. It does mean, however, that reforms are likely to be drawn-out processes of incremental steps in which the historically grown balance of power between military and political elites remains a major factor. Rather than focusing on voluntarist ideas of rational coup-proofing strategies, we need to recognize that patterns of political-military relations are no more the result of rational choice by regime leaders than are other institutional arenas in authoritarian regimes.

Note

1. Lebanon is another Middle Eastern republic that did not experience a military-led regime foundation. Postindependence Lebanon, however, did not follow the same trajectory of authoritarian state formation and regime building as did the other seven Arab republics.

CHAPTER 3

Armed Forces, Internal Security Services, and Popular Contention in the Middle East and North Africa

Fred H. Lawson

One striking result of the wave of popular uprisings that swept across the Middle East and North Africa (MENA) beginning in the winter of 2010–2011 is a marked resurgence of scholarly interest in the political role of the armed forces. With a handful of notable exceptions (Brooks 1998; Kamrava 2000; Bellin 2004; Cook 2007; Droz-Vincent 2007; Lawson 2007; Barak and David 2010), the military establishment disappeared from view in academic writings about Middle Eastern politics after the mid-1980s. In the wake of the uprisings, though, concern for the armed forces came roaring back (Barany 2011; Lutterbeck 2011; Droz-Vincent 2011b). The attention that has been lavished on the actual and potential impact of the so-called security sector on postuprising state institutions and governance processes shows no sign of abating (Bellin 2012; Lachapelle, Way, and Levitsky 2012; Lutterbeck 2013; Nepstad 2013; Makara 2013; Albrecht 2015; Battera 2014).

Lost in the shuffle have been the internal security services that constituted a crucial component of the authoritarian regimes of virtually all MENA countries. Prior to 2011, it was commonplace for knowledgeable observers to refer to political systems in this part of the world as "mukhabarat states," that is, governments dominated by the security and intelligence agencies (*al-Mukhabarat*). For some writers, the decision to ignore the political role of the domestic security apparatus is conscious and deliberate. Oren Barak and Assaf David (2010:806), for instance, warn readers at the outset that

before proceeding further, . . . it is worth explaining our decision to
focus on the military (or the armed forces) and not on the other security agencies (e.g., internal security and intelligence agencies, police
and paramilitary forces, border and coast guards, military industries),
which together with the military, make up the security sector. In most
states of the world, including the Arab States, the military is the primary security service in terms of its size, resources, roles, and association with the process of state formation.

Not the most compelling argument perhaps, but at least the omission of the
security services is explicitly noted. Philippe Droz-Vincent (2011a:3), by contrast, observes that throughout the MENA region

> the police in particular has played an essential role as an administra-
> tive arm of the state, often the ultimate decision-maker in day-to-day
> politics and social life. The police has not only been a repressive body
> (although it has zealously played that role), policing public spaces and
> foiling attempted mobilizations from below. It has also been (along-
> side the secret services, i.e., the dreaded mukhabarat) an essential
> go-between on numerous administrative matters, from solving local
> conflicts to issuing of bureaucratic papers and authorizations.

In fact, he continues, "[Arab] regimes have developed tentacular police
apparatuses that have been at the forefront of social repression, whereas the
army have [sic] remained in a 'quietist' position. In their day-to-day work-
ings, authoritarian regimes have been much more police states than military
regimes" Droz-Vincent (2011a:3). Yet Droz-Vincent's analysis omits any
further discussion of the security services and concentrates exclusively on
dynamics associated with the regular army. Other studies fail to mention the
domestic security apparatus at all or do so only in passing (Lachapelle, Way,
and Levitsky 2012; Lutterbeck 2013:29; Nepstad 2013:347; Makara 2013:347–
50; Barany 2013; Battera 2014).

For once, this aspect of scholarship on the MENA reflects broader conceptual writings in comparative politics. Most—but not all (see Gandhi
and Przeworski 2006)—seminal contributions to the study of persistence
and change in authoritarian regimes include the regular armed forces as a
pivotal actor but ignore the internal security services (Geddes 2004; Pion-
Berlin and Trinkunas 2005; Art 2012). One of the most influential studies of

the formation and durability of authoritarian political systems, Dan Slater's *Ordering Power* (2010), illustrates the general pattern. Extensive attention gets devoted to the ways in which varying degrees of cohesion and institutionalization among the armed forces of Southeast Asia have shaped the structure and complexion of authoritarian regimes in that part of the world. Yet the security services stand missing in action.

Dynamics of Military-Security Relations

In order to analyze relations between the regular armed forces and the internal security services in a systematic way, one must start by spelling out the divergent institutional interests and incentives that drive the actions of these two distinct components of the aggregate security sector in authoritarian polities. Any given country's regular armed forces can be characterized in terms of four analytical variables: (1) whether the armed forces are relatively well institutionalized or instead highly penetrated by nonmilitary actors; (2) whether the armed forces are staffed by means of universal conscription or through volitional recruitment; (3) whether the armed forces concentrate their attention and effort exclusively on military affairs or engages in sustained activity in other arenas, most notably the domestic economy; and (4) whether or not the armed forces provide a substantial proportion of the country's political leadership.

First, whenever the regular armed forces are highly institutionalized, their various component formations have a strong incentive to engage in careful planning and to focus their efforts primarily on operational efficiency. In addition, the activities of the armed forces can be expected to be driven by the institutional priorities of the military establishment, bounded by whatever norms concerning the legitimate role and prerogatives of the armed forces happen to imbue local society. If, on the other hand, the armed forces are highly penetrated by outside actors (whether personalist cliques, sectarian groups, or political parties), then they will most likely tailor their activities in such a way as to conform to the interests of these external actors. The armed forces can be expected to face severe constraints on their routine operations, and the preferences of their primary patron(s) will tend to outweigh broad societal norms in determining these constraints.

Second, whenever the armed forces are staffed by officers and enlisted personnel who enter the ranks through universal (or at least broadly based) conscription, it becomes possible for commanders to screen prospective soldiers according to their aptitude and suitability for military service and to reject or assign to noncombatant duties any individuals who turn out to be unsatisfactory. Qualifications for military service can be set down and maintained at a relatively high level. At the same time, universal conscription raises the likelihood that the actions of the armed forces will be constrained by the norms that enlisted personnel bring with them into the ranks. Whenever the armed forces are staffed instead through volitional recruitment, commanders are apt to try to make enlistment and retention seem as attractive as possible to all citizens. Furthermore, the armed forces will have a strong incentive to expand the mission of the military establishment in order to inculcate greater public awareness of and appreciation for the institution. At the same time, staffing the ranks with volunteers makes it possible for those soldiers whose attitudes deviate from the basic principles of the institution to be weeded out, resulting in greater homogeneity of norms among officers and enlisted personnel alike. Such common values and attitudes give the armed forces wider latitude for action so long as their operations remain congruent with shared notions of institutional loyalty.

Third, in cases where the regular armed forces engage exclusively in military affairs, their commanders have to bargain with political leaders for the resources they need to maintain the institution. Moreover, whatever rewards arise to the military establishment come entirely due to the successful preparation for and implementation of military operations (as well as from a measure of luck on the battlefield). Such armed forces will have a strong incentive to follow whatever orders might be issued by state officials, no matter what impact actions by the armed forces might have on domestic society. By contrast, armed forces that extend their activities to nonmilitary affairs, particularly ones that establish a firm foothold in the local economy, acquire the capacity to generate resources of their own. Such a military establishment will be able to reward troops independently of the actions of the civilian leadership, and such rewards are likely to arise from success in other fields of endeavor besides victory in battle. Furthermore, senior officers who exercise control over commercial, industrial, or agricultural enterprises will tend to take into account whatever disruptions and damage their actions might inflict on those sectors in which they are directly involved as well as on the economy as a whole.

Fourth, whenever the armed forces provide a substantial proportion of a country's political leadership, members of the governing elite can be expected to do their best to monitor and regulate actual and potential rivals inside the officers' corps. In addition, any commander who harbors political ambitions will have a strong incentive to cultivate a favorable reputation among fellow officers and perhaps among enlisted personnel as well. On the other hand, if the military is not a major source of political leadership, then members of the officers' corps who aspire to high state office will have to explore other pathways along which to pursue their political ambitions. More important and politically ambitious officers will find it necessary to cultivate a favorable impression among the general public just as much as, if not more than, inside the military establishment.

Internal security services can also be characterized along four analytically distinct dimensions: (a) whether they are state-affiliated or affiliated with some other organization, such as a political party; (b) whether or not they include armed operational branches; (c) whether they possess a unitary structure or consist instead of multiple agencies; and (d) whether or not they are tightly integrated with the intelligence apparatus of the regular armed forces.

First, whenever the security services are state-affiliated, they can be expected to have a strong incentive to protect and advance the current and future interests of the existing political system. If, on the other hand, they are affiliated with a political party or some other kind of parastate organization, then their overriding interest will lie in ensuring the survival and well-being of that particular entity. Second, if the security services maintain armed operational branches, then engaging in activities that entail the use of force tends to provide a basis for the enlargement of their size and purview. If, however, the security services have no operational branches and engage solely in the gathering and analysis of intelligence, they can be expected to have little or no interest in resorting to force in order to augment or preserve their present and future institutional prerogatives.

Third, whenever a country possesses a unitary security apparatus (or a tightly integrated complex of interlaced security agencies), information will tend to be gathered and disseminated in a comparatively efficient and coherent way. Moreover, no threat arises that competing agencies will take steps to undermine one another's interests or supplant each other's role in the making and implementation of policy. If, however, a number of different internal security services coexist, then each one will be likely to have a strong incentive to withhold crucial information from the others. Each agency will also face the possibility that others might carry out initiatives that threaten its institutional interests or supplant its role in policy making. Additionally, since each agency has an incentive to undercut competing agencies, each one will find itself compelled to open up new areas of operations before its rivals take the opportunity to do so. Competition among rival agencies can be ameliorated, but not eliminated, if all components of the security apparatus are subordinated to an overarching, coordinating body.

Finally, if a country's internal security services are fully integrated with the intelligence branches of the regular armed forces, they will have little if any capacity to withhold information from the military establishment. On the contrary, there will be a strong incentive for the security services to accept a fundamental division of labor in which they focus on nonmilitary intelligence gathering and analysis and leave military aspects of intelligence gathering and interpretation to the armed forces. If, however, the security services operate independently from military intelligence, then there is a potential for the armed forces to engage in activities that threaten the institutional prerogatives of the security services or diminish their role in policy making and implementation. Security agencies will then have an interest in withholding information from the military and a strong incentive to explore new areas of operations before military intelligence can do so itself. If no overarching administrative body exists that can coordinate relations between the security services and military intelligence, the level and extent of intersectoral rivalry can be expected to escalate sharply during moments of crisis.

Different combinations of these eight variables produce contrasting modes of military-security structure, which have a direct impact on the armed forces' decision making in the face of severe challenges to the regime. More specifically, varying configurations of military-security relations help to explain why the regular armed forces exhibit a high tolerance for contentious action by antiregime protesters in some cases but in other cases act quickly and forcefully to suppress the opposition. This question has direct implications for the larger puzzle of why, in some cases, the armed forces defect from the political leadership and align with the challengers rather than staying loyal to the existing leadership.

Responses to Popular Disorder

Countries' regular armed forces and internal security services can be expected to respond to large-scale popular disorder in divergent ways. Their respective reactions depend not only on the mix of features that characterizes relations between the military establishment and the domestic security apparatus but also on the distribution of power that exists between these two major components of the aggregate security sector at the time that a severe challenge to the regime takes shape.

Whenever the armed forces occupy a dominant position in the military-security sector, their response to serious outbreaks of public disorder will be determined by the four variables outlined above. Militaries that are well institutionalized can be expected to act in such a way as to maximize the security of the nation as a whole, whereas those that are highly penetrated by personalist cliques, sectarian communities, or political parties have a strong incentive to protect the narrow interests of their patron(s). Armed forces made up of conscripts will tend to take into account the willingness of soldiers in the ranks to use force against protesters, whereas ones that consist entirely of volunteers (or foreign mercenaries) will exhibit much less empathy for citizens who take to the streets to challenge the regime. Regular armies that focus exclusively on military matters will be less likely to restrain themselves by taking into consideration any resultant disruption or damage to the domestic economy. On the other hand, militaries that operate economic enterprises of their own, particularly companies that play a role in the civilian market, are likely to worry about the effect that their actions will have on labor relations, supply chains, or present and future investment. Finally, if the armed forces provide a substantial proportion of a country's political leaders, then any officers who aspire to high posts in government can be expected to weigh the repercussions that using force against protesters will have on their subsequent careers; if, by contrast, political leaders tend not to come from the military, decisions to adopt coercive tactics against the opposition will be taken on the basis of calculations about short-run efficacy rather than longer-term political expediency.

By the same token, if the internal security services dominate the military-security sector, they can be expected to act in the interests of either the state or the ruling clique, sect, or party, depending upon whether or not they are state-affiliated. Agencies that have operational branches will tend to deploy armed personnel against antiregime activists and to do so with substantially less restraint than the regular armed forces. If multiple security services compete with one another for influence and resources, then it is likely that one agency or another will try to gain an advantage over its rivals by targeting protesters and will do so relatively soon after the protests begin. Finally, the security services will tend to undertake more aggressive initiatives toward antiregime activists if they have few or no institutional links to the military establishment.

On the whole, this logic implies that popular uprisings will elicit quicker and more forceful responses from military-led regimes whenever the regular armed forces are highly penetrated, not staffed by conscripts, uninvolved in the domestic economy, and not a major supplier of political leaders. Countries in which the leadership relies more heavily on internal security services than it does on the regular army will exhibit considerably less tolerance for popular revolt whenever the security services are instruments of a personalist clique, sectarian community, or political party; possess armed, operational branches; compete among themselves for influence over the making and implementation of state policy; and have minimal connections to military intelligence.

One further consideration makes things even more complicated. The interests and incentives of these two analytically distinct components of the military-security sector are likely to change whenever antiregime activists turn from peaceful protest to large-scale organized violence. Even conscript soldiers can be expected to rally behind their officers and defend the existing order if they find themselves under attack by armed rebels. Similarly, the outbreak of large-scale violence poses a direct threat to military-run economic enterprises as well as to nonmilitary companies, so commanders who hold a direct stake in the local economy will most likely take steps to crush armed opposition using any means available. On the other hand, regular armed forces that are highly penetrated by a clique, sect, or party might well hesitate to escalate the level of internal conflict whenever resorting to force to crush an armed opposition would endanger their patron(s), especially if higher levels of overall violence are likely to cause the citizenry to polarize along religious, linguistic, racial, or other ascriptive lines.

Illustrative Cases

Paying close attention to military-security relations can shed new light on regime responses to the rebellions that erupted across the MENA region during the winter of 2010–2011. All of these uprisings initially took the form of peaceful demonstrations, marches, and rallies in which protesters demanded an end to endemic infringements on civil rights and pervasive official corruption. Political leaders uniformly dismissed or ignored the demands for reform that were voiced by antiregime activists and deployed riot police and security forces to crush the early protests, at times backed up by units of the regular army. Yet outcomes diverged sharply from one case to another. In Tunisia, Egypt, and Algeria, the military refrained from using indiscriminate force against the protesters; in Yemen and Libya, the armed forces quickly splintered, with some units attacking the demonstrators and others opting to protect those who were challenging the authorities; and in Bahrain and Syria, the military almost immediately deployed indiscriminate force to deal with challengers. How one might explain these varying outcomes in terms of variations in relations between the regular armed forces and the internal security services can be illustrated by revisiting the uprisings in Algeria and Yemen.

Algeria

From the moment of independence in July 1962, the regular armed forces have played a pivotal role in Algerian politics. Military officers seized control of the central administration in June 1965, and senior commanders exercised firm control over public policy making throughout the subsequent quarter century (Roberts 2007:8). The army's political predominance was reaffirmed in January 1992, when the military high command ousted President Chadhli Ben Jadid and replaced him with a High State Committee, which canceled the ongoing parliamentary elections and reimposed a state of emergency. As fighting escalated between the police and Islamist militants during the early 1990s, however, the military establishment split into two camps. The first, which Hugh Roberts (1994) calls "eradicators," included most of the country's senior officers and was led by the chief of staff, General Muhammad Lamari; the second, which Roberts labels "conciliators," gravitated around the minister of defense, General Liamine Zeroual.

In January 1994, Zeroual was nominated to act as interim state president by the High State Committee. He was confirmed in that post by a popular referendum in November 1995. Nevertheless, as attacks against government installations and civilian targets continued to rage during the mid-1990s and as Zeroual found himself unable to issue orders that would be obeyed by other members of the military high command, the influence and prestige of the regular armed forces waned. By the end of the decade, the Directorate of Counterespionage and Internal Security (DCE) had supplanted the regular army in prosecuting the struggle against the Islamists (Benramdane 2004).

The shift in power was confirmed by the wholesale reshuffling of the council of ministers and the general staff that was carried out by President 'Abd al-'Aziz Bouteflika in December 1999.

Riots that occurred in the predominantly Berber region of Kabylia in the spring of 2001 further entrenched the DCE at the expense of the regular armed forces. In the weeks leading up to the presidential elections of April 2004, Lamari announced that the military would take no part in the contest, despite the preference of many influential commanders for Bouteflika's primary rival, former prime minister 'Ali Ben Flis (Mortimer 2006:166). When the ballots were tallied, Ben Flis came away with no more than 6 percent of the total votes, an outcome that most observers attribute to active intervention by the security services. President Bouteflika flexed his overwhelming electoral mandate to force Lamari to resign, then appointed more compliant officers to the posts of chief of staff and minister of defense (Roberts 2007:11).

From the summer of 2004 to the winter of 2010–2011, the armed forces all but disappeared from sight in Algerian politics. Successive parliamentary and presidential elections grabbed the headlines, along with intense rivalry between the resurgent National Liberation Front (FLN) and a handful of newly established political parties (Mortimer 2006:168–69). In the background, however, hovered the DCE and its parent organization, the Department of Intelligence and Security (DRS), keeping close watch over political activists of all stripes and taking steps to harass and even eliminate any actual or potential challenger who posed a serious threat to the regime (Werenfels 2009:181; Addi 2006). Friction between President Bouteflika and the head of the DRS, General Muhammad "Tawfiq" Mediene, heated up during 2009–2010, when it became obvious that the president's health was failing and equally clear that his younger brother Sa'id was being groomed to be the next president (Keenan 2010). The assassination of the country's longtime chief of police, General 'Ali Tunsi, was widely reported to have been bound up with the burgeoning conflict between Bouteflika and Mediene.

Meanwhile, Algeria's armed forces captured a major stake in lucrative sectors of the domestic economy. Military officers tightened their grip on industrial and commercial enterprises throughout the 1990s. Bradford Dillman (2000:134) remarks that compared to the Algerian case, "there are few parallels in the rentier world, save perhaps in Nigeria and Indonesia, to the wide-scale conversion of army officers and high-ranking [FLN] cadres into pseudo-private entrepreneurs and predators through privatization, deregulation of importing, liquidation of local public companies, and joint ventures between multinationals and the remnants of state companies." Consequently, when popular discontent exploded into widespread public protest in January 2011 (Roberts 2011), Algeria's regular armed forces found themselves predisposed to restrain themselves.

In the first place, Algeria's military establishment enjoyed a substantial degree of institutional autonomy and thus had the capacity to act in the interests of the nation as a whole rather than being compelled to protect the prerogatives of a specific clique, sect, or party. Second, because military units were staffed through universal conscription, commanders were forced to consider the possibility that soldiers in the ranks might empathize with the protesters. Third, the military's extensive involvement in the local economy gave senior officers a strong incentive to keep the extent of societal disruption and physical destruction to a minimum. And finally, all of Algeria's presidents from 1970 to 1998 had come from the senior ranks of the armed forces, a pattern that both inspired political ambitions in the minds of senior officers and led them to take into account the impact their actions might have on their postmilitary careers.

On the other hand, by the winter of 2010–2011 the armed forces had found themselves largely eclipsed by the Department of Intelligence and Security. Algeria's primary internal security service had no institutional connection to any of the parties that engaged in electoral politics, including the FLN, and can thus be considered a state-affiliated agency. Furthermore, there were no other security services that competed with the DRS, so no incentive existed for the DRS to raise the level or broaden the range of operations against antiregime activists in an attempt to outbid rival agencies. Yet the DRS did possess significant operational capabilities, which gave its leaders an incentive to deploy armed agents to harass and suppress anyone who ventured into the streets.

Taken together, this admixture of military-security characteristics generated a comparatively moderate reaction to Algeria's 2010–2011 uprising. In the words of one observer, "the state response was generally careful and limited— only three rioters were killed [that January] and the military was never involved" (Brown 2011). Roberts (2011) concurs: although the January 2011 rioting turned out to be "far wider and more genuinely national in scope [than the popular disorders of October 1988 had been], the army has not acted; no state of siege has been declared. The Police, and occasionally the gendarmerie, have been responsible for coping with the unrest. They have, so far, exercised restraint and have undoubtedly been ordered to do so." As a result, the Algerian rebellion was suppressed without precipitating the kind of conflict spiral that would have entailed a sustained, and almost certainly more violent, counter-attack on the part of those who were challenging the existing order.

Yemen

Military commanders overturned Yemen's monarchical political system in September 1962 and ousted the leaders of the initial coup d'état five years later. A third coup in June 1974 put a group of officers headed by Lieutenant Colonel Ibrahim al-Hamdi in power in Sana'a; the new leadership initiated an ambitious program of administrative reform that was intended to augment the institutional capacity of the central government and thereby supplant the tribal chieftains (sheikhs), who had exercised control over crucial aspects of domestic politics prior to that time. Khaled Fattah (2010:32) reports that al-Hamdi's regime "believed that the military was the only national body that was capable of weakening the tribal institution and its skeikhly symbols. Reorganizing and equipping the military [therefore became] al-Hamdi's top priority" (see also Peterson 1981:258). This project was largely abandoned after al-Hamdi's assassination in October 1977 and the subsequent ascent to the presidency of Lieutenant Colonel 'Ali 'Abdullah Salih.

In place of the rationalization campaign, Salih and his allies took steps to meld the armed forces together with long-standing practices associated with "tribal" governance (al-Shurbagi 2013:4). By the mid-1980s, the Yemeni military "at its top levels [had] turned into a base for tribal power, while at its lower levels, it [had] turned into a wide arena for recruiting tribesmen as a part of the regime's politics of survival and co-optation" (Fattah 2010:34). After the unification of the Yemen Arab Republic and the People's Demo-cratic Republic of Yemen (PDRY) in May 1990, the PDRY's comparatively rationalized armed forces were broken up and dispersed throughout the ter-ritory of the new Republic of Yemen. When former PDRY officers revolted four years later, their scattered and severely degraded units turned out to be no match for the quasi-tribalist formations fielded by the authorities in Sana'a, which were heavily reinforced by clusters of armed Islamist militants (Fattah 2010:39–40). In the aftermath of the 1994 civil war, the Yemeni mil-itary establishment's fundamental nature as "a military-tribal complex of patron-client relationships" became even more firmly consolidated (Fattah 2010:41; Knights 2013:265).

At the same time, President Salih appointed blood relatives and close comrades to key posts in the military command structure. A retired senior officer told the International Crisis Group that as soon as Salih took over as president, he "brought his family and his tribe to prominent positions in the military regardless of levels of professionalisation or education." In addition, Salih "chose a sampling of officers from different regions so that all areas of the country would have token representation, but the most important factor was always personal loyalty" (International Crisis Group 2013:2). By 2010, the president's oldest son, Ahmad 'Ali 'Abdullah Salih, had been put in command of the elite Republican Guard; a younger son, Khalid 'Ali 'Abdullah Salih, led the newly formed Mountain Armored Infantry Division; a half brother, Muhammad Salih 'Abdullah al-Ahmar, was in charge of the air force; a nephew, Tariq Muhammad 'Abdullah Salih, led the Presidential Guard; a cousin, Muhammad 'Ali Muhsin al-Ahmar, was commander of the strife-torn eastern military district; and a longtime comrade and distant cousin, 'Ali Muhsin Salih al-Ahmar, headed the First Armored Division. Midlevel positions in the officers' corps tended to be assigned to individuals from the predominantly Zaidi northern highlands, the president's ancestral homeland (International Crisis Group 2013:3).

Latent animosity between more experienced commanders and younger officers who had been awarded key posts due to their personal connections to the president flared into overt antagonism after a large-scale revolt erupted in the northern province of Sa'dah in 2004. President Salih took advantage of the rebellion by the Believing Youth (commonly called the Huthis, after their leader) to strengthen military formations loyal to himself and undercut units whose loyalty seemed questionable (al-Shurbagi 2013:8; Phillips 2011). At the same time, the internal security services expanded in both size and purview. Mohamed Ahmad Ali al-Mikhlafi and Abdul Kafi Sharaf al-Din al-Rahabi (2012:3) report that by 2011, "the security forces and officers affiliated to the Interior Ministry [were] estimated at over 100,000 individuals and officers, distributed among all the various security organs and institutions under the ministry's authority."[1] Such agencies included the Central Security Units, the General Security Agency, the General Administration to Counter Terrorism and Organized Crime, the Coast Guard, and a number of separate police forces. In addition, the Ministry of Defense housed Military Intelligence, the Counter-Terrorism Unit of the Republican Guard, and the Special Forces. These agencies were supplemented by a handful of "supra-ministerial" security services, including the National Security Bureau and the Central Agency for Political Security (al-Mikhlafi and al-Rahabi 2012:4).

All the internal security services competed with one another for influence over policy as well as for material resources and personnel. "Overall," al-Mikhlafi and al-Rahabi (2012:5) remark,

> the most important characteristics of the security sector are: swelling in terms of the number of apparatuses and individuals; an overlap in their functions and powers; high levels of politicisation among members of the PSO [Political Security Office] and the National Security Bureau; the special privileges they receive that are not granted to members of the police force or the General Security Agency; reliance by all the security services on personal or regional loyalties in appointments, promotions and tenure; and a lack of professionalism and training.

Intense competition among these agencies gave them an incentive to operate in secret not only in their interactions with one another but also in their dealings with the regular armed forces. More important, inter-security service rivalry resulted in a pronounced tendency toward the deployment of force against peaceful protesters, as each agency did its best to assert itself when responding to potentially threatening situations (al-Mikhlafi and al-Rahabi 2012:9).

Yemen's armed forces have occupied a central place in the local economy since the mid-1980s, when well-connected senior officers were awarded licenses to import scarce commodities and were granted preferential access to profitable real estate projects (International Crisis Group 2013:4). The economic role of the armed forces was bolstered by the activities of the Military Economic Corporation (MEC), which had been set up in the late 1970s to provide soldiers with essential provisions and equipment but subsequently moved into food distribution, agricultural production, and commercial fishing. By the early years of the twenty-first century, the MEC was actively engaged in the manufacture of textiles, furniture, and pharmaceuticals as well. In 2007, President Salih further reinforced the centrality of the MEC, now designated the Yemen Economic Corporation (YEC), by ordering all foreign companies to set up joint ventures with the YEC to manage their local operations (Phillips 2011).

When university students and factory and transportation workers took to the streets of Sana'a, Taiz, Aden, and al-Hudaidah in January 2011, riot police, backed up by elements of the regular armed forces, attacked the protesters. After snipers from the internal security services and the Republican Guard shot into the crowd on March 18, killing fifty-two people, the protests exploded in size and intensity. More important, the shooting prompted several senior military officers, including Generals Muhammad 'Ali Muhsin al-Ahmar and 'Ali Muhsin Salih al-Ahmar, to express support for the protesters and order the soldiers under their command to protect civilians. Guarded by these troops, antiregime activists in Sana'a, Taiz, and Aden gained strength and confidence, and the protests soon spread to the city of Ibb in the central highlands and the districts of al-Jawf and Marib in the Eastern Desert.

Army units loyal to President Salih routinely used force against demonstrators during the spring, resulting in hundreds of additional deaths. At the same time, proregime commanders encouraged Islamist militants, including cadres of the Supporters of the Islamic Way (Ansar al-Shar'ah), a group loosely connected to al-Qaeda on the Arabian Peninsula, to target dissident troops in the southern districts of Abyan and Zinjibar. Meanwhile, fierce fighting erupted around the capital between military formations led by the president's supporters and units allied to the two 'Ali Muhsins. "As the conflict escalated," the International Crisis Group (2013:12) observes, "both sides suffered defections and recruited thousands of new soldiers." Skirmishes persisted until mid-November, when Salih signed a document in which he relinquished office and recognized Vice President 'Abd al-Rabbu Mansur Hadi as his legitimate successor. Large-scale protests persisted for the remainder of the year, but clashes involving the armed forces largely disappeared in the wake of the president's resignation.

As in Algeria, the regular armed forces in Yemen in 2010–2011 consisted primarily of conscripts, whose willingness to open fire on unarmed protesters was open to question. The military also held a sizable stake in the Yemeni economy, both overtly through the operations of the YEC and covertly through a wide range of more or less illicit activities. Moreover, the military establishment had been the source of all of Yemen's presidents after 1962 as well as most of the heads of powerful state agencies. All of these factors predisposed commanders to restrain themselves in the face of the protests that erupted that January.

Nevertheless, Yemen differed from Algeria in two crucial respects. First, the regular armed forces and internal security services alike had become highly penetrated by kinfolk and close comrades of President Salih. Key military units thus had an overriding interest in defending the existing political leadership rather than in safeguarding the interests of the nation as a whole. Second, a large number of rival security services—most of which possessed operational branches—competed with one another for influence over policy making and scarce material resources. Each of these agencies had a strong incentive to take quick and forceful action against antiregime activists, as was proven by the March 18 incident in Sana'a. Such unrestrained and indiscriminate use of force elicited immediate condemnation from senior military officers, who calculated that the nation as a whole, and the military establishment in particular, would be better served by more measured tactics if not in fact by accommodating the demands of the opposition. Under these circumstances, the armed forces fractured, and two opposed camps quickly settled into an internecine war of attrition, which after ten months of fighting convinced the president to step down.

Conclusion

Existing studies of the popular uprisings that swept across the MENA starting in the winter of 2010–2011 demonstrate a marked resurgence of interest in the political importance of the armed forces. However, current scholarship underplays or ignores the crucial role that the internal security services play in shaping the activities of the aggregate security sector. Conflating the regular army and internal security agencies paints a distorted picture of governance processes in authoritarian regimes in this region of the world and lays the foundation for a misleading analysis of the ways that authorities in the MENA react to severe domestic challenges.

Whether popular protests elicit quick and forceful reactions from the regular armed forces is determined largely by the institutional interests of the military establishment but is also influenced by structured relations between the military and nonmilitary security agencies. Throughout the MENA, the mukhabarat have played an active part in shaping and carrying out the leadership's response to antiregime activists, and they did so as well during the recent uprisings in Algeria and Yemen. Exploring the complex dynamics of rivalry and collaboration that exist between these two central components of the aggregate security sector sheds new light on these particular cases and opens the door to innovative investigations of the military and politics in authoritarian systems elsewhere.

Note

1. Yemen's regular armed forces were estimated to consist of just 90,000 soldiers, according to the Arab Center for Research and Policy Studies (2011:2).

CHAPTER 4

A Shifting Role of the Military in Arab Politics? Cross-Regional Perspectives and Implications for the Future of Civil-Military Relations in the Region

Robert Springborg

Both *inter-* and *intra*regional perspectives are relevant for understanding the role of the military in Arab politics. The interregional perspective is important, if only to emphasize what should be obvious about the military's role, but is frequently downplayed or altogether ignored—namely, that in Arab countries the military is far more expansive than in other global regions. Specialists in the Arab world have grown so accustomed to the military elephant in the political salon that they tend not to find it as peculiar as it is in reality, nor—until recently—to attribute to it the political and economic importance it deserves. Upheavals that commenced in Tunisia in December 2010 and the "Arab Thermidor" that ensued stripped away much of the camouflage carefully constructed by Arab authoritarian regimes to disguise their "deep states" and the roles of armed forces within them.[1]

This presents a unique opportunity to draw upon new information to improve theorizing about the roles of militaries in Arab politics. The aims of this chapter are to highlight by global standards the extraordinary nature of contemporary Arab armed forces and their relations to civilian political actors and institutions, provide some comparative observations about the political roles of militaries in other regions, and speculate briefly on the impacts of Arab upheavals on civil-military relations. In order to do so, the chapter proceeds in five steps. The following section describes the particular nexus of persisting authoritarianism, high levels of casualties in war and civil unrest, and widespread use of coercion in domestic politics that characterizes the Arab exceptionalism in political-military relations. This will be followed by a cursory overview of political-military relations in four different regions of the globe: Africa, Latin America, Asia, and postcommunist Europe. The third section discusses lessons from the study of civil-military relations in these regions that may be of use for investigating the Arab world. The final two sections discuss the apparent paradox that the recent upheavals in many places in the region actually reinforced status quo ante and their implications for the future of Arab civil-military relations.

Interregional Comparison: Arab Exceptionalism

Global comparisons suggest the particular nexus of persisting authoritarianism, high levels of casualties in war and civil unrest, and widespread use of coercion in domestic politics that characterizes the Arab world. Elbadawi and Makdisi (2013) summarize the relevant evidence, noting that the frequency of "sustainable" democratic transitions is the lowest in the Arab region, that the occurrence of external or civil wars there is surpassed only by sub-Saharan Africa, and that other than the member states of the Gulf Cooperation Council, Arab countries are on average the world's most repressive. The related findings about the comparatively large size of Arab armed forces and the lack of civilian control of them are therefore not surprising. Middle Eastern armed forces are the world's largest, as measured by size in proportion to population and by spending as a percentage of gross domestic product (GDP) (World Bank 2015).[2] Over the first decade of the twenty-first century, countries in the Middle East and North Africa spent more than twice as much on defense as a percentage of GDP than South Asia, the next highest-spending region.[3] Other indicators, such as the Global Militarisation Index calculated by the Bonn International Center for Conversion (BICC 2015), also reveal the high levels of militarization of economy, society, and the state in the Middle East and the lack of effective political control over the armed forces. Transparency International's Government Defense Anti-Corruption Index, first issued in 2013, ranks eighty-two countries according to the measures in place to prevent corruption in their armed forces. Since these measures reflect specific aspects of institutionalized civilian control, this new index is in effect a surrogate measurement for civilian control of the armed forces (Transparency International 2013). Of the five regions in the world assessed on this index, the Arab region scores the lowest, with thirteen of nineteen countries receiving the scores of E or F, the bottom two grades on the scale. By contrast, no country in the Americas, the Asia Pacific region, or Europe and Central Asia received a grade of F. The fourteen sub-Saharan African countries ranked had a modal score of E+, whereas the modal score for Arab countries was an E−. Of the nine of eighty-two countries ranked that received a grade of F, five are Arab (Algeria, Egypt, Libya, Syria, and Yemen). They are those whose militaries are largest in proportion to their respective populations. Of the ten countries of eighty-two evaluated that spent more than 4 percent of their GDP on their militaries, seven are in the Arab world. The only Arab country in which the parliament oversees the military budget is Kuwait.

A particularly useful interregional comparison arises between Latin America and the Arab world. South America has grappled with the issue of democratic control of the armed forces longer and more continuously than any other emerging region. In part because of that, data on its militaries— their size, organization, and relations to civilian political institutions—is especially reliable and readily available, thanks in part to the combined efforts of nongovernmental organizations' (NGOs) activists in the region. Led by Red de Seguridad y Defensa de America Latina (RESDAL) in Buenos Aires, an NGO network produced the first edition of *A Comparative Atlas of Defence in Latin America and the Caribbean* in 2005, which by 2012 was in its fifth edition and had added the Caribbean subregion (RESDAL 2012).[4] The near total absence of Arab NGOs dedicated to imposing civilian control on militaries, not to mention an institutionalized intra-Arab network, is itself a measure of the comparative lack of centrality of the issue in the Arab world. It should also be noted that the atlas does not contain data on the economic roles of Latin American militaries, reflecting their near total absence from that vital sphere and possibly suggesting why civilians in South America have been more successful than Arabs in subordinating their militaries. An equivalent publication for the Arab world would necessarily have to include sections on military economies in order to provide an accurate portrayal of the breadth and depth of military penetration of Arab political systems.

In the absence of similar data for the Arab world as a whole, Egypt, for which the most information is available, can serve as the region's exemplar (see Chérine Chams El-Dine's contribution to this volume). Comparisons between Egypt and Latin American countries suggest the existence of an inverse correlation between the size of militaries and the degree of democratic control—the larger a military, the less it is controlled by civilians. The degree to which especially the Egyptian military is disproportionately large is suggested by reference to some comparable Latin American countries in which the military previously exerted political power. Brazil's military, for example, has 339,000 officers and men, while the country's GDP in 2012 was some $2.5 trillion, roughly ten times greater than that of Egypt. Egypt's military, however, is about 40 percent larger than Brazil's. Argentina, with a GDP of $473 billion in 2012 compared to Egypt's $229 billion, has a total military strength of some 75,000 personnel, which amounts to about one-sixth of that of Egypt's, despite Argentina's GDP being more than twice as large. Venezuela, under quasi-military rule at present, in 2012 had a GDP some 50 percent larger than that of Egypt's, with a total military strength of 113,000 personnel, about one-quarter of that of Egypt's.[5] So, while Venezuela's military is comparatively large in relation to the country's economy, thus confirming the overall inverse relationship between size and civilian control, it is proportionately distinctively smaller than Egypt's. The number of regular force members for every 10,000 inhabitants is on average less than 30 for Latin American countries, the highest ratio being 66 in minuscule Uruguay. Egypt, by contrast, has almost 190 members of its military for every 10,000 of its citizens, a proportion that would rise to an astounding 415 if the Interior Ministry's forces were also included.

The most recent edition of *A Comparative Atlas of Defence in Latin America and the Caribbean* contains a list of measures of civilian control of militaries that provide useful bases for comparison to Egypt as the Arab exemplar. Since Latin America is a region in which the military has a long, if also discontinuous, history of involvement in politics, its standards of civilian control of the military are particularly relevant as comparators. Of the seventeen South American countries analyzed in the volume, in fourteen the military criminal justice system has no jurisdiction over civilians. In Bolivia, Brazil, and Venezuela, the military's jurisdiction extends to civilians but under strictly defined, limited conditions related directly to military matters. By contrast, in Egypt's constitution, ratified in December 2012, Article 198 specified that civilians can be tried in military courts in cases of "crimes that harm the armed forces." In no previous constitution dating back to the first in independent Egypt in 1923 was the military justice system's jurisdiction extended over civilians. Article 20 of the 1954 constitution, previously the most authoritarian in

Egypt's constitutional history, explicitly prohibited prosecution of civilians in military tribunals (Shams El-Din 2013). That this is not an idle matter is suggested by the fact that within a year from the fall of Hosni Mubarak, at least 12,000 civilians had been tried in military courts, most of them in the period immediately following his removal. The rate of referral of civilians to those courts spiked again following the election of President Muhammad Mursi in June 2012 and then yet again after the military overthrew him.[6] Military judges are assessed as being "highly politicized and not independent" (Abdel-Tawab 2013). The corollary of Article 198 is that military matters and personnel are not under the jurisdiction of civilian courts. In the constitutional committee formed under the military government that seized power in July 2013, the issue of the jurisdiction of military courts was among the most controversial. After much discussion in the preparation of the January 2014 constitution, the decision was made to tighten up the wording of Article 198 of the 2012 constitution, but the final product is in reality no more restrictive. As stated in Article 204,

> Civilians cannot stand trial before military tribunals except for crimes that represent a direct assault against military facilities, military barracks, or whoever falls under the authority of the military; military or border zones, military equipment, vehicles, weapons, ammunition, documents, secrets, general property, or factories; crimes related to conscription; or crimes that represent a direct assault against military officers or personnel in the course of performing their duty.

In Egypt's 2012 constitution, Article 195 required the minister of defense to be an active-duty officer, a condition not specified in the constitution or laws of any Latin American state. In ten South American countries officers may legally serve in that capacity only after retirement, while in seven South American countries active-duty officers can serve in that manner. In 2012 in the seventeen Latin American countries for which the *Atlas of Defence* provides data, 60 percent of serving ministers of defense had military backgrounds, while 40 percent were civilians. In just over half of those countries, more civilians had served as ministers of defense than had officers. In contrast, Egypt's 2014 constitution and its enabling legislation further tightened the military's control over the position of minister of defense, requiring that he be an active-duty general who had served in that capacity for at least five years and be from the military's high command. Moreover, the constitution further specified in Article 234 that he be chosen by the Supreme Council of the Armed Forces (SCAF) for the next two presidential terms (eight years) and that he, not the president, be the supreme commander of the armed forces (Article 201).

A third indicator of civilian control of the military is the nature of the role and the powers of what are typically called national defense or national security councils. Such councils exist in all South American countries and are directly attached to the presidency. Their role is typically defined as to "advise the president on national security."[7] None are vested with the power to declare war, and all have a majority of civilian members. In the current Venezuelan Constitution, for example, the National Defense Council is made up of the president, the vice president, the Speaker of the parliament, the chief justice, and ministers of defense, internal security, foreign affairs, and planning. Civilians thus outnumber officers three to one in the National Defense Council even in this specific country, where the military's influence under President Hugo Chavez came to permeate the entire state structure, very similar to how it has in Egypt. By contrast, Article 197 of the 2012 Egyptian Constitution vests the National Defense Council with exclusive power to draft and oversee the military budget, a power that no Latin American equivalent has. It is to this council, not the parliament, that the president must turn if seeking to declare a state of war. Finally, and most important, the majority of members in Egypt's newly created National Defense Council must be active-duty military officers, a provision that was extremely controversial in the Constituent Assembly charged with drafting the constitution. In an argument on the assembly's floor, the military's representative, General Mamduh Shahin, shouted at a delegate of the Muslim Brotherhood, "If you put one of yours, I will put one of mine" (Ashour 2012). With that exclamation, the dominance of the military over the National Defense Council, hence over much of the state and the nation, was written into the constitution. That dominance was yet further reinforced in the 2014 constitution and its enabling legislation decreed by the interim president appointed by the military, not passed by parliament. Together they solidified control over the military's own affairs through the National Defense Council, most notably by empowering it to approve the military's budget and to forward to parliament not the budget itself but only its total amount (Article 203). This National Defense Council has to have a majority of active-duty officers. The National Security Council was empowered by the 2014 constitution in such a way as to extend the military's power over the cabinet and, by implication, the government as a whole. Headed by the president, its key members are the head of General Intelligence, who is always a military officer; the chairman of the parliamentary defense and security committee, who is also always a retired officer; the minister of defense; and the minister of the interior. Other key cabinet ministers are clearly included as a means to render them subordinate to the military core of the council. Enabling legislation specifies that the council is "to develop and approve national security strategies, set policy aims for the various ministries, approve plans for national development and the comprehensive enforcement of national strengths, adopt measures that aim to safeguard the identity and sovereignty of the state, and steer foreign policies and international cooperation in areas of concern to security."[8]

Finally, a few other indirect indicators suggest that Egypt lags well behind Latin America in asserting civilian control of the military. Defense budgets in relation to GDP and to government budgets have declined over the past several years in Latin America, averaging 1.26 percent of the former and 3.73 percent of the latter in 2012 (RESDAL 2012:35). Egypt's defense budget is essentially a state secret. The nominal budget, which the Ministry of Defense provides to the Stockholm International Peace Research Institute and other foreign organizations, is typically just below 3 percent of the GDP and some 2 percent of government expenditures, so taken together proportionately about two and a half times greater than in Latin America. In all Latin American countries, women are admitted into the armed forces. In the all-volunteer Uruguayan Army, for example, 128 of the 811 new recruits in 2011 were women. By contrast, the Egyptian military does not draft women, nor does it accept them as volunteers. In nine of seventeen Latin American countries, military service is obligatory, with the maximum period of conscription being in Cuba and Bolivia, where it is two years. Several Latin American countries, including Brazil and Bolivia, offer civilian service as an alternative to the military draft. Egypt, by contrast, has universal male conscription, with no civilian service alternative, for a period of up to three years, a provision that was written into the 2012 constitution principally to guarantee the continued supply of low-cost labor to the military economy. It was removed from the 2014 constitution but remains enshrined in legislation. Finally, whereas in Latin America noncommissioned officers can aspire to promotion into the ranks of commissioned officers, although that is difficult, there is virtually no possibility of becoming a commissioned officer in Egypt without passing through one of the military academies. A noncommissioned officer has to serve twenty-four years before becoming eligible for admission to a military academy, so virtually none ever receive commissions. In sum, these indicators suggest that by comparison to Latin America, the Egyptian military and, by extension, many if not most of those in the Arab world remain overly large, and their personnel are more traditional and stratified and, at least in the republics, less subject to civilian control.

By global standards, then, Arab countries are exceptionally undemocratic, authoritarian, and repressive, with associated high levels of coercion. It is therefore not surprising that their armed forces are comparatively large and expensive, with relatively little control exerted over them by civilian institutions. But this aggregation of Arab countries disguises the substantial differences in civil-military relations that exist between them, a subject that will be dealt with by various other contributions to this volume; this is why it will not be taken up systematically in this chapter. Instead, some additional insights into the unique nature of Arab civil-military relations may be gained by briefly reviewing the evolution of those relations in different regions.

Interregional Comparisons:
Patterns of Civil-Military Relations

Latin America

Latin America is the true heartland of the military's involvement in politics, both in the classic form of seizure of powers by coups d'état and in the weight of scholarly literature. Despite substantial differences between countries, some regional commonalities can be discerned. The historical pattern of alternating civil and military rule reflects and embodies the legacies and institutional powers of Latin American militaries, on the one hand, and their civil/political societies, on the other. Both sides can claim to embody much of the history and spirit of the nation and to have demonstrated a capacity to lead it. Despite the caudillo, or "man on horseback," tradition, Latin American historical reality recounts much more institutionalized political power than those of Arab countries. While military strongmen such as Chile's General Augusto Pinochet and Argentina's General Leopoldo Galtieri populate Latin American political history, what is notable in comparison to the Arab world is the relatively coherent corporate power of the military. This is indicated, for example, by the fact that none of these caudillos handed the reins of power on to their sons, which is the normal pattern of Arab succession until the Arab

Spring. Moreover, civil and political societies in Latin America have components, such as the church, labor unions, and political parties, that claim both venerable traditions and contemporary power and relevance. Constitutionalism, the rule of law, and the institutional capacities of legislatures, judiciaries, and local governments have frequently been undermined by Latin American military juntas, but they also have contributed to the political histories of their nations and provided benchmarks and ideals against which to measure military rule and stimulate opposition to it.

At the operational level, military rule in Latin America has been characterized by its comparative simplicity and directness. In most cases it is military officers in uniform who have called the shots. They have moved into the institutions of governance and either taken control of statist economies, such as in Peru, or forged working relationships with business elites where private sectors predominate, as was/is the case in Brazil (Stepan 1973). Most important, military officers have usually subordinated security and intelligence services to their will and rendered individual political leaders more or less responsible to the collective will of the military or its leading service's commanders.

Latin American military interventions in politics, in sum, have taken a relatively pure form and have alternated with civilian rule, thereby enabling a legacy of constitutional government to persist even if it has been interrupted. Military government typically has not degenerated into either despotic one-person rule or into a police state, in which the security and intelligence agencies really call the shots—the partial exception of Chile's regime of Pinochet notwithstanding. The exercise of power by Chavez and his successor Nicolas Maduro, for example, has been constrained by the constitution; Venezuelan political institutions, which retained some autonomy; and civilian political actors, individual and collective. The Venezuelan security services are not running rampant in the polity. Even in the darkest hours of Argentina's military rule, it was that institution that was liquidating its opponents, real and imagined, not an independent undercover security agency (Antunes and Carlos 2007; Koonings 2003). The reluctance of Brazil's business elites to accept subordination to the military contributed in no small measure to the restoration of civilian rule there, as did division within the ranks of that military. These and other examples give account of a military corporatism operating within a flawed but still recognizable civilian-based constitutional legacy and legitimacy.

It is therefore the differences and contrasts that make comparisons with Latin America relevant to the Arab world. Latin American caudillos have more than met their match with their Arab counterparts. Individual rather than corporate rule characterizes military-backed government in the Arab republics, whereas family rule with direct control over military establishments characterizes the monarchies. Civil and political societies are weak and are now further weakened by profound divides between Islamists and anti-Islamists, not to mention divides between Sunnis and Shi'ites. These societies have little if any historical legacy on which to draw for inspiration and models. Constitutionalism and rule of law have nowhere been established, and the ongoing efforts to do so only in Tunisia suggests how profoundly difficult that task is in the Arab world. Security services, the third element of ruling troikas that also include presidents and militaries in the Arab republics, typically have lost some power to militaries in the wake of the uprisings since 2010, but they are far from being spent forces, with the exception of those Arab states that have essentially collapsed, including Libya, Syria, and Yemen. Arab business elites have nowhere successfully opposed the exercise of military power. Indeed, when businessmen have been able to profit from relationships with officers, they have done so. Contextual factors have been less supportive of military rule in Latin America than in the Arab world, which is beset with intra- and interstate conflict. In Latin America, by contrast, interstate warfare is absent, and external support for returns to civilian rule, most notably by the United States, has frequently played a vital role, whereas there is no equivalent American pressure on Arab militaries to withdraw to their barracks. Indeed, the United States has systematically prioritized Arab militaries over civilian institutions, as reflected by the profound imbalance in military as opposed to civilian foreign assistance.

Eastern Europe

Prior to the collapse of the Soviet Union and its East European satellite states, the games of national politics therein were simpler, even if murkier than those in Latin America. Whereas the latter typically has had multiple actors, including external ones and those in domestic economies, Russia and Eastern Europe basically have had three or four actors, including communist parties, militaries, security-intelligence agencies, and in some cases, such as Joseph Stalin's Russia and Nicolae Ceausescu's Romania, dictators. The general theme running through the political games during the lifetime of these regimes was the steady erosion of power away from the party toward the security-intelligence agencies, which typically gained the upper hand against the head of state. As the ideological and economic bases of party control dwindled, the only base left was the coercive, within which the security-intelligence agencies, being closer to the ruler and having primary responsibility for domestic security, usually gained the upper hand against the military, the professionalization and corporate power of which in some settings made it less useful for arbitrary, coercive rule and possibly less pliable. A comparison to Tunisia springs to mind here. The various labels for these regimes reveal their nature—posttotalitarian party states, police states, national security states, and counterintelligence states.

Transitions to democracy in this region, which have achieved varying degrees of success, reveal different relationships between civilians and armed forces. In Russia the security services triumphed, ultimately placing one of their own in the all-vital presidency.[9] This reflected the comparative advantages of such agencies in times of political confusion and transition, when their informal networks, knowledge of political and economic actors, ability to forge clandestine political alliances, and coercive capacities rendered them truly potent political actors.[10] It also reflected the cult of intelligence and the vital role it ostensibly played in defending the nation against all manner of threats. This myth was a staple of KGB-backed propaganda during the declining years of the Soviet Union, by which time that agency had displaced the Communist Party and its top figures as the real locus of power in Russia. That artfully constructed if fraudulent historiography was hastily rekindled in the mid-1990s by Vladimir Putin and his colleagues in the Federal Security Service (FSB), the successor to the KGB and their vehicle to power.[11]

Fortunately, security-intelligence agencies did not fare so well elsewhere in Eastern Europe, but in many countries they are still a force subject to inadequate civilian control. In Romania, Ceausescu's dreaded Securitate was trumped by the military following his overthrow in 1989. Those leading the transition reasoned that by placing the Securitate under the not too tender mercies of professional soldiers, they would have solved the problem at least for the time being. During the communist era and especially the Ceausescu era, the military had been degraded and largely de-professionalized, so its members had good reason to get even with security henchmen. This stop-gap measure brought some breathing room, time in which civilians were able to establish a new regime that in the long run would develop more sophisticated constitutional and institutional means of control of both the military and the reformed security agencies (Matei 2007; Watts 2006). Elsewhere in Eastern Europe, security-intelligence agencies and militaries have either been brought under reasonably effective civilian control, such as in the Czech Republic and Slovenia, or have managed to remain important, semiautonomous, clandestine players linked to incumbent civilian elites, especially in the executive branch, such as in contemporary Bulgaria and in Poland prior to 2005 (Bozhilov 2007; Zybertowicz 2007).[12]

Several lessons can be drawn from the collapse of communist rule in Eastern Europe. First, transitions to democracy in most countries of the region were the product of the collapse of the Soviet Union, which made it possible for domestic actors, strongly and effectively supported by the West, to wrest power from the security-intelligence agencies, the military, and the politically comatose Communist Party. Second, in the Russian heartland of the former empire, the comparative weakness of Western actors combined with the residual power of the KGB/FSB, including its popular legitimacy, caused the transition to abort. Third, in all of these pretransition political games, economic actors were notable in their absence; because the struggle for and exercise of power had been reduced to its coercive essence, no economic actors enjoyed substantial autonomy. Finally, with few exceptions, the tale of East European communism is largely one of gray men whom history has almost already forgotten, with the only the memorable ones, such as Stalin and Ceausescu, standing out for their exceptional brutality. These were largely impersonal regimes in which the real sinews of power tended to pass through the hands of security-intelligence operatives, who were in turn linked to their fellow operatives elsewhere in the communist bloc.

So, as with Latin America, comparisons to the Arab world reflect more differences than similarities, although the East European archetype may be closer to the Arab one than is that of Latin America. The obvious similarity is the expansive role of security-intelligence agencies, but the balance of power between them, on the one hand, and militaries and rulers, on the other, differs. In the Arab world, no such agency has managed to gain the upper hand at the expense of a ruler. The balance of power between those agencies and the military tends to favor the latter except in Ben Ali's Tunisia. There is no Arab equivalent to East European communist parties, and Arab economic actors play more important political roles than their East European counterparts did under communism. Hatred of an occupying power, which drove much of Eastern Europe's democratization, has no equivalent in the Arab world, despite allegations of American neoimperialism. Finally, the vital role of external actors in supporting transitions to democracy and civilian control of the armed forces is absent in the Arab world, for the alleged neoimperialist Uncle Sam has deemed it too risky and uncertain to act decisively there to try to tilt the balance away from militaries and toward civilians. The bottom line, then, is that while many observers of Arab politics have spoken of police or national security states, these Arab versions have not been equivalents of the East European prototype. Most important, their security services have been neither as autonomous nor as powerful, even though they might have been just as brutal. Nevertheless, their brutality is typically exercised on behalf of regimes in which other actors are really calling the shots.

Asia

The diversity of Asia is reflected in the wide variation of civil-military relations, both before and after democratic transitions. In Indonesia under Suharto (1966–1998), the military was the predominant political force within the regime, second only to the president. While the military had substantial influence over elite politics and even took over administrative functions at the subnational level, Suharto slowly shifted this influence over the next three decades toward individual military officers loyal to himself, thereby transforming his regime from military domination to personalistic, authoritarian rule (Mietzner 2009; Slater 2010; Croissant et al. 2013:chap. 5). Simultaneously, existing institutions regulating civil-military relations were turned into a Suharto-controlled franchise system (McLeod 2008:200). In the Philippines, the tradition of civilian control rooted in the legacies of American colonialism had dramatically eroded under President Ferdinand Marcos's authoritarian government (1972–1986). Both Marcos's personalization of control over the military and his efforts toward politicization of the Armed Forces of the Philippines (AFP) (Croissant et al. 2013:chap. 7) came at the expense of military professionalism and cohesion such that in the last years of his dictatorship, "the AFP looked more like Marcos's Praetorian Guard than a properly professional military" (Hedman 2001:178). However, the transition to democracy in both countries parallels the Brazilian case, with divisions in the military, mobilization of civil and political societies, preferences of key economic actors, and the relative quiescence of security services all contributing to those transitions (Lee 2015). The Taiwanese case is distinctive in that the gradual inclusion of native Taiwanese into the body politic paved the way for a democratic transition in which the military, like in Romania, was assigned the task of corralling the key politically relevant security service. Once that had been accomplished, again similar to Romania, civilians could then go on to establish direct control of the means of coercion (Phillips 2007). In Thailand, the absorption of Chinese into the country's sociocultural fabric further empowered a civil society led by "urban middle class elements, workers, and rural activists" that has for more than a generation struggled to establish permanent civilian control over the military but ultimately failed to achieve it, as the coups d'état of 2006 and 2014 indicate (Case 2007; Croissant 2015).

By contrast, in South Korea during the authoritarian regimes of former generals and coup leaders Park Chun-Hee (1961–1979) and Chun Doo-Hwan (1980–1988), government and military alike had been dominated by members of the Hanahoe, an elite faction of military officers consisting mainly of graduates of the Korean Military Academy's eleventh class of 1955. Its members occupied strategically important posts in key military units, military intelligence agencies, and countercoup units, such as the Defense Security Command, and they staffed the formally nonmilitary security services such as the Korean Central Intelligence Agency (renamed Agency for National Security Planning after the 1979 coup). Retired military officers took over essential posts in the presidential secretariat, the ruling Democratic Justice Party, and the intelligence service (Croissant 2004; Kim 2008; Moon and Rhyu 2011; Croissant et al. 2013).

However, the steady politicization and mobilization of the populace, driven by one of the most rapid industrializations ever recorded, greatly increased pressure on the military. Internal divisions within the armed forces, especially in the army between the dominant Hanahoe faction and the large majority of marginalized officers who felt excluded from military leadership positions, resulted in officers having little incentive to defend the military government against its opponents during the 1987 mass demonstrations (Kim 2008:14; Croissant and Selge in this volume). This raised the political and institutional costs of continuing the militarized dictatorship to levels that even the ruling generals could not tolerate, regardless of the capacities of the security services. So, as in Taiwan and Romania in the 1990s, some prominent Korean generals even called for stricter oversight of the armed forces. This case in particular highlights potentially important divisions between intramilitary factions as well as the contextual factor of rapid economic growth, especially industrialization, in the democratic transitions of East and Southeast Asia. Again, this latter feature does not have its equivalent in the Arab world, where industrialization in general is underdeveloped and those sectors that are globally competitive and integrated are concentrated in capital-intensive hydrocarbon extraction and processing, which does not stimulate the growth of broadly based worker solidarities.

Coming closer to the Middle East, the Pakistani case is more similar to Arab realities. The power balance between individual heads of state, such as Zia ul-Haq (1977–1988) and Pervez Musharraf (1999–2008), and the military has typically not strongly favored the former. The institutional strength of the Pakistani military, as with those in many Arab countries, also rests heavily on its direct control of the economy, so much so that the term "Milbus" has been coined to describe the sprawling industrial and trading conglomerates that constitute the network of military owned and operated businesses.[13] That this pattern has been typical in Arab republics as well is indicated almost coincidentally by the name of the Syrian military's construction conglomerate, "Milihouse."[14] By comparison, farther to the East in Asia, military relations with the economy have tended to be those of either individual officers being parachuted into state-owned enterprises or military alliances with business elites, both of which point to the greater autonomy of East and Southeast Asian economies from militaries. Another similarity between Pakistan and the Arab world is that there has been only tepid, intermittent external support for civilians seeking to bring the armed forces under control.

Finally, the balance of power in Pakistan between the ruler, the military, and the key security-intelligence agency, although murky, appears reasonably similar to that which obtains within this triumvirate in Arab republics. Pakistan's notorious Interservices Intelligence (ISI), disbanded by the new civilian government in November 2008, was, as the name suggests, a child of the Pakistani military. But it was also a child that outgrew its parents, as symbolized by its lavish headquarters in Islamabad's Aabpara district and other sprawling facilities and its ever-expanding writ into both internal and external security issues. Its prodigious growth after 1977 resulted from Zia ul-Haq having relied upon it to destroy the political opposition then led by Zulfikar Ali Bhutto. The ISI became a pillar of executive power, which even the civilian Prime Minister Nawaz Sharif came to rely on. Patronized by the Pakistani leadership, by the United States, and by sympathetic Arab states, especially Saudi Arabia, the ISI outgrew the military and operated with at least partial autonomy from the executive as well. Although security-intelligence agencies in the Arab world have yet to reach this point, for in all cases they remain subordinate to executives, the Pakistani case could suggest future developments.

Pakistan also differs from the Arab archetype on the key dimensions of the capacity of political opposition and resultant legacy of civilian rule, at least quasi constitutionalism, and rule of law. Pakistan has had intermittent civilian government since 1947. A usual response of opposition rallying cries when the military has been in power has been to return it to the barracks, a call that Arab oppositions rarely uttered prior to the Arab Spring and even then in an intermittent, ineffectual manner. Pakistan, in sum, has a four-actor political game that includes civilian political society, the military, security-intelligence services, and the (frequently military) ruler. In Arab republics, by contrast, while civil society has demonstrated its mobilizational power by virtue of upheavals it spawned, it has yet to mature into a political society with strong, capable, and democratic organizations, the last criterion not being met by the preeminent Islamist organization—the Egyptian Muslim Brotherhood and its offshoots in other Arab countries.

The diversity of Asia renders generalization especially difficult, but the fact that armed forces in Asian countries have been more successfully subordinated to civilian control than their counterparts in the Arab world suggests that there may be some common factors at work in Asian countries. Two in particular seem to be relevant. The first is the comparative strength of civil and political societies, which in virtually all cases of termination of rule by Asian armed forces have played a vitally important role. Like in Latin America, armed forces in Asia have to contend with civilian oppositions that have real political roots and capacities. The second commonality may underpin the first. It is widespread economic growth to which industrialization is the chief contributing factor. Samuel Huntington (1995) observed many years ago that there is a direct correlation between income levels and demilitarization of politics.[15] Asia in general has witnessed sustained industrialization, which in turn has broadened and deepened working and middle classes that serve as the socioeconomic foundations of political organization.[16] By contrast, the Arab world has certainly enjoyed economic growth, which, however, results from hydrocarbon abundance, not from industrialization. As a consequence, Arab class structures are less well formed and coherent than their counterparts in many Asian states. The Arab world lacks "classes for themselves" capable of sustaining political organizations that in turn have the will and the power to stand up to the armed forces.

Africa

Most of sub-Saharan Africa has also had more success in countering armed forces' political influence than has the Arab world. South Africa is the most dramatic example, but that transformation was the side effect of the termination of apartheid. Elsewhere, such as in Nigeria and Ghana, military rule was ended seemingly as a result of factors at both the bottom and top ends of their body politics. At the bottom end, political mobilization, based in some measure on primordial loyalties but inspired also by profound desires to rein in arbitrary, corrupt military rule, provided a serious challenge to incumbent officers. At the top end the armed forces appear to have suffered from more internal dissension and division than has usually been the case elsewhere, including the Arab world. In Ghana, for example, the powerful security-intelligence agency basically imploded, leaving the door open to civilian challengers. In Nigeria, it was possible to play the security forces against the military and thereby achieve civilian hegemony (Fayemi 2003; Hutchful 2003). While Africa's partial success in bringing armed forces under control has resulted from numerous factors, thus rendering generalizations difficult, it does seem to be the case that paradoxically, the relative lack of institutionalization accounts to some degree for the termination of military rule. Having undermined their own legitimacy and credibility through poor governance and corruption, African militaries and security agencies, at least in some instances, have had insufficient coherence to withstand popular challenges to their authority, which are themselves based more in organic than civil society solidarities.

Lessons from These Regional Cases

The preceding cursory overview of civil-military relations in different regions of the globe suggests some tentative hypotheses that may be of use for investigating the Arab world and the comparatively retarded nature of civil-military relations within it. As regards interactions between militaries, security forces, and rulers, a general trend appears to be that security-intelligence agencies tend to become more powerful in the continued absence of civilian rule. Presumably, their cancer-like political growth in authoritarian political systems results from their utility to incumbent rulers, based in turn on their internal coherence, extensive personal networks, possession of information, and capacities for coercion. Indeed, with the exception of Ghana, divisions within security-intelligence services have not played vital roles in transitions to civilian rule. Moreover, even after civilian rule has been established, security-intelligence agencies have frequently continued to elude effective civilian control as new rulers have turned to them as allies in their political struggles in transitional democracies. In the case of Russia, the key security agency managed to gain absolute control of the government. But in numerous other settings, the skills, information, and connections of security agents enabled them as individuals to land on their feet in new civilian political orders, thereby opening up the possibility that networks of former agents play important roles in civilianized political economies.[17] In sum, once security intelligence agencies have been empowered as a result of authoritarian governments requiring their services, their power tends to grow at the expense of both individual rulers and militaries. It can even persist after their original patrons have been displaced by democratically inclined civilians.

As for militaries, the easiest form of rule by them to displace seems to be the purest one, whereby officers in uniform move directly into government positions. Unless militaries burrow down into political economies and create a layer of civilian political camouflage, they are vulnerable to pressures that force them back into the barracks, including those of internal divisions between services. As direct military rule becomes ever more anomalous globally, its surviving examples steadily become more likely to either evolve into more sophisticated subterranean forms of rule by armed forces or be replaced by civilians. Similarly, individual strongmen, emerging from officer corps and then establishing their personal power as paramount, are also an increasingly scarce species outside the Arab world. Examples of their demise, such as those of Musharraf and Pinochet, are possibly deterrents to such ambitions, at least in their crudest forms, while this type of rule may also be more vulnerable to civilian resistance, as Venezuela under Chavez might suggest. General 'Abd al-Fattah al-Sisi therefore appears to be a historical anomaly if viewed in global perspective. His continued widespread support in Egypt following his election as president in May 2014 attests to that country's arrested political and economic development.

The consequences for national elite political games of the contexts within which they are played seem also to exhibit some regularities. Rule by armed forces is unlikely to persist in those settings where the capacities of civil and political societies steadily expand as a result of broad-based economic growth and where key external actors are ready, willing, and able to support transitions to civilian rule. Conversely, if one or more of the factors of (1) coherent and capable civil/political societies, (2) economic growth based in expanding industrialization, and (3) external support are missing, then such transitions are substantially less likely. There are, of course, anomalous cases, such as where economic stagnation undermines military rule, as occasionally has been the case in Africa, but generally, if these key elements are missing, it requires a breakdown in the national political game—due, for example, to intra- or interservice rivalries—to open the door to civilian control of ruling armed forces.

The contemporary Arab political environment is in this case not conducive to bringing armed forces under civilian control. Civil and political societies are weak and divided, polarized between ethnic, religious, linguistic, and tribal identities. Industrialization other than downstream hydrocarbon processing is proceeding slowly if at all, so potential class-based solidarities are attenuated by a variety of vertical cleavages and by the predominance of manufacturing employment in informal, micro, and small enterprises that are typically family-based. The globalized middle class that has emerged remains largely politically inchoate. Its members tend to perceive the fragmented lower classes as potential threats, especially in their Islamist sociopolitical variant, and typically seek political shelter under the umbrella of authoritarian, military-backed regimes. Potential external support for civilian rule, whether provided by the United States or the European Union, is deterred by worries about Islamism and terrorism, the need for cooperation on regional issues, energy concerns, and calculations of the limited potential for successful transitions. External pressure for change is thus weak. So, if real change is to come in the near future, it will most likely be as a result of conflicts between players of the game of elite politics rather than broad sociopolitical developments or external factors. For civil and political societies to become decisive factors in subordinating militaries to democratic control, their further development will be necessary prior to that.

The Arab Spring: Reinforcing the Status Quo Ante

The cruel paradox of the Arab Spring to date is that it has reinforced the exceptionalism of the region as manifested by the nexus of authoritarianism, casualties, and coercion, which in turn is both a consequence and a cause of the lack of democratic control of armed forces. The upheavals either blew away the soft state infrastructure sitting atop deep states, leaving only the bedrock of armed forces intact, as in Egypt; empowered paramilitaries and militias, as in Libya; or both, as in the case of Syria. Rulers from Rabat to Riyad, who have not been swept aside by the upheaval, have employed carrot-and-stick strategies, the latter of which has further empowered their coercive forces. Indeed, Max Weber's "paradox of the sultan," whereby the ruler's increasing use of coercive force diminishes his authority over the armed forces, might come to constitute a second stage of the upheaval, particularly in the monarchies.[18] Jordan's King Abdullah stands out as a possible candidate among family monarchies, but even the tribal monarchies, led by Saudi Arabia, have come to lean more heavily on their armed forces, hence rendering these monarchs more vulnerable to the sultan's paradox. Deployment of army units in Bahrain in 2011, followed by direct military interventions into Libya in 2014 and Yemen in 2015, reflects the external power-projection component of royal counterrevolutionary strategies. The flip side of those strategies is internal repression, as reflected not only by its intensification by the Al-Khalifa monarchy in Bahrain and the Al-Saud monarchy in Saudi Arabia, long the most repressive of monarchies in the Gulf Cooperation Council, but also by the historically more benign Emirati and Kuwaiti ruling families, which have also deemed it necessary to rely ever more heavily on internal security forces. The growing militarization and securitization of monarchial politics, including the increasing appointment of members of royal families into key positions in militaries and security forces, threaten to transform heretofore largely nonviolent intrafamily political struggles into violent ones.

In the republics, the "sultans"—whether Saddam Hussein, Muammar Qaddafi, Ben Ali, 'Ali 'Abdullah Salih, or Hosni Mubarak—have already been swept aside, while Bashar al-Assad hangs on to his power stubbornly. In all these cases, with the exception of Tunisia, it is both the residual deep states and their Hegelian antitheses of opposing coercive forces that have been empowered. In Iraq, Nuri al-Maliki's and then Haidar al-Abadi's regimes have drawn upon the U.S.-retrained military and security services as well as Shiite militias in thus far vain attempts to subdue their enemies, which are themselves steadily coalescing into the ISIL (Islamic State) "caliphate," a sprawling militia cum wannabee state. In Syria, the regime's coercive capacities also consist primarily of militaries and irregular units backed by external powers, principally Iran and Russia in this case, and of sectarian-based militias augmented by Hizbullah, the very progenitor of that model in the Arab world. The Hegelian dialectic of coercion there has given rise to a gaggle of militias, including ISIL, while totally eviscerating nonviolent opposition forces. In Yemen, the sectarian militia, known commonly as the Houthis, has managed to best the regime's forces backed by the United States and the Saudis, largely because of support provided it by elements of the military loyal to ousted former president 'Ali 'Abdullah Salih. In Libya, the sultan and his deep state were swept away by militias backed by external sovereign powers, with the ensuing power vacuum filled by tribal, regional, and Islamist paramilitary forces, in turn backed by competing sovereign external actors. In Egypt, the military is the big winner in the struggle to control the nation's destiny. It has vanquished its primary civilian challenger, the Muslim Brotherhood; subordinated the Ministry of the Interior's various security and intelligence forces to its control; eroded the networks and bases of the Mubaraks' various crony clients, thereby rendering their assets ripe for the picking; reinforced its standing as the country's most popular institution; and put forward a new man on horseback to cash in on the longings of the population for security and a return to the imagined, glorious Nasser era.

In no Arab republic have institutions of civilian government been empowered, and indeed, parliaments, courts, local governments, and so on are still weaker at this point than prior to the upheaval. Constitutional government seems as far or even farther away than it did in 2010, despite what so far have been, again with the exception of Tunisia, fruitless exercises in constitution writing. Underlying these failures of civilian political will is the profound divide between Islamists and anti-Islamists, which militaries and security forces have successfully exploited.

Contextual factors have reinforced the rebalancing of Arab civil-military relations in the latter's favor, so long as military is understood to include militias. Regional tensions, whether resulting from sectarian or ethnic differences, Islamist violence, the civil war in Syria, the never-ending Israeli-Palestinian conflict, or the competition between Iran and Saudi Arabia, undermine appeals from civilians to scale back overblown militaries and security services. Indeed, civilians for the most part have bought into narratives about these various challenges facing themselves; fellow members of their organic religious, ethnic, tribal, or regional solidarities; and their nations. Civilians have therefore largely assented to yet more power for armed forces, whether militaries or militias. The United States, following its brief and ineffectual flirtations with civilians, including Islamists, is drifting back to its natural local allies in Washington's securitized view of the Arab world, which are armed forces preferably of the sovereign military type but, in their absence, such as in Libya, or their unacceptability, as in Syria, are militias. So, whether driven by domestic, regional, or global factors, the forces unleashed by the Arab Spring have extended, not ended, Arab exceptionalism.

Implications for the Future of Arab Civil-Military Relations

Scholars of the Middle East and North Africa are again forced to return to the question that preoccupied them prior to the Arab Spring—namely, how long can Arab exceptionalism last? Is the political resurgence of Arab armed forces—regular or irregular, military or security-intelligence, and their encroachment on even royal power—a temporary or a lasting phenomenon? Can civil-military relations in the Arab world remain globally unique in an increasingly interconnected world that shares ever more norms about acceptable forms and methods of governing?

The answer depends on both civilians and the military. If the former remain divided along ethnic/sectarian and Islamist/anti-Islamist lines and hence are consumed by resulting political struggles, they are unlikely to come together against the common enemy of coercive forces, as they have done in Latin America, Asia, Eastern Europe, and even Africa. As for the armed forces in the republics, both their civilian fellow-citizens and global actors have cut them a lot of slack, but that slack is not infinitely elastic. If militaries do not adequately cloak their rule with civilian garb, they will become much more vulnerable when and if the upheavals in the wake of the Arab Spring subside. Even triumphant militias will ultimately face pressures to at least partially civilianize. But both Arab militaries and empowered militias, whether in suits or khaki, are for the foreseeable future unlikely to be subordinated to effective civilian control. As for royal armed forces, not having tasted real power yet, they would be more likely to want to exercise it while still in uniform if indeed they were to seize it. In that case, one could anticipate that antiroyalist sentiments would be stoked to such a pitch that the generals would be accorded substantial domestic political legitimacy. Since many of them would be in control of large hydrocarbon reserves, the international community would likely acquiescence in their rule. But even absent antiroyalist coups, monarchial militaries are likely to increase their powers as ruling families or just members of them become steadily more reliant upon coercion. The Arab world, in sum, is likely to continue waiting for its Godot of democratic control of the armed forces.

Notes

1. "Deep states" refers to informal links and ties between security officials and their partners in various civilian spheres that have an impact on policy making and concrete policies in the state. See Söyler (2013).

2. It is interesting to note that Egypt's military spending of 3.4 percent of GDP ranks it thirty-fifth in the world, and Algeria's spending at 3.3 percent ranks it thirty-sixth.

3. For a review of the data, see Malik and Awadallah (2013:6). They note that "in comparative terms, defense spending is high even in resource-scarce countries (e.g., Morocco, Jordan, Syria, and Lebanon) and even after accounting for the large outlay in internal security."

4. Publication of *A Comparative Atlas of Defence in Latin America and the Caribbean* was assisted by the Open Society Institute, the National Endowment for Democracy, and the Center for Civil-Military Relations of the U.S. Department of Defense, based at the Naval Postgraduate School in Monterey, California.

5. President Hugo Chavez vastly enhanced the role of the military in Venezuelan politics. At the time of his death, eleven of twenty state governors and a quarter of cabinet ministers were former military officers. Leading state-owned enterprises, such as the Guayana Corporation, are headed by retired officers, who also play a key role in the underground economy, especially in drug trafficking. A key question concerning the country's political future is whether or not Chavez's chosen successor, Nicolas Maduro, who unlike Chavez was not formerly an officer, will be able to contain the military.

6. See also Stacher (2013). All the scores of members of the Muslim Brotherhood tried in the wake of the July 3, 2013, military takeover have been subjected to the military justice system.

7. This is the wording, for example, in the Chilean Constitution (RESDAL 2012:15).

8. For online access to the Egyptian Constitution, see Marsad Egypt (2014), a site sponsored by the Geneva Center for the Democratic Control of Armed Forces.

9. Under Vladimir Putin, the security-intelligence agencies came to dominate not only the office of the presidency but also government more generally. *Siloviki*, as they are termed, have been appointed as head of the presidential administration, chief of staff for the cabinet of ministers, chief of personnel of the presidential administration, first deputy chief of the president's office, deputy director of the Russian news agency TASS, etc. More than one-third of deputy ministers appointed by Putin were *siloviki*. They reached their apogee in 2007, at which time two-thirds of top state posts were held by them. That proportion subsequently declined to about half under Putin's successor, Dimitry Medvedev (Tsypkin 2007; see also Glover 2009).

10. It is interesting to note the correlation between the rise of *siloviki* and the decline of the Soviet Union. In 1988, only 5.4 percent of government positions were occupied by KGB and military officers, a proportion that rose to 11 percent in 1993, 22 percent in 1999, and 32 percent in Putin's first term. The decline of the Communist Party clearly

paved the way for the rise of the agencies of coercion (Kryshtanovskaya and White 2003). Zybertowicz (2007) uses the term "dirty togetherness" to describe the networks and attitudes of security agents in these settings.

11. On myth making by the KGB and the FSB, see Dziak (1988) and Tsypkin (2007).

12. For good assessments of these relationships in various East European countries, including the Czech Republic and Slovenia, see Born et al. (2007).

13. On this term and the economic underpinnings of military rule in Pakistan, see Siddiqa (2007). A similar expansion into the Iranian economy by the Islamic Revolutionary Guards Corps (Pasdaran) has also occurred, thereby suggesting that this might be a common phenomenon in the Middle East (Wehrey et al. 2009).

14. On Milihouse, or Sharikat al-Iskan al-'Askari (Military Housing Company), see Lawson (1993) and Picard (1993).

15. This finding has been reinforced by other studies that reveal negative correlations between income and authoritarianism. See, for example, Barrow (1999), Boix and Stokes (2003), Epstein et al. (2006), and Przeworski et al. (2000).

16. For the application of this argument in the broader Asian context, see Alagappa (2001). For a variation of the argument that stresses the importance of including the military itself in the benefits of rapid economic growth, see Beeson (2008).

17. The case of Poland from 1990 to 2005, in which incumbent governments came to rely heavily on intelligence operatives active in the former communist regime, is a particularly interesting case in point. See Zybertowicz (2007) and Gogolewska (2006).

18. See especially the description of sultanism in Weber (1978 [1921]:231–32).

PART II

Military Engagement
in the Arab Uprisings

CHAPTER 5

Should I Stay or Should I Go?
Comparing Military (Non-)Cooperation
During Authoritarian Regime Crises
in the Arab World and Asia

Aurel Croissant and Tobias Selge

Control of the military by the political leadership is a crucial prerequisite for the stability of any political regime. However, in authoritarian regimes this "civil-military problematique" (Feaver 1996) is particularly relevant. Due to the high vulnerability of authoritarian regimes to horizontal (from inside the regime coalition) threats to their survival (resulting from challenges of authoritarian power sharing) and vertical threats from below (resulting from violent or nonviolent forms of mass contention; see, for instance, Gandhi and Przeworski 2007; Schedler 2009; Svolik 2012), all autocracies must guarantee the continuous loyalty and willingness of their militaries to defend the regime against these challenges. Particularly in situations of nonviolent revolutions and anti-incumbent mass mobilization, the dictator's ability to guarantee the loyalty of the military is crucial for his political survival (Skocpol 1979; Goldstone 2001; Chenoweth and Stephan 2011; Nepstad 2011; Croissant 2013b; Croissant and Kuehn 2015). The factors, however, that determine the military's loyalty and the causal mechanisms behind these factors have so far mostly been disregarded. In particular, the current literature on civic resistance, nonviolent revolutions, and other forms of nonviolent antiregime contention (see Schock 2005; Ulfelder 2005; Chenoweth and Stephan 2011; Nepstad 2011) provides ample evidence for the crucial importance of "loyalty shifts" within the security apparatuses (Chenoweth and Stephan 2011) but almost exclusively view the military (and security services) as reacting to the tactics and repertoires of contention employed by protesters or opposition movements. Our contribution aims to tackle these shortcomings and focuses particularly on when the military decides in favor of defending a dictator (cooperation) and grants the regime leader its repressive capacities during an authoritarian regime crisis triggered by mass mobilization[1] as well as when the military decides in favor of defection and denies the regime said capacities.

The model that we develop in the following section argues that the decision of the military to defend the dictator or to defect from the regime is a result of a two-step cost-benefit analysis. This model suggests that military leaders calculate the expected utility of the two strategic choices with regard to their autonomy from the authoritarian regime and the effect of their choice on the maintenance of military cohesion. As the reader will note immediately, the main differences between our approach and, for instance, the explanatory framework presented by David Pion-Berlin in his contribution to this volume are twofold. First, while his explanation is based on a careful reading of empirical episodes of what he calls the "endgame" and is hence an example of inductive theorizing, our theoretical framework is the result of deductive theorizing. Both inductive and deductive theory building have advantages and disadvantages. We see the advantage of a deductively induced model in the fact that the analysis of empirical cases does not lead to the formulation of the theoretical model and does not build the fundament for the selection of explanatory factors. Hence, the model as such does not suffer from the more typical problems of inductive theorizing such as selection bias, right-censored samples, or omitted variables.

In the empirical section, the model will be tested against a number of cases in the Middle East and North Africa (MENA) as well as in Asia. The variance in the outcome as well as in other factors such as regime type, geopolitical context, timing, and economic, cultural, and historical factors provide our findings with a high degree of plausibility and robustness. We conclude with a short summary and an outline of the next steps in building on our findings.

The Model

Our analysis focuses on the question of why the armed forces choose to defend (cooperate) or to defect during an authoritarian regime crisis.[2] To answer this question, we develop a theoretical model that considers the decisions made by the military during a specific decision-making situation. We develop this model in three steps. First we conceptualize the decision-making situation (dictator's endgame), then we conceptualize the dependent variable (cooperation/defection), and finally we develop our hypotheses, which will be tested in the empirical sections.

The Decision-Making Situation: The Dictator's Endgame

The dictator's endgame is characterized by three individually necessary and jointly sufficient conditions:[3] (1) the dictator is challenged by predominantly nonviolent oppositional mass mobilization, (2) the nonmilitary security apparatus is unable to contain unrest, and (3) the survival of the dictator therefore depends on the military's disposition and capability to cooperate or defect from the regime. While military action in order to defend the dictator does not necessarily guarantee his or their political survival, as the outcome of antiregime contention depends on many other factors as well, military noncooperation and defection from the regime's leadership will end the ruler's term in office (and perhaps even cause his death, exile, or incarceration). Finally, our model omits any further discussion of the security services and concentrates exclusively on dynamics associated with the regular army. This is not because we believe that security services do not matter; obviously they do, especially in the Near and in the Middle East where many states may rightfully be described as "security states" (see, for instance, Droz-Vincent's contribution to this volume). Moreover, as Fred Lawson points out in his chapter, state-affiliated security services "can be expected to have a strong incentive to protect and advance the current and future interests of the existing political system." Yet, the dictator's endgame, as described above, is characterized by the failure of security services to contain and disperse antiregime protests. Hence, in a dictator's endgame, the ball is already in the court of the regular armed forces.[4]

The Explanandum: Military Defection and Cooperation

In our analysis, the dependent variable is the military's decision to cooperate with the dictator (that is, to defend the ruler) or to defect from his rule (Lee 2015). This will be measured by observations of the actual behavior of the military's leadership. While we agree with Ohl and Albrecht in this volume that military reactions to regime crises may include episodes of large-scale desertion by military personnel (both lower ranks and officers), we assume that in the modern world national armed forces are at least in a formal sense hierarchical organizations with a sufficient degree of organizational coherence and cohesion. Of course, armies such as the ones to be found in Qaddafi's Libya and in Yemen suffered from the eroding influences of tribalization, compartmentalization, and the ruler's divide-and-rule tactics. Nevertheless, the unitary actor assumption on which our model rests is a methodologically useful tool for formulating clear (and testable) hypotheses; it is a well-established assumption in game theory and rational choice literature (including civil-military relations literature) that aims to model and explain the behavior of collective actors (such as political parties, unions, bureaucracies, or, as in this chapter, the armed forces); and, as we see it, it also makes sense empirically, as most if not all military organizations in the modern world are led by the commanding generals and follow their orders. The breakdown of military order or the collapse of the military-as-institution usually is the result of military defection during episodes of regime crisis and anti-incumbent mass mobilization but is not a cause for defection.

Military cooperation occurs when the military engages in political repression of the protestors. The military defects from the dictator when it does not comply with a regime's order to suppress mass protests or when key individuals and groups within the military organization signal to the dictator that they would be unwilling or unable to do what the government asks of them.

Hypotheses

We explain the military's decision to shoot or not to shoot based on a decision theoretical model. Following Samuel Finer (1962) and Jonathan Powell (2012a), we distinguish between the capability of the military to defect from the dictator and its disposition to do so. In other words, we ask whether a military is able to defect from the regime and under which circumstances it wants to do so. Only a military that has both the capability *and* the disposition to defect from the authoritarian regime will actually opt for the strategy of defection. A military that lacks either the capability or the disposition to defect will, in contrast, cooperate with the dictator.

Military Capability to Defect:
The Autonomy from the Dictator

The military's capability to defect is determined by its autonomy from the dictator. However, the autonomy of the military is not contingent. Dictators know that their political survival depends to some extent on the loyalty of the military (Brooks 1998:9; Bellin 2004). Accordingly, they have an incentive to use coup-proofing strategies (Quinlivan 1999; Pilster and Böhmelt 2011; Powell 2012a, 2012b) to prevent the military from political interventions. Similarly, Michael Makara (2013) has differentiated between different types of coup-proofing that have different implications for the question of loyalty or defection during mass uprisings. These strategies work as a device to weaken military autonomy, thus providing incentives to military officers not to defect from the regime coalition. Regarding the impact on the autonomy of the military from the regime, the most important coup-proofing strategies are counterbalancing, ascriptive selection (aimed at creating nonmaterial bonds between regime and military elites), and appeasement (which serves to create and strengthen material bonds between the regime leadership and the regular armed forces).[5]

Through counterbalancing, regime leaders attempt to balance the coercive capacities of the military by compartmentalization of the regular army, creating rivalries between military units, or by building up multiple internal security agencies and parallel organizations with command structures outside the army (Belkin and Schofer 2003:613; Pilster and Böhmelt 2011:336). These counterunits do not possess any degree of autonomy, but the survival of these units (and, more important, their members) depends on the continuation of the regime. This is especially the case if these units have been employed to defend the regime against threats from below in the past.

Ascriptive selection refers to a regime's ability to control personal decisions within the armed forces and to reduce the probability of military insubordination by recruiting and promoting military personnel from the members of a certain ethnic or religious group, clan, class, or region into the military leadership (Croissant et al. 2011:87; Roessler 2011; Powell 2012a). While this recruitment policy creates tight bonds between military and nonmilitary regime leaders, it also raises the potential costs of a regime breakdown for the military in terms of the organizational (or individual) survival of the military (McLauchlin 2010; Makara 2013). However, ascriptive selection can also (unintentionally) have the consequence of weakening the internal coherence

of the military if the highly politicized system of military reshuffling and promotions divides the military into factions of losers and winners (Lee 2015).

Appeasement increases benefits of cooperation with the government by
maintaining policies to protect military autonomy, prerogatives, or economic
benefits (Croissant et al. 2011:87). However, appeasement remains a double-
edged sword for authoritarian regimes. Although it may help to "buy" military
loyalty, the effectiveness of this strategy always depends on the regime's ability to deliver private goods to the military. Furthermore, the strategy might
actually enhance the military's autonomy from the authoritarian regime if the
military is granted economic, administrative, or political resources that it can
develop independently from the authoritarian regime (Pion-Berlin, Grisham,
and Esparza 2014).

Overall, counterbalancing and ascriptive selection serve as rather robust
control strategies, whereas appeasement must be qualified as nonrobust.
Hence, the following hypotheses are posited:

> Hypothesis 1: Counterbalancing and ascriptive selection strategies by
> autocratic rulers will decrease the autonomy of the military, and
> therefore the military will choose to cooperate with the dictator.
>
> Hypothesis 1.1: If a regime uses counterbalancing and ascriptive
> selection, it is also to be expected that the regime will primarily
> use those loyal paramilitary and regular military units for repres-
> sion that do not possess autonomy from the regime.
>
> Hypothesis 1.2 (null hypothesis): If a regime uses only nonrobust
> control strategies, which do not tie the military to the political
> survival of the dictator, the military will only fully cooperate if this
> is in line with its institutional interests (which need to be analyzed
> in a second step).

By identifying the control strategies employed by the regime, it is possible to
determine the extent of autonomy of the military from the regime: where the
regime uses robust strategies, its autonomy is low. On the other hand, weak
strategies will result in a higher degree of autonomy of the military.

While low autonomy is the sufficient condition for military cooperation
during a regime crisis, high autonomy is only a necessary condition for military defection. A nonautonomous military has no capability for defection,
but a highly autonomous military does not necessarily have the disposition
to defect from the regime.

Military Disposition: Effects on Military Cohesion

The disposition of an autonomous military to defect is a function of the costs of such a decision in terms of its core institutional interest. As Barbara Geddes (1999:25–26) writes, "there is . . . a consensus in the literature that most professional soldiers place a higher value on the *survival and efficacy* of the military itself than on anything else." The function of a modern military organization is the use of force (Huntington 1957:11). The direction, control, and implementation of operations that involve the use of military force, however, require a coherent military organization (Janowitz 1960:42–48; Finer 1962:7–12; Siebold 2007:292; Lee 2005:4–87). While we agree with Ohl's observation in this volume that the study of military cohesion suffers from some problems of underconceptualization and "that it is difficult to measure whether cohesion exists on an institutional level," we believe that there is abundant evidence in the literature on civil-military relations to assume that maintaining organizational cohesion ranks as the prime interest of military officers. Therefore, with regard to our model we assume the following hypothesis:

> Hypothesis 2: As the sufficient condition for defection, military cooperation must entail high institutional costs for the military in terms of its organizational cohesion. This is the case if an autonomous military is factionalized or otherwise characterized by important internal conflicts, which may erupt if the military leadership decides to defend a dictator against the nonviolent popular movement.

The degree of institutional cohesion of the military, in turn, is a consequence of the control strategies used by the authoritarian regimes. Appeasement strategies can have adverse effects on military cohesion (Stepan 1988). Counterbalancing and ascriptive selection can create losers in the military but—if applied to the majority of the officer corps or entire units—will also create cohesive forces that the dictator can use for repression without risking the cohesion of these units. From these assertions, we form a further hypothesis:

> Hypothesis 2.1: A military cooperates with a dictator if cooperation does not threaten the cohesion of the forces used for repression.

To sum up, a lack of autonomy from the dictator is sufficient to explain military cooperation during a dictator's endgame. The degree of autonomy is a consequence of the coup-proofing strategies used by the regime. Cooperation is then to be expected if repression causes low or no costs for the military. Organizational cohesion is only relevant to explain why an autonomous military may decide to cooperate or to defect: Defection occurs if (a) the military is autonomous from the regime and (b) military officers assume that cooperation with the regime will threaten the cohesion of the military organization. In that case, cooperation entails greater expected costs than defection. Whether cooperation will threaten military cohesion depends then again on the regime's coup-proofing strategies.

Empirical Analysis

The following analysis applies our model first to three cases in the MENA region (Egypt, Syria, and Tunisia in 2011). This is followed by the analysis of four country cases in Asia (Bangladesh in 1990, South Korea in 1980, South Korea in 1987, and the People's Republic of China in 1989). Testing the proposed model requires a two-step approach consisting of, first, the classification of the military's behavior in each dictator's endgame as (a) defection or (b) cooperation; second, we test the relevant hypotheses concerning (a) the relationship between military autonomy and the outcome as well as (b) the relation between military cohesion and outcome. The case studies serve as "plausibility probes" or "pilot studies" (Eckstein [1975] 1992; Ragin 1997) that will provide proximal evidence for the plausibility of our theoretical assumptions. Conclusions must remain tentative, however, since despite the high degree of variance in both the dependent and the independent variables, the countries under study are but seven of more than forty autocracies that have experienced a dictator's endgame since 1946 (Croissant and Kuehn 2015).

Tunisia 2011

The self-immolation of street vendor Muhammad Bouazizi in late 2010 started a series of protests that eventually grew into a nationwide protest wave against President Ben Ali. After mass mobilization had reached a degree that could not be controlled anymore by the internal security apparatus, Ben Ali ordered the military to repress the demonstrations. However, chief of staff

General Ammar explicitly refused the firing order. Even more, during the demonstrations the military protected the population from assaults by the security apparatus (Lutterbeck 2013:35) and eventually also took violent military action against the police and the Presidential Guard Forces (PGF) before it returned to the barracks (Droz-Vincent 2011a:7; Brooks 2013).

Theoretical Expectations

As Tunisia is a clear case of military defection during a regime crisis, we would expect the following empirical observations according to the theoretical model: Since the military opts for the strategy of defection, we can expect a high autonomy of the Tunisian armed forces from the regime as the necessary condition for this strategy. Thus, we expect the regime to have used only nonrobust control strategies (Hypothesis 1.2). Additionally, we expect that as the sufficient condition for defection, the potential strategy of cooperation must entail high institutional costs for the military for its organizational cohesion (Hypothesis 2).

Testing the Hypotheses

(a) *Autonomy*. We argue that the military first assesses its autonomy from the dictator, which in turn is a function of the employed control strategies. For Tunisia, we identify only a low degree of counterbalancing (Croissant 2013b; Makara 2013; Lutterbeck 2013). The only relevant counterbalancing force, the PGF, lacked the capacities necessary to repress the mass demonstrations. Thus, Ben Ali had no counterbalancing forces at his disposal that were tied to the regime *and* had the capabilities to guarantee regime survival through effective repression. Also, ascriptive selection as an equally robust control strategy cannot be identified in the Tunisian case. Due to the homogenous nature of the Tunisian society, Ben Ali was not able to exploit primordial ties to connect the survival of the officer corps to the survival of his regime. Thus, the military was not separated from the population along ethnic or sectarian lines (Bellin 2012:134; Brooks in this volume). Ben Ali did not even employ appeasement strategies to control the military. On the contrary, compared to the internal security apparatus, the armed forces had been systematically disadvantaged under Ben Ali (Springborg and Henry 2011) and instead belonged to the losers of the appeasement strategies (Bellin 2012:134; Hanlon 2012a:4).

The behavior of the military confirms the theoretical expectations: The regime had only employed nonrobust strategies to control the military. Furthermore, these strategies even alienated the armed forces from the regime (Hypothesis 1.2). Thus, the military was autonomous from the dictator (but not depoliticized), which in our model is the necessary condition for the strategy of defection.

(b) *Cohesion.* To explain the military's defection, the potential costs of the military's actions for its organizational cohesion have to be analyzed. Such costs resulting from cooperation with the regime can be identified in the Tunisian case. The Tunisian military was tightly connected to the Tunisian society through conscripts, who in most cases even shared the grievances of the protestors (Lutterbeck 2013:35). Additionally, since mass demonstrations were peaceful, repression of the demonstrations could not be framed within a national security imperative for the conscripts (Bellin 2012:134). Compliance with the shooting order given by the dictator most likely would have led to mass defections among the conscripts. Anecdotal evidence supports this assumption, as the military protected the demonstrators from the security forces and even fought the PGF (Amara and Lowe 2011). This demonstrates the military's rejection of the Ben Ali regime and renders the actual implementation of any firing order highly improbable.

Thus, we also find the theoretical expectations with regard to the military cohesion confirmed. The decision to defend the dictator would have entailed high institutional costs for the military leadership through the potential erosion of military cohesion. In order to maintain cohesion, the military leadership had to refuse Ben Ali's firing order and opt for defection (Hypothesis 2). The potential threat to the military cohesion inherent in the strategy of cooperation thus constitutes the sufficient condition for the military's decision to defect.

Egypt 2011

In Hosni Mubarak's Egypt, the armed forces also defected from the dictator. When the internal security apparatus eventually failed to contain the mass demonstrations in any part of the country, Minister of the Interior Habib al-Adly ordered the security forces to retreat (International Crisis Group 2011b;

El-Ghobashy 2011). In order to guarantee the survival of his rule, Mubarak was by then completely dependent on the military. However, on January 31 the military announced that it would not use violence to repress the demonstrations (BBC Online January 31, 2011). This announcement already constituted the refusal of the military's repressive capacities for the regime. Yet in the face of the continuing demonstrations, the general strike, and the possibility of a direct confrontation with demonstrators, the military's behavior changed to open defection. Finally, on February 11 Vice President 'Umar Sulaiman announced Mubarak's resignation and the formal takeover by the Supreme Council of the Armed Forces (Albrecht and Bishara 2011).

Theoretical Expectations

Since the Egyptian armed forces opted for defection, our theoretical model predicts the following: a high autonomy of the Egyptian armed forces from the dictator. Thus, we expect the regime to have used only nonrobust control strategies (Hypothesis 1.2). Additionally—as the sufficient condition for defection—we expect to find factions or at least significant structural tension within the military that would lead to high institutional costs for the military for its organizational cohesion in case of the potential strategy of cooperation (Hypothesis 2).

Testing the Hypotheses

(a) *Autonomy.* We expect a relatively high degree of autonomy of the Egyptian military from the regime leadership, which in turn is a function of the control strategies employed by Mubarak. Like Ben Ali, Egyptian president Mubarak only made little use of counterbalancing. The only relevant counterbalancing force, the Central Security Forces, was poorly equipped and trained and thus lacked the necessary capacities to successfully contain regime-threatening mass mobilization (Gotowicki 1997; for a more historically informed comparison, see Koehler's contribution in this volume). The PGF likewise did not serve as a significant counterbalancing force, as it was subordinate to the Ministry of Defense (Brooks 1998:39). Moreover, there is only little empirical evidence for a routinized and systematic use of ascriptive selection by Mubarak. Instead, he heavily relied on appeasing the armed forces by providing the military with vast economic prerogatives. In return for a decreasing military budget (but still high in absolute numbers and completely off the books), Mubarak allowed the generals to create an economic empire appropriately described as "military inc." by Robert Springborg (2011b). Mubarak also created a cradle-to-grave welfare system for the officer corps (Abdul-Magd 2012; Springborg 2011a). Additionally, US$1.3 billion in U.S. foreign military aid were directly provided to the military. Nevertheless, appeasement had also lost its effectiveness, as the rise of the business elite around Mubarak's son Gamal constituted a real threat to the economic activities of the military (Lutterbeck 2013:37). Thus, Mubarak was no longer able to credibly guarantee the military the long-term flow of private goods.

Overall, the Egyptian case confirms Hypothesis 1.2: The regime only employed nonrobust control strategies, which left the military relatively autonomous from the dictator, thus constituting the necessary condition for the decision of the military to defect.

(b) *Cohesion.* Similar to the Tunisian case, cooperation would have entailed high institutional costs for the Egyptian military (Hypothesis 2). The Egyptian military as an institution was highly cohesive, but several structural tensions flared under the surface that threatened to erupt in case of a firing order by the military leadership. Ironically, it was the control strategies employed by the regime that created vertical tensions between the military leadership and the junior officers through forestalled career possibilities for the younger officers, a perceived threat to military professionalism (*New York Times* 2011), and grievances of junior officers who felt economically deprived by their senior officers (International Crisis Group 2011b:16). Universal conscription worked in a similar direction (Lutterbeck 2013:37). The potential danger of erosion of military cohesion in case of a firing order can be evidenced by incidents during the Supreme Council of the Armed Forces regime, when junior officers staged mutinies (Awad 2012) or even defected from the military (Steavenson 2011).

These institutional costs serve as the sufficient condition for the strategic decision of the military. In order to maintain military cohesion, the military leadership opted for defection. Additionally, our model can partly explain the time lag between the military's refusal of its repressive capacities on January 31 and its actual defection on February 11. With its announcement on January 31, the autonomous military had realized its organizational cohesion appropriate to the degree of threat without having to cause the breakdown of the regime (Lutterbeck 2013:38). However, due to the continuing mass mobilization and the rising possibility of a violent confrontation between the demonstrators and the PGF, the military could only realize its cohesion by open defection.

Syria 2011

While in Syria the first incidents of mass mobilization were successfully repressed by the internal security apparatus, mass demonstrations did not stop but instead spread and even moved toward Damascus (Shadid 2011; Droz-Vincent in this volume). Thus, on April 22, 2011, in Dara'a, the regime resorted to the repressive capacities of the military for the first time and conducted military operations in order to permanently contain mass mobilization (Al Jazeera English 2011). As of May 2011, military repression of the demonstrations had spread almost nationwide (for more detail, see Droz-Vincent's chapter in this volume).

Theoretical Expectations

Obviously, the military leadership in Syria cooperated with the regime in its attempt to repress the opposition. According to our theoretical model, we would expect the following: As the military opts for the strategy of cooperation, our model predicts a low autonomy of the military from the regime. Thus, we expect the Syrian regime to have used robust control strategies (Hypothesis 1). Accordingly, we expect that repression is carried out by those regular and paramilitary units that are particularly dependent on the dictator through counterbalancing and ascriptive selection (Hypothesis 1.1). Finally, we expect that cooperation does not threaten the cohesion of the armed forces used for repression due to the control strategies employed by the regime (Hypothesis 2.1).

Testing the Hypotheses

(a) *Autonomy.* In contrast to the governments in Tunis and Cairo, ascriptive selection played a central role for Hafiz al-Assad's rule of a religiously and ethnically heterogeneous Syria. As a result, by the time of Bashar al-Assad's presidency, roughly 90 percent of the Syrian officers were Alawi (Brooks 1998:32; Zisser 2002:119). Unlike the Tunisian and Egyptian officer corps, their Syrian counterpart was tightly bound to the survival of the dictator. In addition to their historical socioeconomic deprivation (Hinnebusch 1990:62–66), the Alawis had already experienced religiously motivated terrorism (Hinnebusch 1990:291–99). Moreover, the Lebanese and Iraqi examples of a (partly) sectarian civil war were in their immediate vicinity. Ascriptive selection was combined with counterbalancing, as the two major counterbalancing forces, the Republican Guard and the Fourth Armored Division (both division-sized and equipped with modern heavy weapons), were staffed with Alawis in the rank and file and commanded by Assad's brother Mahir (Quinlivan 1999:142, 147). As Droz-Vincent aptly notes in his chapter in this volume:

> The regime's "social engineering" in the officers' corps had been systematic and scrupulous for four decades, and hundreds of Alawis rose in one generation from an impoverished childhood to much more prestigious social positions as military officers.

Thus, at the outset of the crisis, the regime could rely on powerful counterbalancing forces whose survival was tied to the Alawi regime of Bashar al-Assad. In addition to counterbalancing and ascriptive selection, the regime also relied on appeasement strategies that were mostly directed at the individual (mostly Alawi) officers who controlled large parts of the Syrian economy through connections with the state bourgeoisie and the private sector (Mora and Wiktorowicz 2003:13).

Thus, the Syrian case confirms the model's theoretical expectations. The regime employed a mix of counterbalancing, ascriptive selection, and appeasement to decrease military autonomy (Hypothesis 1). Hence, the sufficient condition for the cooperation of the Syrian military during the regime crises is fulfilled. Accordingly, the regime primarily deployed elite units to repress the demonstrations, such as the 4th Division and the 14th and 15th Special Forces Divisions, which were not only the best-equipped troops but were also staffed with Alawi trained officers, sometimes with a whole Alawi rank and file (see Droz-Vincent in this volume)—units with very low autonomy from the dictator (Hypothesis 1.2).

(b) *Cohesion.* Although the behavior of the military is already explained by the regime's control strategies, the cost-benefit analysis of the military with regard to its cohesion allows for further testing of the hypotheses. Military operations in April 2011 demonstrated that the counterbalancing forces as well as the armed forces as a whole remained cohesive (Hinnebusch

2012:110), at least until the Syrian civic resistance turned violent and the state collapsed in civil war. In fact, as Droz-Vincent (in this volume) argues, in 2011, "[d]efections occur as the result of individual or small group decisions, not whole units choosing to side with the opposition."

This confirms the expectations that correspond with the observed strategy of cooperation: The deployment of the Alawi counterbalancing forces did not threaten the cohesion of these units due to the robustness of the control strategies employed by the regime. Consequently, in these units, we did not find defections (Hypothesis 2.1).

Bangladesh in December 1990

Bangladesh became independent from Pakistan on December 16, 1971, as the result of a civil war within Pakistan. After independence, conflicts arose between the Freedom Fighters and those members of the Bangladesh Armed Forces (BAF) who had remained in (West) Pakistan during the war and were repatriated to Bangladesh. The assassination of Prime Minister Sheikh Mujibur Rahman in 1975 marked the beginning of almost seven years of extreme instability, which included a series of twenty-two coups, counter-coups, and mutinies (Codron 2007). It was only under President General H. M. Ershad (1982–1990) that the vicious cycle of factional coups and countercoups came to an end (Croissant et al. 2013). In December 1990, civil protests broke out against the regime of Ershad. When he ordered the army to suppress the demonstrations, senior officers worried that a crackdown on civilians would disrupt the military's hard-won institutional integrity. Instead, they declared that the army was no longer willing to defend the dictator (Wilkinson 2000). Faced with military defection, Ershad was eventually forced to hand over power to the chief justice of the Supreme Court.

Theoretical Expectations

Bangladesh is a case of military defection during a dictator's endgame. According to the theoretical model, we would expect the following: Since the military opts for the strategy of defection, we expect a high autonomy of the BAF from the Ershad regime as the necessary condition for this strategy. Thus, we expect the regime to have used only nonrobust control strategies (Hypothesis 1.2).

Additionally, we expect that—as the sufficient condition for defection—the potential strategy of cooperation would have entailed high institutional costs for the military in terms of organizational cohesion (Hypothesis 2).

Testing the Hypothesis

(a) *Autonomy*. Ershad had come to power through a military coup in 1982. To prevent military factions from staging a coup against his government and in order to preserve the BAF's loyalty, he adopted a three-pronged strategy of increasing the military's internal cohesion, satisfying its economic interests, and institutionalizing its political role (Mohsin 2001:211). At the same time, Ershad did not try to build any meaningful counterbalancing capacity. Moreover, he only intervened rarely and carefully in military promotions and reshuffles. President Ziaur Rahman (also called "Zia") had already eliminated the paramilitary threats to the armed forces, purged radical junior and midrank officers from the military, and marginalized the Freedom Fighters. Ershad decided to continue Zia's strategy of turning the BAF into a vertically and horizontally integrated military. Using appeasement strategies, Ershad also continued to militarize the state apparatus by institutionalizing military officers' privileged access to positions of political and economic power (Hakim 1998:289; Kochaneck 1993:58–63; Mohsin 2001:215). During his tenure, Ershad, like his predecessor Zia, significantly increased defense expenditures. Salary and other benefits of the army personnel were disproportionately increased, and military officers were appointed to head most of the public companies and enterprises. Furthermore, Ershad not only followed his predecessor's policy of appointing military personnel to crucial civilian jobs but even went a step further by creating a quota system that formalized the entry of military officers in the Foreign Service and other civilian positions.

However, as the military institution increased in robustness and became well entrenched in state and economy, it became autonomous from the dictator (Hypothesis 1.2). In our model, this constitutes the necessary condition for the decision of the military for the strategy of defection.

(b) *Cohesion*. Ershad lost the support of the armed forces in 1990 because military officers realized that taking any action in support of him might risk sparking a return to the bloodletting of the late 1970s. In particular, junior and midrank officers within the army opposed the military's involvement in the political crisis. The fear that supporting Ershad would risk a return to the brutal and devastating intramilitary factional fights of the pre-Ershad era made the military much more willing to support democratization (Wilkinson 2000). Thus—in a paradigmatic case of an extrication coup (Stepan 1988)—we find the theoretical expectations with regard to the military cohesion confirmed: Cooperating with the Ershad regime would have entailed high institutional costs for the military (Hypothesis 2). The potential threat to the military cohesion inherent in the strategy of cooperation thus constitutes the sufficient condition for the military's decision to defect.

South Korea in May 1980 and June 1987

In the 1980s, South Korea experienced two episodes of mass mobilization and authoritarian regime crisis that qualify as a dictator's endgame. The first episode occurred in May 1980, the second in June 1987. In October 1979, President Park Chung-Hee (1963–1979) was fatally shot by his own intelligence chief. Two months later, Major General Chun Doo-Hwan staged a military coup with the support of General Roh Tae-Woo and other members of his military fraternity society called Hanahoe (Group One) (Kim 1997:1138). This triggered mass protests, first in Seoul and then in the southwestern city of Kwangju, the hometown of opposition leader Kim Dae-Jung (Cumings 2005:381–82). When antigovernment protests escalated in Kwangju, with citizens taking up arms to oppose the government and the local police, the Chun government deployed five elite divisions in the Kwangju vicinity. On May 21, 1980, about 20,000 elite combat troops stormed the city and suppressed the revolt in a brutal crackdown (Croissant et al. 2013).

The second episode took place in June 1987. In August 1980, Chun was elected president by an electoral college. In 1987 toward the end of his single seven-year term as president, Chun nominated Roh Tae-Woo as his successor, triggering a new wave of antiregime protests. Unlike prior instances of dissent, this time the middle class sided with workers and students in huge mass rallies in Seoul and other major cities. In early June, President Chun ordered the military to prepare to enforce martial law (Kim 2000). However, the military leadership refused to deploy troops to suppress demonstrators. Because many in the military opposed another massacre among civilians, the regime gave in, and Roh Tae-Woo publicized the "Declaration of Democratization and Reforms," which marked the end of the authoritarian regime and the beginning of Korea's democratization (Bedeski 1994).

Theoretical Expectations

In 1980, the South Korean military did cooperate with the dictator. Accordingly, we expect the following for the 1980 endgame: As the military opts for the strategy of cooperation, our model predicts a low autonomy of the military from the dictator. Thus, we expect the Chun Doo-Hwan regime to have used robust control strategies toward the military (Hypothesis 1). Likewise, we expect that repression is carried out by those regular or paramilitary units that are particularly dependent on the dictator through counterbalancing and ascriptive selection (Hypothesis 1.1). Finally, we expect that cooperation did not threaten the cohesion of the forces used for repression due to the control strategies employed by the regime (Hypothesis 2.1). With regard to 1987, our model predicts a high autonomy of the South Korean armed forces. Thus, we expect the regime to have used only nonrobust control strategies (Hypothesis 1.2). Additionally—as the sufficient condition for defection—we expect to find factions or at least significant structural tension within the military. This would lead to high institutional costs for the military for its organizational cohesion in case of cooperation (Hypothesis 2).

South Korea in 1980

(a) *Autonomy.* After a successful military coup, the coup leader General Park Chung-Hee became president in 1963. The military formed the backbone of his government and permeated all aspects of society and politics. Park relied on three instruments in order to control the military. The first approach was appeasement: By providing posts in the administration and economy to retired officers, the regime offered career chances outside of the military. This significantly reduced the danger of promotion bottlenecks that had been one of the core grievances of the coup makers of 1961 (Roehrig 2002:146). Second, President Park also exercised counterbalancing. He established or strengthened the Capital Defense Command, the Army Security Command, and Special Warfare Command (SWC), the latter of which controlled paratroopers, as the prime countercoup units. These were the only military forces that the Korean president could use without the potential interference of the U.S. government and the U.S. military's command in Korea (Wickham 1999). Third, in a move of ascriptive selection, Park used his personal control over military promotions to systematically groom supporters within the officer corps (Oh 1999:58). Of particular importance was the rise of the so-called Hanahoe (Group One) faction, a group of classmates from the Korean Military Academy that was almost exclusively composed of officers from Park's home province of Taegu-Kyongsang (Kim 2008, 2012). When Park was assassinated in October 1979, Hanahoe quickly moved to fill the power vacuum and had eventually seized all critical positions in the military command in a "multi-stage military coup" (Kim 1997:1138). Thus, Chun Doo-Hwan and his Hanahoe comrades had full control over the essence of the regime's repressive capacity, thereby effectively limiting the autonomy of the military. As the survival of the Hanahoe faction was tied to the survival of the new Chun Doo-Hwan regime, the sufficient condition for the strategy of cooperation of the South Korean military (controlled, at that time, by Hanahoe members) during the regime crisis of 1980 was fulfilled.

(b) *Cohesion.* The behavior of the military is already explained through the effect of the regime's control strategies on the autonomy of the South Korean military. However, the full control of Hanahoe over the regime's countercoup units, which were used to break mass protests in Kwangju, also meant that cooperation did not threaten the cohesion of the units tasked with suppression. Moreover, the counterbalancing forces as a whole remained cohesive. The non-Hanahoe officers, on the other hand, were the losers of the regime's control strategies. Yet, the Chun regime did not need to deploy those troops due to the restricted geographic scope of the demonstrations.

South Korea in June 1987

(a) *Autonomy.* While President Chun Doo-Hwan had exercised counterbalancing, ascriptive selection, and appeasement of the military, it is important to keep in mind that it was not the military as a whole that intervened in 1979–1980 but rather members of a single military faction. Accordingly, the military regime that followed the 1979 coup was a "military minority regime" rather than a corporate military regime (Kim 2008). Furthermore, members of the Hanahoe faction were almost uniformly promoted to the rank of general, as compared to only a quarter of their classmates. Therefore, most officers had nothing to gain from supporting the Chun Doo-Hwan regime (Kim 2008:72). While in the short run ascriptive selection helped to rescue the regime from mass mobilization, in the long run it became the most important source of intramilitary conflict and undermined military support for the regime. In addition, Hanahoe members did not depend on the continuation of the Chung regime for self-preservation. Instead, these officers had an exit option: If the two leading opposition figures, Kim Dae-Jung and Kim Young-Sam, were unable to overcome their differences and split the vote, this would enable Roh Tae-Woo (himself a Hanahoe man) to win the 1987 presidential election and become the country's next president. In fact, this was precisely what happened and what preserved the political prowess of Hanahoe until Kim Young-Sam became president in 1993 (Croissant et al. 2013).

(b) *Cohesion*. The attempt to consolidate control over the military by consciously exerting a considerable influence on military reshuffling, promoting some officers at the expense of others, was based on a system of favoritism that marginalized midranking officers. This undermined the esprit de corps within the military. As a result, intramilitary conflict between privileged Hanahoe officers and the majority of marginalized officers played an important role in determining whether the South Korean military became disengaged from the regime. In 1987, it became rapidly clear that Hanahoe lacked the loyalty of the broader Korean military and even those units that in 1980 had suppressed the opposition movement. The surge of popular uprising in 1987 gave many politically isolated and disadvantaged officers the opportunity to act against the regime by preventing the military government's attempt to repress the push for democratization (Kim 2012). At the same time, mass protests had reached a massive extent, so it seemed highly unlikely that deploying Hanahoe-controlled units would be sufficient to break the mass movement. Thus, from the view of the Hanahoe-dominated military leadership, the cohesion of the institution was at risk in case of a firing order, which constitutes the sufficient condition for the 1987 case of defection.

People's Republic of China in June 1989

In contrast to South Korea in 1987 and Bangladesh in 1990, the People's Liberation Army (PLA) of China did not defect from the regime in June 1989 when Deng Xiaoping and the Chinese Communist Party (CCP) leadership ordered it to crack down on the protestors at Beijing's Tiananmen Square. Rather, on June 3 and 4, 1989, troops moved into the square and forcefully ended the protests, killing hundreds of demonstrators, injuring several thousand others, and arresting hundreds of prodemocracy supporters (Lee 2015).

Theoretical Expectations

The PLA's reaction to the regime crisis in 1989 is a case of military cooperation. Accordingly, we expect the following for the Chinese 1989 dictator's endgame: As the military opts for the strategy of cooperation, our model predicts a low autonomy of the military from the regime in terms of its institutional and physical survival. Thus, we expect the CCP regime to have used robust control strategies (Hypothesis 1). Likewise, we expect that repression is carried out by those regular or paramilitary units that are particularly dependent on the authoritarian regime through counterbalancing and ascriptive selection (Hypothesis 1.1). Finally, we expect that cooperation did not threaten the cohesion of the forces used for repression due to the control strategies employed by the regime (Hypothesis 2.1).

Testing the Hypotheses

(a) *Autonomy*. As the PLA complied with orders to suppress the demonstrations, the theoretical expectation is that Deng Xiaoping and the CCP possessed the requisite institutional capacity to prevent military autonomy. This reflects the successful execution of robust control strategies, that is, counterbalancing and ascriptive selection. In fact, there is universal consensus among China experts that Deng and the party elders stressed their direct control over the armed forces by constraining the discretion of all levels of the military command chain and institutionalizing its control over the PLA down to the platoon level. They did so by using political commissioners who held a disciplinary status equal to the respective military commanders but were solely responsible to the CCP (Shambaugh 1991:546). Since 1949, the Chinese military was subordinated in a system dominated by powerful, paramount leaders with personal connections to the senior party leadership and was penetrated from top to bottom by a political work system intended for maintaining the military's loyalty to the party. As a consequence, the military did not possess any autonomy from the regime (Scobell and Wortzel 2004:12; Croissant and Kuehn 2011). However, it is important to note that this has not been a consequence of deliberate counterbalancing (as, for example, in Syria). Rather, it results from the specific conditions of civil-military relations under Communist Party rule, especially the CCP's political commissar system and the party leaders' (to be precise, Deng Xiaoping's) uncontested control over military promotions and appointments.

(b) *Cohesion.* Although the behavior of the military is already explained through the effect of the regime's control strategies on the autonomy of the PLA, the cost-benefit analysis of the military with regard to its cohesion is instructive, as it allows for further testing of the hypotheses and thus increases the robustness of the model. According to the control strategies employed by the regime, we expect that the strategy of cooperation does not threaten the cohesion of the units tasked with the repression, since their survival is tied to the fate of the regime. Consequently, the PLA's resolute reaction to the Tiananmen protests demonstrates that despite the massive use of violence, there were only very few (if any) defections from the ranks of the deployed units (Lee 2006, 2015)—the PLA remained cohesive. This provides support to the assumption that the deployment of military troops did not threaten the cohesion of these units due to the robustness of the control strategies employed by the regime (Hypothesis 2.1). However, after Tiananmen, the military leadership urged the party leadership to make sure that it would not have to deploy any regular units for the suppression of protests again. Therefore, the paramilitary units of the armed police were reorganized after 1989, and military influence over these troops increased significantly in the 1990s (Tanner 2002).

Conclusion

The aim of this chapter was to explain why in some cases militaries cooperate with dictators and support the regime against mass mobilization, whereas in other cases the military decides in favor of defection. It contends that the control strategies employed by the authoritarian regime explain the military's decision for cooperation or defection. These strategies determine the autonomy of the military from the regime. A low degree of autonomy is sufficient to explain the strategy of cooperation. A high degree of autonomy, however, is only a necessary condition for defection. The strategy of defection itself can only be explained through the high institutional costs for the cohesion of the military, which can derive from the decision for cooperation.

Table 5.1 summarizes the findings of the analysis of the six countries and seven empirical cases analyzed in this chapter.

This analysis finds that the differing outcomes can be explained by analyzing how autocrats employed control strategies such as counterbalancing,

Table 5.1. Summary of Findings

| | Relevance of Regime Strategies | | | | | Outcome | |
	Counterbalancing	Ascriptive Selection	Appeasement	Autonomy	Cohesion	Expected	Real
Egypt (2011)	Low	Low	High	High	Threatened	Defection	Defection
Tunisia (2011)	Low	Low	Low	High	Threatened	Defection	Defection
Syria (2011ff.)	High	High	Medium	Low	Not threatened	Cooperation	Cooperation
South Korea (1980)	Medium	High	High	Low	Not threatened	Cooperation	Cooperation
South Korea (1987)	Medium	High	Medium	Medium	Threatened	Defection	Defection
Bangladesh (1990)	Low	Medium	High	High	Threatened	Defection	Defection
China (1989)	Low*	High	Medium	Low	Not threatened	Cooperation	Cooperation

* The CCP uses mostly monitoring, sanction, and political socialization as functional equivalents to counterbalancing.

ascriptive selection, and appeasement and how these control strategies shaped the autonomy and organizational cohesion of the armed forces. In every case, we found the hypotheses derived from the theoretical model confirmed by the empirical reality with regard to both autonomy and cohesion, which accounts for a high robustness of our explanatory model. Three caveats must be mentioned, however.

First, the evidence derived from the case studies in this chapter need to be compared to evidence from additional cases, as the cases under study are but seven of several dozen cases that have experienced a dictator's endgame since the beginning of the so-called third wave of democratization. What is more, the dictator's endgames presented in this chapter might not be the only instances of endgames in the countries under study. In the case of Egypt, the bread riots of 1977 and the revolt of the Central Security Forces in 1986 immediately come to mind as two cases of military intervention. However, the 1986 revolt does not qualify as a dictator's endgame, as it was not an instance of peaceful popular mass mobilization but rather a revolt of some 20,000 Central Security Forces members—that is, a challenge from within the coercive apparatus itself (Harb 2003:287). As for the 1977 bread riots, again, it was not the goal of our chapter to provide a comprehensive explanation for the Egyptian cases over time but rather to test the robustness of our model against several empirical cases that serve as mere plausibility probes. With regard to 1977, our model would therefore simply assume different values for the explanatory variables—to be more precise, since 1977 serves as a case of cooperation, the use of robust control strategies.

Cursory empirical evidence seems to suggest that robust ascriptive selection mechanisms in fact were in place, as Anwar al-Sadat had removed his (Nasserist) rivals from the military leadership during several rounds of reshuffling within the officers corps after he took office in 1971 (Harb 2003:282; Hashim 2011:73); at the same time, he continued to appease the military professionally and, at least in the view of the Egyptian public, finally restored its institutional reputation in the 1973 war against Israel. Furthermore, the Egyptian military—reluctant to intervene—only acted *after* the cuts in subsidies that had sparked the protests had been reversed, which constituted the complete political concession to the demands of the protestors by the regime leadership, and quickly returned to the barracks. This requires, however, the collection and evaluation of empirical data and the construction of a comprehensive database on political-military relations in all modern autocracies experiencing one or more regime crises since 1946 that qualify as a dictator's endgame (Croissant and Kuehn 2015).

Second, the dictator's decisions to employ control strategies and their results are influenced by the resources available. Robust strategies require a better endowment with material and institutional resources than nonrobust strategies (Trinkunas 2005; Croissant et al. 2013; Kuehn and Lorenz 2011). This resource endowment, in turn, depends on specific historical and structural contexts, in which the interactions between the political leadership and the military take place. The contrasting regime types of the cases under scrutiny seem to be important to explain the forms of control strategies employed by the authoritarian regimes. The People's Republic of China as a Communist Party regime has some mechanisms of political control in place, which, as other scholars have demonstrated (Perlmutter and LeoGrande 1982) and is confirmed by this analysis, seem to be an effective instrument for ensuring political acquiescence within the armed forces. To our best knowledge, there has not been any case of military defection in a communist single-party regime.

Third, our model can only partly explain the cases of Libya in 2011 and Yemen, where the armed forces split into various factions during the dictator's endgame. On the one hand, our model does successfully predict the cleavages along which the splits in the armed forces materialized. The units, whose autonomy from the regime was low, as they were tied to the dictator through robust ascriptive selection mechanisms and were the beneficiaries of the control strategies, chose to cooperate, while the losers of the control strategies of the regime defected. But what accounts for their respective motivation? The strategic choice of the cooperators is explained by our model: Since the survival of these units was tied to the regime, they chose to fight with it. As a low autonomy is the sufficient condition to explain the strategic choice for cooperation, concerns for organizational cohesion did not enter the cost-benefit analysis of those officers, according to our model. Consequently, they were willing to accept an erosion of institutional cohesion when the marginalized factions within the military defected. But what about the motivation of the defectors? According to our model, the defectors were highly autonomous from the regime and thus capable of defecting from the regime, but a preference for institutional cohesion (as predicted by our model) cannot have motivated their strategic choice. Is mere deprivation in the ancient regime— that is, being on the losing side of the regime's control efforts—sufficient to account for their behavior? Or does the underlying reason lie in the fact that neither the Libyan nor the Yemeni military were modern professional military institutions with a corporate interest? In the latter case, the deprivation argument would hold some plausibility, as in a nonprofessional military without a corporate interest, the marginalized factions would not have a reason to stick with their antagonist for the sake of maintaining institutional cohesion. At any rate, the curious cases of splits within the military such as Libya and Yemen remain an urgent desideratum for the academic community.

Finally, it is important to emphasize that although in a number of cases discussed in this chapter the instruments employed by authoritarian rulers to proof their rule against the threat of military intervention backfired during the "stress test" (Droz-Vincent in this volume) of anti-incumbent mass contention does not mean that these regime-stabilizing techniques of authoritarian rule failed. Rather, it is important to keep in mind that coup-proofing per definition is a risky undertaking. As Powell (2014:2) argues, it always involves a certain paradox:

> Leaders face threats to their survival from sources as diverse as foreign invaders, popular uprisings, military coups, armed insurgents, and even an electorate. Leaders would, no doubt, prefer to have a blanket policy that would stamp out any threat to their continued tenure. Unfortunately, the multitude of threats and the different actors that a leader must consider will force him or her to make trade-offs. In the end, a policy that increases security against one set of actors might decrease security against another, as executives engage in a balancing act for political survival.

The means employed to minimize the threat arising from military coups d'état may work very well in regard to this particular problem of authoritarian power sharing when there is no popular mass mobilization. In fact, why should dictators worry much about events such as the Arab Spring if one keeps in mind that during the second half of the twentieth century, only very few dictators (in the Arab world and elsewhere) had been irregularly removed from office by civic resistance and nonviolent revolutions, but many more had lost their office (and sometimes their life as well) due to military coups (Goemans et al. 2009; Svolik 2012; Powell 2012a)?[6] But the unlikely cases of powerful mass mobilization as they are discussed in this chapter (and in other contributions to this volume) constitute a different kind of threat to leadership survival. In this case, the threat does not come from within the ruling coalition but from below. The question of military defection from or cooperation with autocrats in a dictator's endgame is, as we argued in this chapter, inherently different from other sorts of regime crises. Defection creates a window of opportunity for military leaders, which provides them (under the conditions exemplified above) with opportunities for shirking that are not available during normal times of authoritarian rule. Moreover, regimes are expected to be more likely to break down in the very early years and after prolonged rule (Geddes 2003; Svolik 2012). Therefore, it should come as no surprise that coup-proofing strategies, which worked well in preventing the military from organizing and implementing a coup d'état in one situation, backfire and lead to unintended consequences when the political opportunity structure change and a new situation such as the endgame scenario becomes a political reality—especially if mass contention occurs after several decades of authoritarian or personalist rule, as was the case in Arab countries such as Libya, Egypt, Tunisia, and Yemen.

Notes

1. In this chapter, the terms "dictator," "regime leader," and "ruler" are used synonymously. The "dictator" can be an individual or a collective decision-making body, such as a military junta (Bueno de Mesquita et al. 2003).

2. We use the terms "cooperation" and "defending" as well as "defection" and "non-cooperation" synonymously. We rely on Peter Feaver's (2003) pathbreaking theory of military working (cooperation) and shirking (noncooperation) as well as Terence Lee's (2015) differentiation between defection and defending a dictator.

3. This is necessary in order to analytically distinguish the dictator's endgame from other forms of intrastate conflicts (civil wars) or authoritarian regime crises (military coups *without* prior mass mobilization, civilian coups, etc.; see also Pion-Berlin and Trinkunas 2010:398–402).

4. Our model simply assumes that the military perceives cooperation as an effective strategy to secure regime survival. On the other hand, the military will assume that defection will lead to regime collapse. In reality, cooperation may fail, and a dictator falls despite the disposition of military officers to defend it. As the reader will note, we exclude democratic regimes from the definition of the dictator's endgame. For an analysis of endgames in both democratic and authoritarian regimes, see Pion-Berlin's contribution to this volume.

5. For an in-depth discussion of coup-proofing strategies, see Brooks (1998), Quinlivan (1999), Belkin and Schofer (2003), Pilster and Böhmelt (2011), and Powell (2012a). With regard to military behavior during authoritarian regime crises, see Lee (2015), Kim (2012), Lutterbeck (2013), Gaub (2013), and Makara (2013).

6. A recent data collection effort by Goemans et al. (2009) shows that overall, coups d'état accounted for 70 percent of the 489 leader exits that came about through irregular means between 1875 and 2005. This is in in stark contrast to other means of removal, such as foreign intervention (9 percent), civil wars (10 percent), assassinations (5 percent), and popular protests (6 percent). See also Powell (2012a:17).

CHAPTER 6

Cain and Abel in the Land of Sheba:
Elite Conflict and the Military in Yemen

Holger Albrecht

One of the main aims of this book is to emphasize the role of Middle Eastern armies in the popular insurgencies that came to be known as the Arab Spring. Apart from various contributions to this volume, earlier works established the contention that the immediate trajectory of the popular mass uprisings had been ultimately shaped by the military's reaction (Barany 2011; Bellin 2012; Lutterbeck 2013; Nepstad 2013; Makara 2013). Most of these works employ a neoinstitutionalist perspective and hold the type of military organization responsible for whether the military would side with embattled authoritarian incumbents or dispose of them. In simplifying an admittedly more complex argument, the common denominator in these works is that militaries would stand by incumbents in times of crisis when the procedures of recruitment and promotion were ultimately characterized by personal relations in what is coined "patrimonial" or "communal" military organizations. The internal fabrics of these organizations would then be characterized by kin, family, tribe, or religion. In turn, "institutionalized" armies would have established a hierarchical chain of command and were characterized by professionalism and merit-based appointments. Such militaries, the argument goes, would refrain from exercising excessive force against mobilizing societies on the grounds that they had pledged allegiance to state and nation rather than the regime's incumbencies. These cases would therefore witness defections, mutinies, and coups d'état.

There is strong theoretical appeal in these approaches, as they facilitate structured comparison (Pion-Berlin in this volume). Yet a closer look at

Middle Eastern armies would lead us to cast doubt on the empirical applicability of a mutually exclusive categorization of patrimonial and institutionalized military apparatuses. Egypt—while certainly one of the more institutionalized and cohesive fighting forces in the region—exhibits strong personal ties between the higher officer corps and the political incumbency (Bou Nassif 2013; Sayigh 2012). In turn, Syria—where the vast majority of the officer corps is of the Alawite religious sect—has a large army of conscripted soldiers representing a socially fragmented society (Ohl, Albrecht, and Koehler 2015; Droz-Vincent in this volume).

Yemen is the most challenging case for conventional interpretations in the civil-military relations literature, which is perhaps one reason why the country is often ignored in comparative accounts.[1] While its military presents a textbook case for communal organization, the army's reaction somewhat defies conventional wisdom about such patrimonial militaries. Rather than staying loyal to embattled president 'Ali 'Abdullah Salih, senior officers and rank-and-file soldiers defected from the regime early on in the country's popular uprising. Most important was the defection of 'Ali Muhsin, one of the most powerful political-military elite members as well as a distant relative and king maker of the president. 'Ali Salih and 'Ali Muhsin have been brothers in arms ever since the former rose to power in 1978.

This chapter tells this modern Cain and Abel story and argues that military behavior in authoritarian regimes is often contingent upon political elite interest rather than the type of military organization. It is the quality and strength of those personal ties within patrimonial networks, not the mere presence of a communal military organization, that determine military behavior (Decalo 1990; Schiff 1995; Albrecht 2015). Simply said, if personal relations between incumbents and officers are based on trust and common interests, loyalty is the norm irrespective of whether militaries are institutionalized or organized along patrimonial fabrics.

Civil-military relations in authoritarian regimes and military cohesion remain difficult to study in times of domestic peace and stability. Owing to the sensitive nature of elite competition in autocracies, much of these struggles take place behind the scenes, in the "black box" of authoritarian regimes. Yet open elite struggle, external shocks, and domestic political strife bring these fissures in elite coalitions to the fore and become triggering causes for military defection. I depart from the dominant theme in the literature on civil-military relations during the Arab Spring. Rather than asking how the military's reaction to the Yemeni uprising has shaped its trajectory, I inquire into the effects that elite conflict and political shocks have on military organization and behavior. Studying Yemen is useful as an empirical illustration that military apparatuses in authoritarian regimes are vulnerable to penetration by political elites. When elite coalitions change, so does the military—both in personnel and organizational infrastructure. And when social mass mobilization, as witnessed in the 2011 uprising, triggers elite conflict, military behavior is a catalyst of such elite conflicts.

Civil-Military Relations and Elite Change

Most scholars treat military organization as a constant, slow-moving explanatory factor. Categorizations such as "professionalized" (Stepan 1988; Kamrava 2000), "institutionalized" (Bellin 2012; Lutterbeck 2013), "cohesive" (Lee 2005; Gaub 2013), and "communal" militaries (McLauchlin 2010; Makara 2013) facilitate structured comparison and help develop generalizing arguments. Scholars typically employ "the" military as an independent factor for explanations of puzzling empirical phenomena, including democratization, coups d'état, revolution, and war (Russell 1974). There is not only methodological and theoretical promise in such approaches but also supportive empirical evidence. First, all military apparatuses develop a strong hierarchical, top-down chain of command, irrespective of their degree of cohesion and professionalism. Second, despite significant cultural and political differences across countries, the vast majority of military apparatuses would typically develop their own ethos, including a strong esprit de corps, obedience to the chain of command, national duty, comradeship, trust, and heroism. Third, major features of military recruitment usually remain constant in rank-and-file employment (general conscription vs. voluntary recruitment) but also concerning the social background of soldiers and officers.

Hence, there is reason in and merit to treating militaries as slow-moving empirical phenomena. But this also presents us with analytical challenges when studying civil-military relations in nondemocratic contexts. More often than not, militaries are integral parts of the institutional infrastructure of such authoritarian regimes, including certainly those where juntas occupy incumbencies but also other types of authoritarian rule, whether in a more personalist or bureaucratic guise (Geddes 1999). In the majority of such autocracies, the higher officer corps are parts of political elite coalitions (Svolik 2012; Koehler in this volume). To what extent would officers shape and influence political decision making? At which point will officers have to be treated as politicians? And will individuals make decisions based on their position in the military hierarchy or because they are inspired by their interests as political elite members? Such questions are difficult and often impossible to answer, since authoritarian regimes and militaries tend to maintain a "black box" and block penetration by the outside observer. Despite very practical challenges posed to the study of internal military politics, it is intuitively compelling to assume that a military's contribution to, and influence over, political decision making is not a one-sided form of communication. As long as politics and military affairs are intertwined, militaries influence politics, but the inverse statement also holds true.[2]

If military apparatuses are parts of the dynamics of authoritarian politics, they are vulnerable to frequent and often substantial changes, which somewhat undermines their analytical treatment as stable, constant, and slow-moving organizational entities. Two areas are particularly vulnerable to dynamic and frequent changes irrespective of the degree of institutionalization, professionalism, effectiveness, or patrimonial features: organization and recruitment.

First, in authoritarian regimes, the organizational and physical infrastructure of a military apparatus is not as durable as implied in most of the civil-military literature. Changes in military doctrines and threat perceptions and the greater likelihood of authoritarian armies to engage in violent conflict—both internally and externally—lead to frequent organizational changes in military apparatuses. Economic boosts and shocks have a direct impact on military budgets and hence on the army's size and equipment. And changes in international relations may lead incumbents to renegotiate the availability of financial, technical, and logistic support provided by foreign allies.

Second, security establishments in authoritarian regimes often do not consist of coherent organizations where the military, tasked to defend the nation against external threats and reporting through a clear-cut chain of command to the ministry of defense, could easily be distinguished from the police, established to preserve domestic peace and stability and reporting to a ministry of the interior. Rather, autocracies tend to develop a whole array of special forces, militias, and security forces in their attempts to both keep their societies in check and counterbalance security forces in a coup-proofing effort (Al-Ahram 2011 and italized Lawson in this volume). Hence, it is often difficult, sometimes futile, to distinguish between the formal military and other security forces.

Third, as an important part of authoritarian coup-proofing, officers are subject to frequent reshuffling. This is to avoid power centers within the armed forces, but it also bears witness to changes in the quality of personal relations between incumbent elites and serving military personnel. Those relations may well be organized through patrimonial and communal fabrics, but the strength of personal ties may well differ from one case to another. Examples abound where officers of the same kin, family, tribe, ethnicity, or religion stood by authoritarian incumbents in active support, but we are also reminded of a multitude of cases where splits appeared within social groups, leading to factionalism, defections, and palace coups. Evidence can be found in several coups and coup attempts executed by members of the same family or social community characterizing a patrimonial relationship between the respective incumbents and his officers. In Oman in 1970 and in Qatar in 1995, sons deposed their fathers in bloodless coups to take over power; in Syria in 1982, it was Hafiz al-Assad's brother Rif'at who attempted to oust the incumbent in the aftermath of the Hama crisis and when Hafiz encountered serious health problems. Libya's Qaddafi had his own cousin, Hassan Ishkal, assassinated in 1985 in a move to rid the military of an internal rival.

Such incidents encourage us to reconsider assumptions held in the civil-military literature. First, in authoritarian regimes, one will typically find features of professionalism, cohesion, fragmentation, and patrimonialism present within the very same military apparatus (Ohl in this volume). Second, rather than preventing coups, mutinies, and other forms of insubordination altogether, the patrimonial organization of a military apparatus increases the likelihood of coups and mutinies *within* the family or ethnic or religious community. Rallying behind the flag is likely whenever the patrimonial military is challenged by an out-group threat, such as in an uprising or mutiny carried out by a different interest group, social class, or religious sect (McLauchlin 2010). But this does not necessarily apply to cross-sectoral insurgencies of the kind we witnessed in the Middle East and North Africa in 2011.

It is worth employing a strand of the theoretical literature on civil-military relations that looks at the fabric of relations between officers and political decision makers. Rebecca Schiff (1995) used the term "concordance" to denote the degree of conformity, congruence, and agreement among politicians and officers.[3] Schiff (1995:7) identifies the "high level of integration between the military and other parts of society" as a component of concordance. Welch (1992:328) mentions the "fragmented boundaries" characterized by "comparatively numerous, unregulated interchanges between roles and structures in the military and in the wider society." Huntington (1957:350–54) speaks of the "fusion" of military and civilian realms.

The greater the ties, personal bonds, organizational analogy, and strategic interests between political elites and military officers, the greater is the likelihood that officers will actively support incumbents under stress. The difference between institutionalized and communal militaries is that the former tend to develop a stronger corporate interest than the latter. Patrimonial militaries witness the allocation of "private benefits" rather than "corporate benefits" (Lee 2005:82). Patrimonial practices therefore aim to strengthen personal ties and contribute to the weakening of a corporate ethos. A binary perspective comparing institutionalized militaries (supporting the people) with patrimonial militaries (supporting autocrats under stress) ignores the fact that patrimonial militaries can hardly ever be perceived as corporate actors but instead are perceived as a conglomerate of agents who are bound to the political incumbency through personal ties of different qualities. Since those ties are often not unequivocally strong, the question here is not *if* the military supports the autocrat but rather *who* within that military does so.

Popular mass uprisings appear as domestic "stress tests" for authoritarian regimes, of which militaries are part and parcel.[4] And they serve to catalyze existing conflicts in elite coalitions—a perspective that is often ignored in studies on mass mobilization. But as Richard Lachmann (1997:73) emphasizes, "Mass mobilization occurs most often during periods of unusually intense elite conflict." If military officers are members of such elite coalitions, one would assume that insurgencies have as much of an impact on military apparatuses—and relations among individuals within that apparatus—as the military has on the trajectories of the insurgencies. Rather than asking how the military has shaped events when people take to the streets, I am concerned here with the impact that uprisings have on the military: who within the military supports insurgencies, and why? What are the patterns of loyalty and defection triggered by popular revolts? And how do insurgencies catalyze changes in the military apparatus and in its relations with the political incumbency?

The Arab Spring in Yemen: Popular Mobilization as a Catalyst for Elite Conflict

The Yemeni uprising began on January 15, 2011, the day after former Tunisian president Zine al-Abidine Ben Ali departed Tunis (Phillips 2011:123–33; Durac 2012; Day 2012; International Crisis Group 2012; Knights 2013).

Anecdotal evidence suggests that ʿAli ʿAbdullah Salih was on high alert and anticipated a diffusion of protests from the Tunisian uprising, quite unlike the presidents in Egypt and Libya who were apparently surprised by demonstrations in their own countries.[5] Initially a gathering of youth groups in Sanaʿa, protests swept across the country in the following days especially in Taiz, where popular protests were a new phenomenon, and in Aden, where youth groups were supported by an ongoing southern protest movement called al-Hirak. Various human rights activists as well as an alliance of opposition groups organized in the Joint Meeting Parties (al-Mushtarrak) also supported the uprising, including its poster child Tawwakul Karman, a young activist affiliated with the Islah Party who would later be a Nobel Peace Prize winner. The regime's repression grew increasingly uncompromising and on March 18 led to the killing of at least thirty demonstrators in Sanaʿa. The event provoked the resignation of dozens of political elite members and the defection of General ʿAli Muhsin, commander of the 1st Armored Division, known in Yemen simply as the Firqa (military division). ʿAli Muhsin—the president's king maker, cousin, and second most powerful man in the elite—and his Firqa were the main military force in support of the subsequent mutiny.[6]

As Vincent Durac (2012:167) explained, ʿAli Muhsin's move "transformed the situation from one in which a popular challenge to the regime was overtaken by a cleavage in the ruling elite which saw rival units of the national army massed in the streets of the capital." The defection split the armed forces into two equally strong camps. The most important loyalist forces included the Republican Guard, under the command of the president's son Ahmad ʿAli Salih; the Central Security Forces, a paramilitary riot police; parts of the infantry; and most air force brigades. The popular mass protests in Yemen thus turned into a protracted low-level armed conflict between rivaling elite factions. This standoff culminated in an attempt on President Salih's life, leaving him seriously wounded on June 3, and finally in his resignation, brokered by the Gulf Cooperation Council, on November 23, 2011.

The trajectory of the Yemeni insurgency, and particularly the reaction of the military and security forces, is somewhat counterintuitive to assumptions drawn from the civil-military literature: the Yemeni security establishment—including military and domestic security forces—are overwhelmingly recruited from among the northern tribes, in particular the Hashid confederation. The social base of the higher officer corps is even smaller and is dominated by members of the Sanhan tribe—the tribe of former president ʿAli ʿAbdullah Salih. Hence, in 2011 we witnessed the fragmentation of a communal army, with a substantial part of the political and security establishment defecting from the president. Former brothers in arms and family members 'Ali 'Abdullah Salih and 'Ali Muhsin led rival elite camps, which created a standoff triggered by popular mobilization. This is all the more intriguing because at the time when intraelite splits occurred, popular mobilization did not appear as serious a threat to the survival of the regime as in Tunisia, Egypt, and Syria. Elite members therefore did not defect because they anticipated the sinking of the ship but for other reasons. Despite—or perhaps because of—the socially homogeneous composition of the political-military elite, intraelite rifts had appeared prior to the uprising, which served as a catalyst for bringing these elite struggles to the fore.

The Military and Security Establishment in Yemen: Coercive Institution in Flux

It is worth recalling the early military career of former president 'Ali 'Abdullah Salih in order to understand the fabric of the political-military establishment in Yemen (Fattah 2010; Knights 2013; International Crisis Group 2013). At the foundation of the Yemen Arab Republic—or North Yemen—in 1968, Salih was a young military commander of the Bab al-Mandab Brigade and a member of the Security Committee (al-Lajna al-Amniya).[7] A member of the Sanhan tribe, part of the northern tribal confederation of Hashid, Salih at the time was a token figure in a committee dominated by figures from the country's south. Becoming the army commander of the Taiz province presented Salih with the opportunity to bolster his position and, most important, attract substantial financial resources. This was made possible by his control over land, the physical infrastructure in the center of the country, and the trade and smuggling routes in the port city of Mokha. Salih's influence grew under President Ibrahim al-Hamdi (1974–1977), and Salih successfully introduced his own loyalists, particularly from the Sanhan tribe, into the security establishment. After the assassinations of al-Hamdi and his successor, Salih assumed the presidency, backed by a small clique of fellow Sanhanis who henceforth came to control politics and the security apparatus. The inner circle of the security regime at the time of Salih's takeover in 1978 included his brother Muhammad Salih al-Ahmar as well as Ali Muhsin, Mahdi Mukawallah, 'Abdelillah al-Qadi, Muhammad Isma'il, and Ahmad Faraj.[8]

The main ingredients for the consolidation of the Salih regime in North Yemen also made the recipe for future civil-military relations: the fusion of politics with military affairs, a development that had already begun under al-Hamdi; tribal allegiances for recruitment and Sanhani dominance in the military; a power-sharing agreement among the main Sanhani figures and their economic self-sustenance through smuggling; and control over state funds, land, and water resources. Most important, a deal of sorts was struck between 'Ali 'Abdullah Salih and 'Ali Muhsin, widely believed to be the second most powerful man in the country, at the center of which was the mutual understanding that Muhsin was to be next in line for presidential succession.[9] Moreover, military organization in Yemen has been historically characterized by institutional fragmentation. In the 1950s, it was the last Zaidi imam in North Yemen, Imam Yahya, who established overlapping units, including a regular army and a praetorian guard, to counterbalance officers in Yemen's first standing army (Fattah 2010).

Pedigree Politics as a Catalyst for Military Recruitment

Since the mid-1990s, behind-the-scenes power struggles within the incumbent elite had an imprint on the military in terms of size, recruitment, civil-military relations, and the military's organizational infrastructure. Changes are characterized by two aspects: the recruitment of the president's family members in leadership positions of the coercive establishment and an accelerating organizational fragmentation of the state's coercive forces.

The unification of the two former independent Yemeni states—the Yemen Arab Republic (North Yemen) and the People's Democratic Republic of Yemen (South Yemen)—in 1990 was followed by a brief civil war between the political-military establishments of both sides in 1994 that saw the northern elite around Salih, his Sanhani clique, and a tribal coalition appear victorious (Kostiner 1996). With his personal position strengthened—not only against his southern rivals but also within the Sanhani elite coalition—Salih began to introduce his own family members of the next generation into the military establishment. For ten years beginning in 1995, family members assumed high positions in the military and security establishment.[10] The president's half brother Muhammad Salih commanded the air force; another half brother, 'Ali, took over as the regular army's chief of staff to oversee the four regional commands; most important, the president's son Ahmad became commander

of the elite Republican Guard (Haras al-Jumhuriya), which was developed as
the most capable fighting force in the country. Nephews of the president also
made it into the security establishment. Yahya was commander of the Central
Security Forces (al-Amn al-Markasi), a paramilitary force that operated as a
political police; Tariq was in command of the Presidential Guard (Haras al-
Riasi); Ammar took over the National Security Bureau (al-Amn al-Qawmi),
an intelligence agency; presidential cousin Muhammad Muhammad Salih
was the head of an elite combat unit within the Special Forces of the Republican Guard; and Taysir Salih, another of the president's nephews, became
military attaché in Washington, D.C.

These appointments of members of the president's core family bear witness to important changes in the Sanhani elite coalition (International Crisis Group 2013:7–10). Horizontal recruitment of various representatives
of extended family networks characterized the post-1977 regime and was
replaced by a more vertical pattern of elite recruitment, introducing primarily Salih family members, including the younger generation. Most important
was the alleged grooming of Ahmad 'Ali as the most likely successor of his
father in the presidential palace.[11] The simmering power struggle between the
Salih camp and other members of the Sanhan elite was fueled by a helicopter
accident in 1999 that killed Muhammad Isma'il al-Qadhi and Ahmad Faraj.
The incident produced rumors of an assassination, and so did an attempt on
'Ali Muhsin's life in his northern military headquarters in 2010.[12] Whether
true or not, these rumors show an awareness among the political establishment in Yemen that a power struggle within the Sanhani elite unfolded, which
at the time had not broken out openly but was fought behind the scenes over
upper positions in the security establishment and the financial privileges
and political influence associated with these positions. While the political-
military elite still maintained its narrow social base, cracks appeared within
the Sanhani leadership.

Changing Organizational Infrastructure

While intraelite competition could be witnessed in the recruitment for military posts, it also led to significant changes in the physical infrastructure
of the military and security forces. The introduction of Salih family members was not carried out to replace established Sanhani elites but instead was
done in a more complementary fashion. More often than not, powerful elite

members maintained their positions in the military and security apparatus and saw the establishment of new rivaling organizations headed by members of the Salih family connection. The latter refrained from confronting the old elite openly and instead established a fragmented, fragile network of parallel organizations. The balancing act between these singular units worked well as long as the factions in the political elite had a common interest in maintaining the status quo, but it already contained the seeds of open conflict that only needed a trigger to fully erupt.

Units in the security and military apparatuses were extended or newly created, which contributed to an overall expansion in terms of size and equipment (Knights 2013:269). This did not lead to greater operational and combat effectiveness but may have in fact further compromised the coercive capacities of the state, as shown by the unsuccessful attempt to put down an al-Qaeda-inspired Islamist insurrection. The challenge posed by Yemen's al-Qaeda branch led the United States to strengthening its efforts at improving counterinsurgency capacities of the Yemeni state by establishing new security branches in both the military and the domestic security forces. The United States therefore actively contributed to the fragmentation of the Yemeni security sector prior to the 2011 uprising.

In 2002, for instance, a new intelligence organization was formed with the financial and logistical support of the United States: the National Security Bureau (NSB) was created as an antiespionage agency and also included an antiterrorist unit. The NSB was officially headed by the staunch Salih-loyalist 'Ali al-Anisi, and the president's nephew Ammar Salih became its deputy head. The NSB reportedly engaged in fierce competition about funds, technical resources, and access to field intelligence with the older security agency, the Political Security Office (PSO). The PSO suffered from uncertain loyalties, may have experienced Islamist infiltration, and "was supported by key figures within the regime; one of them is General 'Ali Muhsin."[13] Another well-equipped antiterrorism unit was formed within the Central Security Forces, a political police unit under the command of Yahya Salih. Yet another Special Forces Unit was integrated in 1999, with the Republican Guard, under the command of Ahmad 'Ali, as an elite fighting force almost entirely recruited from among the northern tribes and supported by the United States to contain al-Qaeda activities in Yemen after the September 11, 2001, attacks.

Among already existing units, the Republican Guard was expanded into an army in its own right. It was by far the best-equipped and most well-funded combat force and reportedly had around 30,000 men under arms. The

Republican Guard had its units stationed in Sana'a as well as throughout the whole country, thereby creating an independent fighting force that has operated parallel to the regular army. To make matters more complicated, a third army of sorts existed apart from the regular forces and the Republican Guard: the 1st Armored Division under the command of 'Ali Muhsin was essentially a private tribal militia of similar size as the Republican Guard.

Figure 6.1 visualizes the military and security establishment in Yemen prior to the uprising in 2011. Changes in military organization witnessed three interrelated dynamics: institutional fragmentation, the weakening of a clear-cut chain of command, and aggravating rifts between political elite factions.

In an attempt to exert stronger personal control, 'Ali 'Abdullah Salih weakened the functional chain of command, according to which domestic security forces should report to the Ministry of the Interior and the military should be organized under the regular chief of staff and politically under the Ministry of Defense. Yemen had never fully established such modern organizational structures. Yet until the late 1990s and in the early years of the Salih regime, the regular armed forces were more clearly organized in their functional parts (infantry, navy, air force, border guard, military police) and regional commands (south, east, central, northwest). Posts such as regional commanders came with substantial economic perks and political clout, indicated by the fact that the core figures of the inner circle of the early Sanhani regime occupied such posts: 'Ali Muhsin was commander of the northwestern military zone, and the boundaries between his Firqa and the regular units stationed in the country's northern regions have always been somewhat fluid. Mahdi Mukwallah was the commander of the southern military zone, 'Abdelillah al-Qadi was commander of the Taiz military district (central command), Muhammad Isma'il was commander of the air defense and later of the Hadramut sector, and Ahmad Faraj at the time of his death in 1999 was commander of the Taiz zone.[14]

These regional commands were weakened by the establishment of special units that were well equipped, often propped up by U.S. military assistance, and directly or indirectly placed under the authority of Salih family members. Hence, by the late 2000s, Yemen's military and security establishment had evolved into a collection of more or less independently operating units under the command of powerful elite members, with the Ministry of Defense "little more than an administrative appendage . . . that disburses salaries and manages pensions" (Barany 2012:331). Overlapping competencies existed

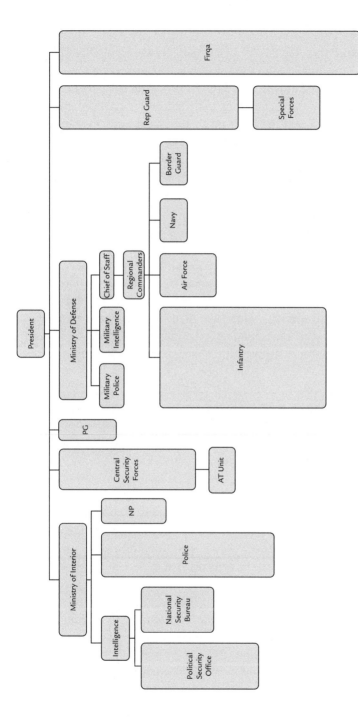

Figure 6.1 Security Sector in Yemen, 2010

Notes: Figure 6.1 was compiled on the basis of information gathered in multiple interviews with security experts, political observers, and military personnel, conducted in January 2013.

Acronyms: NP = Najda ("emergency") Police, a special security force in charge of the protection of government buildings and foreign embassies; AT Unit = Anti-Terrorism Unit; PG = Presidential Guard; Rep Guard = Republican Guard.

in almost every task associated with the coercive apparatus. The regular police, the Najda Police, the Presidential Guard, the Military Police, the Border Guard, and the Republican Guard served for the protection of the state's physical infrastructure but with very little success. Combat forces included the infantry and the air force under the leadership of regional commanders, the Republican Guard, and the Firqa. Antiterrorist missions were executed by the antiterrorism unit of the Central Security Forces, the Special Forces of the Republican Guard, the Military Police, and the Firqa. And domestic political opposition and dissent was contained by a variety of organizations, including the regular police, the PSO, the National Security Office, the Central Security Forces, and Military Intelligence.

'Ali 'Abdullah Salih tried to keep most of the singular organizations under his direct control. The Central Security Forces and the Republican Guard, for instance, were created through presidential decree, which served as a legal justification for direct presidential supervision rather than integration into the respective Ministry of the Interior and Ministry of Defense.[15] Rifts in the organizational infrastructure of the security sector were even institutionalized through the formation in 2005 of the High Central Command (al-Qiyada al-Markaziya al-Awliya, HCC), including the commanders of the Republican Guard, the Central Security Forces, and the NSB. While meetings of the HCC were essentially Salih family gatherings, 'Ali Muhsin responded in kind and established his own command structure, including the Firqa; the leaders of the Islah-affiliated tribal militias, Hamid al-Ahmar and Muhammad al-Yadumi; the head of the PSO, Ghalib al-Qamish; and the commander of the 310th Armored Brigade in 'Amran, Hamid al-Qushaibi.[16]

Upon the outbreak of the 2011 uprising, all those units where family members were in leadership posts were safely in the Salih camp (with the air force as an exception): the Republican Guard, the Central Security Forces, the NSB, and the Presidential Guard. Yet the Sanhani elite around 'Ali Muhsin also had its forces to rely on: the Firqa, the air defense, some regional commands, the PSO, and irregular tribal militias affiliated with the Islah Party.

Concerning the social composition of the military and security establishment, both officers and subordinates were predominantly recruited from among the northern tribes. While military recruitment was technically organized through general conscription, this was in practice often not implemented. The social composition was quite uniform across units and ranks, but grievances persisted owing to the unequal distribution of resources

(International Crisis Group 2013:10). The NSB, for instance, was much better equipped and personnel were better paid than in the PSO, which also suffered from its negative reputation as a repressive force associated with human rights violations. While the Republican Guard and the Firqa were almost equally strong in terms of manpower, the former was privileged over the latter in military equipment and resources for the salaries of personnel. The Republican Guard had an official monthly budget of twelve billion Yemeni riyals, whereas the Firqa received only four billion.[17]

Protracted Elite Conflict After Salih

Apart from national reconciliation and the strengthening of state capacities, changes in the military and security-sector reforms have been identified as a third pillar of reform in the post-Salih transition period, beginning with the takeover of former vice president 'Abd Rabbu Mansur Hadi on February 25, 2012. The immediate post-Salih transition period was short-lived and gave way to violent conflict, initiated by the Houthi takeover of Sana'a in September 2014 and large parts of the Yemeni territory in the spring of 2015. The successful Houthi initiative was in great part made possible by the crumbling security establishment of the state—in itself a telling judgment of the planned reforms of the military and the domestic security forces. In fact, security-sector reforms during 2012 and 2013 were in reality the poorly concealed continuation of power struggles among political rivals. As April Longley Alley (2013:724) observed, "violent conflict is a product of competition between distinct branches of the security apparatus for power and resources in the post-transition era."

One of the first moves of the new president, Hadi, was the formation of the fourteen-member Military Committee (al-Lajna al-'Askariya), supported by U.S. and Jordanian advisers as well as United Nations special envoy Jamal Benomar, which was tasked with security-sector and military reforms. The official aim of reforms included the professionalization of the armed and security forces, the strengthening of the chain of command, curbing sectarian domination of the security forces and the military, and the centralization of civil authority in the Ministry of Defense and the Ministry of the Interior.[18] In conjunction with the transitional government in 2012 and the National Dialogue Conference in 2013, the Lajna served as an important institution to counterbalance camps in the security establishment, namely former

president 'Ali 'Abdullah Salih, his rival 'Ali Muhsin, and interim president
Hadi. The balancing act was represented in the Lajna's composition: Hadi
as an ex-officio member was supported by his close ally, Minister of Defense
Muhammad Ahmad Nasr; the Salih camp was represented by former chief of
staff and then adviser to Hadi for security affairs, Muhammad al-Qasimi; and
'Ali Muhsin's man in the Lajna was Minister of the Interior 'Abdulqadir al-
Qahtan, who also has a political background as a member of the opposition
Islah Party.

Besides practical problems owing to resistance from within the
bureaucratic apparatus,[19] measures that were introduced in the context of
security-sector reforms shrouded more significant political developments
(International Crisis Group 2013:14; Albrecht 2013): protracted struggles
between political elite factions and the attempt, only poorly disguised, by
new president Hadi to strengthen his position vis-à-vis his predecessor 'Ali
Salih, who continued to exert strong influence (Transfeld 2014). While the
head of the military committee, 'Ali Sa'id Obaid, related in January 2013 that
most of the tasks had been accomplished,[20] "security-sector reforms" basically served as a label under which the grip of the Salih connection was to be
gradually loosened. During 2012, most of Salih's men were dismissed from
their leadership positions in the military and security apparatuses, including
nephews, half brothers, and the former president's son and commander of the
Republican Guard, Ahmad 'Ali. Most of these posts were occupied by Hadi
associates. Hadi therefore also strengthened his position not only relative
to his predecessor but also vis-à-vis the éminence grise in Yemen's political
establishment, 'Ali Muhsin.

Two patterns have emerged in the immediate post-Salih transition period.
First, the replacement of Salih loyalists with Hadi's men is indicative of an
attempt, supported by international advisers, at counterbalancing elite factions and of subtle but significant changes in the officer corps. As an active-
duty military officer related in January 2013, 80 percent of new recruitment
among higher officers came from Hadi's Abyan province in the south.[21] A
second pattern witnessed in the immediate post-Salih era is the disintegration of within-unit loyalty among rank-and-file soldiers and personnel in the
security forces. Military behavior during the 2011 uprising was characterized by vertical defections; that is, whole units expressed loyalty or defected
from the political incumbency. Within-unit loyalty is perhaps somewhat
counterintuitive against the backdrop of a largely uninstitutionalized army
that consists basically of a loosely connected network of tribal militias. It was

direct economic dependence of soldiers to their commanders that increased incentives to follow their commanders' lead. Moreover, the decision to follow commanders was made easier by the low-level nature of the 2011 conflict that witnessed a protracted standoff in Sanaʿa but with few casualties on both sides. Hence, risks and costs decreased for soldiers to engage with rival units where soldiers often had a similar tribal origin (Albrecht and Ohl 2016).

Patterns of loyalty and defection seem to have become much more ambiguous in the immediate post-Salih era, which was characterized by an ongoing elite struggle and insecurity among political observers and military personnel alike. The immediate post-Salih era, in 2012 and 2013, saw a competitive broadening of the elite coalition, which again resulted in changes in the upper officer corps. At a time when institutional military reforms were still in the making and the ultimate success of such reform efforts was highly questionable, long-established allegiances were renegotiated, political and military fiefdoms were contested, and hence commander-soldier dependencies were compromised.

Various incidents during 2012 illustrate that in-group loyalty has been disintegrating in the Yemeni military and security force. In early 2012, various units of the air force staged a mutiny against its supreme commander, the former president's half-brother Muhammad Salih, resulting in his dismissal on April 26 after several weeks of negotiations (*Yemen Times* 2012a). In May 2012, a higher officer of the 3rd Brigade of the Republican Guard, ʿAbdulhamid Maqwala, refused to obey presidential orders to replace its commander, a Salih relative. Yet the subsequent mutiny saw splits within the 3rd Brigade, resulting in junior officers publicly declaring their loyalty to the new president. The standoff finally resulted in Maqwala's dismissal in mid-June of that same year (*Yemen Times* 2012c). On July 2, 2012, Murad al-Awbali, a brigadier general of the Republican Guard's 62nd Brigade and a staunch Salih loyalist, was abducted, apparently by other personnel of the Republican Guard who were identified as members of the Khawlan tribe (*Yemen Times* 2012b). It is not known whether the incident was triggered by intertribal rivalries or al-Awbali's role in the suppression of the 2011 popular uprising, but the episode is indicative of splits and rivalries within the Republican Guard, which had stood firm by Ali ʿAbdullah ʿSalih when he was still in power. In late July 2012, clashes at the Ministry of the Interior were not necessarily sparked by political power struggles but instead by economic grievances among police forces resulting in their demands to the ministry to deliver outstanding payments. The ease with which Republican Guard recruits overpowered forces of the

Najda Police, tasked with defending the ministry, raised doubts about Najda soldiers' loyalty to their new commander.[22]

Conclusion

This chapter has argued that a military's involvement shapes the trajectory of an insurgency as much as events prior, during, and after popular mobilization would leave their imprint on military organization, civil-military relations, and patterns of loyalty and defection among armed and security forces. In authoritarian regimes, where officers are members of elite coalitions, not only are recruitment patterns contingent upon elite change, but so is the military's institutional infrastructure. Empirical events in Yemen defy neoinstitutionalist perspectives that use military organization as the main explanatory variable for military behavior. Relations between members of the political-military establishment had soured earlier, which led to ambiguous loyalty patterns within a communal military.

The Yemeni case presents a number of lessons for the topic studied in this book but also for prominent broader literatures in political science. Scholars of civil-military relations often take for granted a high degree of cohesion within a state's security establishment, citing the specific organizational features and command structure of the military as reasons to take the assumed positions of higher officers as aggregated interests for the military.[23] Studying security establishments in authoritarian regimes, however, demands a more cautious perspective on often fragmented security establishments, characterized by blurred boundaries between officers and political elites and the militia-ization of security regimes as a consequence of elite struggle or coup-proofing. The revolutionary situation in Yemen, in 2011 and the subsequent two years, brought such fissures to the fore and serves as a laboratory of sorts to study agents within the military rather the military as a unitary actor.

Accordingly, scholars of regime change will find support in their quest to employ agency perspectives, using a microlens on the interests of political elites during revolutionary processes rather than big structures and processes. Military cohesion—and, in the Yemeni case, the disintegration of the security establishment—should be brought in as a factor to explain why the breakdown of an authoritarian regime precedes the breakdown of the state rather than negotiated democratic transition. While in most works on democratic transition the military was studied in the process of democratic consolidation—with democratization well on its way—Yemen reminds us to consider the military as a venue for elite struggle for one of those factors preventing democratization in the first place.

Notes

1. Notable exceptions are Barany (2011) and Makara (2013).

2. The literature on coup-proofing assumes conscious decisions of incumbents to reshape militaries with the aim of avoiding coups d'état (Quinlivan 1999; Belkin and Schofer 2003; Powell 2012b; Makara 2013; Albrecht 2015). Apart from politicians' attempts to reorganize militaries for power maintenance, militaries are not always reshaped due to intentional innovation. Events such as political and economic crises and war affect military organization as much as political elites, ruling coalitions, and state-society relations.

3. Concordance theory builds on the writings of Janowitz (1960) on military professionalism. In his understanding, a country's military organization mirrors the society from which it originates and is invited to protect. In response to Huntington's (1957) separation hypothesis, Janowitz maintains that the modernization of warfare and the professionalization of military apparatuses catalyze similarities between societies and military apparatuses. Corresponding patterns emerge in recruitment and career paths, organizational and technical skills, and political and ideological views.

4. See the contributions by Droz-Vincent, Croissant and Selge, and Pion-Berlin in this volume for a conceptualization of authoritarian endgame scenarios.

5. Observers reported that Salih immediately requested the mobilization of supporters to rally on Sana'a's Tahrir Square when he learned of Ben Ali's dismissal (author interviews, Sana'a, January 2013). Even in early 2013, Salih loyalists continued to occupy part of the square in the heart of the capital (author's observation). Antiregime mobilization in Sana'a originated outside of Sana'a University, close to the headquarters of the 1st Armored Division that later came to support the uprising.

6. Apart from Muhsin, 'Abdullah al-Qadhi, commander of the Taiz military district and a member of the Sanhani core elite, defected (Phillips 2011:90). Moreover, almost all air defense brigades across the country defected. Various air force brigades—the 4th Brigade (Sana'a), the 101st Mountain Infantry Brigade (Sana'a), the 122nd Infantry Brigade (al-Hudaida), the 314th Armored Brigade (Hadramawt), the 1st Artillery Brigade (Sa'adah), and the 127th Infantry Brigade ('Amran)—all defected from the central command (Gordon and Zimmerman 2012).

7. Author interview with deputy director of Yemeni NGO, Sana'a, January 2013.

8. Ibid.

9. Author interview with expert of Yemeni politics, Sana'a, January 2013. See also Knights (2013:265).

10. Various author interviews with observers, military personnel, and NGO representatives in Sanaʻa, January 2013; see also Knights (2013:274).

11. Author interview with security expert, Sanaʻa, January 2013.

12. Author interview with deputy director of Yemeni NGO, Sanaʻa, January 2013.

13. Author interview with director of a Yemeni think tank, Sanaʻa, January 2013.

14. Author interview with deputy director of a Yemeni NGO, Sanaʻa, January 2013.

15. Author interview with a security expert, Sanaʻa, January 2013.

16. Author interview with deputy director of a Yemeni NGO, Sanaʻa, January 2013.

17. Author interview with deputy director of a Yemeni NGO, Sanaʻa, January 2013.

18. For the planned restructuring of the Ministry of the Interior (in Arabic), see Al-Masdar Online (2013).

19. The merging of departments and units in the security sector was met with opposition, particularly in the concerned ministries; author interview with security expert, Sanaʻa, January 2013.

20. Author interview, Sanaʻa, January 21, 2013.

21. Author interview, January 2013. Rumor has it that Hadi made his own son commander of the Presidential Protection Unit within the Republican Guard, which would indicate the repetition of his predecessor's pedigree politics (International Crisis Group 2013:20).

22. Author interview with security expert, Sanaʻa, January 2013.

23. For a sophisticated, critical discussion of this literature, see Dorothy Ohl's chapter in this volume.

CHAPTER 7

Bahrain's "Cohesive" Military and Regime Stability amid Unrest

Dorothy Ohl

On February 14, 2011, 6,000 protestors hit the streets in Bahrain. On the tenth anniversary of Bahrain's National Action Charter referendum—which had laid out plans for the island state's political development—they called on the Al-Khalifa ruling family to follow through with reform promises. Demonstrators were met with a swift police response, which resulted in the death of at least one individual (Al-Ghasra 2011). In the following days, protests grew and began coalescing around the public square of Pearl Roundabout. By February 17, forces from the Ministry of the Interior, the Bahrain Defense Forces (BDF), and the National Security Agency were clearing the public square, with National Guard members brought in to occupy the space thereafter (BBC Arabic 2011; Al Jazeera 2011a).[1] When the state allowed protestors to retake Pearl Roundabout in the coming days, unrest grew. On February 21 and 22 and again on March 2, more than 100,000 persons were in the streets—nearly one-fifth of the Bahraini population was out demonstrating, mainly peacefully (Al-Wasat News 2011).[2] By March 9, there were popular calls for not only regime reform but also regime removal.[3] Through one month of domestic unrest, however, the security forces remained resolute in containing the demonstrations and supporting the Al-Khalifa monarchy.

What determines whether a regime stands or falls during a domestic crisis, such as that which struck Bahrain in 2011? In the wake of the Arab Spring, observers have often identified military cohesion as a clear predictor of regime restabilization. In a first attempt to distinguish patterns among the uprisings, Barany (2011:28) wrote that "support from a preponderance of the armed forces is surely a *necessary* condition for revolutionary success." It was similarly observed that "where internal [military] divisions are present, they will inhibit the successful execution of presidential orders to repress. Where divisions are either absent or well contained, armies will be able to fulfill such orders" (Pion-Berlin, Grisham, and Esparza 2014:235). Indeed, in this volume many chapters implicitly or explicitly point to the importance of military cohesion in understanding the consequences of mass mobilization. According to Croissant and Selge (in this volume), cohesion is a military preference—a corporate interest that the military seeks to maintain when responding to demonstrators. Lawson highlights how scholars' renewed focus on militaries in the wake of the Arab Spring has come at the expense of studying internal security services as well. His chapter prompts us to consider whether it is strictly military cohesion that is consequential amid unrest or whether unity of the coercive apparatus as a whole is determinative during these regime crises. Given that military cohesion is intimately linked to significant outcomes—ranging from regime change to regional instability and international responses to unrest—it is imperative that we have a clear understanding of the sources of cohesion.

This chapter uses the case of Bahrain to critically assess the cohesion literature. Amid the abundant discussion of military loyalty in the Arab Spring, Bahrain's armed forces have been highlighted as a cohesive military par excellence. The military earned its high-cohesion label by virtue of the fact that its members share a Sunni religious identity. According to Bellin (2012:133), "in Bahrain . . . the military elite and rank and file are predominantly Sunni while the majority of the Bahraini population is Shia"; the military was "primordially distinct from the protestors," and "consequently, in Bahrain the army did not hesitate to shoot" at them. Barany (2011:35) agrees, emphasizing that the "key thing to grasp about the Bahraini military, however, is that it is *not* a national army. Rather, it is a fighting force of Sunni Muslims who are charged with protecting a Sunni ruling family and Sunni political and business elites in a country . . . where about three of every four or five people are Shia." Lutterbeck (2013:42) follows the same thread: "Even though some two-thirds of Bahrain's population is Shia, their presence in the country's security forces has been minimal." And Gaub (2013) characterizes the Bahrain military as cohesive/professional with allegiance to the regime rather than the state.

This chapter reflects on literature concerning the origins of military cohesion using evidence from contemporary Bahrain. It first summarizes how scholars have connected military cohesion to regime durability amid domestic unrest. Second, it presents three areas of scholarly research on the origins of cohesion—those focusing on military norms, institutional design, and nonmaterial bonds—critiquing the diffuse literature on cohesion's sources. To highlight this conceptual weakness, the chapter draws on substantial evidence gained from author interviews conducted in Bahrain on the 2011 uprising. I find ample data that would support labeling the Bahraini military as highly cohesive and also find equally robust evidence labeling it a fragmented force. The cohesion argument is thus found to have theoretical weaknesses that hamper its ability to shed light on military reactions to unrest and therefore regime durability and the trajectory of mass mobilizations. To counter these challenges, the chapter concludes by suggesting that scholars further investigate the microfoundations of military cohesion and more clearly connect these to an understanding of how cohesion is a necessary condition for regime restabilization.

Military Cohesion and Regime Durability

Middle East observers in the Cold War era were struck by the coup cascades that characterized politics in the region. Between 1949 and 1970, there were fifty-five coup attempts in the Middle East and North Africa, many of which displaced ruling regimes (Quinlivan 1999). Syria alone experienced eight successful military interventions in governance between 1951 and 1970. There was a precipitous drop, however, in coups after this period. Many scholars attributed military subordination to authoritarian learning—autocrats had developed strategies to maintain power by insulating themselves from the military threat (Brooks 1998). Such coup-proofing often entailed the "reliance on groups with special loyalties to the regime and the creation of parallel military organizations and multiple internal security agencies" (Quinlivan 1999:131). It seemed as though coup-proofing was yet another tool by which autocrats maintained their power and yet another reason the Middle East remained authoritarian.

Outside the region, however, scholars argued that coup-proofing did not always support an autocrat's resilience and that it might in fact undermine regime durability. According to their logic, widespread social mobilization represented a grave threat for authoritarian leaders. Such events are rare, as authoritarian regimes strive to increase barriers to mass collective action. But as individuals cannot channel their demands through functioning democratic institutions and as mobilization can spiral quickly (Kuran 1991), tensions that are sparked can spread unexpectedly. This produces an "end-game scenario," a context in which the autocrat can no longer rely on his internal security services for protection but instead has to call on his military to suppress citizen demonstrations (Pion-Berlin and Trinkunas 2010).

The type of military on which an autocrat relies differs between normal and such extraordinary times, highlighting the role of military cohesion amid an uprising. When domestic unrest is low, an autocrat relies on a broad distributed security network to monitor the population, infiltrate the opposition, and coerce citizens into supporting the regime. Once unrest breaks out, however, a very different kind of security service is needed to ensure the autocrat's survival. Using force against a mass of citizens necessitates "high degrees of *cohesion* or compliance within the state apparatus" (Way and Levitsky 2006:387). Thus, according to some scholars, the "key to authoritarian stability" amid domestic unrest is "the autocrat's command over an extensive, cohesive, well-funded, and experienced coercive apparatus that can reliably harass opposition and put down protest" (Way 2008:63). In other words, although a fragmented military may make the autocrat's exit by coup less likely, it could make an autocrat's exit by social unrest more likely.

This highly influential cohesive military is described as "one that in spite of differences is capable of confronting another actor in a united fashion, sticking tightly together in order to win certain shared goals. It is an elite that in times of crisis is capable of concerted effort" (Rice 1982). From a military psychology perspective, cohesion "pertains to the extent to which the parts come together to form the social group and hold together under stress to maintain the group" (Siebold 2011:450). This definition of coercive apparatus cohesion runs parallel to the description by Levitsky and Way (2012:870) of ruling party cohesion: "Where cohesion is high, ministers, allied legislators, and local officials routinely support and cooperate with the government. Internal rebellion and defection are rare, and when they occur, they attract few followers." If a highly cohesive apparatus is conceived of as a unified actor with the capability of defending the authoritarian regime, the opposite is a fragmented military. Lack of cohesion is exhibited if "cliques or groups exist within the organization, possess goals, and hold beliefs that are inimical or contrary to the prevailing military organizational culture" (Lee 2005:85). The problem for authoritarian regimes is that with noncohesive forces, marginalized officers and factions can defect to the opposition or simply refuse to participate in quelling domestic dissent. It is then argued that fragmented militaries will not have the cohesion necessary to put down threatening domestic unrest under authoritarianism (Lee 2005, 2009).

In some ways, the cohesion argument represents a divergent vein in scholarly research on military subordination to civilian rule. Founding studies of military intervention in politics focused on societal-level variables to explain military behavior (Huntington 1968). When scholars did take up military organization as an independent variable, the focus was often on military "professionalism" (Huntington 1957). Yet as Lee (2005:83) points out, "While a fair amount of scholars have suggested that an organizational trait—level of military professionalism—can explain the behavior of armed forces, it should be highlighted that these accounts are tautological; the outcomes to be explained and the extent of politicization and intervention are also measures for the explanation." The renewed intellectual focus on military cohesion reenvisions how organization variables affect military behavior, particularly during domestic unrest. Yet despite this progress, this chapter pinpoints a key weakness in the cohesion literature: opacity regarding the sources of military cohesion.

Cohesion's Origins

Scholars utilizing the military cohesion concept have not converged on its fountainhead—arguments have variously contended that cohesion results from a military norm, institutional design, or nonmaterial bonds. In this section, I synthesize leading explanations of military cohesion and critique these components of the literature and then consider how we would identify the Bahraini military's level of cohesion in 2011. I conclude that is difficult to assign cohesion explanatory power without a consensus as to where cohesion comes from and how it operates.

Military Norms

The military cohesion norm argument is typically focused on the unit or institution level. In general, however, the focus is on a context variable influencing individual-level decision making. Military norm explanations are similar in that they argue that organizational culture explains military personnel behavior.

A discussion of unit cohesion focuses on life at the most basic level of military organization. According to Henderson (1985:4), "cohesion exists in a unit when the primary day-to-day goals of the individual soldier, of the small group with which he identifies, and of unit leaders are congruent—with each giving his primary loyalty to the group so that it trains and fights as a unit with all members willing to risk death to achieve a common objective." Such cohesion, or group loyalty, is fostered when soldiers have their "physical, security, and social needs" met and when they "identify with their immediate unit leaders" (Henderson 1985:13). In this argument, unit leadership is consequential. Officers can improve unit cohesion if they are professional, have face-to-face interaction with their unit members, and show the soldier that his service is appreciated. The cohesion norm is strengthened when soldiers increasingly depend on their unit. For instance, connection to the unit intensifies when soldiers are physically separated from the communities in which they grew up (Henderson 1985:41). Combat experience aids cohesion as well; in particular, "international conflict should be expected to increase cohesion within small units as well as service branches" (Belkin and Schofer 2005:154–55). Unit cohesion is established in this way and becomes a norm; social stigma attached to defection is one piece of evidence that the cohesion norm is operating (Henderson 1985). Unit-level arguments suggest that cohesion is undermined when soldiers' basic needs are not met and when competing loyalties arise.

Others contend that a study of military cohesion should focus on the institution level, especially when considering military effectiveness during domestic unrest. According to Lee (2005:84–85), military task cohesion "sets and enforces group standards of behavior" and "sustains the individual in the face of stress." This task cohesion is underpinned by the military's organizational culture: "symbols, rituals, myths, discourse, and heroes" provide evidence of the "basic assumptions, values, norms, beliefs, and formal knowledge that shape the collective identity of an organization" (Lee 2005:85). High institution-level cohesion produces military-wide, norm-governed action, which leads to operational effectiveness and the capacity to repress demonstrators. Broader organization-level arguments suggest that certain types of regime institutional controls undermine cohesion, a topic discussed in the following pages.

A central challenge for the military norm argument is that it is difficult to measure whether cohesion exists on an institutional level. It is unclear how a scholar would assess cohesion, apart from observing an outcome of authoritarian durability or collapse and imputing a post hoc cohesion value. Even if one could judge ex ante that a military was highly cohesive due to its institutional culture, the argument would be unable to explain divergences in loyalty and defection at subgroup levels, which often exist during domestic unrest (Henriksen 2007). Moreover, it would be challenging to test the mechanism at work—the military norm. For instance, Chandra and Kammen (2002) show that when domestic unrest hit Indonesia in 1998, the most highly cohesive groups were not units or the military as a whole but rather officer classes from the military academy. They argue, however, that

> While the formation of tightly knit peer groups, a common development to military organizations, provides the informal structures through which intramilitary cleavages develop, these cleavages must develop in conjunction with individual and group incentives that vary systematically across them in order for one or more groups to take a decisive stand on an issue as important as a transition. (Chandra and Kammern 2002:119)

In other words, the existence of potential divisions within the military is not sufficient to explain the degree of group cohesion; these groups must be made salient. In the Indonesian case, the academy class divisions overlapped with different promotion opportunities, leaving some cohesive classes with a pro-status quo preference and other cohesive classes with a proreform preference. In this way, individual military decision making was not influenced by considerations about military norms or the military institution's broad interests. Instead, for certain officer classes "reform would have meant the loss of jobs and led to retirement" (Chandra and Kammen 2002:114). Material factors and personal power considerations undermined cohesion at the institution level but enhanced solidarity at the academy class level. If military cohesion is based on military norms, these processes remain underspecified.

Institutional Design

Scholars have also studied how autocrats manipulate military institutional design and the potential consequences for military cohesion. They find that when autocrats adopt coup-proofing via institutional fragmentation, military cohesion is undermined. In contrast, if coup-proofing is sought by way of institutional incorporation—layered political and military organizations—military cohesion tends to be supported.

Lee (2005:86) has argued that "divide-and-rule strategies" break down the military's organizational culture, a culture that would foster the norm that soldiers sacrifice their lives to protect the regime. When other scholars focus on coup-proofing, however, they are referencing not only interest convergence and norms but also military capacities. As Brooks (1998:19) states, "Ensuring political control over the military entails depriving it of both the means and the motives to challenge the regime." Whereas democracies prevent coups by punishing soldiers and officers who deviate from civilian control, authoritarian regimes prefer coup-proofing techniques that prevent officers from having the disposition and ability to deviate in the first place (Pilster and Böhmelt 2012). Coup-proofing is the effort to insulate a regime from military takeovers and "may involve the creation of additional (possibly redundant) military branches that prevent any one part of the military from controlling too many resources," as well as "the creation of special paramilitary forces of extremely loyal troops for the sole purpose of protecting the leader" (Belkin and Schofer 2005:149–50). This "counterbalancing has the advantage that it does not only manipulate the military's disposition to intervene, but also that it checks the ability of any other military organization to engage in a coup d'état" (Pilster and Böhmelt 2012:9). Coup-proofing by institutional fragmentation is intended to undermine the military's desire and ability to challenge authoritarian rule.

Quinlivan (1999) has argued that to insulate themselves from coups, many Middle East authoritarian regimes have undertaken extensive efforts to reorganize their armed forces and internal security services along these lines. In particular, they have created parallel security services—such as the National Guard, the Royal Guard regiment, the Ministry of the Interior, and the Religious Police in Saudi Arabia—with overlapping missions and to actively spy on one another. Outside the Middle East, North Korea is often cited for its extensive coup-proofing. Byman and Lind (2010:68) explain that the Kim Jong-un regime has relied "on multiple and competing internal security agencies to reduce the unity of the security forces. . . . Internal security, intelligence, and espionage missions (both foreign and domestic) are distributed across several branches of the government and military." Coup-proofing by way of institutional counterbalancing is seen as undermining military cohesion, resulting in factional defection or paralysis in cases of domestic unrest.

For instance, as Cook (2007:142) has stated regarding Iran's 1978–1979 revolution, "years of the Shah's meddling in the military's affairs to ensure against a coup so compromised the cohesion and professionalism of the officer corps that the military could not act decisively and with a sense of purpose even during a period of grave crisis." Rather than fragmenting the coercive apparatus to prevent coups, another approach is to control the coercive apparatus by incorporating it completely into a dominant party. For example, in reflecting on the role of the People's Liberation Army (PLA) during China's 1989 Tiananmen Square unrest, Scobell (1992:207) argues that the institutional design of the party-army state led to a coercive apparatus with sufficient capacity and civilian oversight to put down the unrest:

> A crucial indicator of the PLA's role in another crisis is the degree of party-army interpenetration. If it is strong, the PLA should function as the "party in uniform" and move to bolster a faltering CCP [Chinese Communist Party]; if it is weak, the PLA's role will be less predictable; if this interpenetration ceases to exist, the PLA might assume a role more like that of the military in many Latin American states.

In other words, the Chinese Communist Party would enhance its durability by continuing the interpenetration of the party-military state. Such an institutional design produces not just a more cohesive coercive apparatus but one that is completely dependent on the regime and thus has high loyalty during domestic crises.

In assessing these arguments, an initial question is whether military cohesion can be assessed in absolute terms or is conceptualized as relational. First, turning to the coup-proofing via institutional fragmentation literature, some scholars focus on intramilitary divides. Yet others discuss how the coercive apparatus as a whole (including, for instance, paramilitary and police forces) is divided and how power is distributed across those groups. If this latter conceptualization was more tightly linked to the outcome of authoritarian durability, studies would need to expand to coercive apparatus coherence rather than military cohesion. Second, the coup-proofing by institutional incorporation literature does not consider military cohesion in isolation. Instead, the key is party-military connections, or political-military cohesion. The institutional design literature is connected to a military cohesion argument, but in many ways, it goes beyond a simple explanation highlighting intramilitary variables.

Nonmaterial Bonds

A growing argument is that military bonds and material incentives are not sufficient to ensure military cohesion during domestic unrest. Instead, nonmaterial loyalties are key to enhancing military solidarity and thus supporting authoritarian durability amid popular rebellion. Scholars in this vein have focused on revolutionary, ethnic, and religious bonds as important sources of military cohesion.

One argument is that shared experience in a violent liberation movement fosters cohesion. "Security forces run by veterans from the liberation struggle are less prone to coups or insubordination" (Levitsky and Way 2012:872), as these forces maintain a shared memory of the past, vision of the future, and view that the regime is legitimate. Indeed, in discussing China's response to the Tiananmen Square demonstrations in 1989, Thompson (2001:77) argues that although elites were divided on a host of specific matters, "the CCP still enjoyed considerable internal party legitimacy through the revolutionary credentials and ideological conviction of the old guard." The argument is that such shared experiences result in military camaraderie, which may reinforce coercive apparatus cohesion and loyalty.

Ethnicity and religion are other nonmaterial bonds that may increase military cohesion. According to Enloe (1980:163), "One of the principal vehicles for creating and sustaining . . . bonds of trust and cooperation among persons of the same ethnic group has been the political party. . . . If a ruling party is perceived to be tied to one ethnic group, it may facilitate intra-state cooperation between civilian and military elites." Focusing on the military, McLauchlin (2010) argues that recruitment on the basis of ethnicity creates a sense of in-group solidarity that limits defections during times of crisis. Investigating the Syrian regime's response to the uprising in Hama in 1982, McLauchlin (2010:342) argues that Hafiz al-Assad's policy of creating an in-group of ethnic and religious Alawites within the armed forces "helped ensure Alawi cohesion, and the presence of an almost entirely Alawi elite unit, in combination with superior firepower, ultimately ensured the regime's victory at Hama and over the rebellion in general." He contrasts this with the Iranian regime's lack of ethnic recruitment in the 1970s and the fall of that regime amid protests at the end of the decade. This is similar to the argument made by Harkness (2012:8), who suggests that for the regime, "an ethnically-based military, loyal to a co-ethnic leader, would be a stable institutional arrangement—for it would be in the military's interests to defend a system that granted them preferential access to such an important source of power and patronage." In Harkness's account, however, neither solidarity nor camaraderie explains cohesion. Instead, cohesion simply represents a group of people who individually agree that the status quo is likely to personally benefit them.

In contrast to ethnic similarities, policies of universal conscription or an unbalanced ratio of ethnic in-group to out-group might undermine coercive cohesion. For instance, Barany (2011:32–33) has argued in the wake of events in 2011 that "Egypt's conscript army has so many ties to society at large that, even had the generals been willing to shoot demonstrators, many officers and enlisted men would probably have refused to obey such an order." The Lebanese officer corps has become more ethnically balanced over time as well (Barak 2006). Such observations have led some scholars to argue that in a diverse society, an autocrat should either chose military members who are "ethnically similar and share other major cultural characteristics" or work to incorporate social minorities so that they "share and adhere to dominant secondary and primary group norms" and "do not form autonomous minority groups with separate norms incongruent with army norms" (Henderson 1985:26). Scholars have pointed to ethnic balancing and conscription as creating a coercive apparatus lacking a potentially strong source of cohesion.

There are evident limitations to such hypotheses, however. With respect to the revolutionary bonds argument, the clearest question is how long cohesion and loyalty persist after a revolutionary juncture. Levitsky and Way (2012:872) anticipate this critique and state that the "effects of violent origins on ruling party cohesion and regime durability are not permanent. Rather, they degrade over time, particularly after veterans of the liberation struggle die or cease to dominate the ruling party." At the heart of this question is the issue of reproduction, the mechanisms that perpetuate cohesion and loyalty based on ideology or shared revolutionary past. If the reproduction avenue is institutional (such as a ruling party or more specifically a party-army state), then the mechanism is not a nonmaterial factor per se. If one insists that it is the ideology or shared history that is consistently bolstering cohesion, the difficulty becomes assessing how actors perceive identities based on such nonmaterial factors. For instance, being part of an ethnic minority attached to a regime may cause strong cohesion and loyalty, as members feel that regime change would pose an existential threat for them. Yet it is unclear in how many cases the regime and coercive apparatus represent an ideology or shared history that sets them clearly apart from demonstrating masses.

There are further critiques regarding arguments that ethnicity and religion enhance cohesion while diversity undermines it. First, Enloe (1980) points out that a group united by ethnic identity is not without other divides—along class, bureaucratic, ideological, and other cleavages. An argument pointing to ethnicity as a basis for military cohesion should be able to explain why this source of solidarity will outweigh potentially cross-cutting cleavages within armed forces. Second, military service may have an independent influence on such identities by weakening them. Countering the perspective that ethnic diversity irrevocably jeopardizes cohesion, Henderson (1985:37) stated that "over time the various ethnic groups [within the military unit] became closer," and he related in words of a Soviet military soldier that "After the first term of service, the relationship among nationalities becomes more equal; all become more like brothers. During the first term of service, Uzbeks make friends only with Uzbeks, Russians with Russians, Jews with Jews, and so forth. But in subsequent service, this is leveled out."

Indeed, this connects to the military cohesion norm argument concerning the military context's effects on individual decision making. Finally, and related, there is a body of social science literature arguing that ethnic and religious identities are not primordial but rather socially constructed and changeable. Along these lines, in comparing coup-proofing strategies, Pilster and Böhmelt (2012:9) argue that "Ethnically or politically induced loyalties to the head of state may be transitory, while the coercive capacities of other military or paramilitary units cannot be tossed aside." In other words, a common nonmaterial bond within the military does not seem fully capable of explaining loyalty and defection, and ultimately authoritarian durability, during domestic unrest.

Bahraini Armed Forces: A Cohesive Military?

There are thus three main arguments as to the origins of military cohesion. One highlights the development of a cohesion norm at the unit or institution level, a second focuses on institutional design's effects on fragmentation or cohesion, and a third underscores that nonmaterial ties can bind military members together. My data from interviews conducted with Bahraini military personnel, defense lawyers, security experts, and others show, however, that scholars can easily code the Bahraini military as cohesive or noncohesive, highlighting the concept's analytical weakness.

Bahrain's High Cohesion Label

As related at the start of this chapter, many scholars highlight the common Sunni religious affiliation shared by Bahraini military members and suggest this is a nonmaterial bond supporting cohesion. It is empirically true that Sunnis have dominated critical coercive positions in Bahrain, while the majority of demonstrators are Shiites. It is commonly believed that any Shiites in the BDF were moved out of their positions in the 1990s, when they were transferred to other government work or offered retirement.[4] Indeed, a 2011 randomized survey found that 16.7 percent of Sunni males contacted reported working in the security services; in contrast, none of the surveyed Shiite males identified themselves as being employed in this sector (Gengler 2011:155). The most prominent police officer to defect from the regime during unrest, now in prison, is a Shiites. His family has described the pains his father went through to get his son the police job in the first place.[5] Typically, the few Shiites able to find work in defense and security industries are given nonsensitive positions, such as traffic control and community policing opportunities (United States Department of State 2011:7).

Such evidence establishes that Bahrain's security forces share a religious affiliation. The next step, however, is explaining whether and how these sectarian demographics are converted into the military cohesion argued to have fueled loyalty to the Al-Khalifa regime during crisis. Unfortunately, scholars do not currently have data that would shed light on whether and how ethnic religious cohesion was the particular driver of military decision making amid crisis. One hypothesis is that Bahrain may place an emphasis on recruiting Sunni radicals into its security services. It is common to hear anecdotes detailing how Bahrain security force members, originally from Syria, believe that fighting Shiites in Bahrain is equivalent to fighting the Assad regime in Syria, and one is told that Shiites are routinely persecuted in Pakistan, from where other security force recruits are drawn. In addition, some claim that following military recruitment, Bahrain has implemented religious advising services within security units to make sectarian divides more salient. One individual recalled his Shiite neighbor who worked in the BDF two decades ago. This former security service member spoke of "mental advisors" within his organization who gave hateful speeches against Shiites.[6] Others claim that the security forces are not directly trained to discriminate against Shiites, but it is implied in their advising and is framed as combat training,[7] such as against the Iranian military threat. Unfortunately, although such anecdotes circulate, scholars do not have the data needed to test the specific mechanisms by which a common Sunni religious affiliation might lead to military cohesion and in turn authoritarian durability.

Without data to explain the religious and ethnic military cohesion argument's mechanisms, scholars simply observe a common Sunni affiliation, identify the outcome of low military defections and no regime leadership changes, and assume that the Sunni identity led to these outcomes. Yet a particular difficulty with this nonmaterial bond explanation is that its observable implications are equivalent to those of other arguments. For instance, I asked Bahraini interviewees: if a BDF officer is Sunni and injures a Shiite demonstrator, does he do that because of his religious beliefs or because he wishes to maintain his privileged place in society? Many thought that this was the exact question to ask. Their reply was usually that there is a group of true believers within the security apparatus; some members truly think that by killing them they are saving Shiites from a life of sin. At the same time, many said that regime supporters implemented their orders for their salary as well as for God.[8] Interviews with loyal security service members might uncover officers' and soldiers' true motivations. The difficulty, however, is that individuals can easily misrepresent their preferences, consciously or unconsciously, and speaking with loyal military personnel is not a frequent opportunity. In sum, scholars have accurately identified that Bahrain's military is drawn from the Sunni population, that most military members did not side with the opposition during crisis, and that the regime remained standing despite unrest. However, they have failed to provide substantial evidence causally linking common religious identity within the military to cohesion and the regime's stability.

Although observers have argued that nonmaterial bonds supported Bahrain's military cohesion, they have not weighed evidence for an alternative explanation: that institutional design may help explain the military's unified response to domestic unrest in 2011. The Bahraini military featured multiple overlapping branches, yet a ruling family member or close ally headed each in 2011. Moreover, there was an institutional forum within the coercive apparatus to strategize about the crisis once it hit, allowing commanders and their civilian elite peers to communicate during the uprising. Bahrain's Supreme Defense Council (SDC) was established in 1973 and has included members such as "the Commander-in-Chief of Bahrain Defense Force, Ministers of Defense, Foreign Affairs, Interior, Finance, National Economy, Council of Ministers Affairs, Information, National Guard, and Deputy Commander-in-chief of Bahrain Defense Force" (Bassiouni et al. 2011:51). The SDC provided a venue for military commanders to meet with one another and with elite civilians once unrest hit and assess the regime's strategy for responding to demonstrators. In addition, following the king's declaration of a State of National Safety on March 15, the SDC recommended the establishment of the National Safety Council (NSC) to supervise Bahrain's three-month State of National Safety. "The BDF Commander-in-Chief presided over this body in his capacity as the officer assigned the responsibility of maintaining order in Bahrain pursuant to Royal Decree No. 18"; the interior minister, a deputy prime minister, the defense minister, the NSA director, the National Guard commander, and the BDF chief of staff also sat on the NSC (Bassiouni et al. 2011:58). Building on the foundation of the SDC, the NSC provided another institutional avenue for military coordination. As the Bassiouni Independent Commission of Inquiry report details:

> Throughout the period during which a State of National Safety was in force, the NSC acted as a forum for information-sharing and coordination between the agencies involved in implementing the measures prescribed in Royal Decree No. 18 of 2011. The NSC held a total of 12 meetings between 16 March and 30 May 2011. During these meetings, which usually convened on a weekly basis, each of the participating agencies presented its evaluation of the unfolding situation in Bahrain, briefed the other agencies on the measures it had undertaken and outlined its proposals regarding future measures that should be taken to restore order in the country. At the conclusion of these NSC meetings, specific tasks and missions were assigned for execution by these agencies either unilaterally or jointly with other government bodies. (Bassiouni et al. 2011:58)

Such an institutional design feature may have enhanced military cohesion—at the least, among Bahrain's military commanders—amid domestic unrest in 2011.

Institutional design choices may also have increased cohesion among lower-level officers and enlisted personnel. First, the regime appears to have put in place coercion mechanisms to formally monitor soldier behavior and in doing so deter insubordination. A former BDF officer related in an interview that there are intelligence personnel within each BDF unit. These individuals are Bahraini, Syrian, and Jordanian, and there are perhaps nine to fifteen per unit. According to the former officer, these intelligence officials can check a soldier's phone and mail as well as who he talks to, what he says, and more. Intelligence officials are responsible for writing weekly or monthly reports about what they find. If a military member expresses antiregime ideas and intelligence officials have evidence, that member can be imprisoned. Worse yet, the BDF has torture facilities on its premises. If intelligence officers do not have sufficient evidence, they will make a note of the suspected behavior so they can put pressure on the security member in the future.[9]

In addition to institutional avenues for formal monitoring, the regime seems to have enabled the informal scrutinizing of soldiers. It is reported that the regime uses family networks to indirectly coerce security force members into subordination. A former BDF officer explained that when five members of a soldier's extended family are serving, if that soldier steps out of line he will receive a phone call not from an Al-Khalifa member but instead from his own family member advising him to modify his behavior.[10] In addition, the regime has pursued a strategy of composing units of both Bahrainis and non-natives. This seems to achieve two purposes. On the one hand, by decreasing the number of Bahrainis in any one unit, the regime seeks to decrease opportunities for collective action among Bahrainis. While the average Bahraini may grumble about inadequate pay, the necessity of certain reforms, and more, there may not be enough Bahraini soldiers serving together to make their true preferences known or to organize to better evade monitoring and punishment. The mixed composition also serves to keep nonnative Bahrainis loyal, responsible agents. For instance, both Bahrainis and nonnatives are sent out on police patrols. The Bahrainis are not given hard tasks but instead are there to supervise the hired guns and ensure that they use sufficient force against demonstrators.[11] The same is likely true within the military. For instance, it is reported that Pakistanis would not use torture against prisoners unless Bahraini supervisors were in the room monitoring them.[12]

Finally, the focus on sectarian identity also overwhelms any investigation of the second alternative argument—that military norms unified the Bahraini coercive apparatus in 2011. Indeed, one could point to the long-standing Western influence in the Persian Gulf region to argue for the presence of institution-level military norms in Bahrain. The British first became involved in Bahrain's defense in 1861 and had a large role in supporting the Gulf state's police and military development in the twentieth century until withdrawing from Bahrain in 1971 (Onley 2009). Following Britain's withdrawal, U.S. presence expanded. This has included the stationing of the U.S. Navy's Fifth Fleet in Bahrain, the United States recognizing Bahrain as a "Major Non-NATO

Ally" in 2002, and the conclusion of a free trade agreement between the countries in 2006 (United States Department of State 2013). These interactions with Western powers, each possessing a culture of military subordination to civilian decision making, may have influenced Bahrain's coercive apparatus compliance with Al-Khalifa orders in 2011.

In sum, scholars conventionally highlight nonmaterial bonds as bolstering cohesion among Bahraini soldiers. Yet they have not brought evidence to bear that would explain how exactly identity may have strengthened military cohesion in Bahrain in 2011. Moreover, there is potential countervailing evidence that institutional design and military norms may have facilitated united action in the kingdom.

Bahrain's Low Cohesion Label

Scholars highlight how Bahraini military members share a religious affiliation yet less frequently acknowledge possible and simultaneous divisions within the armed forces. In considering nonmaterial bonds, my interviews highlight potential family versus nonfamily, tribal, Bahraini versus nonnative Bahraini, and within-mercenary divides among armed forces personnel. In addition, a brief review of Bahrain's history suggests that the organization was not likely to have developed a strong military culture, which may also undermine cohesion. In the following, my data show how nonmaterial identity markers might easily serve to undermine the Bahraini military's cohesion.

First, in Bahrain, ruling family members have permeated the top echelons of the coercive apparatus. At the highest levels, the BDF commander in chief, the minister of the interior, and the National Guard commander, for example, are all from the Al-Khalifa. According to the Bahrain Center for Human Rights (2009), slightly lower-level branches tend to be led by Al-Khalifa officers as well. This could possibly weaken military cohesion in Bahrain, as ruling family members have a much more privileged standing in the country than do military members outside the Al-Khalifa.

On a second front, it is clear that Al-Khalifa officers cannot lead each unit carrying out orders to suppress protestors. It is claimed that members from mainly Sunni and Arab tribes loyal to the Al-Khalifa fill these more basic positions. According to interviewees, these are the Albuflasa, Al-Neim, and Al-Ka'bi, who have a strong presence in the Gulf region; the Al-Qeedat from Syria; Al-Shammari from Iraq; and Al-Amri from Jordan.[13] While it is commonly thought that conflicting tribal affiliations undermine military cohesion and thus imperil an autocrat in crisis, this reasoning has not been applied to Bahrain. Interviews in the country exposed the possible conditions under which the tribe is not a salient intramilitary divide. A political society member explained that Al-Khalifa have worked to ensure that coercive apparatus tribal affiliations are fractured so that no single personality arises, develops a great following within that tribe, and presents himself as a powerful challenger to the king. For instance, you would not find more than eight hundred security force members from any one tribe.[14] In comparison, shortly after protests erupted in Yemen in 2011, the popular General ʿAli Muhsin defected to the opposition, and an entire division of soldiers joined him (Albrecht in this volume). Tribe is a potential divider of military cohesion in Bahrain, but scholars have yet to provide the preceding evidence that suggests why it did not become salient and lead to military fragmentation during crisis (Albrecht and Ohl 2016).

A third key feature of the security services is that a significant component is not of Bahraini origin. After Bahrain's 1970 independence, recruits were often brought from India, Oman, and Yemen, with supervision by British nationals. Today, many come from Baluchistan, Pakistan, Syria, and Jordan as well.[15] A survey of a 2009 list of 1,000 National Security Agency (NSA) employees found that 64 percent were nonnatives (Bahrain Center for Human Rights 2010). The *Wall Street Journal* reported that in March 2011 in the midst of the uprising, "Bahraini recruiters for the National Guard, a paramilitary body, signed up 1,000 new security personnel during road shows in Pakistan, according to officials with military foundations in Pakistan that organized the recruitment" (Delmar-Morgan and Wright 2011). A proponent of reform in Bahrain has mentioned that he has a list of 116 Jordanian security service members working in Bahrain.[16] These recruits, often termed "mercenaries" by Bahrainis, are said to gain a salary ranging from BD500–700 (US$1,300–1,800) monthly.[17] In addition, foreign recruits are given overtime pay, free housing, and compensation to their families should they die.[18] To receive Bahraini citizenship, they often bring their families to Bahrain for two to three months, receive a nationality number and proof of residence, and then send their families back to their home country.[19]

It is argued that non-Bahrainis are Sunni and thus allied with the ruling family and its tribal network. However, interview data questions this simplified portrait of a cohesive tribal and religious alliance surrounding the

Al-Khalifa monarchy. A former BDF officer related a clear bifurcation between native and nonnative Bahrainis in the security forces. As he described, many Bahrainis do not appreciate state money being used to support nonnatives. He related an anecdote: on one occasion, he and his colleagues were carping about their BDF salaries. Their superiors asked why they were grumbling, especially as the nonnative Bahrainis were not complaining. According to this former officer, the native Bahrainis retorted that they did not receive the same tertiary benefits—such as free housing—as were given to the "merce-naries." Moreover, they pointed out that any salary would be a great improve-ment for many nonnatives, whose Bahraini income was seven or more times that available in their home country. The interviewee confessed that not all Bahrainis questioned the Al-Khalifa family's policy of employing nonnatives. However, he affirmed that others have asked why the government tells Bah-rainis that it does not have enough money to increase Bahrain's security force wages but then hires more outsiders.[20]

Indeed, another Bahraini described the foreign security force members as a third sect—there being Shiites, Sunnis, and expatriates. According to this individual, the nonnatives have their own affinities, live in their own areas, and do not fully integrate with Bahraini Sunnis.[21] In fact, interviewees have related disturbances between naturalized and native Sunni Bahrainis in the neighborhood of Hamad Town.[22] There appears to be a degree of tension within the coercive apparatus between Bahrainis and nonnatives that could undermine cohesion. Indeed, a further point that reinforces this possibility is that some foreign-born members have a severely limited ability to speak most Bahrainis' native language—Arabic. Such anecdotes question the degree to which there is a solid melding of interests among members of Al-Khalifa's reputed Sunni-allied tribal network.

Fourth, there are additional divisions within the "mercenary" aspect of the military community. Although many security force members are not born in Bahrain, some, particularly those working in the BDF, gain citizen-ship once they are in the country. There is uncertainty as to what percentage of nonnative military and security members are newly arrived versus being of families who have worked in Bahrain for more than a generation. Variation in these two factors—citizenship status and length of residency in Bahrain—might influence military cohesion and support for the Al-Khalifa.

There is likely intramercenary variation based on these individuals' coun-try of origin and, relatedly, on the jobs they are given once in Bahrain. There are stories of lower-level nonnative recruits showing small signs of sympathy toward the demonstrators with whom they have contact. One formerly imprisoned man described his torture while in prison. He mentioned that on one occasion, a Yemeni guard gave him and a few other detainees brushes and told them that if they left to go clean a nearby room, they would miss a coming round of torture.[23] Another former prisoner referenced his time in al-Grain military prison. He explained that most of his guards were Pakistani, though he interacted with other Bahrainis and Arabs there as well. The interviewee felt that some Pakistanis were very sympathetic to the inmates and seemed to realize that disproportionate brutality was being used against these Bahrainis.[24] Some individuals have related that Pakistanis would not use torture against prisoners unless Bahraini supervisors were in the room monitoring them. These anecdotes should lead us to question whether there might be a divide between Jordanian and other Arab mercenaries, who tend to be hired following their own military and intelligence careers in their home country and who serve in higher-level positions; Yemeni and Pakistani recruits, who serve in low-level positions in prisons; and, further, those Pakistani and other recruits on the front lines in the streets during the crisis.

In addition to questions regarding the extent to which identities strengthen or undermine military cohesion in Bahrain, there is not substantial evidence to support cohesion based on a strong military culture. Being in the military was a steady job with average benefits for Bahrainis in 2011; however, military service was not a privileged position in Bahrain.[25] In addition, in contrast to the Syrian, Iraqi, and Egyptian militaries, for instance, Bahraini troops did not participate in extensive international military campaigns. Without such deployments, the Bahraini military did not develop a strong martial culture and historical place in the national narrative, argued to contribute to military cohesion at the institutional level. Bonds at lower levels within the military were not strengthened through common experience actively fighting an external enemy. In sum, it does not appear that military norms ensured cohesion and subordination to civilian rule during the 2011 uprising in Bahrain.

Summary

Delving into the Bahrain case exposes how a weak conceptualization of cohesion leads to its imprecise operationalization. Scholars commonly cite

Bahrain as a case in which military cohesion allowed the regime to restabilize amid domestic unrest. Yet, although they typically highlight the power of nonmaterial bonds in strengthening military loyalty, they do not establish how exactly a common Sunni identity bolsters cohesion amid unrest. Moreover, institutional design choices may have had a greater impact on military cohesion than these nonmaterial bonds. Indeed, there is equally robust evidence to categorize the Bahraini military as noncohesive, based on family, tribal, and citizenship differences among its members as well as the lack of a strong military culture and norms. The cohesion variable, as currently outlined in the literature, does not provide scholars with great leverage in explaining the underpinnings of authoritarian durability.

Understanding the Microfoundations of Military Cohesion

As Barany (2011) has pointed out, there is a clear correlation between the majority of military actors using force against demonstrations and an autocratic regime restabilizing. Since this military support is crucial to explaining how authoritarian regimes weather domestic unrest, scholars must clarify their conceptualization of military cohesion. The variable currently rests on weak theoretical foundations. Indeed, as specified now, most militaries could be described as either cohesive or fragmented, and a country expert is likely to find evidence for a particular value of the independent variable based on observation of the dependent variable. Due to the close proximity between the military cohesion cause and the authoritarian durability outcome, separating the two becomes even more important for scholars wishing to avoid tautological claims.

Despite these challenges, there is great potential for scholarship to refine our understanding of military cohesion. After clarifying how one can measure cohesion, a step forward will be to outline specific hypotheses as to when cohesion remains intact and when it dissolves. Importantly, scholars should outline observable implications that can adjudicate between rival hypotheses. Second, and related, scholars should investigate how the sources and durability of cohesion may vary depending on the context in which military personnel make their decisions. There is no reason to expect military cohesion to operate the same when units are deployed against external enemies versus when militaries are used to quell domestic unrest, for instance. By clarifying the conceptualization of military cohesion, its origins, and whether it is a necessary or sufficient condition for regime stability during unrest, the variable can gain meaning in studies of military responses to mass civilian mobilization.

Notes

1. The BDF is composed of approximately 12,000 individuals, the MOI 9,000, and the NG 1,200, in addition to NSA intelligence forces (Cordesman and Al-Rodhan 2006; Bassiouni et al. 2011).

2. Bahrain's 2010 census reported a population of 1,234,571 persons: 568,399 Bahraini citizens and 666,172 non-Bahrainis.

3. This escalation of demands can be seen by comparing news coverage of the protests as they unfolded. Days before the February 14, 2011, protests, Bahrainis voiced their demands in Manama Voice for a more vibrant political life. Indeed, on February 15, Reuters reviewed the reform agenda laid out by protestors. But following the regime's use of lethal force against demonstrations, particularly the clearing of Pearl Roundabout, there were increased calls for the fall of the regime, such as those reported by the *New York Times*. See Alfardan (2011), Reuters (2011), and Slackman and Audi (2011).

4. Author interview with defense lawyer, Manama, Bahrain, March 2013.

5. Author interview with family member of police officer who defected and is serving a prison sentence, Manama, Bahrain, March 2013.

6. Author interview with defense lawyer, Manama, Bahrain, March 2013.

7. Author interviews with defense lawyer and with Bahraini journalist, Manama, Bahrain, March 2013.

8. Author interview with Bahraini journalist, Manama, Bahrain, March 2013.

9. Author interview with former BDF member, Manama, Bahrain, March 2011.

10. Ibid.

11. Author interview with political society member, Manama, Bahrain, March 2011.

12. Author interview with defense lawyer, Manama, Bahrain, March 2011.

13. Author interview with former BDF officer, Manama, Bahrain, March 2013.

14. Author interview with political society member, Manama, Bahrain, March 2013.

15. Useful resources on this issue include International Crisis Group (2005:2), Bahry (2000:133), Cordesman and Al-Rodhan (2006:18), Bassiouni et al. (2011:16), Tharoor (2011), and Human Rights Watch (2010).

16. Author interview with political society member, Manama, Bahrain, March 2013.

17. Author interviews with a secular opposition figure, a human rights activist, and a Bahraini journalist Manama, Bahrain, March 2013.

18. Author interviews with former BDF officer and with Bahraini journalist, Manama, Bahrain, March 2013. See also Bahrain Center for Human Rights (2009).

19. Author interview with former BDF officer, Manama, Bahrain, March 2013.

20. Ibid.

21. Author interview with a secular opposition figure and human rights activist, Manama, Bahrain, March 2013.

22. Author interview with secular opposition figure, human rights activist, Manama, Bahrain, March 2013. Also referenced by Al-Shehabi (2011).

23. Author interview with family member of police officer who defected and is serving a prison sentence, Manama, Bahrain, March 2013.

24. Author interview with defense lawyer, Manama, Bahrain, March 2013.

25. Author interview with current BDF member, Washington, D.C., April 2013.

CHAPTER 8

The Syrian Military and the 2011 Uprising

Philippe Droz-Vincent

In 2010–2011, uprisings across the Arab world highlighted the role of social mobilizations against enduring authoritarian rule. Another essential factor was the authorities' use of repressive tools. Authoritarian regimes countered peaceful demonstrators with police means, and when the police, paramilitary, and riot-control forces were overwhelmed by the massive character of social movements, they then called on the regular armed forces to exert repression. At this stage, the role of the military high command became crucial: either senior officers could disassociate themselves from the regime and adopt the mantra of state defender, ushering in the end of authoritarian rule as exemplified by Tunisia and Egypt, or they could engage in repression on behalf of the regime. Syria singled itself out with fierce military repression during the initial months of the 2011 uprising, laying the foundation for the eruption of civil war.

The Bashar al-Assad regime retained sufficient control over the military to survive the initial "stress test" of the uprising and wage fierce repression against unarmed demonstrators. Why did the regime not follow the fate of other Arab authoritarian regimes where the military fractured or exploded, as in Yemen or Libya (Droz-Vincent 2014c)? The Assad regime sustained a fierce civil war, with increasing clashes between deserters defending their villages and government forces, growing bombings and hit-and-run attacks against military convoys, and the rise of the Free Syrian Army. This suggests the central question: How did the regime manage to retain the loyalty of the Syrian military (or at least significant parts of it) as a repressive tool against an increasingly militarized popular rebellion?

The 2011 Uprising as a Crucial Stress Test for the Military

One of the specific features of the Syrian uprising was the regime's rapid turn to brute force and heavy repression.[1] As in other cases during 2011, the Syrian uprising started with sudden and massive civic demonstrations pouring out in public spaces across Syrian cities—those not sealed off by the deployment of security forces, such as Damascus and Aleppo (Lawson 2013). The Syrian uprising was pacific at the beginning, yet the authoritarian regime would not let public spaces slip out of its grid of control (Wedeen 1999). The Assad regime was taken by surprise after being self-blinded by what it thought were its "specific characteristics."[2] It very early recognized that brute force would have to be the mainstay of its survival strategy. It also discovered the impossibility of a quick reinstatement of the vicious "wall of fear," namely the dissuasive effect of prospective repression acting as a deterrent based on the control of the population by the dreaded security apparatus (*mukhabarat*). The Assad regime therefore reacted with extreme brutality. Scuffles began in Daraʿa and several other cities as the security forces opened fire with live ammunition. When demonstrations continued, some military units cracked down using machine guns, tanks, and snipers, which exacted a high death toll in such northern cities as Homs and Hama.[3]

The wholesale repression represented a strong stress test for the regime and in particular for the whole set of social relations constitutive of the military. Its hierarchical relations, relations with other social sectors, sense of duty and obedience, and links to society became strained beyond normal limits. Three factors are essential for understanding why massive social mobilizations can turn into a stress test for the military.

First, everywhere the military feels charged with several missions: to defend the nation, protect order, and maintain the image as well as the interests of the military under the incumbent regime. However, when the military is called on to carry out crowd control with heavy arms, it threatens its image as the defender of the nation and even its internal coherence and discipline. There is a big difference between repressing an armed uprising and killing largely peaceful protesters, since junior officers and rank-and-file troops are called upon to open fire on individuals with whom they might identify. Mass opposition—especially when it manifests itself in open defiance of political authority and a police-based "apparatus of fear"—severely tests the loyalty of military personnel. Furthermore, the Syrian military is a conscript army (except in some specific units), and conscripts in the rank and file might themselves be disenchanted with the regime's policies but do not express it openly until they face unarmed demonstrations and receive the order to fire.

Second, when the number of protesters is large, repression can turn into a bloodbath. The asymmetry of power between insurrectionist demonstrators without weapons—or protesters who carry just some light weapons, as in the northern countryside where firearms are a sign of social status—and heavily armed military units had a strong destabilizing effect on the armed forces. Hence, when demonstrations began to spread in the spring of 2011, the claims by the official press and proregime television outlets that policemen or army personnel were being killed by unknown snipers or infiltrators (*mundas*) was a way for the authorities to advance an argument to legitimize outright repression that was addressed to the entire Syrian public but was targeted as well to security and military personnel.[4]

Third, repression will be seen everywhere in Syria as well as the outside world due to the rise of social media and mobile phone cameras. New media facilitate collective action by means of coordination and snowballing and make it possible to display the horrors of armed repression. Syria in 2011 was very different from Syria in 1982. In 1982, the Hafiz al-Assad regime besieged the city of Hama, where between 10,000 and 40,000 people were estimated to have been killed without much outside knowledge. In 2011, the Bashar al-Assad regime's propaganda was countered by citizen journalists and informal information coming from below, with images circulated widely across Syria. According to Lebanese officers who know the Syrian military well, soldiers who were ordered to open fire on crowds in 1982 "did not hesitate" (Droz-Vincent 2013). Yet in 2011 the horrors of repression led to cracks in the monolith. Videos aired by defectors on the Internet called the atrocities the main reason that led military personnel to defect.

Stories emerged of splits in the 5th Division stationed along the southern border and around Daraʻa, with soldiers shooting other soldiers for refusing to fire on protesters. More cases were reported in the following months, including clashes between army personnel and security forces in Jisr al-Shughur, Homs, Abu Kamal, and Deir-ez-Zor (Abbas 2011). During the first months of 2011, only the elite 4th Division and the Special Forces were regularly deployed to quell protests. As a result, the regime waged its "war against terrorism" with only a small part of the army, perhaps 60,000 soldiers out of the whole Syrian military. This explains why government forces withdrew from some cities in June 2011, leaving territory open to the protesters whose demonstrations expanded in Hama, Homs, Deir-ez-Zor, and Abu Kamal.

Furthermore, the regime used rogue militias—the so-called Shabihas (Specters) to reinforce the security services and play the role of foot soldiers. They called themselves "Asad's Security" (Amn Asad) and reinvigorated the personality cult of the leader. At the beginning of the uprising, the Shabihas roamed as unorganized gangs of black-clothed thugs who turned peaceful protests into deadly chaos in places such as Latakia.[5] They hailed from networks of smugglers organized on the basis of familial ties, sectarian affiliations, or mercenary interest. Quite different from military units, they were unstructured in organization. Later on when the uprising took deeper roots in Damascus and Aleppo, the Shabihas were increasingly recruited from the Alawi quarters of Damascus and among Sunnis in Aleppo. The Shabihas took orders directly from the intelligence services, especially Air Force Intelligence (Istikhbarat Jawwiya), and their growing operational role created resentment among regular military commanders (All4syria 2012a).

Moreover, the Assad regime made extensive use of snipers. Most of the deaths during the initial months of the uprising were the result not of panicked security personnel firing blindly into crowds but of what Navi Pillay called "an apparent 'shoot-to-kill' policy" (United Nations Human Rights Council 2011).[6] Regime snipers carefully selected their targets on the basis of specific criteria, for example, individuals filming demonstrations with mobile phones, using megaphones, or carrying banners. The snipers were told that there were foreign agents sprinkled among the demonstrations. Snipers had to return their precision weapons empty of ammunition, and those who raised an argument about the target with their officers were immediately killed. Shootings were called beheadings (qata' al-ru'us) by Syrian soldiers and were aimed at midlevel organizers in an effort to reinstate "the wall of fear" by terrifying demonstrators (All4syria 2011).

The "Brutalization" of the Military and the Phenomenon of Defections

The Assad regime's reaction to the 2011 uprising did not just involve the calibrated use of military force as a stress test by engaging in heavy repression against civilians. The regime went further in the direction of wholesale brutalization and exerted as much violence on its own military forces as it did in repressing popular demonstrations.

In authoritarian regimes in general, armies manage their internal affairs by acting apolitically with regard to their professional affairs under the guidance of high-ranking officers loyal to the political leadership. The Syrian military, by contrast, was much more penetrated by security organs. Conversely, numerous security structures that governed the Syrian state originated from the military and used military resources,[7] creating a tight nexus of military-security organs not found to the same extent in Egypt and Yemen. As a consequence, there was less leeway for the Syrian military to move away from the regime. Furthermore, the military-security nexus has been reinforced since the beginning of the uprising. At first, sizable numbers of casualties in the military were reported by official sources, the international press, and Human Rights Watch (Human Rights Watch 2011b). These soldiers and officers were in fact killed by the security forces, in particular by Military Intelligence (al-Amn al-'Askari), for refusing to shoot protesters or harboring sympathy for the demonstrators.[8] The executed soldiers were numbered among the martyrs (*shuhada*) by the regime, and their deaths were blamed on armed gangs.

Security structures have taken a prominent role normal military command structures. Al-Amn al-'Askari has overseen the promotion of officers and the movement of all army units: the military command did not follow orders from the Ministry of Defense but from al-Amn al-'Askari. At least 3,000 officers of various grades, especially non-Alawis, were detained in prison. Air bases have been closely monitored; pilots were mostly Sunnis and might feel a deepening sense of unease about the tactics used by the regime. In addition, the sons of Sunni military personnel were "detained"/"hosted" along with relatives at army camps to discourage defections.

Security units (*lijan amniya*) within military units have watched soldiers closely, reporting what was going on inside the army, including what soldiers were telling or writing to their families, and tapping phones. Their reports were sent directly to al-Amn al-'Askari. In some units, the role of security officers (*dabat lil-amn*) turned out to be more important than that of the commander. From the beginning of the uprising, security officers have increasingly dealt with individuals according to their sectarian or geographic affiliation. For instance, their way of dealing with members of the Sunni community, even if they openly displayed no sectarian affiliation, was different from the way members of minorities were handled. Soldiers from regions that were considered to be disloyal were placed under strict control; sometimes they were not even permitted to carry weapons.

Despite the tight scrutiny of the security services, the stress test has had an impact on the Syrian military. This can be exemplified by defections (*inshiqaqat*) of both officers and rank-and-file troops. According to some sources (All4syria 2012b), 100,000 soldiers defected, and 99 percent of the soldiers from Hawran left military service and fled.[9] Hundreds of officers fled as well, among them fifty non-Alawi generals and senior officers. However, the security-military nexus has proven to be instrumental in maintaining an atmosphere of fear in the Syrian military. Systematic repression acted as a powerful deterrent against massive and coordinated defections in 2011–2012.[10] Security forces and their pervasive grid of control systematically hunted defectors and carried out reprisals against their families. Many soldiers have remained in the army because they are terrified by the consequences of betraying it (*Times of London* 2011). Defectors have needed to carefully plan their actions and find ways to protect their families—hence defections have been easier in areas where families live under the control of armed opposition groups. Defections occur as the result of individual or small group decisions, not whole units choosing to side with the opposition. As a corollary, the main problem facing the Syrian military has been the shortage of officers and manpower rather than the collapse of its organizational structure.

Special focus should be put on defections from the officers' corps. Officers' loyalty or acquiescence is crucial for an authoritarian regime to endure, and conversely, their politicization can be detrimental to the regime. The Syrian army boasted a hierarchical corps with a great gap between officers and the rank and file. Numerous eyes in Syria in March 2011 were turned toward the officers as an agent of change, mirroring events in Tunisia and Egypt. In April 2011, the National Initiative for Change called on the army to protect civilians and facilitate a transition; the opposition singled out respected and supposedly "neutral" figures, such as Minister of Defense 'Ali Habib and Chief of the General Staff Daoud Rajiha, as "representing a background that Syrians can positively relate to."[11] A Friday of protest was even named after "the protectors of the nation," with an explicit reference to the Syrian national anthem. Women and children greeted soldiers with olive branches; people in the streets shouted the slogan "the army and the people are one hand" (*al-jaish wa al-sha'b ayad wahida*) as a way to tilt the military toward regime change. Yet the shift in military allegiance did not take place. There was instead a gradual unraveling of the military in the face of the stress test of coping with mass mobilization through repression.

The loyalty of the Syrian officers' corps can only be understood by understanding how it was rebuilt under Hafiz al-Assad and then inherited by his son Bashar. The Syrian officers' corps was not just the path-dependent end result of the emergence of the "new middle class" as part of the modernization of Arab societies in the 1950s and 1960s that connected new social groups with education and social change and installed the military as a key component of Arab regimes. In another crucial step, the Syrian officers' corps was remade in the 1970s: Hafiz al-Assad coalesced around himself networks of officers, using them as "nerves" for regime consolidation and cementing a coalition of Alawi officers (especially from the air force), some rural Sunni officers, and other minority officers (Druze, Ismailis, and Christians). Promotions based on competence became more common among junior officers under the slogan of promoting professionalism, but at senior levels, appointments were made primarily according to political and familial/sectarian considerations. The regime's "social engineering" in the officers' corps had been systematic and scrupulous for four decades, and hundreds of Alawis rose in one generation from an impoverished childhood to much more prestigious social positions as military officers. Rural Sunnis also enlisted in great numbers in the military, along with other minorities from the periphery of the big cities (Batatu 1999).

But the same sociological and political trends that had created equilibrium for the Hafiz al-Assad regime for four decades contained the seeds for the gradual unraveling of the Syrian military during the 2011 uprising. After a decade of modernization under Bashar al-Assad, those who felt the difficulties most were in the rural peripheries where demonstrations originated, namely Sunni towns that were traditionally strongholds of the Hafiz al-Assad regime and loci of recruitment for the military, such as Dara'a, Deir-ez-Zor, Rastan, and Idlib and the towns around Homs and Hama (Droz-Vincent 2014a). It is thus no wonder that officers hailing from those regions defected to form the backbone of the Free Syrian Army (FSA). Symptomatically, the FSA had no Alawi officers and very few minority officers of any kind at the beginning of the uprising.

A whole social stratum, rural Sunni officers who had been incorporated during the Hafiz al-Assad era, provided most of the defectors. That social feature was also felt as a social clash when the armed opposition entered the big cities. For instance, Aleppo city dwellers, with a tradition of urban life attuned to the rhythms of commerce, witnessed the arrival of former soldiers now turned rebels from semirural, tradition-bound suburbs and Sunni agricultural areas and resented them as an occupying force. These fighters' rural pedigree was distinct from the cosmopolitan, multireligious ethos associated with Aleppo, an ancient trading crossroads (Abdul-Ahad 2012). As a result, the rural Sunni officers who defected to command rebel units were not very different in their behavior toward Aleppo merchants and the middle classes than their counterparts in the loyal military.

Furthermore, the whole Syrian military has been organized since the 1970s around a comprehensive system of checks and balances, with officers in key posts checking each other and some officers duplicating others' functions along more or less shadow or parallel command lines—some were more security-related officers rather than field commanders. This has been complemented by a sectarian equilibrium. For instance, if the commander of a given unit is Sunni, his deputy is Alawi and the security officer from another confession, thereby diminishing the ability of the unit to act as a whole. And defecting was problematic because Alawis controlled the most strategic positions and were the more heavily armed. After 2011, those mechanisms of control and balance were reinforced. They impeded military efficiency and nurtured cautiousness among field officers waiting for orders and authorizations from above, but at the same time they forestalled defections of whole units. As a consequence and despite the stress test of the 2011 uprising, the organizational grid of the Syrian military buttressed by security-military networks was maintained under the control of the regime and its loyalists inside the military.

"Managing" the Syrian Military to Exert Massive Repression

It was one thing for the regime to make the Syrian military and security apparatus sustain the stress test of the uprising in 2011–2012. But how did it managed to transform part of the armed forces into a ruthless killing machine and keep the rest quiet? Three elements explain the ability of the authorities to use the military as a repressive tool: the downsizing and securitization of the regular army, the hegemonic rise of a war narrative, and the exploitation of external lifelines to supplement the military's loss of capabilities.

Downsizing and Securitization of the Military

The dualization of the Syrian military was pushed to a new level with the militarization of the 2011 uprising. The regime consistently relied on a few key units that acted as a strike force. Defectors asserted that only one-third of the army was actively involved in repressing protests, most notably the 4th Division, Unit 549 (the former Special Forces), and the 90th Mechanized Division, along with the secretive Unit 450 tasked with chemical weapons (for a description of military deployments, see Holliday 2013 and Kozak 2015). The rapid cycling of deployments of key units across Syria in 2014–2015 was clear testimony to the limited availability of loyal troops.

The rest of the military, namely those units not considered fully loyal, was in bad shape, with only 30 percent of the troops remaining after desertions and with combat readiness suffering from a lack of equipment and spare parts, and they were plagued by low morale due to exhaustion from months of fighting against an increasingly able rebellion and the arrest or marginalization of most of their officers. Some soldiers and officers were left isolated and in despair in remote areas and even sold part of the ammunition they received just to get money to buy food. That part of the military was used as a reserve force, and the regime recombined existing units to create more effective combat units when it launched counteroffensives. Sunni conscripts were sometimes used as cannon fodder.

High-level officers close to the president were systematically promoted. The regime also promoted young, able, and loyal Alawi field officers looking for a way to display their loyalty to the regime and gain rapid promotion. In addition, the regime recalled retired Alawi senior officers to fill vacant posts.[12] New "heroes" of the war were heralded in the media, such as the famous Colonel Suhail al-Hassan—dubbed "the tiger." The "Alawitization" of key positions in the security and military sectors had been a classic tactic of the Assad regime in times of crisis dating back to the 1970s: senior officers mostly drawn from the Alawi sect trust one another and come from the same region, sometimes the same villages. Some sources close to former minister of defense 'Ali Habib stated that the army in 2012–2013 had 36,000 officers, of which 28,000 were Alawis, some 80 percent of the officers' corps; more than 90 percent of officers carrying the rank of general were of Alawi origin and were even from the Kalbiyya tribe to which the Assad family belongs. Similarly, in 2012 there was a major reshuffle in the leadership of Political Security (al-Amn al-Siyasi) under the guidance of General Rustum Ghazalah, a very new feature in this highly and previously unmovable bureaucratic monolith: numerous cadres in whom the regime lost confidence were moved to less prominent administrative posts (All-4syria 2012b).

Command remained overcentralized. A few loyal officers exercised real control, and the others were under constant surveillance. Military formations were directed by loyal commanders in the field answering calls by high decision makers. An atmosphere of fear prevailed among officers, with a lack of confidence between officers. Officers kept their pistols at hand if there was an officer from another confession in their vicinity. There were extensive problems of communication, and tasks were deeply divided.[13] The prerogatives of the minister of defense were distributed between the incumbent and various deputies to forestall the prospects of a coup d'état.

Finally, the extensive use of militiamen (Shabihas and other irregular units) counterbalanced the regular armed forces. They were often integrated into active military units in order to offset the shortage of fully committed infantry or control potential defectors. The militia-ization of the armed forces expanded in 2012 with the spread of armed fighters without uniform manning checkpoints and then again in 2013–2014 with the setting up of a centralized proregime militia parallel to the country's military command structure. This militia was called the National Defense Forces (Quwwat al-Difa' al-Watani) and reportedly included 20,000 to 50,000 members (*Al-Ahram Weekly* 2013). In this way, the Assad regime reinvigorated the tradition of the Ba'thi "people in arms" that had been practiced during the civil war against the militant Islamists (1976–1982), updating it with the model of the Basij militia introduced by Iranian advisers.

As a result of this deliberate securitization, the Syrian army did not buckle under the pressure entailed by the stress test of the uprising and was transformed in an efficient killing machine. Yet, an essential caveat should be added: the repressive apparatus steadily exhausted itself. Losses turned out to be high. In the immediate area of Qardaha, the birthplace of the Assad family, residents estimated that as many as three hundred men died in 2012. Symptomatically, numbers of martyrs (*shuhada*) in the armed forces were at first announced daily by the official news agency SANA and its "private" mouthpieces, al-Duniya television and the newspaper *al-Watan*. Funerals were systematically publicized by the regime. Then in 2012, such displays were thought to be detrimental to morale, and instead SANA began to broadcast images of dead insurgents. When the tide of events on the ground seemed to tilt in favor of the Assad regime in March 2013, the proregime (Sunni) Higher Council for Fatwas (*majlis al-ifta al-a'la*) issued a religious edict (*fatwa*) broadcast on television urging Syrian citizens to join the military for mandatory enrolment, calling it "a spiritual and national obligation" (*masuliyya imaniyya wa wataniyya*) and stating that "fighting to defend our people (*sha'b*) and our nation (*umma*) under the command of God in our fight (*jihad*) and your defense of Syria follows God's Word and the right (*haqq*) in our homeland (*watan*)."

The New Domineering Narrative of War

The gradual shift of the Syrian uprising from pacific (unarmed) revolt in 2011 to militarization in 2012, with the essential milestone represented by the FSA offensives against Damascus and Aleppo in the summer of 2012, radically changed the conditions of warfare under which officers and the rank-and-file fought. The setting was no longer the use of military force by an authoritarian regime against pacific civilians demonstrating in public spaces. As a consequence, there was a redeployment of incentives to fight. Loyalists fought in a war that vindicated the Assad regime's version of events as a foreign plot against Syria to instill war—an assertion made in 2011 as demonstrations were mainly pacific.

More generally, militarization shifted the narrative from soldiers being repressive actors to soldiers trying to survive in a cruel conflict. And by 2012–2013, low-ranking soldiers and officers in the regular army fought not just out of conviction or love for Bashar al-Assad but also due to fear over the armed opposition and the tricks used by insurgent groups to kill them. According to sociological studies of combat experience, fear is essential in combat, and people most often fight not to be killed (Stouffer 1949). Many soldiers felt abandoned in remote military bases, often encircled by armed groups and resupplied by helicopters. And yet they resisted, which explains the patchwork of governmental positions that could be found scattered across Syrian territory in 2013–2014.

The fear generated by jihadist Sunni extremism played into the hands of the Assad regime to make the "silent majority" stick with the government not out of conviction but because it was the lesser evil. This shift meant that the moment had passed when some Alawis might choose to side with the opposition.[14] Those in top military positions, along with thousands of others who played more modest roles in the state apparatus, realized that it had become impossible to get promises of protection if the regime fell. Elite units, intelligence services, and Shabiha members therefore determined to fight on simply to secure their community; others were prepared to fight on the regime's side not out of conviction but out of fear that if it fell, they and their families would be slaughtered by Sunni extremists simply for their religious affiliation.[15]

Feeling the benefits arising from such polarization, the regime positioned senior officers from the Alawi, Christian, Druze, and Ismaili faiths in a life-or-death struggle with the large Sunni majority. The newly appointed defense minister, Daoud Rajiha, provided a Christian face for the regime. His nomination implicated Syria's Christians in the conflict on the side of the regime and was interpreted as such by both camps. A wave of new promotions in the army during 2012–2013 included a great proportion of officers with Druze, Ismaili, and Christian backgrounds. The end result of this strategy could be seen in the high mortality rates of Druze soldiers from Suwaida and the display of numerous Christian martyrs on Facebook pages. In 2012, Druze soldiers performing their military service in Dara'a, in the context of lethal attacks by jihadist groups and the FSA alike, asked their religious elders (*mashayikh aql*) and prominent retired Druze officers to mediate with the authorities to get them transferred to Druze areas.

Furthermore and more viciously, the Assad regime has played on the fear of minorities concerning the rise of Sunni jihadists after 2013 and manipulated the sectarian tinderbox to recruit additional auxiliary troops. Noncommitted Christians and those who at the beginning had harbored sympathy for demonstrators felt threatened by the rise of jihadist groups and the targeted killings they carried out. Groups of vigilantes (*lijan sha'biya*) appeared in Christian neighborhoods at the security apparatus's directive. The vigilante groups consist of ordinary citizens aware that they could be targeted or embroiled in violence by default.

External Assistance as a Lifeline and Compensating for Weaknesses

Finally, assistance from external allies provided a crucial lifeline to the Syrian regime. Iranian support began with the delivery of weapons, ammunition, and riot gear. This support was upgraded with increasing numbers of trainers and advisers, including a key role after April 2011 for members of the elite al-Quds Force of the Islamic Revolutionary Guards Corps (Pasdaran) (*Washington Post* 2011). At the beginning of 2012, Iran began sending arms in large quantities as well as sophisticated equipment to monitor and penetrate rebel groups, especially surveillance equipment that helped the authorities track down opponents through Facebook and Twitter accounts.

The Syrian army has also had access to ample sources of resupply, with surrounding countries serving as logistical hubs, such as in Iraq in 2012–2013. Iran and Hizbullah trained hundreds of Syrian officers in urban warfare. Numerous tactics used by the Syrian regime, such as the Syrian Electronic Army, showed similarities to tactics used against the Green Movement in Iran in 2009. Russia has also provided ammunition and technical knowledge to refurbish Soviet military equipment (Free Syrian Army 2014). The Syrian military in 2012–2013 seemed to have been trained in Russian siege tactics that had formerly been seen in Chechnya.

More important, Iran and its Lebanese partner, Hizbullah, have given essential organizational help to the weakened Syrian military. They are instrumental in explaining the military's surge in counterinsurgency efficiency during the course of 2013–2014. They built a network of militias modeled after Iran's Basij militia to fight alongside Syria's regular forces and take charge of territory once regular units had shifted to other hot spots (*New York Times* 2012). Qassem Suleimani, head of the Iranian al-Quds Force, has come into close contact with Muhammad Nasif Khairbak, the deputy head of the Syrian National Security Directorate.

Beginning in early 2012, Iraqi Shiite fighters started to trickle into Syria under the auspices of the Islamic Revolutionary Guards Corps. Groups such as Liwa Abu Fadl al-Abbas, Kata'ib Hizbullah, Asaib Ahl al-Haq, Harakat al-Nujaba, Kata'ib Sayyid al-Shuhada, and even the Badr Organization began operating in Syria. Slogans of the Shiite militias, such as *"yali tha'rati al-Hussain"* ("revenge for Hussain") and *"ya Zaynab lan tusbay marratayn"* ("O Zainab, you will not be held captive twice"), mirrored the slogans of the militant jihadist Sunnis that equated Shiite with heretics (*rawafidh*). These militias have been instrumental in compensating for the Syrian military's manpower shortages and heightening its capacity to launch counterinsurgency operations.

As Iranian and Hizbullahi high officers have gradually stepped up the level of assistance, rumblings have grown up inside the Syrian officers' corps, reflecting simmering resentment over the fact that Iranian or Hizbullahi officers are now in direct command in major field operations. There are unconfirmed rumors that Iranian advisers took control of key military decision-making positions inside the regime itself following the elimination of several high regime insiders reputed to be opposed to too much external penetration in Syria.

Conclusion

The Syrian military in 2011 did not reveal itself to be an actor that eased the transition away from authoritarian rule. On the contrary, it rallied behind the Assad regime in the escalating crisis and resultant civil war. This outcome derived mainly from the fact that the regime had accomplished a huge social engineering project in the officers' corps for four decades, in particular by posting Alawi officers in key positions. This made a significant difference when the regime answered popular civic demands with extreme violence. At the same time, the regime brutalized the military to keep it cohesive despite internal rumblings of discontent and a number of defections.

The resulting picture is a complex one in which the Syrian military appears to remain one of the main coercive instruments through which the Assad regime has ensured its grip and was even able to regain some territory during the course of 2013–2014. Conversely, the opposition and its external backers have been eagerly waiting the Syrian military's complete unraveling. This may eventually occur, as the Syrian military finds itself exhausted morally and has suffered huge losses. These trends were evident in the regime's inability to retain the northern provincial capital of Idlib in early 2015, a fundamental setback with regard to its claim of maintaining a united country. The Syrian military has also largely been destroyed organizationally, with the officers' corps fundamentally transformed due to the hectic promotion of young Alawi officers on the battlefield, regime-sponsored militias compensating for the regular army's growing weaknesses, and foreign allies assuming prominent combat roles on the ground and thereby effectively sidelining loyal Syrian commanders.

Notes

1. For lack of space, features of the Syrian military before 2011 will not be dealt with here.

2. See *Wall Street Journal* (2011).

3. In October 2011 even before the beginning of the militarization of the uprising, the death toll was estimated at more than 3,000 (Associated Press 2011).

4. Elite 4th Division troops were said to have dumped dozens of weapons in the main square of Dara'a in front of the 'Umari mosque, the main center of resistance in Dara'a.

5. Latakia, a city of 650,000 that serves as Syria's main port, is dominated by Sunnis and is surrounded by mountain villages that are home to Alawis.

6. The Syrian NGO Insan has been collecting testimonies of witnesses and soldiers in order to indict those who gave orders to kill before the International Criminal Court under charges of war crimes (Droz-Vincent 2014b).

7. Minister of the Interior Muhammad al-Shaar, a Sunni born in 1950 in Latakia Province and appointed in April 2011, is the former head of military police in Tripoli, Lebanon. Former military officers were nominated to be governors in Latakia and Dara'a Provinces soon after the first demonstrations in March 2011.

8. See the documents leaked by the Damascus Center for Human Rights, allegedly from Air Force Intelligence, which state that "it is acceptable to shoot some of the security agents or army officers in order to further deceive the enemy, which will further help the situation by provoking the animosity of the army against the protesters" (*Christian Science Monitor* 2011).

9. Conscription tilted the balance of sectarian composition against Sunnis and among Sunnis against urbanites who could afford exemptions, which was not a bad thing for the Hafiz al-Assad regime, due to its perennial mistrust of urbanites and their tradition of liberal politics.

10. When they begin their military service, conscripts are bereft of their civilian identity card and carry a military identity card. They get the former back at the end of their tour of duty, which is another way to control their movements.

11. Habib is a respected career officer with no known connections to the security services; he led the Syrian troops that were sent in Kuwait in 1991. His term ended in August 2011. In September 2013, he was said to have defected to Turkey. Rajiha was killed in a bombing in the building of the security directorate in July 2012.

12. In March 2012 alone, four general officers (*amid* or *liwa*) and twenty-five colonels (*aqid* or *amid*) were nominated, a clear indication of the high rate of turnover inside the military due to defections and losses.

13. As the joke in the Syrian military puts it, "For the first time in the contemporary history of the Syrian military, officers have learned to be more modest!" (Droz-Vincent 2013).

14. In March–April 2011, many Alawis not connected with the Assad power network harbored resentment toward the Assad regime. During the first months of the uprising, the regime's primary goal was to maintain Alawi solidarity.

15. Alawis in Homs and around Damascus are seen by Sunnis as outsiders; they migrated to the cities to work in the state apparatus or the army. The Alawi presence in Homs is quite recent, stretching back no more than three decades: they came into some peripheral neighborhoods from the rural hinterland (*dakhel*) between Homs and Hama. Alawis in Damascus have often settled on land confiscated from Sunni landowners during the 1980s by the Special Forces led by Rif'at al-Assad, particularly in the districts of Mezze 86, Hayy al-Wurud, Sumariya, Wahid Tishrin, and Ish al-Warwa.

PART III

Trajectories of Political-Military Relations: Beyond the Arab Spring

CHAPTER 9

Egypt: From Military Reform
to Military Sanctuarization

Chérine Chams El-Dine

On June 28, 2013, millions of Egyptians took to the streets to ask for an immediate end to Muhammad Mursi's presidency. This was in response to the Tamarrud (Rebellion) campaign, launched in April of the same year by a group of young activists who began collecting signatures on a petition calling for Mursi's resignation on June 30, the first anniversary of his inauguration. By mid-May when the campaign gathered 2 million signatures, the military seized the opportunity and backed Tamarrud, communicating with it through third parties and connecting it with liberal and opposition-linked businessmen (Hendawi 2013). One month later the campaign claimed to have collected more than 20 million signatures and called for mass demonstrations urging Mursi's resignation. At this point, ʿAbd al-Fattah al-Sisi—then minister of defense and commander in chief of the armed forces—issued a statement giving both sides a week to resolve their differences, with the deadline being the end of June. This was followed by a forty-eight-hour ultimatum on July 1 explicitly urging Mursi to meet the people's demands or the military would be forced to intervene. As the ultimatum came to its end, on July 3 al-Sisi announced the destitution of President Mursi, suspended the 2012 constitution, and promised early elections under the terms of a transition road map. A few hours after Mursi's ouster, ʿAdly Mansur—head of the Supreme Constitutional Court—was sworn in as Egypt's interim president. Mansur named a ten-member expert committee to review controversial articles in the 2012 constitution in order to suggest amendments to a larger fifty-member committee—formed in early September 2013 by presidential decree—in charge of finalizing Egypt's new constitution. On the other hand, an interim government was formed mid-July by Hazem Beblawi,[1] in which al-Sisi combined the functions of minister of defense and first deputy prime minister.

It is worth noting that al-Sisi was appointed by Mursi on August 12, 2012, following a wide reshuffling within the military command. This took place only few days after an attack by some militant groups on an Egyptian border post in northern Sinai that killed sixteen Egyptian security personnel. Almost two hundred senior officers in total (Springborg 2012) were sent to retirement by Mursi, including Muhammad Husain al-Tantawi, then minister of defense and commander in chief of the armed forces, and his chief of staff, Sami 'Anan. This reorganization of the army command was an occasion to get rid of al-Tantawi's supporters and some of the most unpopular military figures involved in the crackdown of protests during the Supreme Council of the Armed Forces (SCAF) direct rule, between the overthrow of President Hosni Mubarak on February 11, 2011, and the assumption of power by President Mursi on June 30, 2012. The Muslim Brotherhood believed that al-Sisi—being the contact person between them and the generals during SCAF's rule—was sympathetic with their Islamist agenda. However, what looked like a negotiated arrangement between the military and Mursi during his early days in office soon turned into major disagreements over policies to be implemented. First and foremost was the security situation in the Sinai Peninsula, as the military believed that Mursi gave free hand to Islamist militants and that his Islamist agenda prevailed over Egypt's national interest, as explained later in this chapter.

Al-Sisi's central role in President Mursi's ousting from power created an aura around him or even a "Sisi-mania" (Kingsley and Awad 2013). Encouraged by his rising popularity—overemphasized by the media—al-Sisi resigned from his position as minister of defense[2] to run for president. This was an unbalanced battle that he won by far against his only rival, the leftist politician Hamdin Sabahi.[3] Al-Sisi's landslide victory in the presidential elections along with the military institution's special status after June 30, viewed as one of the most trusted state institutions by large segments of the population, is calling into question the possibility of a civilian oversight of the military and thus of democratic military reforms in Egypt. The chapter examines the type of civil-military relations currently taking shape in Egypt, especially in light of the 2012 and 2014 constitutions. Both the constitutional texts and the debates they triggered provide a strong indicator of the military's scope of action and the extent to which it has been either contested or "legally" institutionalized since 2012. In this perspective, a distinction is made in the following sections between two major dimensions of the civil-military balance in Egypt, namely zones of military prerogatives and zones of military contestation, in order to depict the type of civil-military relations and limitations of military reforms.

Robert Dahl set a major condition for a polity in order to be governed democratically, which is the military and police organizations' subjection to civilian control.[4] The armed forces' tendency to defend their areas of autonomy, or the so-called military prerogatives during the transition[5] process, has been a constant in every single instance, whether it has been gradual or abrupt, following the collapse of an authoritarian regime. These military prerogatives were defined by Alfred Stepan (1988:93) as those "areas where the military as an institution assumes it has an acquired right or privilege, formal or informal, to exercise effective control over its internal governance, to play a role within extra-military areas within the state apparatus, or even to structure relationship between the state and political or civil society." Even in the absence of conflicts over these prerogatives, they encompass a form of independent latent structural power and are therefore a source of imminent threat within the polity.

While areas of military autonomy will always exist—even in consolidated democracies—the levels of military autonomy should be decided by elected political authorities and not by the military institution itself (Serra 2010:43). Thus, zones of military contestation appear when the military strongly resists attempts by a new civilian government to reduce military prerogatives to areas of autonomy compatible with the state of law. In other words, the zones of military contestation are those areas of contention where the military highly resists any proposals that may curb its power (Stepan 1988; Serra 2010). In regard to the Egyptian context, we can determine zones of "untouched" military prerogatives overlooked by the civilian governments in charge after June 30 and by the constitutional committee in charge of drafting Egypt's 2014 constitution and zones of military contestation, as detailed in the following sections.

Zones of "Untouched" Military Prerogatives

Legislatures and consecutive civilian governments since Mubarak's overthrow have turned a blind eye to a number of military privileges that have not been even questioned by them for a variety of reasons. Thus, despite dissident voices among civil society actors, these privileges remain walled off or untouched prerogatives, namely the military's economy, legacy of human rights abuses, and national security custodianship.

The Military's Economy

The minister of defense retains supervisory control over a wide variety of activities known as the military's economy, which grants him decision-making power over a substantial part of Egypt's economy. This military's economy consists of five main elements: the annual defense budget (EGP 25.7 billion, around 4.7 percent of the 2012–2013 budget),[6] U.S. military assistance (US$1.3 billion[7] received annually by the armed forces, usually in-kind assistance since the aftermath of Egypt's peace treaty with Israel in 1979), arms deals (import and limited export of weapons and ammunition), the factories run by the Arab Organization for Industrialization (AOI) under the supervision of the Ministry of State for Military Production,[8] and the National Service Projects Organization (NSPO), directly overseen by the Ministry of Defense.

The official rationale behind the military's economic activity has been budget relief, based on the argument that the military's self-sufficiency allows Egypt to maintain large military structures without placing pressure on state finances (Cook 2007:19). Initially created by President Anwar al-Sadat in 1975, the AOI provided a base from which arms manufacturing and assembly (weapons, ammunition, tanks) expanded after 1981 under 'Abd al-Halim Abu Ghazala, Egypt's defense minister from 1981 to 1989 (Springborg 1987:8–9). A section of these arms plants is nowadays specialized in the production of household appliances. As for the NSPO, it was established by Sadat's presidential decree number 32 of 1979, according to which its budget is managed by the minister of defense and the profits of its exclusively civilian projects are transferred to an undisclosed bank account. Such civilian activities made the army an integral part of Egypt's development efforts through the armed forces' involvement in the reconstruction of Egypt's infrastructure—damaged by the war against Israel—under the late 1970s slogan "one hand builds and another carries an arm" (Chams El-Dine 2012a). At the same time, it was Sadat's strategy to reduce the army's involvement in politics while rewarding it through the expansion of its role in domestic economic production. Thus Sadat, and Mubarak after him, transformed the military from an active protagonist in the Egyptian political arena into a power operating in cooperation with the president to advance their respective interests. However, the so-called military disengagement from politics, or military depoliticization, has not settled the issue of military subordination to the state. In fact, the military has always retained some bargaining power, and its loyalty took the form of "agreed subservience rather than total submission" (Droz-Vincent 2007:198).

The armed forces started their civilian economic activities with agrarian projects, land reclamation, and civilian public works contracts. They then gradually expanded and diversified their fields of activities through a multitude of income-generating enterprises to include tourism/hotels, construction, maritime transport, production of petrochemicals, and environmental projects such as wastewater treatment and renewable energy (Marshall and Stacher 2012). The military institution is keeping the aforementioned activities completely secret, using "national security" as a pretext. For example, none of these companies is listed on the Egyptian stock market. However, the activities of the AOI and the NSPO are ubiquitous and permeate Egyptians' daily lives, namely army-produced brands such as Queen pasta and Safi mineral water and the services provided by Wataniyya petrol stations and military-managed wedding halls (Abul-Magd 2011). The military institution has thus developed a gray economy that is not subject to any parliamentary scrutiny or the Central Auditing Office. Given this lack of transparency, experts come to very different assessments of the military economy's share, ranging from 5 percent (Al-Naggar 2012) to 15 percent (Faruq 2012) of Egypt's gross domestic product.[9] While these enterprises enjoy lucrative subsidies, tax and licensing exemptions,[10] and some comparative advantages such as the cheap manpower of the military's conscripts, the revenues they generate are returned to the military's own account rather than incorporated into the state's budget.

After Egypt's January 25 revolution, many activists called for civilian oversight of the military's budget by the elected bodies. Others demanded a merger of the army's projects into Egypt's official public sector. The military institution responded harshly to such demands, stressing that the armed forces' economic projects are off limits (*Al-Shorouk* 2012).[11] One reason for the military's attitude is that a portion of the revenue is spent on officers' allowances, housing, and other improvements to their living standards. The remainder is either reinvested or used to complement spending on maintenance, operations, and procurement not covered by the defense budget or U.S. military assistance (Sayigh 2012:17).

During the drafting process of the 2012 constitution, passed into law under President Mursi, some representatives of the opposition proposed to keep some items of the defense budget secret for "national security" reasons and to discuss others in closed sessions by specialized parliamentary committees (namely the Committee of Defense and National Security). However, none of these propositions materialized. According to Article 197 of the 2012 constitution, the National Defense Council has the exclusive prerogative to discuss the armed forces' budget, thus stripping the parliament—the civilian-elected body par excellence—of oversight of the state's nonelected entities. In fact, the rehabilitation and composition of this council is quite telling. Originally set up under President Gamal 'Abdel Nasser and formally established by the 1971 constitution (Article 182), the National Defense Council rarely met or exercised any discernible authority before it was revived by Field Marshal al-Tantawi, then head of the SCAF, on June 14, 2012—a few days before the results of the presidential elections that brought Mursi to power. Headed by the president of the republic and mainly composed of military figures (eleven out of sixteen members came from the army ranks), it could be viewed as a mini-SCAF (Reuters 2012). The composition of the National Defense Council in the 2012 constitution is slightly different. It is still presided over by the president of the republic but is composed of fourteen members, namely the Speakers of the People's Assembly (lower house) and the Shura Council (upper house); the prime minister; the minister of defense; the minister of foreign affairs; the minister of finance; the minister of the interior; the head of the General Intelligence Service (GIS); the chief of staff of the armed forces; the commanders of the navy, the air forces, and the air defense; the chief of operations for the armed forces; and the head of military intelligence. This composition is more balanced than the one created by al-Tantawi (as six of fourteen members are civilians), but still the absolute majority of the military is maintained.[12]

The 2014 constitution, approved by popular referendum in January 2014, introduced some amendments to the 2012 text that only confirmed the status quo. The armed forces' budget is still entirely discussed by the National Defense Council; however, three changes have been introduced to Article 197, which became Article 203 of the current constitution, the first one being that the defense budget should appear as one single figure in the annual state's budget—without further details. Moreover, the composition of the National Defense Council slightly changed, as the Shura Council has been dissolved for good. This amendment makes the National Defense

Council even more predominantly a military body, as the position held by the Shura's Speaker has been removed. Finally, a clause has been added to Article 203 to require the presence of the armed forces' head of financial affairs, along with the heads of the Budget and Planning Committee and the Defense and National Security Committee, during the discussion of the military budget by the National Defense Council. The absence of conflicts over parliamentary oversight of the military's budget and other economic activities implies that they will remain walled off and even institutionalized by the current constitutional text.

The military institution's role became even more central in Egypt's economy following Mursi's ouster. The post-June 2013 successive governments awarded the Ministry of Defense several contracts to carry out infrastructure projects through direct order, that is, without public tenders. These projects are to be implemented by the Armed Forces' Engineering Authority (AFEA) and range from building highways, bridges, and low-income housing to renovating public hospitals. They also include the Suez Canal Area Development megaproject. State officials justify their preference for the AFEA over private companies on the basis of the army engineering corps' rapidity in implementing projects for the lowest cost and with the highest quality (Morsy 2014). Most of these projects are carried out by subcontractors belonging to the private sector. The latter's involvement is essential, as the implementation of these projects goes beyond the AFEA's own capabilities. However, this arrangement grants the military a supervisory role in these projects and, a fortiori, over its private-sector partners.

Legacy of Human Rights Abuses

Popular demands stressed the necessity to hold military officials accountable for serious human rights abuses committed during the January 25 Revolution and its aftermath,[13] including the killing of demonstrators, the excessive use of force in dispersing protesters, torture during detention, corruption, and so on.

In fact, the civilian general prosecutor lacks the power to investigate allegations of corruption against army officials, as the SCAF amended the Code of Military Justice (Article 8A) on May 10, 2011, to limit prosecution of members of the armed forces accused of "illicit gain" to military courts. This includes retirees, which shows the particular concern of former SCAF

leaders (Chams El-Dine 2012b). In November 2012, President Mursi dele-
gated his competencies regarding the lessening and cancellation of sentences
issued against the military to al-Sisi, then the minister of defense, in order to
grant extra immunity to SCAF members (*Al-Hayat* 2012b). Thus, the prosecution of the military for human rights abuses did not go beyond scattered
official declarations and newspapers leaks. Though the military leadership
got offended when a newspaper reported that al-Tantawi and 'Anan, the former commander in chief of the armed forces and his chief of staff, "would
be banned from travel for charges of illicit gains" (*Egypt Independent* 2012).

To satisfy popular demands, President Mursi formed a fact-finding committee[14] in July 2012 to inquire into crimes committed against protesters from
January 2011 to June 30, 2012. At the beginning of 2013, the committee presented its eight hundred-page report to Mursi, who never made its content
public and merely transferred it to the general prosecutor to start an investigation in the report's findings. Leaked experts of the report declared that
Mubarak and his police and military officials were "legally responsible" for
the killing of protesters and thus called for their retrials (*Al-Masry al-Youm*
2013b). After June 30, 2013, the file was closed by the general prosecutor's
bureau, and the committee's report was put away in dusty drawers (Chams El-
Dine 2014). Yet even though the committee gathered evidence charging military officials for crimes against peaceful protesters, according to the Code of
Military Justice all cases involving military personnel would have been subjected to the military prosecutor, which does not guarantee the transparency
of the investigations.

The interim government formed following the ouster of President Mursi
created Egypt's first-ever Ministry of Transitional Justice and National Reconciliation.[15] However, the effectiveness of this initiative has yet to be proven.
The new ministry "does not seem to have a clear action plan and its messages
are mainly addressed to the west" (Chams El-Dine 2014). The 2014 constitution includes Article 241, which makes the promulgation of a transitional
justice law mandatory for the coming elected parliament. Though this could
be considered as a positive step, the formulation of Article 241 remains vague,
which leaves enough room for the legislator, and makes no reference to the
reform of the state institutions as part of the transitional justice process. Thus,
despite official declarations generally in favor of this process, there is a clear
lack of will to push through these efforts and in particular to take the risk of
a confrontation with the military.

National Security Custodianship

The armed forces have always used a nationalist discourse arguing that external defense affairs cannot be left to civilian leaders. In addition, the armed forces have been eager to keep the country out of costly wars with its neighbors, particularly Israel, and to "shield the army from any adventurous foreign policy initiatives that elected civilian politicians may choose to advance" (Brumberg and Sallam 2012:2).

The military's historic self-image as "custodian" of Egypt's security against external enemies has been coupled with its new mission of "war on terrorism" to confront escalating violence from President Mursi's supporters and Islamist allies. The armed forces were almost mandated to sharpen their military operations in order to eradicate Islamist insurgency in the Sinai Peninsula and to stop the flow of arms and fighters along the Egypt-Gaza border. In this respect, the security situation in Sinai, which has experienced a high level of penetration by jihadist groups,[16] and Mursi's relationship with Hamas constituted two major subjects of disagreement between the military command and the former president. These two zones of contention under Mursi turned into zones of military autonomy after his ouster, as explained in the following section.

Following the attack on an Egyptian border post in northern Sinai on August 5, 2012, by militant groups that killed sixteen Egyptian soldiers, the military leadership planned to extend its anti-insurgency campaign[17] to crack down on militant groups in Sinai. At the same time, President Mursi sent an official delegation to initiate a dialogue with relatively moderate jihadist groups, albeit without much success (*Al-Ahram Weekly* 2012). Moreover in November 2012, he asked the military command to stop an offensive in Sinai a day before it was to be launched. This was completely denied by the military spokesman, who asserted the continuation of operations in Sinai and rejected any possibility for dialogue between the armed forces and jihadist groups (Ahram Online 2013c), thus underlying a certain friction between the military and the presidency.

The second source of contention was Mursi's close relationship with Hamas, especially since the armed forces believed that militants from Gaza were involved in the killing of the sixteen soldiers in August 2012 and that Mursi rejected al-Sisi's request to ask Hamas to hand them over for trial (Hendawi 2013). It was clear for the military that the tunnels along the Egypt-Gaza border have become a threat to Egypt's national security, given the flow of weapons and fighters that can go through them. Thus, since August 2012 they have initiated efforts to destroy them. By late December 2012, the minister of defense went further by banning private ownership and rental of land and properties in strategic locations of military importance in Sinai.[18] These military bans aimed to stop land ownership by foreigners, in particular by Palestinians who obtain Egyptian nationality through mixed marriages, and to cut down the "tunnel economy," which thrived through smuggling activities between the Gaza Strip and Sinai. Since the ouster of President Mursi, the military's countertunnel operations have intensified, and the eradication of Islamist groups outlawed in Sinai became one of the top priorities of the military. There is no doubt that the targeting of the army's positions in the Sinai Peninsula made operations there almost a matter of personal revenge for the military.

Given the above-mentioned concerns, the armed forces were particularly keen on keeping the upper hand in military affairs and being consulted for all national security matters. This military claim was not challenged by the civilian interim government or even the committees in charge of the drafting of the 2014 constitution. Civilians are themselves reluctant to see the military's prerogatives diminished in a context of open confrontation with the Muslim Brotherhood and Islamist insurgency in Sinai. This military's special status has already been somehow institutionalized by the prerogatives and composition of the National Defense Council, as stated in the 2012 suspended constitution and enshrined by the current constitution, which kept the council's functions intact.

In addition to discussing the military budget, as explained above, the National Defense Council has "military prerogatives." The latter, which were detailed in Law 86 of 1968, include defining the national defense policy and coordinating it with other relevant ministries' policies, ensuring the country's defense and troop mobilization for war, and determining the number of troops as well as their equipment in times of war and peace (*Al-Ahram* 2012). This council, which cannot convene or make decisions unless a majority of its members are present, must be consulted by the president before declaring war or sending the armed forces outside state territory (Article 146 of the 2012 constitution and Article 152 of the current constitution).[19] The council must also be consulted for draft laws related to the armed forces (Article 197 of the 2012 constitution and Article 203 of the current constitution).

This is not to be confused with another predominantly civilian body called the National Security Council (Article 193 of the 2012 constitution and Article 205 of the current constitution). The latter is presided over by the president of the republic and composed of twelve members, namely the prime minister, the Speaker of the People's Assembly, the minister of defense, the minister of the interior, the minister of foreign affairs, the minister of finance, the minister of justice, the minister of health, the minister of communications, the minister of education, the head of the GIS, and the head of the Committee of Defense and National Security in the People's Assembly.

The creation of a National Security Council in charge of civil defense (for example, preventing food shortages or managing natural disasters) while keeping purely military prerogatives (for example, the armed forces' size and equipment, the military's budget, approval of war) in the hands of the predominantly military National Defense Council is an indicator of the military's resolve to secure its autonomy in security and defense affairs from civilian control and have its reserved domains guaranteed by the constitutional text and unchallenged by civilian control.

Zones of Military Contestation

Zones of military contention are areas where the military highly resisted any proposals that may curb its power. On the contrary, the military pressured to enshrine itself with a special status, institutionalized in a constitutional text to make it immune. These zones of high contestation are namely the military trials of civilians and the designation of the minister of defense.

Military Trials

During the three months following the revolution (January to March 2011), the military used excessive force against civilians and relied heavily on military trials that imposed disproportionate sentences. These abuses were at least partially due to the military's lack of experience in preserving domestic order, as military institutions (military police, military prosecution, and military courts) had replaced the respective civil state institutions in the aftermath of the revolution. Later on, military trials were gradually used as a political tool to intimidate opponents (Chams El-Dine 2012c).

As stated by the head of the Military Judiciary, nearly 12,000 civilians were tried by military courts from January to the end of August 2011—a figure confirmed by relevant civil society organizations (*Al-Ahram* 2011). Most of the cases were related to ordinary crimes, but hundreds of civilian activists were also subject to military trials. Accusations varied from looting to curfew violation, disturbance of public traffic, sabotage of public and private properties, slander of the armed forces, and offensive writings in social media networks. By the end of August 2011, the number of civilians referred to military courts significantly decreased as a consequence of mounting pressure from civil society actors and wide media coverage of some cases. Obviously, the military then took the decision to reduce confrontations with civilians to improve the armed forces' image.

On May 6, 2012, the Egyptian People's Assembly[20] approved the abolition of Article 6 of the Code of Military Justice. This article had allowed the president of the republic to directly refer civilians for trial in front of military courts. The new text restricts the president's powers. However, the military retains its authority to try civilians. In fact, under President Mubarak, Article 6 mainly targeted Islamists, which explains the Islamist-led parliament's endeavors to abolish the article and pave the way for appealing previous sentences against Islamists without touching the military's prerogatives to try civilians.

Upon taking office, President Mursi established a commission to examine all cases of civilians sentenced by military courts from January 2011 to June 30, 2012, the date of the beginning of his term in office. The commission has been criticized by political activists, as its membership was dominated by figures close to the SCAF and because it was to address cases up to June 30, 2012, meaning that cases after this date would remain beyond scrutiny (Ahram Online 2012). On different occasions, civilians tried before military courts were granted amnesty, initially by the SCAF and later, in October 2012, by President Mursi. He granted a general amnesty for "crimes committed to support the revolution" (*Al-Masry al-Youm* 2012b)—a vague formulation allowing the military prosecutor to exclude its application to some civilians tried before military courts (Chams El-Dine 2012b). Despite official denials, military trials of civilians have continued since. For example, on November 18, 2012, military police arrested 25 civilians during an attempted compulsory eviction on al-Qursaya Island (in the Nile-Giza area). The military claimed that they were on military property, despite a 2010 court verdict overruling previous eviction orders and recognizing the inhabitants' right to live and work on the island. The prosecutor charged the civilians with assaulting the military and its properties, and their military trial is still ongoing (Human Rights Watch 2012). Article 198 of the 2012 constitution confirmed the military's right to try civilians before military courts for crimes "harming the armed forces." Such a vague formulation left a wide margin for the legislator to include various cases at the military's discretion and allowed the continuation of military trials for civilians. As of July 2013, 1,101 civilians were detained in custody awaiting military trials (*Egypt Independent* 2013).

Yet things have not improved under the interim government that followed Mursi's ouster, as around fifty civilians were convicted to prison terms by military courts (*Al-Masry al-Youm* 2013a). The fifty-member committee in charge of drafting the 2014 constitution sought to prohibit or at least limit military trials of civilians but faced very high resistance from the military representatives, who insisted on keeping the same formulation as the 2012 constitution. The declaration of the former military prosecutor that "today there is no other force able to protect all citizens except the Armed Forces" (*Al-Shorouk* 2013) reflects not only the military's self-image but also the special status the institution wants to grant for itself. For the military representatives, banning military trials would humiliate the army and undermine its status in a context where the military positions and personnel are constantly targeted by jihadist groups. Thus, they categorically rejected proposals that the constitution completely ban military trials. Other suggestions presented by the committee that civilians face military trials only in case of terrorism or direct assault on military personnel/property as well as the creation of special civilian courts to prosecute attackers of military facilities were similarly rejected by military representatives (Ahram Online 2013b). The military managed to impose its will after rounds of negotiations, and Article 204 of the 2014 constitution came to extend the scope of military trials of civilians unprecedentedly. The article includes crimes committed by "whoever is subject" to the armed forces—in other words, the conscripted—and by members of the general security services during their service. Moreover, Article 204 explicitly details potential crimes against the armed forces leading to military trials of civilians, namely attacks on military facilities, barracks, or whatever falls under their authority; attacks on military zones, equipment, vehicles, weapons, documents, or secrets; attacks on military public funds and factories; and crimes related to conscription or crimes representing direct assault on military officers or personnel performing their duties.

In the same vein, on October 27, 2014, President al-Sisi issued Decree Number 136, which rendered all vital public properties and facilities—including power stations, universities, gas and oil facilities, railway lines, roads, and bridges—as "equivalent to military facilities" for two years. The provisions of the decree imply that any civilian accused of attacking any of these public properties or blocking roads will be tried in a military court. While this move is nominally targeting terrorists, it also makes it easier for the government to try members of the political opposition in military courts (Mohy El Deen 2015).

The Defense Minister's Designation

While it was a tradition in Egypt to appoint a general as minister of defense, the 2012 and 2014 constitutions (Article 195 and Article 201, respectively) enshrined it into law. The current text stipulates that the minister of defense is the general commander of the armed forces and is chosen from among its officers. This implies that the defense minister is necessarily a military officer and that he cumulates both political and military positions. Given the current political instability in Egypt, having a military officer at the head of the Defense Ministry has not even been questioned. However, the suitable way to appoint him was quite problematic. The ten-member expert[21] committee suggested the approval of the SCAF as a condition for the appointment of the defense minister. While the fifty-member committee rejected this proposal, the military representatives demanded that the constitution gives the military the right to "name" the defense minister through the next two presidential terms (Ahram Online 2013b). Article 234 of the 2014 constitution resulted as a compromise between both entrenched positions. It stipulates that the appointment of the defense minister must be approved by the SCAF and that this clause will be valid for two complete presidential terms.

Article 234 gives special status to the SCAF and strips the chief executive (the president) of his full authority over the military as the supreme commander of the armed forces. The military institution was apprehensive about the new constitution and about the results of the upcoming presidential elections. It feared a new president taking revenge on the army, settling old accounts with its leaders, and threatening the armed forces' cohesion and independence. Thus, it sought to immunize itself with a special status in the new constitution; however, by doing so it continued to act as an entity above other state institutions.

Conclusion

"The military has a project and a will. The civilians have neither" (Stepan 1988:127). This quote of a former Brazilian general explaining why the civilians had made no progress toward controlling the military in the 1980s perfectly illustrates the current situation in Egypt, given the civilian political actors' major responsibility for the flawed and shaky military reform. Since 2011, a significant portion of the civilian political actors have been seeking to accommodate the military in order to confront other civilians they highly distrust instead of dealing and negotiating with them. Thus, they have welcomed the military's intervention in politics and have been reluctant to see the military prerogatives diminished, using Egypt's national security as an excuse for maintaining the military's privileges. The same strategy was adopted by the Muslim Brotherhood and proved its failure under President Mursi, who thought that forging an alliance with the military could strengthen his position in order to deal with liberal actors' opposition. Thus, the 2012 constitution enshrined into law a special status for the military institution that did not exist in the 1971 constitution. The civilian political actors have fallen into the same trap following the ouster of Mursi. The absence of consensus among political protagonists has given the military the opportunity not only to bypass civilian oversight but also to acquire privileges they had never enjoyed previously.

The military institution has managed to secure its main interests, despite a few zones of contestation. The civilians have been turning a blind eye to a number of military prerogatives that thus remain walled off. The defense budget (as well as other military affairs) is still discussed in the National Defense Council, where the military has a majority, and the 2014 constitution remains silent on the military's economic projects, which are not subject to parliamentary scrutiny. The military leadership has also successfully kept its leaders safe from being prosecuted on charges of excessive use of force against protesters and corruption. It has become apparent that the civilian political actors are unwilling to enter into confrontation with the military leadership—despite some "media-oriented" actions taken by the post-January 25 successive governments—and thus are keeping the "transitional justice" file pending. This leaves only two zones of conflict between the military and the civilians, namely the trials of civilians before military courts and the appointment of the minister of defense. And in both cases, the military has managed to impose its own views on the civilians.

The election of al-Sisi as head of the Egyptian state in May 2014 renders a civilian oversight of the military wishful thinking. Stemming from the armed forces, al-Sisi cherishes the military institution, considers it a role model for other state institutions, and grants it the status of ultimate arbiter between the people and the regime.[22]

In this perspective, civil-military relations in Egypt are heading toward what Stepan (1988:100–101) called "unequal civilian accommodation" rather than "civilian control of the military" or "military democratic reform," given this combination of low contestation and high military prerogatives, unchallenged by the top political leaders and legislatures due to asymmetric power between the military and the new "civilian" regime. Stepan described it as a highly vulnerable position because of the military's latent structural power entailed in its possession of so many prerogatives. On the one hand, the military might use its prerogatives to impose a series of policy outcomes on the leaders of the new regime. On the other hand, this polity could be transformed into a nondemocratic "civilian-headed garrison state" because of the executive's exploitation of the military's high prerogatives. This situation can end only with the election of a new political leadership with a capacity to impose a series of reforms challenging/reducing military prerogatives, paving the way for more democratic civil-military relations.

Notes

1. Hazem Beblawi and his cabinet resigned at the end of February 2014, and another interim government was formed by Ibrahim Mahlab in March 2014.

2. Al-Sisi was promoted by presidential decree to the rank of field marshal on January 27, 2014, and kept his position as minister of defense until his resignation on March 26, 2014.

3. The presidential elections were held from May 26 to May 28, 2014. Al-Sisi won more than 96 percent of the votes cast.

4. However, Dahl stated that this condition is necessary but not sufficient, as the civilians who control the military and police must "themselves" be subject to the democratic process (Dahl 1989:245).

5. In this chapter, "transition" means the interval between one political regime and another. It is delimited by the launching of the process of dissolution of an authoritarian regime; however, it does not necessarily lead to democratic rule. It is a highly uncertain period characterized by the absence of predictable rules of game and in which actors

struggle not only to satisfy their interests but also to define procedures and set future rules (O'Donnell and Schmitter 1986:6).

6. It is worth noting that since the state's budget for fiscal year 2012–2013, military expenditures have not been clearly stated in the general budget and appear under the rubric "miscellaneous" (Ministry of Finance 2013).

7. In a context of U.S. government shutdown and in disapproval of the Egyptian regime's crackdown on the Muslim Brotherhood, the U.S. government trimmed military aid to Egypt on October 8, 2013. Although the delivery of some big-ticket military hardware (such as Apache helicopters and F-16 fighter jets) has been interrupted, the impact of this partial aid cut seems limited at least in the short term, as much of the U.S. military partnership with Egypt will continue (Radwan 2013). However, al-Sisi inked an arms deal with Russia during his visit to Moscow in February 2014 as minister of defense in order to diversify Egypt's sources of military procurement. Some points of this deal have been finalized by Major General Muhamad al-Assar, the assistant minister of defense, who visited Russia at the end of May 2014 (*Al-Masry al-Youm* 2014). Similarly, al-Sisi sealed a deal in February 2015 to buy twenty-four Rafale fighters, a Fremm frigate, and MBDA missiles from France (Reuters 2015).

8. In November 1986, the new position of minister of state for military production was created. It is a device whereby the minister of defense and military production retains overall supervisory control of military production while the minister of state is managing it. Please note that in this chapter we refer to the Ministry of Defense and Military Production and its minister as Ministry of Defense and the minister of defense.

9. In an interview, al-Sisi stated that the military's economy does not exceed 2 percent of Egypt's economy (*Al-Shorouk* 2014).

10. Decree Number 68 of 2015 granted the military additional tax exemptions, as 574 military properties, including hotels, clubs, apartments, villas, theaters, and supermarkets, have been exempted from property tax (*Al-Masry al-Youm* 2015).

11. This military stance was also clearly expressed in November 2011, when an official committee headed by 'Ali al-Salmi, then deputy prime minister for political affairs, issued a document that would have established a number of supraconstitutional principles. In essence, the so-called Salmi Document would have given the SCAF the sole responsibility for all matters concerning the armed forces, especially with regard to their budget, which was supposed to be incorporated only as a single figure in the annual budget and would not be subjected to discussion in parliament. These supraconstitutional principles were quickly dropped after strong criticism; however, the consecutive constitutional texts retained some of these provisions.

12. The head of the GIS has traditionally (in the absence of a binding constitutional text) been a military figure since its establishment by President Nasser in 1954.

13. Several instances of obvious human rights abuses led to public backlash and pressure on the military. Among these incidents is the so-called Maspero Massacre that took place on October 9, 2011. In front of Maspero's state television building, at least twenty-five

Coptic Christians were killed and more than three hundred injured in violent clashes with the army. Armored vehicles drove over protesters who were marching to protest the authorities' failure to protect churches. Only three soldiers were convicted by a military court in September 2012 and received light sentences of two to three years in prison, which underscores the failure and unwillingness of the military justice to investigate those responsible at senior levels (Human Rights Watch 2011a; Ahram Online 2013a).

14. The committee was composed of sixteen members representing all relevant stakeholders: state institutions, parents of the victims and martyrs, former judges, human rights lawyers, and university professors.

15. A new fact-finding committee was formed in December 2013 to investigate various cases of human rights abuses that took place after June 30, 2013, including the breaking up of the Muslim Brotherhood's sit-ins in August 2013. The committee concluded its work and published a report in late November 2014. Human rights activists considered its findings mild, especially regarding the authorities' responsibility for the high death toll during violent clashes with Muslim Brotherhood supporters in the summer of 2013. The committee concluded its report with a set of over sixty recommendations that so far have been ignored by the authorities (*Aswat Masriya* 2014).

16. Egyptian opposition voices attribute Sinai's increasing lawlessness to the 1979 peace treaty with Israel, which restricts Egypt's military presence in Zone C (stretching along the Israeli border) and only allows the deployment of a rather symbolic and lightly armed Egyptian police force in addition to a multinational monitoring force (*Al-Hayat* 2012a).

17. These operations, initially launched in August 2011 when a group of militants crossed into Israel and conducted an attack, were first called "Operation Eagle" and then "Operation Sinai."

18. Law 14 of 2012 gives the minister of defense the responsibility of setting regulations concerning land attribution on the Sinai Peninsula. The strategic locations in question include Zone C (according to the 1979 Camp David peace treaty) and lands located within five kilometers west of Egypt's eastern border with Gaza/Israel (*Al-Masry al-Youm* 2012a).

19. Article 152 stipulates that the declaration of war requires the consultation of the National Defense Council and the approval of the parliament by a two-thirds majority. In case of dissolution of the parliament, the approval of the SCAF is required, along with the approval of National Defense Council and the Council of Ministers.

20. The People's Assembly was dissolved by the Supreme Constitutional Court on June 14, 2012, as the court found the lower house's election law unconstitutional.

21. This small committee suggested amendments to the 2012 constitution and submitted them to the fifty-member committee, which was in charge of drafting the constitution.

22. This is the author's analysis of several interviews conducted with al-Sisi as presidential candidate.

CHAPTER 10

The Tunisian Military and Democratic Control of the Armed Forces

Risa A. Brooks

Among the Arab states that experienced social uprisings in 2011, Tunisia has the dual distinction of being the first to witness protests as well as the state that emerged best prepared to transition from an autocratic past after the removal of the country's longtime dictator, Zine El Abidine Ben Ali. The ability of the country to endure serious political crises since Ben Ali's ouster, including the assassination of two opposition politicians in 2013, has been a crucial basis for optimism about its future (Gall 2013a).

A second cause for sanguinity, according to many analysts, is the unique character of the Tunisian military and its putative willingness to submit to democratic control of its institutions. Indeed, among its Arab counterparts, the Tunisian military is often cited as the most capable of accommodating to structures and processes of democratic oversight of the armed forces. One analyst, for example, concludes that within the armed forces, there is little change needed to ensure this transition. According to Querine Hanlon (2012b), "Tunisia needs no lessons in subordinating the military to civilian control"; therefore, rendering it accountable to parliamentary control will be straightforward. As another analyst describes it, "the [Tunisian] army is by nature non-interventionist and consequently ready to adapt to democratic politics" (Sayigh 2011). In short, scholars and practitioners can anticipate a smooth transition to democratic control of the armed forces.

If these analysts are correct, Tunisia will prove to be exceptional not only in comparison with its Arab counterparts but also compared with many militaries in autocratic states in Latin America and Asia that have proven to be resilient in maintaining independence from democratic control of their institutions. But is the conventional view correct? Will the transition to democratic control of the military prove to be a relatively smooth and straightforward undertaking? More important, if the conventional view is correct, what factors can best explain why the Tunisian military might easily conform to democratic oversight?

The importance of these issues cannot be underestimated. In autocratic regimes, reform of the military, police, intelligence, and security entities are central to the establishment of institutions that support law and order and are responsive and accountable to a country's citizens. If such reform is successful, "security institutions should not only be effective and efficient in providing security for the country's citizens, but should also be accountable to democratically elected civilian authorities, and should act on the basis of rule of law" (Lutterbeck 2012:3). In the worst cases, failure to reform security institutions can stymie progress in promoting democratic institutions and practices more broadly in the state. For this reason, "it is not an exaggeration to say that security sector reform, particularly police, military, and intelligence reform, will determine the fate of the Arab Spring transitions" (United States Institute of Peace 2012). Put simply, assessing the prospects for reform is central to any assessment of the status of the regime transition occurring in Tunisia.

This chapter addresses the prospects for security-sector reform and establishment of democratic oversight and control, focusing specifically on the Tunisian military. Its aim is to assess the structural and normative basis that could account for why the Tunisian military may be willing to accommodate institutional changes that allow for public and parliamentary oversight. It concludes that, in fact, there are reasons for optimism that the Tunisian military will acquiesce, if not invite, democratic control. There are nonetheless some potential risks that should be considered that could complicate the transition. Tensions among political parties and the elite, civil strife and ongoing security issues related to insurgent and terrorist attacks, the challenges of reforming the Interior Ministry, and the possibility that civilians could aim at politicizing the military present challenges in the transition to democratic control. These challenges generate pressures on the military that could enmesh it in domestic politics and generate other barriers to the institutional reform of the armed forces in Tunisia.[1]

Specifically, I argue that the strategy of political control employed by the country's autocrats, Habib Bourguiba and Ben Ali, has shaped the character of the Tunisian military, rendering it well positioned to accommodate the institutions and structures essential to democratic oversight of the armed forces. That strategy of political control—control by marginalization and exclusion—shaped the incentives and organizational interests as well as the corporate ethos of the military. Consequently, the military has little to lose materially from acceding to democratic control and is likely to be normatively receptive to allowing the imposition of these institutions.

I begin this chapter with a discussion of the nature of political control of the military under the Habib Bourguiba regime and subsequently under Ben Ali's leadership. The chapter then discusses the implications of this particular history and logic of political control for the character of the Tunisian military, including positive implications for reform as well as potential obstacles that could impede the advancement of democratic control of the armed forces. The chapter closes with a discussion of the scholarly implications of the analysis.

The Bourguiba Legacy

Understanding the prospects for democratic reform in Tunisia requires first assessing the historical role of the military and the methods employed by the country's first postindependence leader, Habib Bourguiba, in managing relations with his armed forces.

Importantly, when Bourguiba assumed power in 1956 after Tunisia won independence from the French, he did not do so with the help or at the behest of a powerful army, nor did the military play an important symbolic role in the new state. This distinguishes the country from other republics in the region such as Egypt, where the military brought the Free Officers to power in a coup, and Algeria, where the military fought for independence. The army was created in 1956 with Tunisians who had served in the French Army and the Beylical Guard under French administration (Jebnoun 2014). As James Gelvin (2012:68) aptly captures it, "the Tunisian army is the product of independence, not the progenitor of independence." Bourguiba, a French-trained lawyer, had a particular conception of the military's role in the state in which it would only play a small role in politics (Lutterbeck 2012). He then organized civil-military relations in ways to sustain that marginal role.

For example, rather than accommodating the military to his rule by allowing it to play a role in governance or political institutions, he ensured that it remained politically disenfranchised. Officers were prevented from playing a role in the regime's dominant political party, thereby denying them access to an important institution of elite politics in Tunisia. Bourguiba also sought to deliberately distance the military from daily policing and coercive functions, investing that role with the Interior Ministry and the conglomerate of police, security, and paramilitary forces under its control (Ware 1985).

So notable was the marginalization of military from regime politics that when Ben Ali became minister of the interior in 1986 under Bourguiba, he was the first career military officer to be appointed to a cabinet-level post (Gassner 1987; Bou Nassif 2015). Ben Ali had attended the Saint-Cyr military academy in France and also received intelligence and security training as a young officer in the United States. Early in his career, he served in military intelligence. Later, within the Interior Ministry, he helped coordinate security in the aftermath of the bread riots that occurred in January 1978. After a stint as Tunisia's ambassador to Poland he returned to the Interior Ministry, moving up through its leadership ranks and finally in April 1986 being appointed interior minister (Ware 1985:41; Murphy 1999:164; Gassner 1987). He retained that portfolio when he became prime minister in October 1987. One month later he would maneuver Bourguiba, whose health and erratic behavior had become increasingly serious, out of office through a bloodless coup (Borowiec 1998).[2]

Political Control Under Ben Ali

Ben Ali inherited the structures of civilian control established by his predecessor and innovated within the parameters of these extant structures. Specifically, his method of political control had several key elements.

Unlike most Arab militaries, the military in Tunisia was deliberately limited in size, resources, and missions. In 2011, the regular armed forces included a 27,000-strong army, of which approximately 20,000 were conscripts; a navy with 4,800 personnel; and air force of 4,000 personnel (*Military Balance* 2012). A 12,000-strong paramilitary force, the National Guard, fell under the control of the Interior Ministry. The budget was limited to approximately 1.4 percent of gross domestic product (GDP) so that in 2010, Tunisia ranked 109th in the world in terms of percentage of GDP devoted to defense expenditure—figures that contrast sharply with other states in the Arab world.

Ben Ali also limited the roles of the military within the Tunisian state. The military played a role in infrastructure development, disaster relief, regional peacekeeping operations, and humanitarian assistance. The army operated alongside the National Guard (a paramilitary force under the control of the Ministry of the Interior) in border control and alone in southern parts of the country.[3]

Importantly, the military did not participate in providing domestic security and policing the civilian population. Although some officers under Ben Ali were appointed to key positions within the Interior Ministry and security services, this was not indicative of a larger systematic pattern of incorporating the military as an institution in the provision of domestic security (Bou Nassif 2015:69). The military did not even operate in Tunis, which reflected both its circumscribed mandate in the autocratic regime and also the regime's desire to limit the military's operations to outside the capital. Security in the capital and major cities was provided by police and other forces controlled by the Interior Ministry. Outside of Tunis, the National Guard played a primary policing role in the countryside and smaller cities. When, for example, Ben Ali deployed the army to the capital on January 12, 2011, during the uprising that precipitated his departure from the country, it indicated the severity of the situation facing the regime (*Maghreb Confidential* 2011a, 2011b).[4]

In addition, the military was not accommodated to the regime through the conferring of private or organizational benefits. Unlike in Egypt, where in the 1970s Anwar al-Sadat expanded the military industry in order to help wed the military to the regime, there was no significant arms industry established in Tunisia. Also, the military did not develop a vast infrastructure of industrial and commercial enterprises; the military did not play a substantial role in the economy at large. Tunisian officers under Ben Ali did not enjoy special perquisites or ready access to key positions in state institutions or the private sector upon retirement.

While the military was kept on the sidelines, in contrast, Ben Ali sponsored a significant expansion of security forces housed in the Ministry of the Interior.[5] Beginning in the 1990s, the size of the police and security forces grew substantially, by some accounts quadrupling, and included forces within the formal control of the Interior Ministry as well as militias accountable directly to the presidential residence, Carthage Palace.[6] As Christopher

Alexander (2011) captures it, "The police force, uniformed and plainclothes, became the regime's praetorian guard." The number of police and security services employed has been estimated by some to be as high as 120,000–200,000; these figures are likely overstated but are suggestive of the pervasive security presence in the country of 10 million people (Erdle 2004:214; Goldstein 2011; Henry and Springborg 2011).

Within the Interior Ministry specifically, there were several well-equipped and well-trained specialized forces such as the Public Order Brigade (Brigade de l'Ordre Publique), or riot police, which played an important role in the regime's efforts to repress the 2010–2011 uprising (Amnesty International 2011:2). The Interior Ministry housed the Intervention Forces, which included the Rapid Intervention Response Brigade, the Anti-Terrorism Brigade (BAT), and an elite tactical unit of the National Guard, the National Guard Special Unit. These units benefited from professional training and equipment and were known for their skill and specialization.

Also central to Ben Ali's security forces was his 5,000–6,000-strong Presidential Guard, which was especially well-equipped and well treated.[7] Indeed, within the final days of the Ben Ali regime as the protests escalated in January 2014, the Presidential Guard would stay loyal to the regime but ultimately would prove incapable of protecting it (Walt 2011). Immediately following Ben Ali's departure on January 14, the army and some segments of the police fought fierce gun battles around the capital, including the presidential palace in Carthage and the Interior Ministry. Members of the Presidential Guard and private militia recruited and directed by Ben Ali engaged in looting and violence, which appeared to have been part of a strategy to sow chaos and lay the groundwork for Ben Ali's return to the country, forcing citizen patrols to mobilize to protect their neighborhoods (Al Jazeera 2011c).[8]

In short, Ben Ali's formula for keeping the military subordinate had been largely one of control through exclusion. The military was kept distant from the regime, both literally and figuratively, and its influence was balanced with a large police and security apparatus. Intriguingly, Ben Ali relied on this approach despite the very different patterns of elite control and regime management that he employed more broadly. He ruled through direct control and management of a small cohort of elites, who rotated in and out of government institutions, and a clique of presidential advisers operating out of the palace (Erdle 2004; Murphy 2002; Angrist 2007). Indeed, in its later years, the regime was seemingly largely mobilized to facilitate the personal enrichment of Ben Ali's family.

Explaining the Character of the Tunisian Military

This history and the manner in which political control was sustained in the autocratic decades of the regime had important consequences for the military's organizational interests and corporate identity. Three important implications from the past methods and structures of political control under the Ben Ali and Bourguiba regimes point to the character of the Tunisian military and its receptivity to democratic control and oversight.

Corporate Ethos

Critical to understanding the Tunisian military's character is how the isolation and marginalization of the military provided the foundation for the development of its organizational culture.[9] The relegation of the military to the periphery of the regime effectively granted the military significant organizational autonomy. As a result, the military was able to sustain a corporate ethos that prioritized the cohesion and meritocratic traditions of the institution and its officer corps (Gaaloul 2011). In addition to its isolation from the political institutions and informal and formal channels of influence and power, this ethos was perpetuated by the military's limited mandate, focus on external threats and challenges, and participation in peacekeeping missions. The tasks in which it was engaged therefore reflected and promoted a notion of the military as protecting the security of state from external challenges and militants threatening the state—not protecting the state from its own citizens.

In addition, the exclusion from political institutions limited the vulnerability of the military to the distortions and mixed incentives that can result from participation in elite politics and patronage networks within the state. The military was isolated and removed from direct involvement in the intrigues of regime politics.

Operating at the periphery of politics and insulated from the regime, the military sustained, by many accounts, a corporate ethos or culture that is republican in orientation. Safeguarding and abiding constitutional processes and procedures are viewed as a primary mission and role for the military. As Yezid Sayigh (2011) describes, the Tunisian army is notable for its "adherence to the republican system, in particular the constitutional order and the preeminence of civilian control." As characterized by the former head of Tunisia's National War College, "We are a republican military and we never wanted to become politically hegemonic; this goes against our values" (Bou Nassif 2015). In this view, political engagement in contravention of democratic politics may therefore be less likely because the military explicitly understands this to be outside its mandate and mission.[10] This republican ethos in turn may render the military amenable to laws generated in a democratic process and to oversight by parliament and elected officials.

The origins of this organizational culture may be rooted in a number of factors, including the particular role (or lack thereof) of the military in the origins of the republic in 1956. Far from playing the role of the revolutionary vanguard as did the military in Egypt, the Tunisian military lacked the symbolic role and political influence in the constitutional order throughout Tunisia's modern history. The military also lacked a clear ideological agenda and sectarian divisions. This republican ethos was also likely reinforced during the rigorous education and socialization processes within the officer corps that is characteristic of the Tunisian armed forces.

The interaction of the Tunisian military with foreign military forces and relations with its military counterparts in the United States and France may also have helped reinforce this republican ethos. For example, Tunisia's forces participate in annual meetings of the Joint Military Commission with the United States, are involved in regular training exercises, and receive Foreign Military Financing (FMF) and International Military Education and Training (IMET), which in 2011 amounted to approximately $17 million and $1.7 million, respectively.[11]

Foreign training and contact facilitate interaction with military officers from democratic states and expose them to norms associated with cultivating professional expertise and protecting the integrity of their military institutions. To the extent that these socialization processes are significant, they may serve to reinforce meritocratic norms and support the conception of the military as operating outside of politics (Arieff 2011:21; United States Embassy Tunis 2008). These socialization processes, however, may be important because they reinforce a structural situation in which the military is already isolated from regime politics and also exhibits a particular republican organizational culture, not because they alone are responsible for that noninterventionist culture. These are starkly different circumstances than those found in places such as Egypt, where, for example, there is little evidence that U.S. investment in IMET has socialized the Egyptian officer corps to favor nonintervention in politics.

This corporate ethos and apparent regard for constitutional processes, moreover, should not be misinterpreted so as to say that the military was professional and that its training and skill render it inherently apolitical. Arguing that the Tunisian military reflects a corporate ethos that supports republican institutions is not the same as saying that the military is reflexively apolitical. Discussions of the Tunisian uprisings, however, are replete with references to the apolitical nature of the Tunisian military as shorthand in explaining its leaders refraining from the use of force in defense of the Ben Ali regime during the 2010–2011 protests.[12] Two issues deserve consideration in this regard.

First, to the extent that an organizational culture has evolved in which respect for constitutional processes and principles are paramount, this should be seen not as some inherently apolitical character of the military. Instead, it should be considered as a product of the Tunisian military's particular history in which norms about the appropriate mission of the military developed and the structures of political control through which those norms were sustained. As Taylor (2003) and Pion-Berlin, Grisham, and Esparza (2014) contend, militaries commonly develop and exhibit a particular notion of their roles and missions that reflect a military's unique history and experience. In short, there is a structural basis supporting the military's perception of its appropriate role in society.

Second, contrary to the notion of the military as simply blindly abstaining from politics, examination of the events in 2010–2011 in the aftermath of Ben Ali's ouster reveals that military leaders acted with discernment and a political calculus. The positive normative connotations of events in Tunisia—the military acted to protect the people and safeguard the revolution—should not obscure what in effect was an ineluctably, if perhaps not especially self-conscious, political role played by the military in the regime both before and during the uprising (Angrist 2013). Admittedly, the Tunisian military did not actively oversee the removal of the president and seize power in the transition, as in Egypt. Still, by not actively defending the regime by using force to disperse protesters and only following a stated mandate of protecting state institutions, the military leadership was necessarily making a political decision not to safeguard the autocracy.[13] Given the centrality of the military as the coercive force of last resort in autocratic regimes, not stepping up in defense of the Ben Ali regime—whether or not the use of force was explicitly ordered by Ben Ali—was a decision that was intrinsically political in that it represented a deliberate effort not to act to maintain Ben Ali in office.[14]

In fact, the military's actions in December 2010 and January 2011 were clearly calculated and political in this sense. The military deployed to cities in the south and west and stood by while security forces used extreme tactics, including live ammunition at times, to suppress the demonstrations (Kirkpatrick 2011c, 2011d; Al Jazeera 2011c). While some units and soldiers reportedly tried to calm the volatile situation on the ground by interposing themselves between protesters and the police, the military in January 2011 was sitting on the fence and watching the regime try to suppress the protest, only drawing a line at using force itself. Moreover, this was not the only time the military had behaved in such a passive way toward the regime's efforts to repress protesters. The military had similarly been deployed and stood by while forces under the control of the Interior Ministry violently suppressed labor protests in the interior region of Gafsa in 2008 (BBC Monitoring Middle East 2008; Amnesty International 2009b).

Moreover, the decisions made during the final days of the uprising were also political in the sense that they meant that the army and its leader, General Rashid Ammar, was de facto the key power broker in the country—a role that in the weeks following the protests became manifestly clear. Not only had the military refrained from defending Ben Ali, precipitating his departure from the country, but it subsequently played a vital role in reestablishing control under a new government in the days that followed. Military personnel participated in the arrest of key officials and provided essential backing to the interim government led by Ben Ali's longtime prime minister, Muhammad Ghannouchi. In turn, the military defended the government from threats posed by Ben Ali loyalists by engaging in a series of street battles with members of security forces allied to the leader.[15] In short, when General Ammar famously stated that "the army will protect the revolution," he was essentially admitting to the military's fundamental role as power broker (Kirkpatrick 2011e). What is important in this context is how the military sees its appropriate role within democratic society—not that its leaders somehow are incapable of political decisions and engagement.

The Division of Labor

A second factor that has affected the character of the Tunisian military and is important in understanding the prospects for advancing democratic control of the military relates to the implications of the division of labor in domestic policing that was maintained in Tunisia under the autocratic regimes.

The military's lack of a historical role in domestic policing has important implications for the social esteem and importance of maintaining the standing and reputation of the institution in Tunisian society. For example, in December 2010 and January 2011 when the protests occurred, the military was not identified by Tunisians as being part of the autocracy's coercive apparatus, as were police and other security forces. The military did not have a negative reputation with which to contend. This created an opening for the military to capitalize on these sentiments and enhance its social position and prestige by not using armed force, thereby avoiding the disdain that Tunisians reaped on the police and security forces. The military has been able to maintain that social esteem because it is viewed as an impartial actor in the transition. A Pew Global Survey from October 2014 reports, for example, that 95 percent of respondents felt that the military was having a "good influence" on the "way things are going" in the country (Pew Global 2013).

Consequently, the military does not have to contend with the legacy of domestic repression, unlike the Interior Ministry. The military's forces must develop in a democratic environment clouded by a mistrustful population and an unsavory legacy of acting as the coercive arm of the state. Given that the military is popularly esteemed, it may be easier for its leaders to submit to the authority of institutions accountable to the public.

In addition, the low status of the military within the regime also shaped its (lack of) organizational interests and investment in maintaining the autocratic status quo and preexisting security institutions. Under Ben Ali, the police and the Interior Ministry benefited from growing resources and status in the regime, which by some accounts created resentment and dissatisfaction with the conventional armed forces (Erdle 2010). As Querine Hanlon (2012b:4) reports, military officers were "at the bottom" of the hierarchy of security institutions. As one officer put it, "We were always last . . . the regime did not like us." Hence, there is no loss of status by abandoning a system in which the military was put in competition with a privileged Interior Ministry.

Even more important in considering how officers might view the old regime, there is evidence that the Ben Ali regime also purposely sought to humiliate and subordinate the military leadership. This occurred most notably in an incident in May 1991 known as the Barraket Essehel Affair (Bou Nassif 2015). As cover for a purge of the military, the regime fabricated a coup attempt by military leaders. Up to two hundred officers were taken to the Ministry of the Interior, and some were subjected to torture and forced confessions. The regime maintained that the coup plot was real, and only in the aftermath of Ben Ali's departure did the regime's treachery become known. The incident speaks to Ben Ali's approach to the military and an underlying estrangement between him and its officers.[16] Ben Ali also may have played a role in the downing of a helicopter in 2002 that killed Ammar's predecessor and twelve other senior officers and personnel—an incident, if true, that would have only fueled the alienation of the military from the regime.[17] In short, for all these reasons, the military in Tunisia is likely to have little attachment to the institutions of the country's recent autocratic past.

Civilian Ministry of Defense

A final factor that has shaped the military involves the processes of civilian control that were in place under Ben Ali. Notably, Tunisia had a civilian Ministry of Defense, staffed and run by civilians in charge of formulating and implementing decisions about the policy and administration of the armed forces. Under Ben Ali, the Ministry of Defense was divided into seven directorates responsible for everything from military justice, conscription, and training to technical departments, military schools, and education (Hanlon 2012a). The military command traditionally lacked a unified chief of the services until Rashid Ammar was appointed chairman of the Joint Chiefs of Staff in April 2011. Hence, the military is used to being run by civilians; the practice of civilian control within the actual administration of the armed forces was in place before Ben Ali's departure. The civilian defense minister was, of course, part of the regime and answerable to Ben Ali, which is quite different than the accountability to a democratically elected parliament. However, the structure is essentially in place, and the military is experienced in being accountable to a civilian Ministry of Defense.[18] To the extent that those administrative processes have had some socializing effect, this tradition of a civilian-led defense minister may then render the military amenable to the extension of civilian oversight.

In fact, there is evidence that these processes of administration are firmly established in civil-military relations. One intriguing illustration, for example, occurred during the protests of 2011 and in particular in developments in the final days of the Ben Ali regime.[19] On January 13, 2011, Chief of Staff

Ammar was sent by the minister of defense to the Operations Room of the Interior Ministry to help coordinate efforts to respond to the protests. At this point the army had deployed to the streets and was guarding government buildings (although it would not engage in active defense of the regime). Given the dominant position of the Interior Ministry in the regime, these orders may have been intended to ensure that the armed forces would not act on their own. The fact, however, that Ammar did indeed follow orders to report to the ministry shows how the processes of civilian control were intact and suggests that these routines were deeply entrenched, even during a moment of intense stress on the regime.[20] In short, his actions underscored the degree to which the military had accommodated to conventions of civilian administration and the entrenchment of those practices.

Implications for the Tunisian Military's Accommodation to Democratic Control

This history and the formula of political control initiated by Bourguiba and developed under Ben Ali have several important implications for understanding the Tunisian military's receptivity and willingness to accommodate to institutions of parliamentary oversight and control of the armed forces.

Consider, first, that because of the low status of the military, the limited resources it was granted, and its exclusion from political institutions under the autocratic regime, the military does not have any direct interests at stake in sustaining those autocratic structures. Neither its officers nor the organization had much to lose in the end of the autocratic regime. In fact, by providing protection from the arbitrariness of the autocratic regime, the military may stand to gain under institutions that provide transparent and consistent oversight. The military may also be able to benefit from democratic control if funding increases and better equipment is secured as a result. In this context, democracy could afford some protections and improvements in the organizational status and resources of the military that were absent under Ben Ali.

In addition, these material interests coincide with a corporate ethos in which the military's role and missions are conceived as limited and in which the military has a narrow mandate to safeguard national security—even while, as I describe below, it must play a role in helping to battle an insurgency and ensure civil order during the political transition. Without a prominent role in bringing the regime to power and within the structures of political control subsequently imposed and given the isolation afforded by its relegation to the periphery of the regime, regard for procedure and republican constitutionalism appear to have flourished. In addition, the Tunisian military has been subordinated to a Ministry of Defense staffed and led by civilians. This practical experience of civilian administration may help the ministry accommodate to constitutionally mandated oversight. In short, as a result of the material status and normative commitments to constitutionalism and the rule of law, the military may be organizationally prepared to accept rules and structures imposed by a democratically elected government.

Potential Challenges

The history and character of the Tunisian military provides the basis for confidence that the military will embrace its role within democratic institutions. That transition, however, will not necessarily be smooth or inevitable. Tunisia faces several challenges that could affect the pace and nature of institutional reform and the advancement of democratic control.

A first issue of hindrance is the lagging effort to promote reform of the Interior Ministry and the security sector as a whole. Partly as a result, the police and security forces have been unable to effectively maintain civil order and manage ongoing demonstrations during the transition; the variously brutal and incompetent practices of policing common in Tunisia under autocratic rule have continued. Consequently, the Tunisian military has been called on to help guard buildings and installations, provide local security, and protect law and order (Hanlon 2012a:9, 2012b:2–4). This prevents the military from focusing on traditional security threats and disengaging from participation in maintaining civil order.

In addition, the absence of plans for serious reform of the police has stymied the broader efforts by interim governments to consider security-sector reform. As one Tunisian officer described it, "reform of any one ministry is closely tied to the reform of other ministries" (Hanlon 2012a). Hence, even if the military will accept institutional changes consistent with democratic control and accede to new legislation, the failure by the country's political leaders thus far to address reform in the broader security sector represents a crucial barrier to moving forward (Sayigh 2015).

Reform of the Interior Ministry has proven to be a major and persistent obstacle. The Interior Ministry has not been restructured, and reforms to date have been limited (Sayigh 2015). Early in the transition in February 2011, Interior Minister Farhat Rajhi dismissed a number of officials and the directorate for State Security was formally abolished, but because these efforts occurred without a systematic plan and did not follow regulations in place regarding such actions, they were seen by some as arbitrary and, in any event, had little effect in promoting reform (Ben Mahfoudh 2014:3). In September 2011 a report titled "Security and Development: A White Paper for Democratic Security in Tunisia" was drafted by an official charged with reform efforts in the Interior Ministry. The report was passed to the interim president, Moncef Marzouki, in December 2011, who at the time vowed to pursue reform aggressively (Sayigh 2015). The initiative, however, proved to be a nonstarter, and reform was essentially stymied by the al-Nahda government after parliamentary elections; its officials argued that the plan was the pretext for the reemergence of elements of the former regime (Sayigh 2014, 2015).

On the plus side, there have been changes in laws regarding arrests and detentions by police and security personnel, a procedural handbook on human rights has been adopted, and the Interior Ministry's role in the electoral process has been eliminated (Ben Mahfoudh 2014:5). There have been various educational initiatives and programs sponsored by the Geneva Centre for the Democratic Control of Armed Forces (DCAF), including an extensive effort to map security-sector legislation in Tunisia.[21] Foreign assistance for security-sector reform has also been made available; through various programs, for example, the United States from fiscal year 2011 through fiscal year 2014 provided security and justice aid of $185 million.[22] Despite these bright spots, however, little comprehensive reform occurred in the posttransition period (Ben Mahfoudh 2014; Sayigh 2015; Al Jazeera 2011b).[23]

Indeed, substantial political obstacles to reform remain in Tunisia. There is likely to be substantial push-back to comprehensive reform from within the security edifice, many of whose officials and institutions have remained entrenched throughout the transition. Examples of these were the failure in January 2012 of Interior Minister Ali Laarayedh to sideline the director of the Intervention Forces, Monsef al-Ajimi, who had been implicated in the brutal suppression of protesters in 2011.[24] In response to the effort to remove Ajimi, more than 12,000 police mobilized a demonstration and blocked access to the director. In the process, the police abandoned their posts and key installations, and the minister of the interior was stymied in his effort to remove the director from the Intervention Forces (Perito 2012; Hanlon 2012b). The police and their unions, which are now legal, seem to be caught up in a particular mix of perceived persecution and disenfranchisement by a population that (according to them) fails to appreciate the role of the police in providing security (Ajmi 2012), combined with an ongoing arrogance and impunity in managing civil disturbances and demonstrations (Crane 2014; Hanlon 2012b).

Two additional issues present even more serious obstacles to reform. The first involves a lack of economic reform in addition to ongoing structural problems that especially afflict the center and south of the country. The region where the protests against Ben Ali began in December 2010—the Gafsa mining basin—remains a tense and volatile area, as unemployment remains high (Gall 2014b; Ben Bouazza 2014; Slama 2014). There has been growing popular disillusionment with the status of Tunisian politics and society, including a loss of faith in democracy and the country's political leadership, after the initial highs of the post-Ben Ali era (Pew Global 2013).[25] Consequently, civil disorder and security problems are likely to continue if not intensify (Perito 2015). Even while outsiders continued to laud Tunisia as the poster child for successful management of the Arab uprisings, there have been persistent and regular strikes, demonstrations, and incidents of civil disorder. That Tunisia has provided more recruits than any other Arab or Western state to the ISIL (Islamic State) movement is striking in this context and suggestive of a deep current of disillusionment among the country's youths, a sector where rates of unemployment remain very high even among the well educated (Khatib 2014). It also raises vital questions about future stability as these foreign fighters indoctrinated in extremist ideologies and trained on the battlefields of Iraq and Syria return home to Tunisia.

A second major challenge is the ongoing insurgency in Tunisia on the Algerian border that the Tunisian military and National Guard have been trying to contain. Several extremist militant groups have taken a foothold in this mountainous region in the Kasserine governorate (Moore 2015). Much of that fight has been focused on the border areas, but there have been clashes at times in urban areas and the capital (Gall 2013b, 2014a). The militants have proven resilient, and the military has struggled. Attacks by militants in the border area in July 2013 and July 2014 left eight and fourteen soldiers dead, respectively (Tajine 2014).[26] The military consequently has come under criticism by civilian politicians regarding its ineffectiveness (*Asharq Alawsat*

2013). It has also experienced the resignations of General Ammar in June 2013 and Ammar's successor, Brigadier General Salah Hamdi, in July 2014 under a cloud of questions about their competence in managing the battle against the militants (*Asharq Alawsat* 2014).

The virulence of the extremist challenge has also been demonstrated in the devastating attacks on the Bardo Museum in March 2015 and the deadly shooting spree of a young man at a hotel in the tourist resort of Sousse in June 2015. These attacks are likely to have several implications— none of which bode well for the advance of democratic reform and institutional change of the armed forces and the Interior Ministry. The loss of tourism revenue is likely to add to the country's economic hardships, while the threat to security is likely to harden resistance to change from within the Interior Ministry. Efforts to restructure and dismantle parts of the security apparatus will be subordinated to the perceived imperatives of meeting the country's security challenges. Pressure from civil society for reform is likely to abate as Tunisians call on their government to provide security and stability. Many of Tunisia's politicians, who have heretofore not been seriously engaged in the issues, are unlikely to change course in the intensified security atmosphere.

Even if momentum for a reform movement were to build, there could still be obstacles to the military accommodating to democratic—and not just civilian—control. While the Tunisian military has appeared receptive to the concept of reform and allowing parliamentary oversight and involvement in its affairs, the reality of democratic control as the actual requirements and mechanism are put in place could prove less than appealing to Tunisia's senior officers.

Consider, in this context, the persistence of legal provisions that permit the trial of civilians in military courts and make criticism of the military a prosecutable offense. In January 2015, for example, a Tunisian blogger who posted about potential corruption and financial irregularities within the military was sentenced to prison under Article 91 of the Code of Military Justice, which renders it illegal to "defame the military" (Al Jazeera 2015). Amendments to autocratic laws such as this are essential if democratic reform is to become a reality.[27]

The intrusiveness of democratic oversight necessarily requires changes in a military that has been administered in the past by civilians but not by a potentially fractious parliament or political leadership. One could anticipate some potential tensions, or complexities, in this regard, especially if the civilian politicians in charge are viewed as corrupt or their legitimacy to make laws for the republic is in question.

In addition, while the structural situation is auspicious—in that the Tunisian military does not have a lot to lose and may have something to gain from democratic control—it is important to bear in mind the agency of individual leaders and actors and how it could influence the actions of the military in the future. General Rashid Ammar's actions during and after the ouster of Ben Ali underscore his personal conception of the role of the army and his personal role as its leader. Yet counterfactually, had an individual of different character been in place, would another leader have handled the decisions facing him with the same aplomb and readiness to leave politics to the civilians? Consider, for example, the case of the BAT leader, Samir Tarhouni, in the 2011 regime upheaval. Tarhouni gained notoriety when he spontaneously detained several members of the Trabelsi family at the airport lounge, prohibiting their departure from the country on January 14, 2011, the day that Ben Ali departed for Saudi Arabia. The incident was not organized in advance and did not represent a planned or broad defection of the Interior Ministry.[28] The action was not ordered by his superior and he may have purposely violated the orders of the civilian minister of defense in proceeding with the detention. In short, individuals do and can matter, not only in how they act upon their own preferences but also in how they lead what is a very hierarchical organization like the military.[29]

One final set of challenges may come from civilian politicians, who in the event of another major political crisis could be the impetus for politicization of the military. Historically, civilians have often tried to employ the military for their own ends—a phenomenon common in coups in which segments of the elite coalesce with the military or, in a different manner, across and within many democratic states when civilians try to cultivate alliances with influential military leaders. In the aftermath of President Muhammad Mursi's ouster in Egypt in July 2013, activists sought to mobilize intervention by the military against the Islamist al-Nahda party (Walt 2013)—while the effort failed, it illustrates the dangerous role that civilians can have in advancing military involvement in politics. As Alfred Stepan (2012:5) observed in a 2011 trip to Tunisia, the tendency or potential willingness of some civilians to look to the military to side with them in the event of a regime crisis was a serious concern. In part, future progress in securing the subordination of the military to democratic institutions will require civilians to resist any temptations to politicize its officers.

Implications for Future Research

There are sound reasons for optimism in anticipating that the Tunisian military will accommodate itself to the imposition of parliamentary oversight and democratic controls of its organization and institutions. This is rooted in the history and structural role of the military and in the methods of political control employed under the Bourguiba and Ben Ali regimes. These factors, in combination with the particular history of the Tunisian military, also contribute to an organizational culture that appears amenable to constitutionalism.

The Tunisian case, while unique in some ways, also offers a number of lessons for scholars and practitioners. A first implication of the Tunisian case is that the precise methods and mechanisms of sustaining political control matter in autocracies. Many scholars have studied the variety of methods of coup-proofing available to dictators, which includes developing overlapping security services, relying on favored minority groups in promotions and key appointments, providing perquisites to officers and equipment and resources to the military, centralizing commands, creating shadow commands, and attaching political officers, or commissars, to monitor units (Quinlivan 1999; De Atkine 1999; Picard 1999; Biddle and Zirkle 1996; Brooks 1998).

Rather than conceptualizing methods of political control as a list of interchangeable tactics, scholars might consider conceptualizing alternative strategies or logics of control and identifying empirical variants of these systems or logics. That is, one strategy may involve control through divide and rule (Syria) versus control through a grand bargain (Egypt) versus control through marginalization (Tunisia). Historical development, the presence of external threats, and sectarian and social-structural factors or regime type (whether type or system of semidemocracy or autocracy) might play a role in shaping the strategy observed.

In turn, the strategy of political control might matter in understanding incentives to defect and abandon the political leadership in response to mass uprisings (McLauchlin 2010) and leadership's reaction and role more broadly in democratic transitions or other dimensions of military behavior or activity.

A second set of lessons relates to the concept of professionalism. Professionalism as a concept alone has limited explanatory power to account for the Tunisian case, especially when the political roles played by other professional militaries in the region (i.e., Egypt) are taken into consideration. The Tunisian case instead points to the particularities of the corporate ethos or specific organizational culture of the armed forces, which is historically and structurally bound.[30] That the Tunisian military seems apt to accommodate to democratic institutions is a reflection of its (lack of) material investment in the former autocratic institutions of the state as well as its particular organizational culture and conception of its role in the Tunisian state.

Rather than attributing norms of nonintervention in politics to the development of professional skills and expertise, scholars need to look deeper in probing how and why a military might perceive its appropriate roles and missions in ways that disincline it toward an active role in directing or shaping civilian political life.

Finally, the case highlights the interdependent relationship between reform of the military and of the police and security sectors, more broadly. Often, when studying state militaries and civil-military relations, other armed forces are treated as auxiliary or secondary actors in the analysis—they are not regarded as especially consequential actors in understanding civil-military relations. Yet, especially in efforts to assess the prospects and process of democratic reform in countries such as Tunisia, one must consider the complexity of security forces and how the fate of one set of actors in that sector bears on the others.[31]

Notes

1. Security-sector reform aims to transform security institutions to promote transparency in their activities and structure and accountability of personnel to elected politicians, civil bureaucracies, and ultimately citizens. While the precise set of rules and processes put in place may vary, reform usually involves an array of initiatives, such as efforts to promote civilian expertise and analysis of defense and military issues, establishing control of budgets (both size of funding and allocation), and legislative monitoring and oversight of institutional practices and regulations. For details, see Sean McFate (2008) and Born (2002). For a pre-2011 discussion of the issue in the Arab world, see Kodmani and Chartouni-Dubarry (2009).

2. According to Borowiec (1998), Ben Ali relied on forces from the National Guard and not the regular army to deploy to key sites in the capital, setting the stage for the bloodless coup that ensued. See also Cody (1987).

3. See the description, for example, offered by the minister of defense to American embassy officials and leaked by Wikileaks (2009).

4. The military has only rarely played a role in domestic policing. Exceptions include the 1978 and 1984 bread riots (Kamm 1984). In 2008, the military had been called in to provide reinforcement in the Gafsa region (BBC Monitoring Middle East 2008). See also Amnesty International (2009b).

5. On the coup-proofing tactic of building alternative security forces in the Interior Ministry to balance military influence, see Brooks (1998) and Quinlivan (1999).

6. The police numbered 40,000 under Bourguiba, according to Kallander (2011); see also Alexander (1997:36).

7. Many rank-and-file in the national police, by contrast, were poorly paid and equipped as employment in the police apparently doubled as a kind of jobs program under the regime (Kallander 2011; Amara 2011; Daragahi 2011).

8. Ben Ali did not leave Tunisia on January 14 with the expectation of being gone permanently (BBC Monitoring Middle East 2011).

9. On the importance of how military organizations understand their appropriate roles and missions in society and the state, see Taylor (2003) and Pion-Berlin, Grisham, and Esparza (2014).

10. On the importance of how militaries see and understand their appropriate roles and missions, see Taylor (2003).

11. Total FMF was $12 million in 2009 and $17 million in 2011. Tunisia relied on FMF to maintain its 1980s- and 1990s-era U.S. origin military equipment, which accounts for 70 percent of its total inventory. Since 1994 Tunisian has been one of the top twenty recipients of IMET, which was close to $2 million in 2011. The U.S.-Tunisian Joint Military Commission meets annually, and joint exercises are held regularly (Arieff 2011:24–25).

12. References to the apolitical nature of the Tunisian military are often used as a shorthand explanation for why the military acted as it did in January 2011. What precisely is captured by that concept, however, is rarely explored. For a discussion of events that underscores the military's role as power broker, see Amrani (2011), Murphy (2011), and Cockburn (2011).

13. There remains some ambiguity over what Ben Ali explicitly ordered the army chief of staff, General Ammar, to do and whether Ben Ali told him overtly to fire on protesters and if so the manner in which the orders were conveyed. A lengthy investigation by *Al-Arabiya* (2012) suggests that there was no such order, a position that is supported by solidly researched scholarship by Bou Nassif (2015) and Jebnoun (2014). Bou Nassif (2015) links the origins of the story that Ammar refused orders to fire to a Tunisian activist who was trying to split the military from Ben Ali. The fact remains that the military did not step up in defense of the regime and aid what was clearly a faltering, if not doomed, effort by the police to contain the protests. Regardless, whether or not Ben Ali explicitly ordered the use of force and whether the military simply refused to entertain the idea itself, it is clear that force was not used by the military in defense of the regime. There is no evidence that the army used live ammunition in cities where it was deployed; to the contrary, there were reports that soldiers were interposing themselves between police and protesters to try to protect the latter and calm the situation. See Kirkpatrick (2011a, 2011b, 2011c), International Crisis Group (2011c:11), and *Africa News* (2011).

14. Pachon (2014) has made the argument that the military was not asked to fire (or that there is some uncertainty about interactions between General Ammar and Ben Ali), observing that this meant that no "defection" from the regime occurred. But this

misses the point. It is essential to keep in mind the coercive foundation of an autocratic regime, in which armed forces are the protector of last resort—the ultimate enforcer and safeguard of the regime. Whatever the precise details and regardless of whether and how Ammar explicitly defied Ben Ali's order, by January 11 the situation had become dire. The regime's future was seriously in question. By deploying to the streets ostensibly to provide public order without protecting the regime (as would the militia and elements of the Presidential Guard in the aftermath of what appeared to be Ben Ali's temporary trip to Saudi Arabia), the military failed to fulfill its implicit mandate to protect the regime. The deeper and more important aspect is that the military defected.

15. According to the prime minister, the army was acting in accordance with the constitutional state of emergency declared on January 14 (BBC Monitoring Middle East 2011).

16. For an account of the affair, see Klaas (2013).

17. See BBC News (2002). There were also indications of growing tensions between the regime and military before the protests (Kallander 2011). There was evidence that Ammar was actually going to be replaced before the protests.

18. On the significance of a civilian defense minister, see Stepan (1988).

19. For details on the protests, see Amnesty International (2011) and Chomiak and Entellis (2011:13–15).

20. See the extensive exposé on these events in *Al-Arabiya* (2012).

21. On the DCAF's extensive efforts to support reform in Tunisia, see the website and the programming for Tunisia at dcaf-tunisie.org.

22. Goodman (2014). For fiscal year 2016, the United States planned to increase assistance threefold to nearly $100 million (Goodman 2015).

23. For popular criticism on the absence of reform, see, for example, Samti (2013) and Sahraouni (2013).

24. In addition to this incident, the release of a scandalous video was an effort to disgrace the minister of war in January 2012 (Tunisia-Live 2012).

25. See the polling data in Pew Global (2013).

26. This means that the military retains a significant stake in decisions by the civilian Ministry of Defense about resources and counterterrorism policy, since this affects the efficacy of its efforts to battle the militants.

27. This follows other similar sentences given to other bloggers and critics of the military. See Amnesty International (2015).

28. For details on these events, see the extensive report in *Al-Arabiya* (2012).

29. For details on these events, see the extensive report in *Al-Arabiya* (2012).

30. On the importance of a military's organizational culture and unique conception of its roles and missions, see Taylor (2003); Pion-Berlin, Grisham, and Esparza (2014); Kier (1997); Farrell (2005); and Feaver (1999).

31. For a summary of the debate about professionalism and its implications, see the overview in Koonings and Kruijt (2002).

CHAPTER 11

Building an Army to Build the State? The Challenge of Building Security Institutions in Post-Qaddafi Libya

Virginie Collombier

In sharp contrast to the way the 2011 revolutions enfolded in Tunisia and Egypt, the elimination of Muammar Qaddafi in October of that same year was the result of an armed uprising and a subsequent civil war. In Libya, weapons proved to be the key to bringing about political change. The reorganization of the security sector and the building of national security institutions therefore emerged as crucial political issues after the demise of the leader of the Jamahiriya.

For most Libyans, rebuilding the national army and police has been considered the cornerstone of any effort to construct a new state and establish the rule of law. Two major efforts were to be engaged in parallel: Libya's conventional forces had to be rebuilt, and the multitude of disparate brigades operating autonomously throughout the country had to be brought under the control of the central government and fully integrated into the formal security apparatus or completely dissolved and disarmed. Yet the fragmentation of the security landscape has rapidly come to mirror the security arrangements that existed during the Qaddafi era. The major difference is that there are no longer any central authorities with sufficient capacity and legitimacy to exercise control over these disparate forces.

Out of the War: A Fragmented
Security Landscape

The proliferation of militias in post-Qaddafi Libya has its roots in the means by which the Jamahiriya's leader was overthrown. The nonviolent protests that started on February 15, 2011, to contest the regime were organized on a city-by-city basis and took the form of a multiplicity of local uprisings. When the regime and its security forces attempted to crush the protests, the movement transformed into an armed insurrection that largely kept its distinct local dimensions. One or more military brigades formed at the city level, operating independently even when they professed formal allegiance to the National Transitional Council (NTC). In the territory over which the regime lost control, citizens formed autonomous transitional governing and military councils. The imposition of a no-fly zone in March 2011 enabled anti-Qaddafi cities located in regime-held territory to survive, even though they were isolated from other rebel structures. The brigades were first and foremost loyal to their respective cities rather than to the NTC. The result was a deeply fragmented security landscape consisting of loosely connected armed groups, each of which had developed "its own chain of command, military culture, and narrative of the revolution" (International Crisis Group 2011a).

The post-Qaddafi security landscape was characterized by a lack of trust and growing competition among the armed groups. The most prominent was the new National Army, headquartered in Benghazi and mainly composed of officers who had defected from the former National Army. Other northeastern brigades, mostly based in Benghazi, al-Bayda, and Darna, included the February 17th Brigade headed by Isma'il al-Sallabi, an Islamist commander close to the Muslim Brotherhood, as well as the Abu Slim Martyrs, Omar al-Mukhtar, and Obaida Ibn al-Jarah Brigades. Fighters from the Tripoli Military Council, headed by former Libyan Islamic Fighting Group member 'Abdul Hakim Belhaj, were mostly present in neighborhoods of the capital but with brigades also operating in the east, west, and south. The Western Military Council, whose leadership was dominated by former National Army officers from Zintan, gathered the military councils of approximately 140 localities in the western mountains. The Misrata Military Council, which had grown out of small cells set up by young civilians in that city, was made up of 100 different units in October 2011.

The Challenge of Unifying and Controlling:
A Battle of Legitimacies

After proclaiming the liberation of the country, the NTC claimed to embody the new central authority. It attempted to bring the numerous political and military entities that had emerged amid the uprising under its leadership. Yet it was faced with strong resistance on the part of the irregular militias. Tensions came to the fore between rebels who had been powerless or persecuted under the former regime and former members of the armed forces who looked back on long military careers under Qaddafi. On July 28, 2011, this had already been illustrated by the assassination of the commander in chief of the new National Army, 'Abdul-Fatah Younis, apparently by members of an Islamist revolutionary brigade.

Many of the brigades that had joined the NTC umbrella had considered this to be a temporary arrangement. They could be credited for their military successes and the heavy price they had paid, while the NTC's core was made of former regime officials and longtime reformers, whose legitimacy could easily be challenged. NTC leader Mahmud Jibril, himself a former regime official tied to the reform efforts undertaken by Saif al-Islam Qaddafi, lacked the revolutionary legitimacy enjoyed by most of the rebel commanders.

This rift was superimposed over regional divisions, with the NTC being suspected of an eastern bias, along with divergent views about the role of religion in politics. Competing narratives of legitimacy therefore started clashing with each other, with some groups claiming to represent the revolution's values better than others. Civilian-led brigades refused to obey orders by senior officers who had defected from the former National Army, and young people demanded promotion to the detriment of holdovers of the former regime.

When the time came to form a transitional government, the brigades emerged as a significant political force. The most powerful groups requested substantial compensation in exchange for their "submission" to the NTC, as was shown during the negotiations for the formation of a transitional government under the leadership of 'Abdulrahim al-Keib in November 2011. Zintani and Misratan militias agreed to support the new cabinet only in exchange for large concessions: Zintan was awarded the defense ministry (to Osama al-Jwaili), and Misrata was awarded the interior ministry (to Fawzi 'Abdul'Aal). Similarly, the nomination of a chief of staff turned into a battle between the NTC, the militias, and former military commanders.

Even though he was eventually nominated for the position in January 2012, Yusuf al-Mangush was still rejected by many because he had served as a colonel in the National Army.

The top priority of the al-Keib government, which took office in November 2011, was to restore security in the country. This was seen as the indispensable condition to the building of new state institutions. However, the weakness of the formal security institutions hampered the centralization of security operations, even in Tripoli. The conventional army, which had been significantly weakened and marginalized under Qaddafi, was to be rebuilt—almost from scratch. Many of those within its ranks who opposed the Jamahiriya leader had melted away at the beginning of the uprising, while those who supported him fought until the end and consequently could not participate in the new structures. Moreover, the components of the armed forces that had defected in early 2011 had remained stuck on the eastern front[1] and had not taken part in battles elsewhere in the country. They were perceived as an eastern more than a national force and were not trusted by most of the civilian brigades, who considered them opportunistic.

Against this background, the rebel brigades were quick to fill the vacuum, as the transitional government had no choice but to rely on them to secure the cities and borders. Nevertheless, the militias that were still in the streets in early 2012 were not the ones that had fought the war. While some brigade elements that had assumed the brunt of the fighting against Qaddafi's forces were not ready to leave the ground before a new constitution was drafted for fear that their struggle would have been in vain, many civilians who had taken up arms against Qaddafi went back to their former lives after October 2011. At the same time, many jobless youths, but also adventurers and criminals, realized the many advantages that brigade membership could offer.[2] They thus joined existing groups or took part in the formation of hundreds of new military groups after the death of Qaddafi.

Powerful factions tried to take advantage of the inherent weakness of the transitional government to consolidate their positions within the nascent central institutions. Defense Minister al-Jwaili, for instance, gave preferential treatment to the Zintani brigades, such as al-Q'aq'a, al-Sawa'iq, and al-Madani, by granting their members priority in training abroad and access to equipment. He also ensured that these units were placed directly under his command and not under that of Chief of Staff al-Mangush. Similarly, control over the Supreme Security Committee (SSC) became a major challenge. Created by the NTC in October 2011, the SSC was intended as a temporary structure, tasked with providing security in the capital as well as protecting state and private property and embassies. Revolutionary fighters were hired as the initial personnel in an attempt to absorb them into the national security forces. While the NTC passed a law to dissolve the body as early as December 2011, this piece of legislation was ignored.

After the formation of the transitional government, the SSC was transferred administratively and financially to the Ministry of the Interior and was then restructured and authorized to open branches in other cities. As Interior Minister 'Abdul'Aal attempted to bring the body under his control, brigades were allowed to join wholesale under their previous leadership and were paid generous salaries.[3] As a result, while they were supposed to operate under the control of the Interior Ministry, the brigades remained largely autonomous, and their membership swelled: in October 2012, the SSC was estimated to have over 100,000 members, more than all the people who had fought with the revolutionaries during the uprising (El Mayet 2012).

A comparable experience happened with the creation of the Libyan Shield Force (LSF) by Chief of Staff al-Mangush in 2012. Originally, the LSF was set up as a temporary structure for integrating former rebel fighters into a cohesive national force, with members nominally paid and placed under the authority of the Defense Ministry. In reality, however, the LSF looked more like a bottom-up initiative by the brigade commanders themselves, most notably the Islamists from Misrata and the east, who intended to resist the incorporation of their members into the official army or police (Wehrey 2012). Much like the SSC, the LSF actually operated with a high degree of autonomy.

A Replica of Qaddafi's Militia State?

In 2012, most of the major brigades were incorporated into two umbrella coalitions, the SSC and LSF, and formally brought under government control. Their members had been given official titles and received government salaries in exchange for guarding government property or acting as temporary police forces to deal with local conflicts. In reality, however, efforts to build a national army and police force had failed. The fragmentation of the security landscape instead mirrored the security arrangements that had existed under Qaddafi.

When he came to power in 1969, Colonel Qaddafi was quick to isolate and marginalize the regular armed forces, the institution that had been the source of his power and out of which competitors could emerge. The army, denounced as a corrupt institution that could not be entrusted with the mission of protecting the revolution, was counterbalanced by the creation of a new informal security apparatus, which operated in parallel with the conventional institutions. Structures such as the Revolutionary Guard (charged with protecting the regime), the Jamahiriya Guard (responsible for protecting the leader and his family), the Islamic Legion, and the 32th Brigade (led by Khamis Qaddafi) were actually in charge of all security operations. As a result, even though the National Army was estimated at around 76,000 troops on the eve of the uprising (Cordesman and Nerguizian 2010; Haddad 2012), it was very weak in terms of equipment and training and was marginalized in the face of the plurality of paramilitary forces tasked with domestic surveillance and repression.[4]

Under Qaddafi, though, the center enjoyed the strength to exert domination over the fragmented security landscape. While some argue that the emergence of a strong center after 2011 was deliberately prevented by certain political forces, in particular the Islamists,[5] a major impediment to the effort to build strong national security institutions was the legitimacy deficit of the transitional authorities and the minimal amount of trust that they inspired among many of those who had fought against the old regime.

The General National Congress and the Limits of Electoral Legitimacy

The first legislative elections in July 2012 might have remedied this situation by entrusting the elected General National Council (GNC) with the required authority to initiate a serious security restructuring. But instead of contributing to the legitimacy of the new political leadership and providing it with the authority to rule, the elections deepened the rifts among competing factions. In particular, polarization widened between those who claimed to embody the "real values" of the revolution and those they considered to be opportunists and remnants of the former regime, even if they had defected and joined the revolution early on. Ideological and regional conflicts constituted additional divisive factors, as did a persistent rift between those who considered themselves the victors of the war (i.e., the revolutionary camp) and those considered as the defeated (i.e., the supporters of the former regime).

While the elections drew a large number of voters, they put in parliament factions that had little if any trust in one another. Their primary objective

quickly became the consolidation of their own positions within the nascent
state apparatus rather than the building and consolidating of the state. Outside parliament, armed militias continued to consider themselves to be more
legitimate than any other political actor and therefore empowered to act to
safeguard the revolution if necessary. With the passage of time, some of them
started to exchange favors with parties in the GNC. Moreover, events during
the autumn of 2012 signaled that weapons had entered the political arena.

On September 25, 2012, fighters from Misrata accused local leaders of
the city of Bani Walid of protecting individuals who had been responsible
for the death of Omran Sha'ban, a former Misratan rebel credited with cap-
turing Qaddafi. They vowed to purge the city—considered a pro-Qaddafi
stronghold—of remnants of the former regime if those responsible for this
crime were not immediately handed over. The GNC supported the fighters'
demands and issued GNC Decree 7/2012, which authorized the use of force
by the Defense Ministry and the Interior Ministry. Misratan fighters from
the LSF subsequently imposed a three-week siege on Bani Walid, and talks
between tribal elders and GNC president Muhammad Magarief collapsed.
While the Bani Walid elders refused to hand over their men to what they
considered lawless militias, they did eventually agree to allow the army to
enter the city and to hand over the individuals for whom an official arrest
warrant would be presented. Misratan authorities rejected this proposal,
and on October 17–24 the LSF launched a full-scale military operation, with
army backing, that left around fifty dead, injured dozens, and inflicted heavy
damage on Bani Walid.

This episode, commonly called "the second war" by residents of Bani
Walid, had tremendous impact on popular perception of the state authorities
and of the GNC in particular, especially among the Warfalla, estimated to
be Libya's largest tribe.[6] The bulk of the forces that led the assault on Bani
Walid came from Misrata, a city considered to be one of the spearheads of the
revolution but also a locality with a long history of rivalry with Bani Walid.
The GNC's Decree No. 7 was therefore perceived as the national authorities
taking sides with Misratans against Walidis in a tribal feud but also, and more
crucially, as the new National Army backing and supporting rogue militias
affiliated with one particular political force instead of fulfilling its mission of
ensuring the security of all Libyans.[7] These events echoed other episodes of
conflict and revenge between tribes or cities in which the national authorities' behavior was considered not consistent with the rule of law.[8] Such
events constituted a serious blow to the central authorities' legitimacy in Bani

Walid, which organized itself around its own local institutions, mainly the Social Council of the Warfalla Tribes and to a lesser extent the Local Council appointed by the GNC.

Meanwhile, prolonged negotiations over the composition of the new government in Tripoli[9] signaled that militiamen were not ready to allow politicians to take sole responsibility for the transition. On October 4, 2012, parliamentary proceedings were interrupted by militiamen from al-Zawiya, a city located about forty-five kilometers west of Tripoli, protesting the council of ministers that had been proposed by Prime Minister Mustafa Abushagur. They demanded that Abushagur be dismissed and his government rejected, complaining that al-Zawiya had not been adequately represented. Abushagur eventually withdrew his entire cabinet list, and the government formation process started again from scratch. On October 30, 2012, the GNC hall was stormed, and the proceedings were disrupted once again during the voting to approve 'Ali Zaidan's government. Dozens of militiamen, this time from Tripoli, complained that their region was underrepresented in the new government. While Zaidan's cabinet was eventually sworn in on November 14, 2012, the nomination of some ministers continued to be opposed by politicians who complained that they did not "meet the standards of integrity and patriotism" due to their collaboration with the Qaddafi regime.

Weapons in Politics as a Way to "Resolve" Unaddressed Issues

The transitional authorities were also handicapped in their action by conflict that remained unresolved or improperly addressed. The issue of how to deal with both the legacy of the Qaddafi era and the effects of the civil war came to constitute serious impediments to the building of national security institutions. Judging the action of the transitional authorities to be insufficient, militias and political factions alike started to take matters into their own hands.

Public pressure was particularly heavy to prevent the return of the remnants of the former regime, commonly called *azlam*. Yet because of the collapse of the judicial system, the transitional authorities were forced to resort to alternative ways to deal with the crimes committed under Qaddafi. The NTC at first attempted to bar former functionaries from politics, administration, and the public sector by defining a series of criteria that public officials were required to fulfill. In April 2012, the Supreme Authority for the Implementation of the

Criteria of Integrity and Patriotism, commonly called the Integrity Commission, was established and called upon to rule on the nominations of all new ministers, ambassadors, and high civil servants. In parallel, the first law concerning transitional justice was adopted by the NTC in February 2012, and the Commission for Truth and Reconciliation was appointed in May 2012.

When a revised version of the transitional justice law was submitted to the GNC for ratification, members could not agree on the new text, notably because of major disagreements regarding the question of whether the law should cover crimes committed by the Qaddafi regime up until 2011—as the revolutionary camp was demanding—or those perpetrated by all parties until the end of the transitional period. Lack of trust in the justice system and the police led militias to proclaim themselves defenders of the people's quest for justice, and radical forces started to deal with the situation by themselves. In Benghazi and Darna in particular, dozens of former members of the domestic intelligence service and Revolutionary Committees were killed in what could be interpreted as a response to inadequate action against former regime elements on the part of the transitional authorities (Gall 2014a).

The aim of "protecting the revolution" and preventing the return of former regime remnants was also accorded to a strategy of exclusion and elimination of potential opponents to the new political institutions. The conflict that emerged between Prime Minister Zaidan and GNC president Magarief over key nominations in late 2012[10] mirrored the battle between competing factions within the new state institutions (Mezran and Knecht 2013). Moreover, the resulting power vacuum provided room for a wide range of actors to assert their positions in the new state apparatus, at times through exclusion of their competitors by force. This was illustrated by the conditions under which the Political Isolation Law (PIL) was adopted on May 5, 2013, after months of deliberation. While there was widespread public support for the exclusion of anyone who had worked alongside Qaddafi, heavy pressure was put on GNC members by SSC and LSF elements to influence their decision. On April 30, 2013, parliamentary debates had to be suspended when demonstrators supporting the law barged into the GNC hall (Khan 2013). During the following days, militiamen—reportedly mostly from Misrata—blockaded and attacked government ministries, provoking sharp criticism throughout the country against what was seen as subversion of the democratic process through outright intimidation.

The result was a law that was considered by many analysts to be far too vague, as it potentially barred anyone who had ever worked with the authorities during the four decades of Qaddafi's rule.[11] Yet this proved to be a winning tactic for those who wanted to exclude opponents from the new state's institutions, including positions of power in the new National Army. Despite the adoption of the PIL, militiamen refused to end their siege of government ministries and demanded the resignation of Prime Minister Zaidan. On May 28, 2013, GNC president Magarief announced his resignation, anticipating that he may have to leave his position by virtue of the new PIL. Militias—especially those funded, trained, and armed by the Islamists—now became aware that they had the power to influence the political process. This realization paved the way for further use of force to manipulate the mechanisms of government for political gain, and all camps started to resort to such tactics.

Further Fragmentation of Central Power Encouraged by Political Leaders

Despite renewed protests in Tripoli demanding the departure of the militias and "illegitimate brigades," the creation of a national army and police, and the election of Nuri Abusahmain as the new GNC president in June 2013, no significant change took place in the way the transitional authorities handled the militia issue and the security situation in general. Several international plans to train reconfigured Libyan security forces got under way, but they would take time and suffered various loopholes (Fetouri 2013; Pack, Mezran, and Eljarh 2014:51–52). Moreover, they did not address the underlying political causes of security-sector fragmentation. The formulation and implementation of disarmament and demobilization plans, in particular, were rendered complicated by the pervasive mistrust and hostility that existed between militia members and elements of the former National Army.

Confronted with growing insecurity and violence as targeted killings and bombings multiplied, Prime Minister Zaidan and GNC president Abusahmain proved incapable of agreeing on a common strategy. On the contrary, deepening conflict among rival factions inside the GNC as well as between the GNC and the government resulted in the continuation of a strategy of appeasement toward the militias. This contributed to the further empowerment of the latter, along with a deeper penetration of state institutions by militia-political alliances.

Almost as soon as he assumed his position as the new GNC president, Nuri Abusahmain established the Libyan Revolutionary Operations Room

(LROR), an umbrella grouping for Islamists and Misratan-dominated militias that was formally placed under the authority of the Ministry of Defense. Significant funding was allocated to the LROR,[12] which was entrusted with securing the streets of Tripoli starting in July 2013. Yet the impartiality and motivations of Abusahmain were soon questioned following the alleged involvement of LROR members in the kidnapping of Prime Minister Zaidan on October 4, 2013. The creation of this new security structure was seen as an attempt to counter the influence of Zintani militias in Tripoli and in particular the al-Q'aq'a brigade, known for its links with Mahmud Jibril's National Forces Alliance (NFA). Moreover, multiple militias continued to operate out of the state institutions and took part in the increasingly tense competition for power between the two main political blocs. The Misratan brigades, the February 17th Martyrs Brigade, the Rafallah al-Sahati Brigade, and Ansar al-Shari'ah could be found on the side of the Muslim Brotherhood, while the Zintan Revolutionary Council, the al-Q'aq'a Brigade, and the al-Sawa'iq Brigade aligned with the NFA.[13]

At the end of 2013, despite the central authorities' efforts to centralize the security sector and exert control over the multiplicity of militias operating in the country, the power of the so-called authorized militias (SSC, LSF, LROR, Petroleum Facilities Guard, al-Sa'iqah Forces) had actually increased. The new National Army and police, by contrast, were much weaker in terms of personnel, equipment, and funding and exercised no actual control over the various bodies they were supposed to oversee. The links between the authorized militias and civilian political forces had deepened, as it became clear that weapons could be more efficient instruments than the democratic process to achieve political objectives. A de facto alliance had also emerged between the authorized and nonauthorized brigades. Those having an Islamist bent, in particular, refused to fight against their unauthorized counterparts, most notably the radical Ansar al-Shari'ah, on the pretext that the latter consisted of "genuine revolutionaries" who had fought against Qaddafi.

Continuing Defiance of the Central Authorities at the Local Level

Even in cities where the security situation was considered good, such as Misrata, Zintan, Zuwara, and Bani Walid, the persistent lack of trust in the central authorities led to the prevalence of local security arrangements.

While this was partly the result of the localized character of the insurrection, the transitional authorities who assumed power at the center found themselves incapable of restoring control over these territories. In Misrata, for instance, three years after the war the security infrastructure still depended entirely on the cluster of revolutionary brigades that had defended the city during the bloody siege that occurred in the spring of 2011. Traumatized by this experience, Misratans refused to accept any security institution staffed by people who might have served the former regime. Local militiamen still restrict access to the city.[14] Despite the large number of armed groups based in different neighborhoods, residents consider the mechanisms of coordination established by the Local Council and the Military Council as making their city safe.[15]

Continuing defiance against national conventional forces nevertheless constitutes a serious challenge to the central authorities. In November 2013 after renewed clashes between brigades from Suq al-Jum'a in eastern Tripoli and Misrata, thousands of protesters marched toward the headquarters of the Gharghur-based Misratan militias, demanding that all of the armed groups should be disbanded and that the national security forces should take their place. Forty-seven people were killed as militiamen opened fire on the march with heavy machine guns and rocket-propelled grenades in what has come to be known as the Gharghur Incident. In the aftermath of this event and the ensuing public outcry, Misratan militias found themselves under heavy public pressure to leave Tripoli. Yet it was only after Misrata's Local Council intervened that the Misratan militias agreed to exit the city (British Broadcasting Corporation 2013).

In Bani Walid, similarly, the National Army departed in 2011 and has not returned. Even though many former military officers originate from the city and still live there, they consider the new security apparatus to be a factional organization (Collombier 2014). Tribal elders refused to let militias enter the city during the war and assumed sole responsibility for organizing security in coordination with the Local Council. The new local police force is staffed with almost the same personnel as under Qaddafi. It is now said to include both supporters and opponents of the former regime from the city, which residents explain as a consequence of Decree 7/2012. While security has deteriorated overall in Libya since 2011, Bani Walid is regarded as one of the safest locales in the country.[16] The situation, however, remains outside the control of the central authorities.

Derailment of the Transition Process

Militarization of political infighting reached new levels as the transition went off track in February 2014 with the GNC's decision to extend its term for another six months.[17] This decision, which was widely perceived as a dangerous slip away from the transition framework, provoked an outcry among the militia-political factions that were aligned with the NFA as well as from the general public. It also precipitated two events that signaled that all political factions were now ready to use weapons to support their claims. On February 14, former major general Khalifa Hiftar intervened in the name of "the Libyan National Army" ("the army of the people, guardian of the nation"), calling for the GNC and the government to be dissolved and a new road map for the post-Qaddafi transition to be established. The event highlighted the deepening polarization that was occurring in the country along fault lines that were essentially political and increasingly pitted competing armed forces against one another. This trend was confirmed on February 18 when the Zintani al-Q'aq'a and al-Sawa'iq Brigades issued an ultimatum to GNC members to resign or be arrested.

Meanwhile, developments in the eastern region underlined the importance of the new militia-political alliances throughout Libya. Over the course of 2013, employees of border security and units of the Petroleum Facilities Guard (PFG), which had been set up in 2012 to protect Libya's oil installations,[18] had initiated a large-scale blockage of oil fields and ports. PFG leader Ibrahim Jadhran, a former rebel who had fought against Qaddafi, allied himself with the federalist movement, accused the central government of corruption with regard to oil sales, and demanded that the east be given a larger cut of the revenues. The blockage of oil export terminals culminated in March 2014 with the eastern rebels' attempt to export crude oil illegally from one of the terminals under their control. The central authorities proved incapable of restoring control over the situation, and on March 11, 2014, Prime Minister Zaidan resigned after a no-confidence vote by the GNC. This action paved the way for an escalation of the dispute among competing factions within the GNC, with active support from armed groups outside the assembly.

As the parliament swore in interim defense minister 'Abdullah al-Thinni as acting prime minister, intense jostling broke out between deputies associated with the Muslim Brotherhood and the alliance that opposed the Muslim Brotherhood. Al-Thinni himself resigned two weeks after taking the position, citing threats by a militia against his family. On May 4 after a chaotic voting session in the GNC, Ahmed Maitiq, a Misratan businessman with Islamist leanings, was announced as the new prime minister. However, the legality of the vote was immediately contested by the first Deputy Speaker of the parliament. When al-Thinni responded that he would remain in his position until a new prime minister could be elected, the country found itself torn apart between two competing cabinets. Meanwhile, Benghazi was hit by a wave of violence, which the government blamed on Ansar al-Shariʻah.

It was against this background that Hiftar on May 16, 2014, launched Operation Dignity, a broad air and ground offensive against Islamist militias in Benghazi.[19] The operation, conducted by army units based in the east, tribal militias, and forces loyal to Jadhran's eastern federalist forces, was initiated in complete disregard of the central authorities and national military command structure based in Tripoli. Hiftar and his followers, who justified their move by citing the necessity to restore security in the eastern region and get rid of all of the Islamist militias responsible for violence and terror, were quick to portray themselves as the sole legitimate "Libyan National Army." By making this claim, they surfed on the widespread popular sentiment that a strong national army was needed and that the political leadership had failed to take the most pressing steps toward building a new Libyan state. A few days later, a group of militias affiliated with Zintan launched an assault against the GNC, thereby preventing a vote on the formation of the government led by Ahmed Maitiq. Colonel Mukhtar Firnana, a former military police officer from Zintan, read a statement on behalf of the "Libyan National Army" in which he called for the GNC to disband and hand over power to the Constitutional Committee that had been elected in February 2014.

Although it attempted to present itself as the truly national force that Libyans had been demanding, the coalition that formed around Hiftar highlighted once again the major fault line of the political transition. Operation Dignity gathered members of the former and current National Army, tribal leaders from the east and the south, and Zintani militias as well as the eastern federalist movement. It was yet another attempt by groups that felt marginalized to reverse the political balance and eliminate their rivals. The main feature of this enterprise, through which the militarization of political infighting reached a new climax, was that it played on the demand for a strong national army that was widespread in the Libyan public. Yet instead of attempting to bridge the gap between rival factions and bringing the various components together around trusted central authorities, the operation looked like just another attempt to seize control of the state and enforce a definition of the new political framework that would be favorable to its members, to the detriment of their adversaries.

Conclusion

Contrary to the widespread idea that in contemporary Libya there is little sense of national identity in addition to a deep resistance to the concept of a state, the citizenry has expressed a strong demand for an institutional order that can unite the country and establish the rule of law. To this end, the consolidation of strong security institutions—first and foremost a new national army—is key. In the context of a wide dissemination of weapons after 2011, however, the transitional authorities in Tripoli have failed to accumulate sufficient legitimacy to assert control over the multiple armed groups that were born during the war. As the authorities tried to buy off the militias in order to ensure short-term stability, they ended up empowering those with arms and sent a message that violence could be more effective than formal politics as a means for achieving one's ends.

While Libya remains in need of strong security institutions that might support the structure of a reconfigured state, the primary challenge continues to be political. After decades of repression followed by a chaotic civil war, political competition has been undertaken without a minimal level of trust having been reached among key actors and without a serious effort to engender confidence in the central authorities. The result has been a pronounced militarization of political infighting along with further delay in the emergence of a stable post-Qaddafi order.

Notes

1. The Qaddafi regime confined the National Army to operations in the eastern region. Security in the west was handled by the 32nd Brigade, led by Khamis Qaddafi, which was considered more loyal.

2. The mere fact of leading a brigade allowed them access to cars, money, and influence.

3. The pay for fighters who joined an SSC-incorporated brigade was higher than what most Libyans could hope to make in any other job or in the conventional security forces.

4. Such organization was also characteristic of the security forces before 1969 under King Idriss. The Cyrenaican Defense Force (Cydef), in particular, was a paramilitary

force that was better equipped than the regular army, whose personnel were recruited among tribes considered loyal to the regime.

5. They notably use the assassination of NTC commander in chief 'Abdul Fatah Younis under unclear circumstances in July 2011 to support their claim.

6. Bani Walid is the home to the Warfalla tribe. The city is connected by way of tribal relations to the cities of Sirte on the Mediterranean coast and Sebha, capital of the southwest region.

7. These were arguments developed at length by the residents of Bani Walid in conversations with the author during two visits to the city in early 2014.

8. This was notably reminiscent of the case of Tawergha, a city from which Misratan forces drove out the 30,000 inhabitants in what was described by human rights groups as an act of revenge and collective punishment.

9. Almost three months after the July 7th GNC elections, Libya was still without a government.

10. The August 2011 Provisional Constitutional Charter that was supposed to govern the transitional process quickly appeared vague and insufficient, especially on the distribution of competences among different political bodies.

11. Moreover, on April 9, 2013, the GNC approved an amendment to the Provisional Constitutional Declaration that excluded any possibility of judicial review of the PIL, once it passed. This eliminated the possibility that the Supreme Court could strike the law down.

12. In their report, Pack, Mezran, and Eljarh (2014:47) mention LD900 million, that is, more than $700 million.

13. For a review of the various militia groups operating in Libya as of early 2014, see British Broadcasting Corporation (2014) and Pack, Mezran, and Eljarh (2014).

14. Author's observations in Misrata, December 2013 and February 2014.

15. This assessment should be investigated more thoroughly. A better understanding of the mechanisms of coordination and control of the armed brigades is needed. Analysis of the relationships between militia leaders and local businessmen would be particularly relevant.

16. This was confirmed by the author's personal observations in Bani Walid, February and April 2014.

17. The GNC was elected in July 2012 for an eighteen-month term to supervise the drafting of a new constitution and organize general elections. Its mandate expired on February 7, 2014, without this mission being fulfilled. In this context, many Libyans opposed the GNC's decision to extend its mandate and called for the election of a new representative body.

18. The PFG officially comes under the oil ministry but is funded by the Defense Ministry. For more details, see British Broadcasting Corporation (2013).

19. The operation began with attacks in Benghazi against units of the February 17th Martyrs Brigade, the Libya Shield No. 1 Brigade, and Ansar al-Shari'ah.

CHAPTER 12

Military Prestige, Defense-Industrial Production, and the Rise of Gulf Military Activism

Shana Marshall

Although contemporary studies of civil-military relations in the Middle East tend to overlook the Gulf Arab states,[1] where the armed forces have been politically marginal and operationally weak, Saudi Arabia and the United Arab Emirates (UAE) are taking steps to strengthen the capabilities and institutional prestige of their armed forces. These efforts include significant support for the domestic production of defense material, a shift toward investment in troop training and institutional infrastructure (as opposed to hardware and equipment procurement), and efforts to build prestige and foster a more coherent institutional identity for the armed forces.

When significant material and political resources are redirected to an institution that has traditionally been marginal, we can reasonably expect a concomitant shift in the power and influence of that institution within the structure of the state. This alone makes an examination of these cases worthwhile. However, these militaries have also been involved in serious sustained combat in recent years—a major departure from the past. It may therefore be useful to examine these factors in the context of one another, asking what is the relationship between increased military deployments, increased state support for domestic military-industrial production, and state-led efforts to enhance the prestige and institutional identity of the armed forces.

Many of the authors in this volume examine how the provision of various forms of state support to the armed forces make them more or less likely to support an incumbent regime facing serious opposition. The regional cases we use to examine such questions are typically those whose militaries have large footprints in the domestic economy—countries such as Algeria, Egypt, and Syria. In such cases, the military was typically an integral player during the period of state formation and subsequently to the consolidation of postcolonial regimes. The participation of such militaries in industry and commerce often began with the production of defense material—mostly small arms and ammunition assembled with foreign assistance—but eventually grew to include a range of activities across several sectors, from agriculture and public infrastructure to automobiles and consumer electronics. These militaries also tend to loom large in the histories of regional conflict, participating directly in wars and occupations.

This question is important, because a military with a significant stake in domestic economic activity is more likely to wield influence in domestic politics and elite decision making. The claim is intuitive—and is (or was) an empirical reality for many militaries in developing country, including Egypt, Jordan, Turkey, Indonesia, Pakistan, China, and elsewhere. Theoretical insights from civil-military relations literature tells us that the armed forces often possess this economic stake because incumbent regimes bestow upon them economic privileges and subsidies as part of a coup-proofing strategy. This is done either to encourage the military to remain outside of politics (by buying them off) or to foster cleavages within the military that weaken its ability to act cohesively and decisively against the regime (by using patronage to drive a wedge between the various service units).

Such patronage strategies are designed to redirect the energies of an already large and influential military away from thoughts of political intervention and toward commercial activity. But in Saudi Arabia and the UAE, where the military has traditionally been weak and politically marginal, will support for domestic military industrial production and efforts to enhance institutional prestige promote a more influential and interventionist military? To understand how this might occur, we must examine how political and economic influence might be enhanced through domestic military industrial production, increased military capacity and deployment, and state support for institution building and status within the armed forces.

There are many avenues through which defense industrial production can translate into a nascent military economy. States with military-industrial sectors are more likely to have related infrastructure, from testing facilities and simulation equipment to high-security warehouses, much of which may be maintained or operated by active-duty or retired soldiers. Similarly, officers in such states are more likely to be involved in activities such as export marketing, consulting, and subcontracting, which can form the foundation of a so-called officer economy. Enterprises funded through and/or operated by the armed forces may likewise be used to finance the pension funds and social clubs that form an important part of the military-business landscape in the broader Middle East and elsewhere in the Global South. Additionally, serious regime efforts to increase the prestige of a military career, reduce reliance on foreign-born soldiers, and provide the industrial and regulatory architecture needed to link domestic businessmen to new defense enterprises suggest that we can learn much from examining the cases of Saudi Arabia and the UAE.

Historically Marginal Militaries of the Persian Gulf Region

Many Middle East militaries, such as those of Egypt, Iran, and Algeria, have been central players in the major events shaping their national histories, from violent regime changes (coups d'état) to comprehensive modernization platforms (ISIL [Islamic State] and military-driven industrialization) and the management of extensive state programs of surveillance and repression that contributed to decades of regime stability. However, neither the period of state formation nor subsequent phases of economic and political development presented favorable conditions for an influential military or a nascent defense-industrial capacity in the Persian Gulf region, where sparse populations, bountiful oil revenues, and de-industrialization policies supported by Western patron states mitigated against an industrial state-building role for the army. The result was small apolitical militaries, often composed of minorities, foreigners, or mercenaries, whose commanders were content to rely on off-the-shelf foreign weapons systems and Western security guarantees.

Countries with sophisticated defense industrial sectors typically also possess an influential defense establishment heavily staffed by military elites. But the absence of a politically influential class of men in uniform has long been a primary distinction that sets the oil-rich states of the region apart from their more populous resource-poor neighbors. The armed forces of all the Gulf Arab states have historically been weak political actors, with large segments staffed by third-country nationals or marginalized minority groups.[2] In Saudi Arabia, Pakistani military personnel were employed to build and fly jets for the Royal Saudi Air Force beginning in the 1960s, and some 15,000 troops were stationed there in the years before the Persian Gulf War (Riedel 2008).[3] It was also to Islamabad that the Saudis turned for assistance in their repeated offensives against the Houthi rebels in Yemen.

In the mid-1980s, Omanis made up an estimated 85 percent of the UAE's enlisted ranks, with key staff positions occupied by Jordanians (Middle East Research Institute 1985:7). Twenty years later about 30 percent of the UAE's 50,000 active-duty troops were still expatriates (Cordesman and Al-Rodhan 2006:285), and just a few years ago the UAE added several hundred elite Colombian soldiers to its payroll.

However, these foreign-born troops are giving way to conscription policies meant to more fully staff the military with national citizens. Kuwait, Qatar, and the UAE have all enacted conscription laws. In the UAE, the new conscription law gives those individuals who complete their national service priority in job placements, promotions, access to loans for marriage and the purchase of land, and funding for their continued education (Salem 2014). Salaries and allowances are generous enough (and the definition of those eligible to be conscripted broad enough) to bring in potentially skilled workers who might be integrated into military-industrial projects such as the UAV Research & Technology Centre operated by the UAE Air Force. Equally important, conscript salaries and allowances are funded through the budget of the armed forces, which is significant because it links the recruitment policy itself—and therefore also the training and performance of conscripts— directly to armed forces personnel. The allocation of funds to military projects and initiatives through the formal military budget (rather than other ministerial budgets) signals the transfer of at least some control to military decision makers.

The Changing Nature of Persian Gulf Region Militaries

One of the starkest changes in regional military dynamics is that the Saudi and UAE militaries are playing a direct role in regional military actions. Forty years ago, the UAE armed forces consisted of roughly 10,000 troops whom analysts claimed "could not hope to offer more than a very brief resistance" to any regional aggression (Middle East Research Institute 1985:23). Today, American military generals refer to the UAE as "Little Sparta." Most notable is the UAE Air Force's strikes against ISIL targets in Iraq and Syria in the fall of 2014, against Islamist rebel targets in Libya in August 2014, and as part of a joint force with Saudi Arabia deployed against antigovernment protestors in Bahrain in 2011. In 2014, Saudi Arabia deployed tens of thousands of troops to its 850-kilometer border with Iraq to counter threats from the Sunni militant group ISIL and participated in an air campaign against ISIL targets in Syria (Arab News 2014). Although the Saudi campaign against the Houthis in Yemen was responsible for large numbers of civilian casualties, it was better-coordinated than previous Saudi-led offensives in which soldiers were forced to fall back and evacuate entire towns (Trofimov 2015).

Such deployments are striking for a region whose well-supplied and well-trained forces have remained largely on the sidelines. Although the UAE military has in fact been deployed previously—to protect critical logistics routes in support of the United States in Afghanistan, airlift wounded civilians in Bosnia as a part of peacekeeping forces in the Horn of Africa and the Balkans, and protect shipping traffic from piracy—the Libya event was a watershed moment (Davidson 2013:86). Not only was it an offensive action as opposed to a defensive action or a logistical support effort, it was also largely unilateral. In a region where even routine military exercises are coordinated with major Western coalitions, this is a huge shift.

Military Culture

Another visible change in the Arab Gulf States is the cultivation of a martial culture, including a brand of nationalist patriotism that foregrounds the armed forces. Saudi Arabia's recent—and largest ever—military parade is one example, as is the growing popularity of shooting clubs, mixed martial arts gyms, and jujitsu competitions in the UAE (Khaled 2014; Newbould 2014; Passela 2015).

Much as in the United States, cinemas in the UAE play armed forces promotional videos during the preview period. The videos, some of which are extremely well produced, highlight not only typical combat scenes of urban warfare, naval exercises, amphibious landings, and fighter jet acrobatics but also feature scenes of female medics, military marching bands, and tearful reunions between troops and family members.[4] Such imagery is meant to highlight the linkages that exist between the military and civilian society more broadly, a significant evolution for a region where soldiers have historically been recruited from groups identified explicitly for the lack of social and kinship connections that might complicate their allegiance to the ruling family. Many of these promotional videos are self-conscious in their juxtaposition of modern military warfare and traditional combat scenes, pairing images of a falcon and a fighter jet, a naval frigate and a traditional long boat, and men on horseback alongside tanks in the desert.[5] Similarly, the ubiquitous portraits of leaders adorning the rearview mirrors and windshields of taxis and personal cars in many regional capitals most often feature Abu Dhabi's crown prince Muhammad bin Zayed Al-Nahyan not wearing the traditional white dishdasha but instead in full military regalia.[6]

Arms trade exhibitions—which have become a sort of landmark for aspiring regional powers and a prime forum for enhancing interaction between foreign defense firms, domestic military-industrial producers, and military officers—are also increasingly common in Saudi Arabia and the UAE. The UAE hosts several such exhibitions, including Navdex (Naval Defense Exhibition), ISNR (International Exhibition for Security and National Resilience), the Dubai Air Show, the recently announced Umex (Unmanned Systems Exhibition and Conference), and the International Defense Exhibition and Conference (IDEX), which attracted over 1,100 vendors and some 80,000 visitors in 2013. Saudi Arabia hosted its first trade fair in February 2010, the Armed Forces Exhibition of Materials & Spare Parts. A handful of Saudi companies have also exhibited at these fairs,[7] including items under license that cannot be exported, suggesting that the display is largely for domestic political consumption. This includes the G36 assault rifle, which the German gun maker Heckler & Koch licensed to the state-owned Military Industries Corporation (MIC) on the condition that it not be exported (Overton 2014). Such performative events are an important avenue for enhancing military prestige. As UAE major general Mazrouei stated in reference to the UAE's many exhibitions,

> Our officers would meet with manufacturers and consumers and attend workshops and symposia where high caliber papers are presented. Exhibitions, moreover, offer representatives of top defense corporations a golden chance to exchange ideas and expertise under one roof and to close deals. (*Nation Shield* 2012)

Becoming a patron of other less professionalized and less capable militaries is also an important rite for an aspiring regional military power. To that end, the UAE has increased ties with the Somali Army through construction and training projects.

Increasing the Prestige of Military Careers

Another important element in enhancing military prestige and capacity is the shift in focus from investments in hardware and technology to investments in troop training and institutional infrastructure, especially simulation and training facilities.[8] The publicity and prestige generated by Jordan's special operations training center[9]—and the increasing demand for such facilities, where foreign militaries can send small delegations for specialized training in mock warfare simulations—have not gone unnoticed in the Persian Gulf region.

A number of such projects are currently under way in the UAE, notably the Jaheziya complex, a training facility set to open in 2017 that will provide purpose-built maritime, urban, industrial, and hazardous materials training zones for international military and police as well as private-sector personnel, and the Rabdan Academy, which offers academic and experiential training for Emirati personnel from defense and civil security agencies. The UAE aircraft maintenance company AMMROC (a joint venture with Lockheed Martin) is also set to expand to provide training for military aircrews and maintenance training for military engineers. Increasing demand inside the Persian Gulf region for equipment simulators and training facilities is of course linked to the increasing deployment of national militaries in the region. For decades, the number of complex weapons systems outstripped the number of national military service people trained and qualified to use them. Spending on training and simulations indicates that this imbalance is changing, and more resources are being invested in human capital within the armed forces.

In the UAE, leadership of the military has become a symbol of political power for senior princes in the Nahyan and Makhtoum ruling families (Young 2014:105). In Saudi Arabia, the fact that nonroyals have been implicated in bribery scandals related to the military may itself be a perverse indicator of the increasing social prestige of military positions. This is a significant departure in a region where the military has not traditionally been a channel for social mobility. As Steffen Hertog (2011:401) points out, "Archival records on the Saudi military in the 1960s and 1970s report low levels of motivation and training. . . . The officer corps' 'new middle class' ethos that led to successful military coups in other Arab countries seems not to have taken hold on the Arabian peninsula, where most commoner officers remain subordinate clients to individual princes." Although Saudi recruits did enjoy some perks—including free land, housing allowances, and interest-free loans for officers—there was little "prestige" associated with enlisting.

In the UAE, where the military is facing significant personnel short-ages,[10] the leadership is luring recruits with new training academies (includ-ing the National Defense College, established in 2013 in coordination with the United States National Defense University) and establishing other tra-ditional vestiges of military identity, including institutional journals (e.g., *Nation Shield*)[11] and strategic think tanks (such as the Institute for Near East and Gulf Military Analysis [INEGMA], headed by a retired colonel). Nor is the military a last-ditch career option for wayward young men. One faculty member at the American University of Sharjah (an expensive private univer-sity) reported that when a male student dropped out to join the army halfway through his four-year degree, his peers viewed this as a lateral move, because a military career—even for individuals of substantial means—is a respect-able career path (Young 2014:110). The perception among expatriates living in the UAE is that entry-level salaries and allowances for Emirati nationals who enlist in the military is extremely generous; one individual said that he believed the figure to be equivalent to around $200,000 per year.[12]

Similar efforts in Saudi Arabia are less impressive. Saudi Arabia's armed forces journal, *The Muslim Soldier's Magazine* (*Majallat al-Jundi al-Muslim*), is published by the Saudi armed forces' Religious Affairs department, and the few available references to the publication suggest that it focuses more on religious doctrine than strategic issues or nationalism. The country also has only seven think tanks (Ulrichsen 2015), although one is headed by a member of the armed forces: the Middle East Centre for Strategic and Legal Studies in Jeddah, whose chairman is General Anwar Eshki. The more prom-inent Gulf Research Center, based in Jeddah, does have a large contingent of resident scholars focused on regional defense and security issues, but the only one with a military background is an Iraqi national.

The Role of Domestic Defense Industrial Production in Gulf Militarization

Alongside a growth in deployments and the increasing visibility of a regional military culture, there has also been a major increase in state support for domestic military industrial production. Much of the activity taking place in the Persian Gulf region today is enabled by global factors. The decline of defense budgets in Europe and the United States has increased the lever-age that major customers such as Saudi Arabia and the UAE enjoy in their negotiations with private defense firms. Annual combined military spending by the Gulf Cooperation Council states doubled during the previous decade,[13] with Saudi Arabia's estimated defense spending in 2013 reaching nearly $60 billion (*Global Military Balance* 2013), while the UAE is the largest customer for U.S. military exports, with purchases of about $15 billion annually.

Defense firms are often willing to offer significant incentives to secure contracts with such large buyers. These incentives increasingly center on agreements to transfer defense technologies, production equipment, and even personnel to the purchasing country. These agreements—known as "offsets"[14]—obligate defense firms to invest a specific percentage of the value of their sales contracts in the domestic economy of the procuring country.[15] The vast majority of offset projects implemented in the Persian Gulf region during the 1980s, 1990s, and the early years of the 2000s were of the indirect (i.e., nonmilitary) variety, in sectors such as petrochemicals, pharmaceuticals, financial and health care services, software and communications technology, and real estate.

As late as 2006, the Gulf Arab states still imported roughly 99 percent of their military equipment (Hasbani 2006:75). However, in recent years both the UAE and Saudi Arabia have implemented changes to their procurement policy and domestic industrial and financial regulations in order to create a climate that is more conducive to direct offsets—those that require the defense firm to transfer technology or equipment in order to promote domestic production. A recent industry estimate put the total value of offset agreements globally at about $150 billion between 2010 and 2015 (Chuter 2010), with offsets in Saudi Arabia and the UAE accounting for nearly one-third of this figure.[16] The UAE has relaxed foreign ownership restrictions in order to facilitate the creation of projects with military applications (Wagstaff-Smith 2010), while in Saudi Arabia regulations barring domestic firms from supplying items that would eventually find their way into the kingdom's defense arsenal have been removed.[17]

Saudi officials say that the decision was initiated to encourage foreign suppliers to partner with Saudi firms, with the ultimate aim of establishing a domestic military industry. Colonel Attiyah al-Maliki characterized the new policy as "just the beginning," adding that, "nothing should prevent Saudi Arabia from making its own fighter jets" (Karam 2010). The Saudi Defense Ministry also created a sort of liaison committee to coordinate with local industry. The former head of this committee, Prince Khalid bin Sultan, also at the time the deputy defense minister, told the Saudi-based *Arab News* that private-sector companies should eventually be capable of producing 70 percent of the kingdom's military equipment using technology transferred from abroad (Abdul Ghafour 2011).

Neither Saudi Arabia nor the UAE is close to producing such a significant portion of its defense equipment needs domestically, but both have recently established a number of large enterprises. In the UAE, where the government has built an industrial park specifically outfitted for defense production, these enterprises include ammunition and firearms manufacturing, shipbuilding, maintenance, and repair depots for advanced aircraft, UAV (drone) design and manufacturing, and a host of defense electronics projects. The number of domestic operations is sufficient to have generated $3.8 billion in contracts with the UAE armed forces during the 2015 IDEX held in Abu Dhabi (Mustafa 2015).

Saudi Arabia is likewise stepping up state support for defense production, with funding for the state-owned MIC, which consists of several industrial operations and a military uniform factory, increasing sharply in recent years (Saudi Arabian Monetary Agency 2013:129).[18] Another sign of the increasing importance of the MIC is King Salman's choice for its new chairman— the former chief executive of the consistently profitable petrochemical giant SABIC, one of the world's largest diversified chemical companies and one of the few operations in the kingdom where management and investment decisions are insulated from politics (OECD 2013).

Saudi Arabia is also directing new investment toward a number of nearly defunct defense industrial firms launched by Boeing and other U.S. firms in the mid-1980s under the U.S.-Saudi Peace Shield, including two companies designed to manufacture aircraft parts, an aircraft repair and maintenance firm, a defense electronics company, and a defense technology firm.[19]

Some of these firms have experienced a significant revival, and a recent Boeing contract included an agreement to "jointly grow the aerospace sector in the Kingdom of Saudi Arabia" (*CTO Newsletter* 2008). One of these firms, Alsalam Aircraft, which laid off more than half of its workforce as recently as 2004, has staged an astounding recovery, including the construction of a $40 million maintenance facility and at least six new government contracts.[20] Alsalam is also partnering with another Saudi firm, the Advanced Electronics Company (AEC), to produce electronic components for new Eurofighter Typhoons (Bailey 2010), while another company, the Middle East Propulsion Company (MEPC), has been the subject of significant share acquisitions by two foreign defense firms whose executives cited MEPC's projected work on the kingdom's burgeoning fleet of fighter aircraft as a major driver in their investment decisions (*Arabian Aerospace* 2009).[21] Three of France's largest defense firms have likewise announced the formation of partnerships with these same Saudi firms[22] (*CTO Newsletter* 2006). The government itself is increasingly recruiting domestic oil and gas logistics firms to oversee military contracts. Bahri Shipping—which is partly state owned and has spent the last three decades shipping crude oil and chemicals—was recently awarded a contract to ship military equipment for the Saudi Ministry of Defense. This pattern of Gulf-based conglomerates diversifying into defense-related logistics and support services that were formerly provided by European or American contractors is an increasingly common one.

Although it seems counterintuitive, the purchasing country bears the expense of offset projects because the costs are factored into the sales agreement by the defense firm (Markowski and Hall 2004:52), and since firms employ a range of methods to fulfill offset investment targets with minimal capital outlay, procuring countries pay a high premium for arms deals that involve offsets. These inflated costs are well known to procurement officials, so the shift in Saudi and UAE policy to support domestic military production with offsets suggests an important realignment of interests and influence among power brokers in the Gulf region. These would include the military and civilian defense establishments as well as private-sector businessmen involved in a range of industrial and technological activities that could be incorporated into a program of domestic military production.

At the same time, leaders in the Gulf region are seeking to maximize the political benefits of their sizable defense expenditures, which include the ability to support and subsidize domestic producers by encouraging foreign firms to partner with them. And as these producers become more sophisticated and increasingly networked with military leaders and the civilian defense establishment, the more these parties' financial and professional interests will coalesce around expanded domestic defense production.

The region's new generation of military officers charged with leading these more advanced armies is another constituency with a critical interest in indigenous defense production. Trained in elite (often Western) military colleges, they are increasingly aware of both the strategic needs of their states and the technological specifications of the defense equipment they purchase. As the gap widens between the sophistication of these military elites and the capabilities of their respective national defense industrial bases, they are likely to seek out channels through which the state can subsidize indigenous producers and enhance the overall prestige of the nation's military institutions.

These domestic constituencies, whose interests are shaped by both market conditions and political realities, may work in tandem to catalyze the building of a defense production capability in Saudi Arabia and the UAE.

Domestic production of military industrial equipment can also serve as an important source of career prestige for the military. It provides a source of employment for military-trained engineers and technicians and integrates military personnel more fully into high-level decision-making processes, as they are consulted on issues of technology needs-assessments and related procurement questions, and an effective military-industrial development program can provide a major source of institutional prestige. This is particularly true in the Gulf region, where large budgets have enabled both Saudi Arabia and the UAE to participate in the production and maintenance of the most technologically advanced weaponry.

Influence of Domestic Defense-Industrial Firms/Contractors/Merchants

Decades of large defense expenditures and persistent conflict in the Arab world have created a contingent of powerful domestic elites whose business operations are linked to the defense industry. This includes many large conglomerates that got their start as local agent-distributors for foreign defense firms. And these firms are benefiting significantly from state subsidies designed to secure them a spot in the global military-industrial supply chain.

The UAE's Bin Jabr Group, owned by Saeed bin Jabr Al-Suwaidi, got its start as the local agent for defense communications firms and now has subsidiaries operating in health care, retail, construction, energy, and manufacturing. In addition to supplying uniforms for the UAE military, Bin Jabr Group also coproduced the region's first armored personnel carrier in a joint venture with the Jordanian military.

Trust International Group LLC, owned by Sheikh Tahnoon Bin Zayed Al Nahyan, also got its start as a distributor of foreign supplies to the UAE armed forces. Today the company has joint ventures with numerous defense firms. Retired UAE Air Force general Khalid 'Abdullah Abu Ainnain has at least six joint ventures with French and Italian defense firms through his investment company Baynuna Group. Several other families with connections to the UAE armed forces have also benefited from collaborative production agreements with foreign defense firms. 'Ali al-Dahiri—founder of

Adcom, one of Abu Dhabi's earliest defense production firms—comes from a tribe that has typically dominated the upper-level administrative positions in the UAE's military, the Union Defense Force (UDF) (Davidson 2006:53). Similarly, the Mazariah (or Mazari') tribe has also held many high-ranking posts in the UDF and is well represented within the defense bureaucracy, and Mazariahs are shareholders and board members in a number of enterprises (both military and civilian) set up under the auspices of the UAE's defense offset program. The board of Abu Dhabi Ship Building—an early joint venture set up with Northrop Grumman—includes the names of many powerful families with long military pedigrees, including 'Abdullah Saeed Al-Darmaki, whose extended family holds many of the top posts in military procurement, and former member Salim Rashid Al-Noaimi, whose tribe was a key military ally of Abu Dhabi during the days of border contestation with Saudi Arabia (Davidson 2006:53).

In Saudi Arabia, 'Abdul Rahman Al-Zamil, former deputy minister of commerce and patriarch of one of the kingdom's largest industrial conglomerates, has been a key private-sector partner in official efforts to foster the growth of domestic military production. In addition to being a member of the local industrialization committee created by the Ministry of Defense (Reuters 2010), Zamil has been a domestic partner in many of the kingdom's offset projects and was among those who participated in Saudi Arabia's first defense industry exhibition, held in 2010. The 'Abdullah Al-Faris Company is another Saudi firm that illustrates the methods through which regional governments are supporting the expansion of defense-related production. The firm's eponymous owner brought in an international design and engineering team that developed prototypes for several armored personnel carriers during the 1980s and 1990s. Although the state-owned MIC initially held a 33 percent stake in Al-Faris, in 2003 the Saudi government acquired all the remaining shares (*Arabian Knights* n.d.). This strategy—to consolidate small private operators under the umbrella of the state—is also visible in the UAE, where the government is acquiring entire companies (or units within larger conglomerates) with defense-related applications using various defense-specific investment funds.

The increase in domestic arms production is becoming an avenue for individual military elites to enter Gulf commerce in a way that was uncommon in previous decades. In the UAE, many large conglomerates diversifying into defense-related activities are recruiting executives from the ranks of retired armed forces officers—hoping to capitalize on the connections they have to those still active in the military hierarchy (and presumably still influential in the chain of procurement decision making). Sheikh Tahnoon's Trust International (formerly known as Vallo and before that as Hydra Trading) recently boasted of "beefing up" its management team with the addition of eight retired officers from the UAE armed forces. The aforementioned Bin Jabr Group recently added Yousef al-Shaibah, a retired UAE staff colonel, as the general manager of marketing and development for the company's defense unit.

Meanwhile, high-ranking retired officers with existing defense portfolios are expanding their enterprises as well. In addition to the aforementioned Colonel Abu Ainnain, Homaid Al-Shammari, a former lieutenant colonel in the UAE armed forces, is the executive director of Mubadala's aerospace subsidiary, chairman of three defense-related firms (Abu Dhabi Autonomous Systems Investments, Abu Dhabi Aircraft Technologies, and AMMROC), and a board member for two more (Abu Dhabi Ship Building and Al-Yah Satellite Communications). The International Golden Group, which was founded in 2002 by Fadel Al-Ka'bi and is headed by Fadel's uncle, retired armed forces deputy chief of staff Mohammed Hilal Al-Ka'bi, has signed a number of large contracts with multinational defense firms since the state-owned defense investment fund Tawazun purchased a 26 percent stake in the company in 2011.[23] Retired Special Operations colonel Hussain al-Hammadi is chairman of Emirates Advanced Investments, which owns a number of defense-related subsidiaries, including Knowledge International, which does about US$500 million in business per year as a licensed arms broker and procurement consultant.[24]

In Saudi Arabia, military officers may also be increasingly influential in the economy, though not in precisely the same way, and highlighting a trend is more difficult because business operations are less transparent. Traditionally, licenses to act as local distributors or agents for arms imports have been reserved for members of the royal family, serving as a sort of allowance or pension for the kingdom's many princes. Retired military officers serving as chairman or shareholders in these firms have typically been little more than front men for high-ranking members of the royal family, which may have dozens of such agency agreements. For example, the CEO of Al-Raha Group for Technical Services, which has an agency agreement with Raytheon and acts as an intermediary for U.S. arms transfers, is a retired brigadier general in the Royal Saudi Air Force. Although the company reports being owned by two individual shareholders, U.S. diplomatic sources believe that the company belongs to Prince Khalid bin Sultan, former deputy minister of defense and son of the late Crown Prince Sultan (United States Department of State 2009). Military officers are also frequently appointed to executive posts in business development or as technical advisers, especially if they have been posted overseas and are likely to have useful military and diplomatic connections.

The role of military officers in recent bribery scandals also hints at a potentially more influential role for men in uniform in Saudi Arabia. Revelations about bribes connected with a lucrative weapons sale to Saudi Arabia listed a nonroyal military officer as a major recipient of gifts (including a villa and a luxury sports car), which seems to be a novel trend, as it has traditionally been members of the ruling family who have been the recipients of large bribes associated with defense sales.[25] Prince Bandar—the most influential son of the late Prince Sultan—was recently relieved of his post as intelligence chief by a nonroyal military figure, Colonel Yusuf bin 'Ali al-Idrissi. This was the first time in nearly forty years that the post was held by anyone outside the royal family. Such moves may not be evidence of a military elite or an "officer's economy" but may be an indicator of the growing influence concentrated in the armed forces.

Benefits of Operating in the Gulf Region for Defense Firms

In addition to their purchasing power, there are other factors that make Saudi Arabia and the UAE attractive locations for defense firms, including reliable infrastructure and R&D (research and development) subsidies. The UAE in fact has frequently provided up-front financing to bankroll next-generation weapons development and partially financed R&D for Russia's most advanced antiaircraft system (Antonenko 2002); GEC-Marconi's al-Hakim missiles; internal avionics for the F-16 and the French-built Mirage jet, an F-15 modification; and a defense radar system from Northrop Grumman (Knights 2003). The newly designed F-15 was subsequently exported to additional markets, yielding profits for both Lockheed Martin and the UAE, which received royalties from the deal. In the words of a U.S. diplomatic cable, the UAE's desire for the most advanced weaponry "often includes reaching into the future for systems still under development" (United States Department of State 2006).

The legacy of these investments is visible today in the increasing sophistication of the UAE's own defense electronics industry, including Emirates Advanced Investments, which partnered with Raytheon to develop a laser-guidance kit that can be attached to unguided Talon rockets for use on patrol helicopters.[26] The missiles just passed another round of testing and will likely make it onto global markets in the near future.

Much of the region's newly built technology infrastructure has important defense applications, and some—such as the UAE's Tier 4 data center (one of only four in the world) and the world's sixth-largest supercomputer, housed at the King 'Abdullah University for Science & Technology (KAUST)—have been built in collaboration with foreign defense firms, whose executives cite their capacity to "bring in great minds from around the world . . . and successfully attract world-renowned scientists who are experts in key areas of interest" (*Boeing Frontiers* 2011).[27] Arms sales agreements often contain language about the provision of new industrial infrastructure, as did Riyadh's recent $40 billion purchase of Eurofighter Typhoons that included plans for a "regional defense industrial center" (Abdul Ghafour 2011). The UAE, now a global hub for weaponized drone technologies, recently completed construction of an industrial park in Abu Dhabi dedicated to the research, design, and manufacture of defense material, where the world's largest multinational defense firms are already setting up joint ventures with domestic producers.

The presence of these assets facilitates subsequent sales of advanced weapons and technology transfers, because they establish the necessary physical infrastructure and human capital (technicians, maintenance specialists, and researchers). Many of the institutions where this infrastructure is housed include large academic and vocational departments dedicated to defense-related research and training.[28] Al-Faisal University was partially founded with an initial US$11 million donation from Boeing, BAE Systems, Thales, and United Technologies—and some of these firms also offer scholarships to Saudi students majoring in defense and security-related areas.[29] More recently, Lockheed Martin agreed to capitalize a research investment fund that will make grant money available to Saudi researchers working on applications related to defense and security technologies (Sambidge 2013).

Boeing coordinates with other educational and research entities in Saudi Arabia, including the King 'Abdullah City for Science and Technology (KACST), where the firm is establishing a Decision Support Center to offer modeling, simulation, and analysis services for defense and aerospace firms in the region (*Boeing Frontiers* 2011).[30] Dassault signed an agreement in 2011 to partner with KACST on digital design and engineering programs in the center's Advanced Technology Institute—an expansion of its existing collaboration with KACST's National Satellite Technology Program (*Saudi Gazette* 2011). Both Boeing and Lockheed Martin have recently established partnerships with KAUST to facilitate the transfer of defense technology and conduct unique research and development projects.[31] In the UAE, Boeing and BAE coordinate with the Higher Colleges of Technology, regularly bringing executives to campus to talk to students about pursuing careers in the defense and aerospace industries, showcasing new product innovations to students in relevant disciplines, and offering internships to promising young Emiratis.[32] It is no longer only the big multinational companies promoting education and career training in the military-industrial sector: Emirates Advanced Investments (owned by retired UAE colonel Hussein al-Hammadi) has a formal MoU with the Emirati Ministry of Education to place graduates in EAI companies (Olarte 2011).

The UAE's Higher Colleges of Technology cosponsors an annual competition to design unmanned aerial vehicles (the "Unmanned Systems Rodeo"), along with a firm owned by retired air force general Abu Ainnain; Northrop Grumman pays for the winning student team to present their unmanned aerial vehicle design at the Association for Unmanned Vehicle Systems International Convention held annually in Washington, D.C. (HCT Press Release 2011). Abu Ainnain has also used his considerable defense-related expertise and connections to establish one of the first genuinely indigenous strategic studies centers in the Gulf region, INEGMA. INEGMA provides risk analysis and other defense-related services to the UAE government, and its research staff benefits from U.S.-sponsored engagement with other global strategic think tanks through the U.S. Department of Defense Foreign Military Training program.[33]

Links Between Defense Production, Increased Deployments, and Growing Military Influence

The provision of subsidies to support domestic defense production, a growing contingent of civilian and military elites vested in this expansion, and state-led efforts to enhance the prestige of the military all possess a functional affinity with increasing military activism. Weapons exports and troop deployments are forms of foreign policy; the latter typically represents an escalation of the former, signaling a state's increased commitment to some foreign policy objective. States that have the capacity to export weapons (which is enhanced by a national military industrial base able to manufacture and/or maintain and upgrade those weapons) may therefore be more likely to deploy their armed forces to intervene abroad.

This sheds new light on the UAE's 2014 airstrikes against Islamist targets in Libya, as there is some indication that the UAE had previously shipped arms to anti-Qaddafi rebels in Libya via one of its domestic producers (the International Golden Group) in 2011 and to have used a similar setup to send arms to Syrian rebels in 2012 and 2013.[34] Saudi Arabia's primary means of intervening in regional conflicts prior to its recent deployments has been largely contained to providing financing—the kingdom's repeated efforts to prop up the Lebanese armed forces against Hizbullah is a prime example, as are Riyadh's reported efforts to supply weapons to Syrian rebels via Pakistan. For scholars of civil-military relations, these activities are important because they are all indications of an increasingly influential military and defense establishment in a region where monarchs are known for their efforts to weaken and divide the armed forces as a hedge against antiregime activity.

The examination of these two cases raises important questions for our understanding of civil-military relations. One is the extent to which the economic and political roles of the military during the state-building phase impact subsequent civil-military relations. In the UAE and Saudi Arabia, where both colonial penetration and pressure to industrialize were low, the initiation of efforts to build a domestic defense industrial capacity now precedes the existence of a politically influential or economically consequential military. Both states' efforts to build the prestige and performance of their militaries may yield new insight about civil-military relations within the state-building process. The intensification of activity in any economic sector is likely to generate demand for a type of labor suited to that particular sector. The increasing production of defense material will generate demand not only for defense scientists and military engineers but also for those with qualifications suited to marketing, business development, export promotion and licensing, battlefield testing, logistics, and a range of other associated fields. Many of these qualified individuals are likely to have military backgrounds. In the past, members of the Saudi and Emirati militaries had few such opportunities because there was no significant source of domestic production, and they were unlikely to be recruited to participate in the activities of foreign firms that had established local agency offices to qualify for government contracts. Domestic production is thus likely to generate a significant number of lucrative employment opportunities for military officers and contribute to the growth of the institution's economic and political leverage.

Another key issue is the role of militaries in the Arab Spring. Many analysts point to the region's militaries as the decisive actors in the outcome of the uprisings, as their support for, or defection from, incumbent regimes was critical to the latter's survival. By implication, this suggests that the apolitical militaries of the Gulf Arab states have been a major asset for regime survival or at the very least are not a threat to survival. The fact that these militaries are now the recipients of increasing state support—in the form of prestigious training academies, coordinated displays of public support, and forms of economic enterprise that favor individuals with military backgrounds—may change this dynamic.

For the same reason, the increasing incidence of conscription and nationalization policies is critical to issues of regime survival. The Gulf region's emphasis on purchasing big-ticket weapons systems from foreign patron states has historically compensated for its relatively modest armies, as such purchases are accompanied by a dense web of security guarantees that include foreign military advisers, technicians and maintenance staff, civilian support personnel, and private-sector industry representatives.[35] The number of U.S. defense personnel and contractors officially stationed in Saudi Arabia is probably well in excess of 1,000,[36] and there are nearly 300 United Kingdom personnel stationed in the kingdom in support of several large arms supply agreements.[37] In the UAE, scholars estimate that most of the training and engineer personnel in the UAE air force are still foreigners, despite the fact that most of the federation's defense spending since 2000 has been on aircraft and air defense systems (Young 2014:108).

The long-term results of efforts to nationalize the military through conscription and boost military industrial production by subsidizing domestic firms will phase out these foreign personnel, producing a military and defense establishment that more closely resembles the overall socioeconomic makeup of the nation. To the degree that monarchs could have counted on their militaries' foreign or minority status to prevent them from identifying with potential civilian opposition, this may prove less true in the future. Conversely, empowering the military may also represent an effort to create and nurture a new and perhaps more secular constituency that can counter the growing challenge posed by antiregime opposition from religious conservatives.

Certainly regional threats from extremists—most notably ISIL—might trigger such a buildup, but many of these pro-armed forces policies and projects have been in the works for a decade, long before the most recent threats emerged. Do regimes embark on programs to strengthen and promote their militaries only when confronted with existential threats, or might there be more banal political imperatives behind such strategies? More research must to done to catalogue the range of incentives and forms of support that have been provided to militaries in the Gulf Arab states. Examining the processes through which this takes place will add not only to our understanding of politics in this particular region but also to our understanding of how militaries come to be important political players in the first place.

Notes

1. Quinlivan (1999) is a notable exception.

2. In both Saudi Arabia and the UAE, bedouin populations have been major sources of military manpower, presumably because they lack strong ties to the urbanized civilian population and are less likely to be swayed by opposition movements and other antiregime activities.

3. Virtually all the members of the National Guard battalion that fought under the American Joint Forces Command during the 1990–1991 Persian Gulf War were Pakistani (Hasbani 2006; Al-Najjar 2004).

4. See YouTube (2013).

5. See YouTube (2011).

6. Saudi promotional videos available online are unofficial and splice together stock news footage or still photos. See YouTube (2010).

7. Saudi firms that have exhibited include Armored Vehicles & Heavy Equipment Factory, a company affiliated with the state-owned MIC; Al-Ghuroub Group; Al-Wafa International Co.; and Jadwalean International Operation & Management Company (*Arab News* 2013).

8. Two examples from the UAE are a 2011 training contract with Reflex Resources (owned by Blackwater founder Eric Prince) and a 2014 counterterrorism training contract with the U.S. Marine Corps.

9. The full name of the facility is the King ʿAbdullah Special Operations Training Center, known by its acronym KASOTC.

10. According to Major General ʿIsa Al-Mazruʿi, deputy chief of staff of the armed forces in 2012, "There is a shortage of pilots, engineers and others in various branches of the armed forces" (*Nation Shield* 2012).

11. Both Saudi Arabia and the UAE have publications specifically catering to the armed forces, although the UAE magazine *Nation Shield* resembles a professional bureaucratic journal aimed at institutional technocrats.

12. Author's telephone interview with a young expatriate living in Dubai, July 1, 2015.

13. Spending increased from $35 billion in 1997 to more than $70 billion in 2009 (*Gulf Military Balance* 2010:36).

14. "Defense offset" is the term used to describe a wide variety of mandatory investment agreements that foreign governments impose as a condition of making a purchase from a foreign defense firm. Although "offset" is the term most frequently used by governments, other terms such as "industrial participation," "industrial collaboration," and "economic enhancement" are frequently used by industry to avoid some of the negative connotations associated with outsourcing the production of defense material from their host countries.

15. Foreign defense firms can satisfy these obligations in a variety of ways: coproducing or licensing the production of portions of their weapons systems in-country, launching new joint ventures with domestic entrepreneurs, subcontracting with existing companies, or relocating some components of their R&D (research and development) activities or MRO (maintenance, repair, and overhaul) operations.

16. Projected defense spending for Saudi Arabia and the UAE during the next three to five years is about $100 billion; offset requests emanating from these sales contracts are estimated at $24 billion for Saudi Arabia and $21 billion for the UAE (Wagstaff-Smith 2010).

17. Under the new rules, local firms can bid to supply some 15,000 basic materials used in defense construction (Karam 2010). The previous ban was based on fears that domestic extremists would attempt to sabotage the kingdom's equipment.

18. The report includes a figure for annual state spending on MIC, which was about $730 million in 2013, a 38 percent increase from 2012.

19. These are the Alsalam Aircraft Company (Alsalam), the AEC, the MEPC, the Middle East Battery Company, the Aircraft Accessories & Components Company, and International Systems Engineering. The companies that served as joint venture partners included Boeing, Westinghouse, AT&T, Hughes Aircraft (since acquired piecemeal by Raytheon and Boeing), General Electric, Pratt & Whitney, Rolls-Royce, and Frank E. Basil.

20. These include maintenance for AWACS and C-130s, an engine overhaul of the kingdom's F-15s, assembly of the canopies for HAWK trainers, and upgrades to BAE's tornado fighter aircraft. *Alsalam Horizons* (www.alsalam.aero/news_horizonmagazine .aspx) is a company newsletter that began publishing in 2008; se especially the July 2009 and May 2010 issues.

21. MTU Aeroengines and Wamar International now own a combined 28.6 percent of MEPC shares.

22. These firms are Thales, Dassault, and Snecma, which have formed partnerships with AEC, Alsalam, and MEPC, respectively.

23. These firms include Thales, BAE, Paramount (South Africa), and Selex (Italy). Fadil was formerly an executive at Tawazun.

24. The firm's leadership includes several well-known U.S. military officers, including a former head of Special Operations Command and General Stanley McChrystal, who led NATO's Afghanistan command.

25. In the recent EADS/GPT bribery case, four luxury cars valued at £201,000 were allegedly given to members of the Saudi royal family and the military, and £278,000 was reportedly paid for the rental of a villa owned by a Saudi National Guard general.

26. The Chairman of Emirates Advanced Investments (retired colonel Hussain al-Hammadi) is also on the board of directors of Abu Dhabi Ship Building, which recently concluded an agreement with Raytheon to build a regional maintenance depot for servicing the company's missiles.

27. The UAE's Tier 4 data center is operated by Injazat Data Systems, which was built as an offset by EDS Defense & Security, a U.S. company; many of Injazat's clients are offset-generated ventures, both public and privately owned. Many of the technologies and laboratories available at KAUST were transferred or built by foreign defense companies as part of long-term collaboration deals. These are increasingly replacing traditional offset deals, whereby each individual sale has a corresponding offset contract. Chris Thompson (1994:1) labeled the complex of facilities linking the 1984 defense offsets to Saudi Arabia's nascent research institutions a "Silicon Oasis" (see also Alsharif 2008).

28. These include CERT in the UAE and Dar Al-Faisal University and Knowledge Economic City, both in Saudi Arabia.

29. The Boeing Saudi Arabia Fellowship Program is one such example.

30. Boeing also has partnerships with King Saud University and King 'Abdulaziz University.

31. Boeing is financing projects to develop next-generation composite materials for use in aircraft and the designing of new thin-film solar cell technology (*Boeing Frontiers* 2011). Lockheed Martin's 2013 agreement with KACST targets more generalized technology transfer and skill acquisition; the company also has agreements with KAUST and Al-Faisal University (Al Baqmi 2013).

32. These include the CERT Boeing Academic Excellence Awards, which provides for a one-month internship at Boeing's facilities in the U.S.

33. The 2010 Joint Report to Congress on Foreign Military Training compiled by the U.S. State Department and Department of Defense shows that INEGMA personnel attended the workshop "Emerging Threats in the Gulf," jointly sponsored by the UK International Institute for Strategic Studies and the Near East & South Asia Center for Strategic Studies, part of the U.S. National Defense University, under the auspices of the Department of Defense's foreign military training program.

34. The shipment to Libya also allegedly involved two other intermediary firms: Meico of Albania and DG Arms Corporation of Armenia (Intelligence Online 2013).

35. The sale of certain weapons systems and platforms represents long-term commitments between buyer and seller; for example, the sale of a tranche of fighter jets initiates a relationship that can last upwards of thirty years, since each unit is frequently upgraded several times before a new-generation fighter comes onto the market.

36. There are at least 500 contractors and 215 defense personnel in Saudi Arabia in support of OPM-SANG (Office of the Program Manager, Saudi Arabian National Guard Modernization Program), another 300-plus working under the U.S. Military Training Mission, and an additional unspecified number of military advisers working

with OPM-MOI-SFS (Office of the Program Manager, Ministry of the Interior, Facilities Security Forces). These figures date from 2008, the latest year for which official numbers are available, as reported by Christopher M. Blanchard (2010:22).

37. The UK personnel are stationed in Saudi Arabia in support of two long-term UK-Saudi defense contracts: the Ministry of Defense Saudi Armed Forces Projects and the Saudi Arabia National Guard Communications Project.

REFERENCES

Abbas, Hassan. 2011. *The Dynamics of the Uprising in Syria.* Arab Reform Brief 51, October.

Abdel-Malek, Anouar. 1968. *Egypt: Military Society.* New York: Vintage.

Abdel-Tawab, Nashwa. 2013. "Martyred for History." *Al-Ahram Weekly,* January 23.

Abdul-Ahad, Ghaith. 2012. "Syrian Rebels Sidetracked by Scramble for Spoils of War." *Guardian,* December 27.

Abdul Ghafour, P. K. 2011. "Kingdom to Manufacture 70% of Military Hardware Locally." *Arab News,* January 19.

Abrahammson, Bengt B. 1972. *Military Professionalization and Political Power.* Beverly Hills, Calif.: Sage.

Abul-Magd, Zeinab. 2011. "The Army and the Economy in Egypt." www.jadaliyya.com, December 23.

———. 2012. "The Egyptian Republic of the Retired Generals." www.foreignpolicy.com, May 8.

Acemoglu, Daron, and James A. Robinson. 2006. *Economic Origins of Dictatorship and Democracy.* New York: Cambridge University Press.

Addi, Lahouari. 2006. "Algeria: Islamobusiness as Usual." *Le Monde Diplomatique,* May.

Africa News. 2011. "Unrest Spreads as Protests Hit Capital." January 12.

Ahram, Ariel. 2011. *Proxy Warriors: The Rise and Fall of State-Sponsored Militias.* Stanford, Calif.: Stanford University Press.

Ahram Online. 2012. "Civilians Convicted in Egypt Military Courts Keep Fingers Crossed for Morsi Amnesty." July 17.

———. 2013a. "After Maspero: Have Egypt's Christians Reconciled with the Military?" October 9.

———. 2013b. "Military Articles Still Unresolved: Constitution Amending Committee." October 10.

———. 2013c. "Reports on Halting Operation Sinai Are False: Egypt Military Spokesman." January 6.

Ajmi, Sana. 2012. "In Tunis, Protest Against Security Forces Union Open Strike." www.tunisia-live.net, February 2.

Alagappa, Muthiah. 2001. "Introduction." In *Coercion and Governance: The Declining Political Role of the Military in Asia,* ed. Muthiah Alagappa. Stanford, Calif.: Stanford University Press.

Al-Ahram. 2011. "Milyun Junayh Linadb Muhameen Limutahameen fi 3,863 Qaddiya Munzu al-Thawra" [One Million Egyptian Pound to Assign Lawyers to Accused Persons in 3,863 Cases Since the Revolution]. September 5.

———. 2012. "Majlis al-Difa' al-Watani" [The National Defense Council]. June 20.

Al-Ahram Weekly. 2012. "The State of Sinai." November 21.

———. 2013. "Recruiting Civilians." January 21.

Al-Arabiya. 2012. "Al-Arabiya Inquiry Reveals How Tunisia's Ben Ali Escaped to Saudi Arabia." January 13.

Al Baqmi, Shuja. 2013. "Saudi Arabia Boosts Defense Capabilities Through Specialized US Company After Signing Direct Cooperation Agreements." *Al-Sharq al-Awsat*, February 6.

Albrecht, Holger. 2013. "Consolidating Uncertainty in Yemen." www.foreignpolicy.com, February 22.

———. 2015. "Does Coup-Proofing Work? Political-Military Relations in Authoritarian Regimes amid the Arab Uprisings." *Mediterranean Politics* 20 (1): 36–54.

Albrecht, Holger, and Dina Bishara. 2011. "Back on Horseback: The Military and Political Transformation in Egypt." *Middle East Law and Governance* 3 (1): 13–23.

Albrecht, Holger, and Dorothy Ohl. 2016. "Exit, Resistance, Loyalty: Military Behavior during Unrest in Authoritarian Regimes." *Perspectives on Politics* 14 (1): 38–52.

Alexander, Christopher. 1997. "Authoritarianism and Civil Society in Tunisia: Back from the Democratic Brink." *Middle East Report* 27 (Winter): 36–37.

———. 2011. "Anatomy of an Autocracy." www.foreignpolicy.com, January 14.

Alfardan, Hani. 2011. "Matha nurid fi 14 febriar?" [What Do We Want on February 14?]. Manama Voice (Sawt Manama), February 12, http://manamavoice.com/news -news_read-6477-0.html.

Al-Ghasra, Mohammad. 2011. "Maqtal mutathahar wa juriha 9 fi 'youm ghadab' bi Al-Bahrain" [One Demonstrator Killed and Nine Injured in "Day of Rage" in Bahrain]. CNN Arabic, February 15, http://archive.arabic.cnn.com/2011/middle_east/2/15 /Bahrain.protests/.

Al-Hayat. 2012a. "Intiqadat Limanh Mursi Wazir al-Difa' Haq Waqf Tanfiz al-Ahkam Dhad al-'Askareyeen" [Mursi Criticized for Granting the Minister of Defense the Right to Cancel Sentences Issued Against the Military]. November 20.

———. 2012b. "Sina' al-Ha'ira Bayn Mas'uliyat al-Dawla wa Saif al-Jama'at al-Jihadiya" [Sinai Torn Between State Responsibility and Jihadist Groups' Sword]. November 15.

Al Jazeera. 2011a. "Al-Jaish Al-Bahraini yahthur min al-tajamuat" [Bahraini Military Warns of Gatherings]. February 17, http://www.aljazeera.net/news/arabic/2011 /2/17

———. 2011b. "Tunisia Disbands State Security." March 8.

———. 2011c. "Tunisia Gripped by Uncertainty." January 16.

———. 2015. "Tunisian Blogger Sentenced for Defaming Army." January 20.

Al Jazeera English. 2011. "Fresh Violence Hits Syrian Town." April 30.

All4Syria. 2011. http://all4syria.info/web/archives/175051.

———. 2012a. http://all4syria.info/web/archives/56649.

———. 2012b. http://all4syria.info/web/archives/59978.

Al-Masdar Online. 2013. "Al-Masdar Online Publishes New Organizational Structure of the Yemeni Ministry of Interior." February 6, almasdaronline.com/article/41327.

Al-Masry al-Youm. 2012a. "Al-Mutahadith al-'Askari: Qarar Hazr Tamaluk Araddi Sina' lil Hifaz 'ala al-Amn al-Qawmi al-Misri" [The Military Spokesperson: Banning Land Ownership in Sinai to Preserve Egypt's National Security]. December 24.

———. 2012b. "Qarar al-'Afuw 'an Munaseri al-Thawra Yashmal al-Jinayat wal Junah 'ada al-Qatl al-'amd" [The Amnesty for the Revolution's Supporters Includes Various Crimes Except Premeditated Murder]. October 8.

———. 2013a. "Ra'is al-Qawmi li Huquq al-Insan: Sodur Ahkam 'Askariya Bihaq Khamseen Madani Asabana bil Sadma" [The Head of Human Rights' Council: We Were Shocked by the Conviction of Fifty Civilians Before Military Courts]. October 9.

———. 2013b. "Taqrir Lajnat Mursi Litaqasi al-Haqa'ik: Al-Jaysh wal Shurta Attlaqa al-Nar 'ala al-Muttadhahereen" [Mursi's Fact-Finding Committee: The Army and Police Opened Fire on Protesters]. January 1.

———. 2014. "Wafd 'Askari Misri Yattir ila Mosco fi Ziyara Ghayr Mo'lana." [Egyptian Military Delegation Flew to Moscow for a Secret Visit]. May 23.

———. 2015. "Wazir al-Difa' Ya'fi 574 Munsha'a lil Jaysh min al-Dariba al-'Aqariya" [The Minister of Defense Exempts 574 Military Properties from Property Tax]. June 3.

al-Mikhlafi, Mohamed Ahmad Ali, and Abdul Kafi Sharaf al-Din al-Rahabi. 2012. *Reform of the Security Sector in Yemen*. Arab Reform Initiative, May.

Al-Naggar. 2012. Interview. Cairo, November.

Al-Najjar, Ghanim. 2004. *Challenges of Security Sector Governance in Kuwait*. Working Paper 142. Centre for the Democratic Control of the Armed Forces, Geneva.

al-Sayyid-Marsot, AfafLutfi. 1977. *Egypt's Liberal Experiment, 1922–1936*. Berkeley: University of California Press.

Alsharif, Asma. 2008. "Saudi Supercomputer Lures Researchers." Reuters, October 20.

Al-Shehabi, Omar. 2011. "Demography and Bahrain's Unrest." *Sada*.

Al-Shorouk. 2012. "Al-'Askari: Mashru'atna 'Arak Wizarat al-Difa' Walan Nasmah lil Dawla Biltadakhul Fiha" [The Military: Our Projects Are the Fruits of the Ministry of Defense's Efforts and We Will Not Allow State's Intervention in Them]. March 27.

———. 2013. "Al-Muda'i al-'Askari al-Asbaq: Qada'una Mustaqil wa Nazih" [The Former Military Prosecutor: Our Judiciary System Is Independent and Fair]. October 13.

———. 2014. "Nanshur al-Nas al-Kamel li Moqabalat Reuters ma' al-Sisi" [We Publish the Full Transcript of Sisi's Interview with Reuters]. May 15.

al-Shurbagi, Adil. 2013. *The Restructuring of the Yemeni Army*. Arab Center for Research and Policy Studies. Doha, June.

Al-Wasat News. 2011. "Hashud dukhma tahiyi shuhada Al-Bahrain" [Huge Crowds Salute Bahrain's Martyrs]. February 23, http://www.alwasatnews.com/3092/news/read/528485/1.html.

Amara, Tarek. 2011. "Tunisian Police Protest Ban on Joining Unions." Reuters, September 6.

Amara, Tarek, and Christian Lowe. 2011. "Tunisia Forces Fight Presidential Guards Near Palace." Reuters, January 16.

Amnesty International. 2009a. *Iran: Election Contested, Repression Compounded.* New York: Amnesty International.

———. 2009b. *Tunisia: Behind Tunisia's Economic Miracle; Inequality and Criminalization of Protest.* June 18.

———. 2011. *Tunisia in Revolt: State Violence During Anti-Government Protests.* February 2.

———. 2015. "Tunisian Blogger Should Be Released." January 6.

Amrani, Issandr El. 2011. "Tunisia's Diary: Ammar's Move? (2)." www.arabist.net, January 24.

Anderson, Lisa. 1986. *The State and Social Transformation in Tunisia and Libya, 1830–1980.* Princeton, N.J.: Princeton University Press.

Angrist, Michelle Penner. 2006. *Party Building in the Modern Middle East.* Seattle: University of Washington Press.

———. 2007. "Whither the Ben Ali Regime in Tunisia?" In *The Maghrib in the New Century: Identity, Religion and Politics,* ed. Bruce Maddy-Weitzman and Daniel Zisenwine. Gainesville: University Press of Florida.

———. 2013. "Understanding the Success of Mass Civic Protest in Tunisia." *Middle East Journal* 67 (4): 547–64.

Antonenko, Oksana. 2002. "Russia's Military Involvement in the Middle East." In *Armed Forces in the Middle East,* ed. Barry Rubin and Thomas Keaney. London: Frank Cass.

Antunes, Brandao, and Priscilla Carlos. 2007. "Establishing Democratic Control of Intelligence in Argentina." In *Reforming Intelligence: Obstacles to Democratic Control and Effectiveness,* ed. Thomas C. Bruneau and Steven C. Boraz. Austin: University of Texas Press.

Arab American Institute. 2013. "Egyptian Attitudes in the Post-Tamarrud, Post-Morsi Era." http://www.aaiusa.org/reports/egyptian-attitudes-in-the-post-tamarrud-post-morsi-era.

Arab Center for Research and Policy Studies. 2011. *The Army and Popular Revolution in Yemen.* Doha, April.

Arabian Aerospace. 2009. "Saudis Countdown to Typhoon Service Entry." May 13.

Arabian Knights. n.d. "Knight of Enterprise: Abdullah Othman al-Faris."

Arab News. 2013. "KSA Firms Eye Deals at Abu Dhabi Defense Show." February 18.

———. 2014. "Kingdom Reinforces Border with Iraq." July 18.

Arceneaux, Craig L. 2001. *Bounded Missions: Military Regimes and Democratization in the Southern Cone and Brazil.* University Park: Pennsylvania State University Press.

Arieff, Alexis. 2011. "Political Transition in Tunisia." Congressional Research Service, December 16.

Art, David. 2012. "What Do We Know About Authoritarianism After Ten Years?" *Comparative Politics* 44 (April): 351–73.

Asharq Alawsat. 2013. "Tunisian Army Chief of Staff Announces Resignation." June 26.

———. 2014. "Tunisian Defense Minister: War on Terror Requires Patience." August 20.

Ashour, Omar. 2012. "Egypt's Draft Constitution: How Democratic Is It?" al-monitor .com.

Associated Press. 2011. "UN Says Death Toll in Syrian Uprising Tops 3,000." October 14.

Aswat Masriya. 2014. "Rabaa Leaders Responsible for Sit-in's Victims—Fact-Finding Committee." November 26.

Awad, Marwa. 2012. "Special Report: In Egypt's Military, a March for Change." Reuters, April 10.

Baaklini, Abdo I., Guilain Denoeux, and Robert Springborg. 1999. *Legislative Politics in the Arab World: The Resurgence of Democratic Institutions.* Boulder, Colo.: Lynne Rienner.

Bachman, Jeral, and John D. Blair. 1975. "Citizen Force or Career Force? Implications for Ideology in the All Volunteer Army." *Armed Forces and Society* 2 (1): 81–96.

Bahrain Center for Human Rights. 2009. *The Bahraini Authorities Recruit of Mercenaries from Makran Town, Pakistan.* June 6.

———. 2010. *The King of Bahrain Grants the National Security Apparatus (NSA) Full Power.* August 23.

———. 2011. *Bahrain Urgently Recruits More Mercenaries Amidst Political Crisis.* November 22.

Bahry, Louay. 2000. "The Socioeconomic Foundations of the Shiite Opposition in Bahrain." *Mediterranean Quarterly* 11 (3): 129–43.

Bailey, Robert. 2010. "Local Arms Manufacturing in the Middle East and North Africa Region Is Set to Grow." *Middle East Association*, May 14.

Barak, Oren. 2006. "Towards a Representative Military? The Transformation of the Lebanese Officer Corps Since 1945." *Middle East Journal* 60 (1): 75–93.

Barak, Oren, and Assaf David. 2010. "The Arab Security Sector: A New Research Agenda for a Neglected Topic." *Armed Forces and Society* 36 (October): 800–824.

Barany, Zoltan. 2011. "The Role of the Military." *Journal of Democracy* 22 (October): 28–39.

———. 2012. *The Soldier and the Changing State: Building Democratic Armies in Africa, Asia, Europe, and the Americas.* Princeton, N.J.: Princeton University Press.

———. 2013. *Explaining Military Responses to Revolutions.* Arab Center for Research and Policy Studies: Doha

Barrow, Robert J. 1999. "Determinants of Democracy." *Journal of Political Economy* 107 (6): 158–83.

Bassiouni, Mahmoud, et al. 2011. *Report of the Bahrain Independent Commission of Inquiry.* Manama, November 23.

Batatu, Hanna. 1999. *Syria's Peasantry.* Princeton, N.J.: Princeton University Press.

Battera, Federico. 2014. "Perspectives for Change in Tunisia, Egypt and Syria: The Military Factor and Implications of Previous Authoritarian Regimes." *Contemporary Arab Affairs* 7 (4): 544–64.

BBC Arabic. 2011. "Al-Jaish fi shawaria Al-Manama bad suqut qatla khilal tafriq atisam al-mutathahirin" [The Army in the Streets of Manama After Deaths as Demonstrators' Sit-In Is Dispersed]. February 17, http://www.bbc.co.uk/arabic/middleeast /2011/02/110217_bahrain_crackdown.shtml.

BBC Monitoring Middle East. 2008. "Al Jazeera TV Maghreb Harvest Programme 2130 GMT 6 June 08." June 7.

———. 2011. "Tunisian Interim President Asks Al-Jazeera to 'Contribute to Encouraging Calm.'" January 16.

BBC News. 2002. "Tunisian Army Chief Dies in Air Crash." May 1.

———. 2013. "Libya Clashes: Misrata Militia Ordered Out of Tripoli." November 18.

———. 2014. "Guide to Key Libyan Militias." May 20.

BBC Online. 2011. "Egypt Protests: Army Rules Out the Use of Force." January 31.

———. 2013. "Libya Clashes: Misrata Militia Ordered Out of Tripoli," 18 November.

———. 2014. "Guide to Key Libyan Militias," 20 May.

Bedeski, Robert E. 1994. *The Transformation of South Korea: Reform and Reconsitution in the Sixth Republic Under Roh Tae Woo, 1987–1992.* London: Routledge.

Beeri, Eliezer. 1982. "The Waning of the Military Coup in Arab Politics." *Middle Eastern Studies* 18 (1): 69–81.

Beeson, Mark. 2008. "Civil-Military Relations in Indonesia and the Philippines: Will the Thai Coup Prove Contagious?" *Armed Forces and Society* 34 (3): 474–90.

Belkin, Aaron. 2008. "Don't Ask Don't Tell: Does the Gay Ban Undermine the Military's Reputation?" *Armed Forces and Society* 34 (2): 276–91.

Belkin, Aaron, and Evan Schofer. 2003. "Toward a Structural Understanding of Coup Risk." *Journal of Conflict Resolution* 47 (5): 594–20.

———. 2005. "Coup Risk, Counterbalancing, and International Conflict." *Security Studies* 14 (1): 140–77.

Bellin, Eva. 2004. "The Robustness of Authoritarianism in the Middle East." *Comparative Politics* 36 (January): 139–57.

———. 2012. "Reconsidering the Robustness of Authoritarianism in the Middle East: Lessons from the Arab Spring." *Comparative Politics* 44 (2): 127–49.

Ben Bouazza, Bouazza. 2014. "Riots over Economy Break Out in Tunisia." Associated Press, January 11.

Ben Mahfoudh, Haykel. 2014. "Security Sector Reform in Tunisia." Arab Reform Initiative, July.

Benramdane, Djamel. 2004. "Algeria: A Long and Dirty War." *Le Monde Diplomatique*, March.

Bhave, Aditya, and Christopher Kingston. 2010. "Military Coups and the Consequences of Durable De Facto Power: The Case of Pakistan." *Economics of Governance* 11 (1): 51–76.

BICC. 2015. "Global Militarisation Index 2015." In *Bonn International Center for Conversion*, ed. Jan Grebe and Max M. Mutschler. Bonn: BICC.

Biddle, Stephen, and Robert Zirkle. 1996. "Technology, Civil-Military Relations, and Warfare in the Developing World." *Journal of Strategic Studies* 19 (2): 171–212.

Binnendijk, Anika, and Ivan Marovic. 2006. "Power and Persuasion: Nonviolent Strategies to Influence State Security Forces in Serbia (2000) and Ukraine (2004)." *Communist and Post-Communist Studies* 39 (3): 411–29.

Blanchard, Christopher M. 2010. *Saudi Arabia: Background and U.S. Relations*. Congressional Research Service, February.

Blaydes, Lisa. 2010. *Elections and Distributive Politics in Mubarak's Egypt*. Cambridge: Cambridge University Press.

Boeing Frontiers. 2011. Newsletter, July.

Boix, Charles, and Susan Stokes. 2003. "Endogenous Democracy." *World Politics* 55 (4): 517–49.

Born, Hans. 2002. *Democratic Oversight of the Security Sector: What Does It Mean?* Working Paper Series 9. Geneva Centre for the Democratic Control of Armed Forces, April.

Born, Hans, Marina Caparini, Karl Haltiner, and Juergen Kuhlmann. 2007. *Civil Military Relations in Europe: Learning from Crisis and Institutional Change*. London: Routledge.

Borowiec, Andrew. 1998. *Modern Tunisia: A Democratic Apprenticeship*. New York: Praeger.

Botman, Selma. 1991. *Egypt from Independence to Revolution, 1919–1952*. Syracuse, N.Y.: Syracuse University Press.

Bou Nassif, Hisham. 2013. "Wedded to Mubarak: The Second Careers and Financial Rewards of Egypt's Military Elite, 1981–2011." *Middle East Journal* 67 (4): 509–30.

———. 2015. "A Military Besieged: The Armed Forces, the Police, and the Party in bin 'Ali's Tunisia, 1987–2011." *International Journal of Middle Studies* 47 (1): 66–87.

Bozhilov, Nikolai. 2007. "Reforming the Intelligence Services in Bulgaria: The Experience of 1989–2005." In *Democratic Control of Intelligence Services: Containing Rogue Elephants*, ed. Hans Born and Marina Caparini. Aldershot, UK: Ashgate.

Brooks, Risa A. 1998. *Political-Military Relations and the Stability of Arab Regimes*. Adelphi Paper No. 324. London: International Institute for Strategic Studies.

———. 2006. "An Autocracy at War: Explaining Egypt's Military Effectiveness, 1967 and 1973." *Security Studies* 15 (3): 396–430.

———. 2013. "Abandoned at the Palace: Why the Tunisian Military Defected from the Ben Ali Regime in January 2011." *Journal of Strategic Studies* 36 (2): 205–20.

Brown, Jack. 2011. "Algeria's Midwinter Uproar." *Middle East Report Online*, January 20.

Brownlee, Jason. 2007. *Authoritarianism in an Age of Democratization*. Cambridge: Cambridge University Press.

Brownlee, Jason, Tarek Masoud, and Andrew Reynolds. 2015. *The Arab Spring: Pathways of Repression and Reform*. Oxford: Oxford University Press.

Brumberg, Daniel, and Hesham Sallam. 2012. *The Politics of Security Sector Reform in Egypt*. Washington, D.C.: U.S. Institute of Peace.

Bueno de Mesquita, Bruce, Alastair Smith, Randolph M. Siverson, and James D. Morrow. 2003. *The Logic of Political Survival.* Cambridge, Mass.: MIT Press.

Byman, Daniel, and Jennifer Lind. 2010. "Pyongyang's Survival Strategy: Tools of Authoritarian Control in North Korea." *International Security* 35 (1): 44–74.

Campbell, Kenneth J. 1998. "Once Burned, Twice Cautious: Explaining the Weinberger-Powell Doctrine." *Armed Forces and Society* 24 (3): 357–74.

Case, William. 2007. "Democracy's Quality and Breakdown: New Lessons from Thailand." *Democratization* 14 (4): 622–42.

Central Intelligence Agency. 2013. "The World Fact Book." https://www.cia.gov/library/publications/the-world-factbook/geos/xx.html.

Chams El-Dine, Chérine. 2012a. Interview with military expert. Cairo, November.

———. 2012b. Interview with human rights lawyer. Cairo, November.

———. 2012c. Interview with human rights activist and prominent member of the No to Military Trials group. Cairo, November.

———. 2014. Interview with a member of the July 2012 fact-finding committee and prominent human rights lawyer. Cairo, May.

Chandra, Siddharth, and Douglas Kammen. 2002. "Generating Reforms and Reforming Generations: Military Politics in Indonesia's Democratic Transition and Consolidation." *World Politics* 55 (1): 96–136.

Chenoweth, Erica, and Maria J. Stephan. 2011. *Why Civil Resistance Works: The Strategic Logic of Nonviolent Conflict.* New York: Columbia University Press.

Chomiak, Laryssa, and John P. Entellis. 2011. "The Making of North Africa's Intifadas." *Middle East Report* 259 (Summer): 13–15.

Christian Science Monitor. 2009. "Why Iran's Revolutionary Guards Mercilessly Crack Down." August 6.

———. 2011. "Syria's Military Shows Signs of Division Amid Crackdown." April 25.

Chuter, Andrew. 2010. "Nations Seek More Offsets from Suppliers." *Defense News*, April 18.

Cockburn, Patrick. 2011. "Troubles Like These Are Brewing All over the Middle East." *Independent*, January 15.

Codron, Jérémie. 2007. "Putting Factions 'Back in' the Civil-Military Relation Equation: Genesis, Maturation and Distortion of the Bangladeshi Army." *South Asia Multidisciplinary Academic Journal* (October).

Cody, Edward. 1987. "Tunisian President 'Senile' Is Removed by His Deputy; Habib Bourguiba's 30 Year Rule Ends." *Washington Post*, November 8.

Collard, Rebecca. 2013. "Coup or No Coup Egyptians Love the Military." *Global Post*, July 30.

Collier, Ruth B., and David Collier. 1991. *Shaping the Political Arena: Critical Junctures, the Labor Movement, and Regime Dynamics in Latin America.* Princeton, N.J.: Princeton University Press.

Collombier, Virginie. 2014. Interviews with residents. Bani Walid, Libya, February and April.

Colton, Timothy. 1979. *Commissars, Commanders, and Civilian Authority: The Structure of Soviet Military Politics*. Cambridge, Mass.: Harvard University Press.

Cook, Steven. 2007. *Ruling but Not Governing: The Military and Political Development in Egypt, Algeria and Turkey*. Baltimore: Johns Hopkins University Press.

Cooper, Mark N. 1982. *The Transformation of Egypt*. London: Croom Helm.

Copsey, Nathaniel. 2010. "Ukraine." In *The Colour Revolutions in the Former Soviet Republics*, ed. Donnacha O. Beachain and Abel Polese. London: Routledge.

Cordesman, Anthony H., and Aram Nerguizian. 2010. *The North African Military Balance*. Washington, D.C.: Center for Strategic and International Studies.

Cordesman, Anthony H., and Khalid R. Al-Rodhan. 2006. *Gulf Military Forces in an Era of Asymmetric Wars*. Washington, D.C.: Center for Strategic and International Studies.

Crane, Emily. 2014. "Protesters and Police Clash in Tunis Neighborhood," www.tunisia-live.net, January 13.

Croissant, Aurel. 2004. "Riding the Tiger: Civilian Control and the Military in Democratizing Korea." *Armed Forces and Society* 30: 357–81.

———. 2013a. "Coups and Post-Coup Politics in Southeast Asia and the Pacific: Conceptual and Comparative Perspectives." *Australian Journal of International Affairs* 67 (3): 264–80.

———. 2013b. "Militar und Politik in den Arabischen Autokratien." In *Friedensgutachten 2013*, ed. Marc von Boemcken et al. Hamburg: LIT Verlag.

———. 2015. "Southeast Asian Militaries in the Age of Democratization: From Ruler to Servant?" In *Routledge Handbook of Southeast Asian Democratization*, ed. William Case, 314–32. London: Routledge.

Croissant, Aurel, et al. 2011. "Theorizing Civilian Control of the Military in Emerging Democracies: Agency, Structure and Institutional Change." *Zeitschrift für Vergleichende Politikwissenschaft* 5 (1): 75–98.

Croissant, Aurel, et al. 2013. *Civilian Control and Democracy in Asia*. Basingstoke, UK: Palgrave Macmillan.

Croissant, Aurel, and David Kuehn. 2011. *Militär und zivile Politik*. München: Oldenbourg.

———. 2015. "The Military's Role in Politics." In *Handbook of Comparative Political Institutions*, ed. Jennifer Gandhi and Rafael Ruiz-Rufino. New York: Routledge.

CTO Newsletter. 2006. August 14.

———. 2008. February 11.

Cumings, Bruce. 2005. *Korea's Place in the Sun*. New York: Norton.

Dahl, Robert. 1989. *Democracy and Its Critics*. New Haven, Conn.: Yale University Press.

D'Anieri, Paul, Robert Kravchuk, and Taras Kuzio. 1999. *Politics and Society in Ukraine*. Boulder, Colo.: Westview.

Daragahi, Borzou. 2011. "A Tunisian State Police Officer Shares Harrowing Inside View." *Los Angeles Times*, February 3.

Darchiashvili, David Georgian. 2005. "Defense Policy and Military Reform." In *Statehood and Security: Georgia After the Rose Revolution*, ed. Bruno Coppieters and Robert Legvold. Cambridge, Mass.: MIT Press.

Davidson, Christopher M. 2006. "After Sheikh Zayed: The Politics of Succession in Abu Dhabi and the UAE." *Middle East Policy* 13 (1): 42–59.

———. 2013. *After the Sheikhs: The Coming Collapse of the Gulf Monarchies*. London: Hurst.

Day, Stephen. 2012. *Regionalism and Rebellion in Yemen: A Troubled National Union*. Cambridge: Cambridge University Press.

De Atkine, Norvell. 1999. "Why Arabs Lose Wars." *Middle East Quarterly* (December).

Decalo, Samuel. 1990. *Coups and Army Rule in Africa*. New Haven, Conn.: Yale University Press.

Deeb, Marius K. 1979. *Party Politics in Egypt: The Wafd and Its Rivals 1919–1939*. London: Ithaca.

Delmar-Morgan, Alex, and Tom Wright. 2011. "Bahrain's Foreign Police Add to Tensions." *Wall Street Journal*, March 25.

Devlin, John F. 1976. *The Ba'th Party: A History from the Origins to 1966*. Palo Alto, Calif.: Hoover Institution Press.

Dillman, Bradford L. 2000. *State and Private Sector in Algeria*. Boulder, Colo.: Westview.

Doucet, Lyse. 2011. "Egypt Protests: Army Rules Out the Use of Force." *BBC News*, January 31.

Droz-Vincent, Philippe. 2007. "From Political to Economic Actors: The Changing Role of Middle Eastern Armies." In *Debating Arab Authoritarianism: Dynamics and Durability in Nondemocratic Regimes*, ed. Oliver Schlumberger. Stanford, Calif.: Stanford University Press.

———. 2011a. *A Return of Armies to the Forefront of Arab Politics?* IAI Working Paper 11/21. Rome: Instituto Affari Internazionali.

———. 2011b. "Authoritarianism, Revolutions, Armies and Arab Regime Transitions." *International Spectator* 46 (2): 5–21.

———. 2013. Interviews with Syrian activists, citizens, and military officers. Paris, Brussels, Istanbul, Geneva, The Hague.

———. 2014a. "State of Barbary (Take Two): From the Arab Spring to the Return of Violence in Syria." *Middle East Journal* 68 (1): 33–58.

———. 2014b. Interviews with Syrian activsts, citizens, and military officers. Paris, Brussels, Istanbul, Geneva, The Hague.

———. 2014c. "Prospects for 'Democratic Control of the Armed Forces'? Comparative Insights and Lessons for the Arab World in Transition." *Armed Forces and Society* 40 (October): 696–723.

Durac, Vincent. 2012. "Yemen's Arab Spring: Democratic Opening or Regime Endurance?" *Mediterranean Politics* 17 (2): 61–78.

Dziak, John. 1988. *Chekistry: A History of the KGB*. Lexington, Mass.: D. C. Heath.

Eckstein, Harry. [1975] 1992. *Regarding Politics: Essays on Political Theory, Stability, and Change*. Berkeley: University of California Press.

Economist. 2009. "Iran's Revolutionary Guards: Showing Who's Boss." August 27.

Egypt Independent. 2012. "Al-Gomhurriya Editor Suspended for Reporting SCAF Travel Bans." October 17.

———. 2013. "Rights Group: Constitutional Declaration Grants Military Absolute Powers." July 11.

Elbadawi, Ibrahim, and Samir Makdisi. 2013. "Understanding Democratic Transitions in the Arab World." Working Paper 765, Economic Research Forum. Cairo, September.

El Deber. "Goni Se Desentiende de Muertes de Octubre, 2003," July 27, 2015.

El-Ghobashy, Mona. 2011. "The Praxis of the Egyptian Revolution." *Middle East Report,* no. 258.

El Mayet, Ibrahim E. L. 2012. "The Supreme Security Committee—Guardians of the Revolution?" *Libya Herald,* October 16.

Enloe, Cynthia H. 1980. *Ethnic Soldiers: State Security in Divided Societies.* Athens: University of Georgia Press.

Epstein, David L., et al. 2006. "Democratic Transitions." *American Journal of Political Science* 50 (3): 551–69.

Erdle, Steffen. 2004. "Tunisia: Economic Transformation and Political Restoration." In *Arab Elites, Negotiating the Politics of Change,* ed. Volker Perthes. Boulder, Colo.: Lynne Rienner.

———. 2010. *Ben Ali's "New Tunisia" (1987–2009): A Case Study of Authoritarian Modernization in the Arab World.* Berlin: Klaus Schwartz.

Farrell, Theo. 2005. "World Culture and Military Power." *Security Studies* 14 (3).

Faruq, Abdel Khaleq. 2012. Interview. Cairo, November.

Fattah, Khaled. 2010. "A Political History of Civil-Military Relations in Yemen." *Alternative Politics* 1 (November): 25–47.

Fayemi, J. Kayode. 2003. "Governing the Security Sector in a Democratic Polity: Nigeria." In *Governing Insecurity: Democratic Control of Military and Security Establishments in Transitional Democracies,* ed. Gavin Cawthra and Robin Luckham. London: Zed.

Feaver, Peter D. 1996. "The Civil-Military Problematique: Huntington, Janowitz and the Question of Civilian Control." *Armed Forces and Society* 23 (Winter): 149–78.

———. 1999. "Civil-Military Relations." *Annual Review of Political Science* 2: 211–41.

———. 2003. *Armed Servants.* Cambridge, Mass.: Harvard University Press.

Feaver, Peter D., and Richard H. Kohn. 2001. *Soldiers and Civilians: The Civil-Military Gap and American National Security.* Cambridge, Mass.: MIT Press.

Fesiak, Andrew. 2002. "Nation-Building in the Ukrainian Military." In *Dilemmas of State-Led Nation-Building in Ukraine,* ed. Taras Kuzio and Paul D'Anierieds. Westport, Conn.: Praeger.

Fetouri, Mustafa. 2013. "Ill-Conceived Army Foreign Training Threatens Libya." *The National* (UAE), November 20.

Finer, Samuel E. 1962. *The Man on Horseback: The Role of the Military in Politics.* London: Pall Mall.

———. 1988. *The Man on Horseback: The Role of the Military in Politics*. Rev. ed. Boulder, Colo.: Westview.

Finkel, Evgeny, and Yitzhak M. Brudny, eds. 2013. *Colored Revolutions and Authoritarian Reactions*. London: Routledge.

Fitch, J. Samuel. 1998. *The Armed Forces and Democracy in Latin America*. Baltimore: Johns Hopkins University Press.

Fleishman, Jeffrey. 2013. "Army Ousts Morsi." *Los Angeles Times*, July 4.

Frantz, Erica, and Natasha Ezrow. 2011. *The Politics of Dictatorship: Institutions and Outcomes in Authoritarian Regimes*. Boulder, Colo.: Lynne Rienner.

Free Syrian Army. 2014. "Report: The Regime's Military Status After 100 Days of War." January 16.

Gaaloul, Badra. 2011. "Back to the Barracks: The Tunisian Army Post Revolution." *Sada*, November 3.

Gall, Carlotta. 2013a. "A Political Deal in a Deeply Divided Tunisia as Islamists Agree to Yield Power." *New York Times*, December 16.

———. 2013b. "Tunisia Faces More Anger After an Ambush Kills Soldiers." *New York Times*, July 29.

———. 2014a. "Despite Signs of Progress, Security Issues Rise in Tunisia." *New York Times*, February 7.

———. 2014b. "Tunisian Discontent Reflected in Protests That Have Idled Mines." *New York Times*, May 13.

Gambill, Gary C. 2002. "The Military-Intelligence Shakeup in Syria." *Middle East Quarterly* 4 (2).

Gandhi, Jennifer, and Adam Przeworski. 2006. "Cooperation, Cooptation and Rebellion Under Dictatorships." *Economics and Politics* 18 (March): 1–26.

———. 2007. "Authoritarian Institutions and the Survival of Autocrats." *Comparative Political Studies* 40: 1279–301.

Gassner, Robert J. 1987. "Transition in Tunisia." *International Review* (May–June).

Gaub, Florence. 2013. "The Libyan Armed Forces Between Coup-Proofing and Repression." *Journal of Strategic Studies* 36 (2): 221–44.

Geddes, B., E. Frantz, and J. G. Wright. 2014. "Military Rule." *Annual Review of Political Science* 17: 147–62.

Geddes, Barbara. 1999. "What Do We Know About Democratization After Twenty Years?" *Annual Review of Political Science* 2: 115–44.

———. 2003. *Paradigms and Sand Castles: Theory Building and Research Design in Comparative Politics*. Ann Arbor: University of Michigan Press.

———. 2004. "Authoritarian Breakdown." Unpublished paper. University of California, Los Angeles.

Gelvin, James. 2012. *The Arab Uprisings: What Everyone Needs to Know*. Oxford: Oxford University Press.

Gengler, Justin. 2011. "Ethnic Conflict and Political Mobilization in Bahrain and the Arab Gulf." Doctoral dissertation, University of Michigan, Ann Arbor.

George, Alexander L., and Andrew Bennett. 2005. *Case Studies and Theory Development in the Social Sciences.* Cambridge, Mass.: MIT Press.

Global Military Balance. 2013. London: International Institute for Strategic Studies.

Glover, Charles. 2009. "Shift to the Shadows." *Financial Times,* December 17.

Goemans, Henk E., Kristian Gleditsch, and Giacomo Chiozza. 2009. "Introducing Archigos: A Dataset of Political Leaders." *Journal of Peace Research* 46 (2): 269–83.

Gogolewska, Agnieszka. 2006. "Problems Confronting Civilian Democratic Control in Poland." In *Civil Military Relations in Europe: Learning from Crisis and Institutional Change,* ed. Hans Born, Marina Caparini, Karl Haltiner, and Juergen Kuhlmann. London: Routledge.

Goldstein, Eric. 2011. "Dismantling the Machinery of Oppression." *Wall Street Journal,* February 16.

Goldstone, Jack A. 2001. "Toward a Fourth Generation of Revolutionary Theory." Annual Review of Political Science 4: 139–187

Goodman, Colby. 2014. "Security Sector Reform a Key Issue to Watch in Tunisia." *Security Assistance Monitor,* December 19.

———. 2015. "U.S.-Tunisia Security Cooperation Escalates to Nearly $100 Million." *Security Assistance Monitor,* May 19.

Gordon, Joel. 1989. "The False Hopes of 1950—the Wafd Last Hurrah and the Demise of Egypt's Old Order." *International Journal of Middle East Studies* 21 (2): 193–214.

Gordon, Sasha, and Katherine Z. Zimmerman. 2012. *2012 Yemen Order of Battle.* http://www.criticalthreats.org. April 12.

Gotowicki, Stephen. 1997. *The Role of the Egyptian Military in Domestic Society.* Institute of National Strategic Studies, National Defense University. May 30.

Gulf Military Balance. 2010. Washington, D.C.: Center for Strategic and International Studies.

Haddad, Saïd. 2012. "Les forces armées libyennes de la proclamation de la Jamahiriya au lendemain de la chute de Tripoli: Une marginalization paradoxale." *Politique Africaine* 125.

Hakim, Muhammad A. 1998. "Bangladesh: The Beginning of the End of Militarized Politics?" *Contemporary South Asia* 7 (3): 283–300.

Halpern, Manfred 1963. *The Politics of Social Change in the Middle East and North Africa.* Princeton, N.J.: Princeton University Press.

Hanlon, Querine. 2012a. *The Prospects for Security Sector Reform in Tunisia: A Year After the Revolution.* Strategic Studies Institute. Fort Leavenworth, Kans.: U.S. Army War College. September.

———. 2012b. *Security Sector Reform in Tunisia: A Year After the Jasmine Revolution.* Special Report 304. Washington, D.C.: United States Institute of Peace.

Harb, Imad. 2003. "The Egyptian Military in Politics: Disengagement or Accommodation?" *Middle East Journal* 57 (2): 269–90.

Harkness, Kristen A. 2012. "The Origins of African Civil-Military Relations: Ethnic Armies and the Development of Coup Traps." Unpublished doctoral dissertation, Princeton University.

Hasbani, Nadim. 2006. "The Geopolitics of Weapons Procurement in the Gulf States." *Defense and Security Analysis* 22 (1): 73–88.

Hashim, Ahmed S. 2011. "The Egyptian Military, Part One: From the Ottomans through Sadat." *Middle East Policy* 18 (3): 63–78.

Hauslohner, Abigail. 2013. "Egypt Military Re-enters the Political Fray." *Washington Post*, July 2.

HCT Press Release. 2011. "HCT Launches Inaugural Unmanned Systems Rodeo Competition at IDEX." February 22.

Hedman, Eva-Lotta. 2001. "The Philippines: Not So Military, Not So Civil." In *Coercion and Governance*, ed. Muthiah Alagappa. Stanford, Calif.: Stanford University Press.

Heinecken, Lindy. 2009. "Discontent Within the Ranks? Officers' Attitudes Toward Military Employment and Representation—A Four-Country Comparative Study." *Armed Forces and Society* 35 (3): 477–500.

Hendawi, Hamza. 2013. "Disputes Between Morsi, Military Led to Egypt Coup." Associated Press, July.

Henderson, William D. 1985. *Cohesion: The Human Element in Combat*. Washington, D.C.: National Defense University Press.

Henriksen, Rune. 2007. "Warriors in Combat—What Makes People Actively Fight in Combat?" *Journal of Strategic Studies* 30 (2): 187–223.

Henry, Clement M., and Robert Springborg. 2011. "The Tunisian Army: Defending the Beachhead of Democracy in the Arab World." Huffington Post, January 26.

Hertog, Steffen. 2011. "Rentier Militaries in the Gulf States: The Price of Coup-Proofing." *International Journal of Middle East Studies* 43 (3): 400–402.

Heydemann, Steven. 1999. *Authoritarianism in Syria: Institutions and Social Conflict, 1946–1970*. Ithaca, N.Y.: Cornell University Press.

Hilal, Ali El Din. 2006. *Tatawwur Al-Nizam Al-Siyasi Fi Misr, 1805–2005* [The Development of the Egyptian Political System, 1805–2005]. Cairo: Jami'ah al-Qahirah, Kulliyah al-Iqtisad wa-al-'Ulum al-Siyasiya, Markaz al-Buhuth wa-al-Dirasat al-Siyasiya.

Hinnebusch, Raymond A. 1990. *Authoritarian Power and State Formation in Ba'thist Syria: Army, Party, and Peasant*. Boulder, Colo.: Westview.

———. 2001. *Syria: Revolution from Above*. London: Routledge.

———. 2012. "Syria: from 'Authoritarian Upgrading' to Revolution?" *International Affairs* 88 (1): 95–113.

Holliday, John. 2013. *The Assad Regime*. Middle East Security Report No. 8. Institute for the Study of War, Washington, D.C., March.

Human Rights Watch. 2003. *Letter to President Carlos Mesa Gilbert*. New York, December 22.

———. 2010. *Torture Redux: The Revival of Physical Coercion During Interrogations in Bahrain*. New York, February 8.

———. 2011a. Egypt: Don't Cover Up Military Killing of Copt Protesters: Official Denials Suggest Investigation Will be Flawed. New York. October 25.

———. 2011b. *We Have Never Seen Such Horrors: Crimes Against Humanity by Syrian Security Forces.* New York, June 1.

———. 2012. "Egypt: Forced Eviction by Military Leaves One Dead." November 21.

Huntington, Samuel P. 1957. *The Soldier and the State: The Theory and Politics of Civil-Military Relations.* Cambridge, Mass.: Harvard University Press.

———. 1968. *Political Order in Changing Societies.* New Haven, Conn.: Yale University Press.

———. 1995. "Reforming Civil-Military Relations." *Journal of Democracy* 6 (4): 9–17.

Hutchful, Eboe. 2003. "Pulling Back from the Brink: Ghana's Experience." In *Governing Insecurity: Democratic Control of Military and Security Establishments in Transitional Democracies,* ed. Gavin Cawthra and Robin Luckham. London: Zed.

Intelligence Online. 2013. "Al Kaabi Family Profile." October 23.

International Crisis Group. 2005. *Bahrain's Sectarian Challenge.* Brussels.

———. 2011a. *Holding Libya Together: Security Challenges After Qaddafi.* Middle East/North Africa Report 115. Brussels, December 14.

———. 2011b. *Popular Protests in North Africa and the Middle East III: The Bahrain Revolt.* Middle East/North Africa Report No. 105. Brussels, April 6.

———. 2011c. *Popular Protest in North Africa and the Middle East IV: Tunisia's Way,* Middle East/North Africa Report No. 106. Brussels, April 26.

———. 2012. *Yemen: Enduring Conflicts, Threatened Transition.* Brussels.

———. 2013. *Yemen's Military-Security Reform: Seeds of New Conflict?* Middle East/North Africa Report 139. Brussels, April 4.

Jamestown Foundation. 2011. "Alawi Control of the Syrian Military Key to Regime's Survival." *Terrorism Monitor,* June 9.

Janowitz, Morris. 1960. *The Professional Soldier: A Social and Political Portrait.* Glencoe, Ill.: Free Press.

Jaskoski, Maiah. 2012. "The Ecuadorian Army: Neglecting a Porous Border While Policing the Interior." *Latin American Politics and Society* 54 (1): 127–57.

Jebnoun, Noureddine. 2014. "In the Shadow of Power: Civil-Military Relations and the Tunisian Popular Uprising." *Journal of North African Studies* 19 (3): 296–316.

Johnson, Thomas H., R. O. Slater, and Pat McGowan. 1984. "Explaining African Military Coups d'État, 1960–1982." *American Political Science Review* 78 (3): 622–40.

Kallander, Amy Aisen. 2011. "Tunisia's Post Ben Ali Challenge: A Primer." Middle East Research and Information Project, January 26.

Kamm, Henry. 1984. "Tunisia Appears to Halt Wave of Rioting with Show of Troops and Armor." *New York Times,* January 5.

Kamrava, Mehran. 2000. "Military Professionalization and Civil-Military Relations in the Middle East." *Political Science Quarterly* 115 (Spring): 67–92.

Kandil, Hazem. 2012. *Soldiers, Spies, and Statesmen: Egypt's Road to Revolt.* London: Verso.

Karam, Souhail. 2010. "Saudi Arabia Opens Military Supply to Local Firms." Reuters, February 7.

Keenan, Jeremy. 2010. "General Toufik: 'God of Algeria.'" Al Jazeera, September 29.

Khaled, Ali. 2014. "Martial Arts Opening New Doors for People in the UAE." *National* (UAE), June 6.

Khan, Umar. 2013. "Demonstration in Support of Isolation Law." *Libya Herald*, April 30.

Khatib, Lina. 2014. "Tunisia's Security Challenge." Carnegie Middle East Center, November 26.

Kier, Elizabeth. 1997. *Imagining War: French and British Military Doctrine Between the Wars*. Princeton, N.J.: Princeton University Press.

Kim, Insoo. 2008. *Bringing the Military Back in Political Transition: Democratic Transition by and for Powerless Officers in South Korea*. Madison: UMI Dissertation Publishing.

———. 2012. "Intra-Military Divisions and Democratization in South Korea." *Armed Forces and Society* (August).

Kim, Sunhyuk. 1997. "State and Civil Society in South Korea's Democratic Consolidation: is the battle really over?" *Asian Survey* 37 (12): 1135–45.

Kim, Su-whan. 2000. "Former KMA Superintendent Min Byeong-Don." *Monthly Chosun*, September.

King, Stephen J. 2009. *The New Authoritarianism in the Middle East and North Africa*. Bloomington: Indiana University Press.

Kingsley, Patrick, and Marwa Awad. 2013. "Egypt's Army Chief Rides Wave of Popularity Towards Presidency." *Guardian*, October 20.

Kirkpatrick, David D. 2011a. "Protests Spread to Tunisia's Capital and a Curfew Is Decreed." *New York Times*, January 13.

———. 2011b. "In Tunisia, Clashes Continue as Power Shifts a Second Time." *New York Times*, January 15.

———. 2011c. "Military Backs New Leaders in Tunisia." *New York Times*, January 16.

———. 2011d. "In Tunisia, New Leaders Win Support of Military." *New York Times*, January 17.

———. 2011e. "Chief of Tunisian Army Pledges His Support for the Revolution." *New York Times*, January 25.

Klaas, Brian. 2013. "The Long Shadow of Ben Ali: How a Decades Old Fake Coup Attempt Is Taking its Toll on Tunisia." *Foreign Policy*, December 17.

Knights, Michael. 2003. "Future Development of GCC Air Forces; Part 2." Air Combat Information Group, December 18.

———. 2013. "The Military Role in Yemen's Protests: Civil-Military Relations in the Tribal Republic." *Journal of Strategic Studies* 36 (2): 261–88.

Kochaneck, Stanley A. 1993. *Patron-client politics and business in Bangladesh*. New Delhi: Sage.

Kodmani, Bassma, and May Chartouni-Dubarry. 2009. "The Security Sector in Arab Countries: Can It Be Reformed?" *IDS Bulletin* 40 (2).

Koehler, Kevin. 2013. "Military Elites and Regime Trajectories in the Arab Spring: Egypt, Syria, Tunisia and Yemen in Comparative Perspective." Doctoral dissertation, European University Institute.

Kolkowicz, Roman. 1967. *The Soviet Military and the Communist Party*. Princeton, N.J.: Princeton University Press.

Koonings, Kees. 2003. "Political Armies, Security Forces and Democratic Consolidation in Latin America." In *Governing Insecurity: Democratic Control of Military and Security Establishments in Transitional Democracies*, ed. Gavin Cawthra and Robin Luckham. London: Zed.

Koonings, Kees, and Dirk Kruijt. 2002. *Political Armies: The Military and Nation Building in the Age of Democracy*. London: Zed.

Kostiner, Joseph. 1996. *Yemen: The Tortuous Quest for Unity, 1990–1994*. London: Royal Institute of International Affairs.

Kozak, Christopher. 2015. *An Army in All Corners*. Middle East Security Report No. 26. Institute for the Study of War. Washington, D.C., April.

Kryshtanovskaya, Olga, and Stephen White. 2003. "Putin's Militocracy." *Post Soviet Affairs* 19 (4): 289–306.

Kuehn, David, and Philip Lorenz. 2011. "Explaining Civil-Military Relations in New Democracies: Structure, Agency and Theory Development." *Asian Journal of Political Science* 19 (3): 231–49.

Kuran, Timur. 1991. "Now Out of Never: The Element of Surprise in the East European Revolutions of 1989." *World Politics* 44 (1): 7–48.

Kuzio, Taras. 1995. "Ukrainian Civil-Military Relations and the Military Impact of the Ukrainian Economic Crisis." In *State Building and Military Power in Russia and the New States of Eurasia*, ed. Bruce Parrott. Armonk, N.Y.: M. E. Sharpe.

Lachapelle, Jean, Lucan Way, and Steven Levitsky. 2012. *Crisis, Coercion and Authoritarian Durability: Explaining Diverging Responses to Anti-Regime Protest in Egypt and Iran*. CDDRL Working Paper No. 127. Center for Democracy, Development, and the Rule of Law. Stanford University, Palo Alto, Calif.

Lachmann, Richard. 1997. "Agents of Revolution: Elite Conflicts and Mass Mobilization from the Medici to Yeltsin." In *Theorizing Revolutions*, ed. John Foran. London: Routledge.

La Nación. 2000. "Para el ministro, son las fuerzas armadas más chicas del mundo." September 4.

———. 2001a. "La Justicia rechazó un pedido de excarcelación para Massera." July 11.

———. 2001b. "De la Rúa derogó el estado de sitio." December 20.

Lawson, Fred H. 1993. "Neglected Aspects of the Security Dilemma." In *The Many Faces of National Security in the Arab World*, ed. Bahgat Korany, Paul Noble, and Rex Brynen. London: Macmillan.

———. 2007. "Intraregime Dynamics, Uncertainty and the Persistence of Authoritarianism in the Contemporary Arab World." In *Debating Arab Authoritarianism*, ed. Oliver Schlumberger. Stanford, Calif.: Stanford University Press.

———. 2013. *Global Security Watch Syria*. Santa Barbara, Calif.: Praeger.

Lee, Terence. 2005. "Military Cohesion and Regime Maintenance: Explaining the Role of the Military in 1989 China and 1998 Indonesia." *Armed Forces and Society* 32 (1): 80–104.

———. 2006. "The Causes of Military Insubordination: Explaining Military Organizational Behavior in China, Indonesia, the Philippines, and Thailand." Doctoral dissertation, University of Washington.

———. 2009. "The Armed Forces and Transitions from Authoritarian Rule: Explaining the Role of the Military in 1986 Philippines and 1998 Indonesia." *Comparative Political Studies* 42 (5): 640–69.

———. 2015. *Defect or Defend: Military Responses to Popular Protests in Authoritarian Asia*. Baltimore: Johns Hopkins University Press.

Levitsky, Steven, and Lucan A. Way. 2010. *Competitive Authoritarianiam*. Cambridge: Cambridge University Press.

———. 2012. "Beyond Patronage: Violent Struggle, Ruling Party Cohesion, and Authoritarian Durability." *Perspectives on Politics* 10 (4): 869–89.

Longley Alley, April. 2013. "Assessing (In)security After the Arab Spring: The Case of Yemen." *PS: Political Science and Politics* 46 (4) (April): 721–26.

———. 1999. *For La Patria: Politics and the Armed Forces in Latin America*. Wilmington, N.C.: Scholarly Resources.

Loveman, Brian 1999. *For la Patria: Politics and the Armed Forces in Latin America*. Wilmington: SR.

Lowenthal, Abraham F., and J. Samuel Fitch. 1986. *Armies and Politics in Latin America*. New York: Holmes and Meier.

Lust-Okar, Ellen. 2005. *Structuring Conflict in the Arab World: Incumbents, Opponents and Institutions*. Cambridge: Cambridge University Press.

Lutterbeck, Derek. 2011. *Arab Uprisings and Armed Forces: Between Openness and Resistance*. SSR Paper No. 2. Geneva: Centre for the Democratic Control of Armed Forces.

———. 2012. *After the Fall: Security Sector Reform in Post-Ben Ali Tunisia*. Arab Reform Initiative, September.

———. 2013. "Arab Uprisings, Armed Forces and Civil-Military Relations." *Armed Forces and Society* 39 (1): 28–52.

Maghreb Confidential. 2011a. "Army Serves as Ben Ali's Last Rampart." January 13.

———. 2011b. "Has Ben Ali Played His Last Cards." January 6.

Makara, Michael. 2013. "Coup-Proofing, Military Defection and the Arab Spring." *Democracy and Security* 9 (4): 334–59.

Malik, Adeel, and Bassem Awadallah. 2013. "The Economics of the Arab Spring." *World Development* 20: 1–18.

Mantle, Craig Leslie. 2006. *The Unwilling and the Reluctant: Theoretical Perspectives on Disobedience in the Military*. Kingston, Ontario: Canadian Defense Academy Press.

Markowski, Stephan, and Peter Hall. 2004. "Mandatory Defense Offsets: Conceptual Foundations." In *Arms Trade and Economic Development*, ed. J. Brauer and J. Paul Dunne. London: Routledge.

Marsad Egypt. 2014. "Constitution of the Arab Republic of Egypt 2014." March 14, http://www.marsad.eg/en/constitution-of-the-arab-republic-of-egypt-2014/.

Marshall, Shana, and Joshua Stacher. 2012. "Egypt's Generals and Transnational Capital." *Middle East Report* no. 262: 12–18.

Matei, Christiana. 2007. "Romania's Transition to Democracy and the Role of the Press in Intelligence Reform." In *Reforming Intelligence: Obstacles to Democratic Control and Effectiveness*, ed. Thomas C. Bruneau and Steven C. Boraz. Austin: University of Texas Press.

McFate, Sean. 2008. *Securing the Future: A Primer on Security Sector Reform in Conflict Countries*. Special Report, United States Institute of Peace. Washington, D.C., September.

McLauchlin, Theodore. 2010. "Loyalty Strategies and Military Defection in Rebellion." *Comparative Politics* 42 (3): 333–50.

McLeod, Ross H. 2008. "Survey of Recent Developments." *Bulletin of Indonesian Economic Studies* 44 (2):183–208.

Mezran, Karim, and Eric Knecht. 2013. *Libya's Fractious Politics*. The Atlantic Council, January 9.

Middle East Research Institute. 1985. *United Arab Emirates*. Dover, N.H.: Croom Helm.

Mietzner, Marcus. 2009. *Military Politics, Islam, and the State in Indonesia*. Singapore: Institute of Southeast Asian Studies.

Military Balance. 2012. International Institute for Strategic Studies. London, March.

Ministry of Finance. 2013. *Financial Statement of State's General Budget for the Fiscal Year 2013/2014*. Cairo: Ministry of Finance Publications, October 22.

Mohsin, Ahmed. 2001. "Bangladesh: An Uneasy Accomodation." In *Coercion and Governance: The Declining Political Role of the Military in Asia*, ed. M. Alagappa. Stanford, Calif.: Stanford University Press.

Mohy El Deen, Sharif. 2015. "Fair Trials for All." Arab Reform Initiative, June.

Moon, Chung-In, and Sang-Young Rhyu. 2011. "Democratic Transition, Persistent Civilian Control over Military and the South Korean Anomaly." *Asian Journal of Political Science* 19 (3): 250–69.

Moore, Clement H. 1964. "The Era of the Neo-Destour." In *Tunisia: The Politics of Modernization*, ed. Charles A. Micaud. New York: Praeger.

Moore, Jack. 2015. "The Lawless Hotbed of Jihadism in Tunisia's Western Mountains." *Newsweek*, March 20.

Mora, Frank, and Quintan Wiktorowicz. 2003. "Economic Reform and the Military: China, Cuba, and Syria in Comparative Perspective." *International Journal of Comparative Sociology* 44 (2): 87–128.

Moran, Jonathan. 2005. "The Role of the Security Services in Democratization: South Korea's Agency for National Security Planning." In *Who's Watching the Spies? Establishing Intelligence Service Accountability*, ed. Hans Born, Loch K. Johnson, and Ian Leigh. Washington, D.C.: Potomac Books.

Morsy, Ahmed. 2014. "The Military Crowds Out Civilian Business in Egypt." Carnegie Endowment for International Peace, June 24.

Mortimer, Robert. 2006. "State and Army in Algeria: The 'Bouteflika Effect.'" *Journal of North African Studies* 11 (June): 155–71.

Moskos, Charles C., and Frank R. Wood. 1988. *The Military: More Than Just a Job?* Washington: Pergamon-Brassey's.

Mullins, Lisa. 2011. "Egyptian Military's Role in the Crisis." Public Radio International, the World, February 7.

Murphy, Emma. 1999. *Economic and Political Change in Tunisia: from Bourguiba to Ben Ali.* New York: Palgrave Macmillan.

———. 2002. "The Foreign Policy of Tunisia." In *The Foreign Policies of Middle East States*, ed. Raymond Hinnebusch and Anoushiravan Ehteshami. Boulder, Colo.: Lynne Rienner.

———. 2011. "Exit Ben Ali, but Can Tunisia Change." BBC News Africa, January 15.

Mustafa, Awad. 2015. "UAE Contract Awards Favor Joint Ventures." *Defense News*, March 1.

Nation Shield. 2012. "UAE Armed Forces: A Shield to Defend the Nation." May 10.

Nepstad, Sharon Erickson. 2011. *Nonviolent Revolutions: Civil Resistance in the Late 20th Century*. New York: Oxford University Press.

———. 2013. "Mutiny and Nonviolence in the Arab Spring: Exploring Military Defections and Loyalty in Egypt, Bahrain and Syria." *Journal of Peace Research* 50 (May): 337–49.

Newbould, Chris. 2014. "Popularity of Dubai-Based Mixed Martial Arts TV Programme Grows with the Sport." *The National* (UAE), April 8.

New York Times. 2009a. "Hard-Line Force Extends Grip over a Splintered Iran." July 20.

———. 2009b. "Layers of Armed Forces Wielding Power of Law." June 22.

———. 2011. "Academics see the Military in Decline, but Retaining Strong Influence." June 11.

———. 2012. "Soldier Says Syrian Atrocities Forced Him to Defect." February 1.

Nordlinger, Eric. 1977. *Soldiers in Politics: Military Coups and Governments.* Upper Saddle River, N.J.: Prentice-Hall.

Odom, William E. 1998. *The Collapse of the Soviet Military.* New Haven, Conn.: Yale University Press.

O'Donnell, Guillermo, and Philippe C. Schmitter. 1986. *Transitions from Authoritarian Rule: Tentative Conclusions About Uncertain Democracies.* Baltimore: Johns Hopkins University Press.

OECD. 2013. "State-Owned Enterprises in the Middle East and North Africa: Engines of Development and Competitiveness?" October 21.

Oh, John Kie-Chiang. 1999. *Korean Politics: The Quest for Democratization and Economic Development.* Ithaca, N.Y.: Cornell University Press.

Ohl, Dorothy, Holger Albrecht, and Kevin Koehler. 2015. "For Money or Liberty? The Political Economy of Military Desertion and Rebel Recruitment in the Syrian Civil War." Carnegie Middle East Center, November 24.

Olarte, Olivia. 2011. "Students to Be Directed to Right Career Path." *Khaleej Times*, June 6.

Onley, James. 2009. "Britain and the Gulf Shaikhdoms, 1820–1972: The Politics of Protection." Occasional Paper No. 4, Center for International and Regional Studies, Georgetown University School of Foreign Service in Qatar.

Overton, Iain. 2014. "Death Is German: Die Zeit Exposé on Heckler and Koch's Shady Dealings in Mexico." *Action on Armed Violence*, January 7.

Pachon, Alejandro. 2014. "Loyalty and Defection: Misunderstanding Civil-Military Relations in Tunisia During the Arab Spring." *Journal of Strategic Studies* (April).

Pack, Jason, Karim Mezran, and Mohamed Eljarh. 2014. *Libya's Faustian Bargains: Breaking the Appeasement Cycle*. The Atlantic Council.

Parchomenko, Walter. 2000. "The State of Ukraine's Armed Forces and Military Reform." *Journal of Slavic Military Studies* 13 (3): 63–86.

Passela, Amith. 2015. "Emiratis Help Push Jiu-Jitsu as Category at Jakarta Asian Games." *The National* (UAE), January 25.

Perito, Bob. 2012. "Reforming the Security Sector in Tunisia and Libya." February 7.

———. 2015. "Security Sector Reform in North Africa: Why It's Not Happening." Security Sector Resource Centre, January 7.

Perlmutter, Amos. 1974. *Egypt: The Praetorian State*. New Brunswick, N.J.: Transaction Books.

Perlmutter, Amos, and W. M. LeoGrande. 1982. "The Party in Uniform: Toward a Theory of Civil-Military Relations in Communist Political Systems." *American Political Science Review* 76 (4): 778–89.

Peterson, John E. 1981. "The Yemen Arab Republic and the Politics of Balance." *Asian Affairs* 12 (November): 254–66.

Pew Global. 2013. "Tunisians Disaffected with Leaders as Conditions Worsen." December 12.

Phillips, Sarah. 2011. *Yemen and the Politics of Permanent Crisis*. Adelphi Paper No. 420. London: International Institute of Strategic Studies.

Phillips, Steven E. 2007. "Taiwan's Intelligence Reform in an Age of Democratization." In *Reforming Intelligence: Obstacles to Democratic Control and Effectiveness*, ed. Thomas C. Bruneau and Steven C. Boraz. Austin: University of Texas Press.

Picard, Elizabeth. 1990. "Arab Military in Politics: From Revolutionary Plot to Authoritarian State." In *The Arab State*, ed. Giacomo Luciani. Berkeley: University of California Press.

———. 1993. "State and Society in the Arab World: Towards a New Role for the Security Services?" In *The Many Faces of National Security in the Arab World*, ed. Bahgat Korany, Paul Noble, and Rex Brynen. London: Macmillan.

———. 1999. *The Demobilization of the Lebanese Militias*. Oxford, UK: Centre for Lebanese Studies.

Pilster, Ulrich, and Tobias Böhmelt. 2011. "Coup-Proofing and Military Effectiveness in Interstate Wars, 1967–99." *Conflict Management and Peace Science* 28 (4): 331–50.

———. 2012. "Do Democracies Engage Less in Coup-Proofing? On the Relationship Between Regime Type and Civil-Military Relations." *Foreign Policy Analysis* 8 (4): 355–72.

Pion-Berlin, David. 1997. *Through Corridors of Power: Institutions and Civil-Military Relations in Argentina.* University Park: Pennsylvania State University Press.

———. 2011. "The Study of Civil-Military Relations in New Democracies." *Asian Journal of Political Science* 19 (3): 222–30.

Pion-Berlin, David, Kevin Grisham, and Diego Esparza. 2014. "Staying Quartered: Civilian Uprisings and Military Disobedience in the Twenty First Century." *Comparative Political Studies* 47 (2): 230–59.

Pion-Berlin, David, and Harold Trinkunas. 2005. "Democratization, Social Crisis and the Impact of Military Domestic Roles in Latin America." *Journal of Political and Military Sociology* 33 (Summer): 5–24.

———. 2010. "Civilian Praetorianism and Military Shirking During Constitutional Crises in Latin America." *Comparative Politics* 42 (4): 395–411.

Powell, Jonathan. 2012a. "Coups and Conflict: The Paradox of Coup-Proofing." Unpublished paper, University of Kentucky, Lexington.

———. 2012b. "Determinants of the Attempting and Outcome of Coups d'Etat." *Journal of Conflict Resolution* 56: 1017–40.

———. 2014. "Trading Coups for Civil War: The Strategic Logic of Tolerating Rebellion." http://ssrn.com/abstract=2466225.

Przeworski, Adam, Michael E. Alvarez, Jose Antonio Cheibub, and Fernando Limongi. 2000. *Democracy and Development: Political Institutions and Well-Being in the World, 1950–1990.* New York: Cambridge University Press.

Quinlivan, James T. 1999. "Coup-Proofing: Its Practice and Consequences in the Middle East." *International Security* 24 (2): 131–65.

Quintana, Juan Ramón. 2004. "Policías y militares: Memorias y escenarios de conflictoen Bolivia." RESDAL, February.

Rabinovich, Itamar. 1972. *Syria Under the Ba'th, 1963–66: The Army-Party Symbiosis.* Jerusalem: Israel Universities Press.

Radwan, Tarek. 2013. *The Almost-Aid Cut to Egypt.* The Atlantic Council, October 9.

Ragin, Charles. 1997. "Turning the Tables: How Case-Oriented Research Challenges Variable-Oriented Research." *Comparative Social Research* 16: 27–42.

Rand Corporation. 2009. *The Rise of Pasradan: Assessing the Domestic Role of Iran's Islamic Revolutionary Guard Corps.* Santa Monica, Calif.: Rand.

Remmer, Karen. 1985. *Military Rule in Latin America.* Boston: Unwin Hyman.

RESDAL. 2012. *A Comparative Atlas of Defence in Latin America and the Caribbean.* Buenos Aires: Red de Seugirdad y Defense de America Latina.

Reuters. 2010. "Saudi Arabia Opens Military Supply to Local Firms." February 7.

———. 2011. "Factbox: Demands of Bahrain's Protestors." February 15.

———. 2012. "T'adat Tashkil Majlis al-Difa' al-Wattani fi Misr" [The Reconstitution of Egypt's National Defense Council]. June 18.

———. 2015. "French Rafale Fighter Jet Sale to Egypt 'Imminent': Source." February 10.

Rice, Condoleezza. 1982. "The Problem of Military Elite Cohesion in Eastern Europe." *Air University Review* (January–February).

Riedel, Bruce. 2008. *Saudi Arabia: Nervously Watching Pakistan*. Washington, D.C.: Brookings Institution.

Roberts, Hugh. 1994. "Algeria Between Eradicators and Conciliators." *Middle East Report* 189 (July–August): 24–27.

———. 2007. *Demilitarizing Algeria*. Carnegie Papers 86. Carnegie Endowment for International Peace. Washington, D.C., May.

———. 2011. "Algeria's National 'Protesta.'" *Foreign Policy*, January 10.

Roehrig, Terence. 2002. *The Prosecution of Former Military Leaders in Newly Democratic Nations: The Cases of Argentina, Greece, and South Korea*. Jefferson, Mo.: McFarland.

Roessler, Philip. 2011. "The Enemy Within: Personal Rule, Coups, and Civil War in Africa." *World Politics* 63 (2): 300–46.

Rouquie, Alain. 1987. *The Military and the State in Latin America*. Berkeley: University of California Press.

Russell, Diana E. H. 1974. *Rebellion, Revolution, and Armed Force: A Comparative Study of Fifteen Countries with Special Emphasis on Cuba and South Africa*. New York: Academic Press.

Sahraouni, Hassiba Hadj. 2013. "Time for Security Reform in Tunisia." www.tunisia-live.net, August 7.

Salem, Ola. 2014. "Benefits Await Emiratis Who Complete Military Service." *National* (UAE), March 4.

Sambidge, Andy. 2013. "US Defense Giant Launches Saudi Tech Partnership." *Arabian Business*, October 13.

Samti, Farah. 2013. "Tunisian Civil Society Lambasts Police Reform Process." www.tunisia-live.net, January 25.

Saudi Arabian Monetary Agency. 2013. *49th Annual Report*. SAMA: Riyad.

Saudi Gazette. 2011. "Saudi Arabia: KACST, Dassault Systems in Deal at the Paris Air Show." June 25.

Sayigh, Yezid. 2011. "The Tunisian Army: A New Political Role?" *Cairo Review*, October 31.

———. 2012. *Above the State: The Officers' Republic in Egypt*. Carnegie Papers, August.

———. 2014. *Arab Police Reform: Returning to Square One*. Carnegie Papers, January.

———. 2015. *Missed Opportunities: The Failure of Police Reform in Egypt and Tunisia*. Carnegie Endowment for International Peace, March 17.

Schedler, Andreas. 2006. *Electoral Authoritarianism*. Boulder, Colo.: Lynne Rienner.

———. 2009. "The New Institutionalism in the Study of Authoritarian Regimes." *Totalitarismus und Demokratie* 6 (2): 323–40.

———. 2013. *The Politics of Uncertainty: Sustaining and Subverting Electoral Authoritarianism*. Oxford: Oxford University Press.

Schiff, Rebecca. 1995. "Civil-Military Relations Reconsidered: A Theory of Concordance." *Armed Forces and Society* 22 (1): 7–24.

Schock, Kurt. 2005. *Unarmed Insurrections: People Power Movements in Nondemocracies*. Minneapolis: University of Minnesota Press.

Scobell, Andrew. 1992. "Why the People's Army Fired on the People: The Chinese Military and Tiananmen." *Armed Forces and Society* 18 (2): 193–213.

Scobell, Andrew, and Larry M. Wortzel. 2004. *Civil-Military Change in China: Elites, Institutes, and Ideas After the 16th Party Congress*. Strategic Studies Institute, http://www.strategicstudiesinstitute.army.mil/pubs/display.cfm?pubID=413.

Seale, Patrick. 1988. *Asad of Syria: The Struggle for the Middle East*. London: Tauris.

Serra, Narcis. 2010. *The Military Transition: Democratic Reform of the Armed Forces*. Cambridge: Cambridge University Press.

Shadid, Anthony. 2011. "Security Forces Kill Dozens in Uprisings Around Syria." *New York Times*, April 22.

Shambaugh, David. 1991. "The Soldier and the State in China: The Political Work System in the People's Liberation Army." *China Quarterly* 127 (September): 527–68.

Shams El-Din, Mai. 2013. "Under New Constitution, the Battle Continues Against Military Trials of Civilians." *Egypt Independent*, January 17.

Siddiqa, Ayesha. 2007. *Military Inc: Inside Pakistan's Military Economy*. London: Pluto.

Siebold, Guy L. 2007. "The Essence of Military Group Cohesion." *Armed Forces and Society* 33 (2): 286–95.

———. 2011. "Key Questions and Challenges to the Standard Model of Military Group Cohesion." *Armed Forces and Society* 37 (3): 448–68.

Singer, J. David, Stuart Bremer, and John Stuckey. 1972. "Capability Distribution, Uncertainty, and Major Power War, 1820–1965." In *Peace, War, and Numbers*, ed. Bruce Russett. Beverly Hills: Sage.

Singh, Naunihal. 2014. *Seizing Power: The Strategic Logic of Military Coups*. Baltimore: John Hopkins University Press.

Skocpol, Theda. 1979. *States and Social Revolutions*. Cambridge: Cambridge University Press.

Slackman, Michael, and Nadim Audi. 2011. "Security Forces in Bahrain Open Fire on Protesters." *New York Times*, February 18.

Slama, Nissaf. 2014. "As Tunisia Marks Revolution, Clashes Continue." www.tunisia-live.net, January 15.

Slater, Dan. 2010. *Ordering Power*. Cambridge: Cambridge University Press.

Sly, Liz. 2011. "In Syria, Defectors Form Dissident Army in Sign Uprising May Be Entering New Phase." *Washington Post*, September 26.

Smith, Charles D. 1979. "4 February 1942: Its Causes and Its Influence on Egyptian Politics and on the Future of Anglo-Egyptian Relations, 1937–1945." *International Journal of Middle East Studies* 10 (4): 453–79.

Söyler, Mehtap. 2013. "Informal Institutions, Forms of State and Democracy: The Turkish Deep State." *Democratization* 20 (2): 310–34.

Springborg, Robert. 1987. "The President and the Field Marshal: Civil-Military Relations in Egypt Today." *Middle East Report* 147 (July–August): 4–16.

———. 1989. *Mubarak's Egypt: Fragmentation of the Political Order.* Boulder, Colo.: Westview.

———. 2011a. "Armes reiches Land: Ohne einen wirtschaftspolitischen Neustart kommt Ägypten nicht auf die Beine." *Internationale Politik* (May–June): 96–104.

———. 2011b. "Economic Involvements of Militaries." *International Journal of Middle East Studies* 43 (3): 397–99.

———. 2012. "The View from the Officers' Club." *Egypt Independent*, November 29.

Springborg, Robert, and Clement Henry. 2011. "Army Guys." *American Interest*, May–June.

Stacher, Joshua. 2012. *Adaptable Autocrats: Regime Power in Egypt and Syria.* Stanford, Calif.: Stanford University Press.

———. 2013. *Deeper Militarism in Egypt.* The Middle East Institute. Washington, D.C.

Steavenson, Wendell. 2011. "Who Owns the Revolution?" *New Yorker*, August 1.

Stepan, Alfred. 1971. *The Military in Politics: Changing Patterns in Brazil.* Princeton, N.J.: Princeton University Press.

———. 1973. "The New Professionalism of Internal Warfare and Military Role Expansion." In *Authoritarian Brazil: Origins, Policies, and Future*, ed. Alfred Stepan. New Haven, Conn.: Yale University Press.

———. 1988. *Rethinking Military Politics: Brazil and the Southern Cone.* Princeton, N.J.: Princeton University Press.

———. 2012. "Tunisia's Transition and the Twin Tolerations." *Journal of Democracy* 23 (2): 89–103.

Stouffer, Samuel A. 1949. *The American Soldier.* Princeton, N.J.: Princeton University Press.

Sunday Telegraph. 2012. "Interview with Brigadier General Mustafa al-Chaykh." February 6.

Svolik, Milan W. 2012. *The Politics of Authoritarian Rule.* Cambridge: Cambridge University Press.

Tajine, Synda. 2014. "Tunisia Suffers Bloodiest Day in 50 Years as Terror Strikes." *Al Monitor*, July 21.

Tanner, Murray. 2002. "The Institutional Lessons of Disaster: Reorganizing the PAP After Tiananmen." In *The PLA as Organization*, ed. James Mulvenon and Andrew Yang. Santa Monica, Calif.: Rand.

Taylor, Brian. 2003. *Politics and the Russian Army: Civil-Military Relations, 1689–2000.* Cambridge: Cambridge University Press.

Tharoor, Ishan. 2011. "A History of Middle East Mercenaries." *Time*, February 23.

Thompson, Chris. 1994. "Planned International Technology Transfer: The Economic Offset Example in Saudi Arabia." *Digest of Middle East Studies* 3 (1): 1–28.

Thompson, Mark R. 2001. "To Shoot or Not to Shoot: Post-Totalitarianism in China and Eastern Europe." *Comparative Politics* 34 (1): 63–83.

Times of London. 2011. "Syrian Regime Hunts Army Defectors Who Seek to Save Civilians." August 18.

Transfeld, Mareike. 2014. *Yemen's GCC Roadmap to Nowhere.* SWP Comments 20. May.

Transparency International. 2013. *Government Defense Anti-Corruption Index 2013.*

Trinkunas, Harold A. 2005. *Crafting Civilian Control of the Military in Venezuela.* Chapel Hill: University of North Carolina Press.

Trofimov, Yaroslav. 2015. "Saudis Show Their Military Might in Yemen Conflict." *Wall Street Journal*, April 23.

Tunisia-Live. 2012. "Release of Unauthenticated Prison Sex Video Denounced in Defense of Tunisian Interior Minister." January 19.

Tsypkin, Mikhail. 2007. "Terrorism's Threat to New Democracies: The Case of Russia." In *Reforming Intelligence Obstacles to Democratic Control and Effectiveness*, ed. Thomas C. Bruneau and Steven C. Boraz, 269–300. Austin: University of Texas Press.

Ulfelder, Jay. 2005. "Contentious Collective Action and the Breakdown of Authoritarian Regimes." *International Political Science Review* 26 (3): 311–34.

Ulrichsen, Kristian Coates. 2015. "An Opportune Time for New Think Tank in Saudi Arabia." *Al-Arabiya*, March 26.

United Nations Human Rights Council. 2011. "Statement by Ms. Navi Pillay, UN High Commissioner for Human Rights to the Human Rights Council 17th Special Session on 'Situation of Human Rights in the Syrian Arab Republic, in Geneva." United Nations, http://www.ohchr.org/en/NewsEvents/Pages/DisplayNews.aspx?NewsID=11321&LangID=E.

United States Department of State. 2006. "UAE Defense Spending." October 2.

———. 2009. "Saudi Arabia Response to Blue Lantern for License 05014165." August 17.

———. 2011. "Bahrain." In *International Religious Freedom Report for 2011.*

———. 2013. "U.S. Relations with Bahrain: Fact Sheet." September 13.

United States Embassy Tunis. 2008. "Africom Visit Strong U.S. Tunisian Relations." May 30.

United States Institute of Peace. 2012. "The Challenge of Security Sector Reform in the Arab World," http://www.usip.org/events/the-challenge-security-sector-reform-in-the-arab-world.

van Dam, Nikolas. 2011. *The Struggle for Power in Syria: Politics and Society under Asad and the Ba'th Party.* 4th ed. London: I. B. Tauris.

Wagstaff-Smith, Keri. 2010. "Briefing: Offset Policies of Saudi Arabia/UAE on Course for Major Overhaul." *Jane's*, April 22.

Waldman, Peter. 1995. "Strife in Bahrain Focuses Attention on Persian Gulf Recent Street Riots Have Been Met by the Ruling Family with Armies of Foreign Mercenaries." *Globe and Mail* (Toronto), June 14.

Wall Street Journal. 2011. "Interview with Syrian President Bashar al-Assad." January 31.

Walt, Vivienne. 2011. "Chaos Threatens Tunisia's Revolution." *Time*, January 16.

———. 2013. "After Morsi Ouster in Egypt, Tunisia's Islamists Fear a Similar Fate." *Time*, July 16.

Ware, Lewis B. 1985. "The Role of the Tunisian Military in the Post-Bourguiba Era." *Middle East Journal* 39 (1).

Washington Post. 2011. "Syria Sends Tanks to Crack Down on Protesters." May 28.

Watts, Larry L. 2006. "Stressed and Strained Civil-Military Relations in Romania, but Successfully Reforming." In *Civil Military Relations in Europe: Learning from Crisis and Institutional Change*, ed. Hans Born, Marina Caparini, Karl Haltiner, and Juergen Kuhlmann. London: Routledge.

Way, Lucan. 2008. "The Real Causes of the Color Revolutions." *Journal of Democracy* 19 (3): 55–69.

Way, Lucan A., and Steven Levitsky. 2006. "The Dynamics of Autocratic Coercion After the Cold War." *Communist and Post-Communist Studies* 39 (3): 387–410.

Weber, Max. 1978 [1921]. *Economy and Society: An Outline of Interpretive Sociology*, Vol. 1. Berkeley: University of California Press.

Wedeen, Lisa. 1999. *Ambiguities of Domination*. Chicago: University of Chicago Press.

Wehrey, Frederic. 2012. "Libya's Militias Menace." *Foreign Affairs*, July 15.

Wehrey, Frederic, et al. 2009. *The Rise of the Pasdaran*. Santa Monica, Calif.: RAND.

Welch, Claude. 1992. "Military Disengagement from Politics: Paradigms, Processes, or Random Events." *Armed Forces and Society* 18 (3): 323–42.

Werenfels, Isabelle. 2009. "An Equilibrium of Instability: Dynamics and Reproduction Mechanisms of Algeria's Political System." *Confluences Mediterranee* 71 (Autumn): 179–94.

Wickham, John. 1999. *Korea on the Brink: From the "12–12 Incident" to the Kwangju Uprising, 1979–80*. Washington, D.C.: National Defense University Press.

Wikileaks. 2009. "Codel Schiff Meetings with the Defense Minister and Parliamentarians." https://wikileaks.org/plusd/cables/09TUNIS506_a.html.

Wilkinson, Steven I. 2000. "Democratic Consolidation and Failure: Lessons from Bangladesh and Pakistan." *Democratization* 7 (3): 203–26.

Willis, Michael J. 2012. *Politics and Power in the Maghreb: Algeria, Tunisia and Morocco from Independence to the Arab Spring*. New York: Columbia University Press.

Worboys, Katherine. 2007. "The Traumatic Journey from Dictatorship to Democracy: Peacekeeping Operations and Civil-Military Relations in Argentina, 1989–1999." *Armed Forces and Society* 33 (2): 149–68.

World Bank. 2015. *World Development Indicators 2015*. Washington, DC: World Bank.

Yemen Times. 2012a. "Dismissed General Al-Ahmar Finally Leaves Office." April 26.

———. 2012b. "3rd Republican Guard's Mutiny Ends." June 14.

———. 2012c. "Republican Guard Commander Abducted, Sparks Tension Between Khawlan and Sanhan." July 2.

York, Steve. 2007. *Orange Revolution*. New York: Cinema Guild.

Young, Karen. 2014. *The Political Economy of Energy, Finance, and Security in the United Arab Emirates*. London: Palgrave Macmillan.

YouTube. 2010. "Saudi Armed Forces," November 22, https://www.youtube.com /watch?v=TUo8vddTPsM.

———. 2011. "Promotional Video for UAE Armed Forces," June 23, https://www.you tube.com/watch?v=XehrQusF8Po.

———. 2013. "UAE Armed Forces." September 15, https://www.youtube.com /watch?v=V3kuqVvFHwY.

Zisser, Eyal. 2002. "The Syrian Army on the Domestic and External Fronts." In *Armed Forces in the Middle East: Politics and Strategy*, ed. Barry M. Rubin and Thomas A. Keaney. London: Frank Cass.

Zybertowicz, Andrzej. 2007. "Transformation of the Polish Secret Services: From Authoritarian to Informal Power Networks." In *Democratic Control of Intelligence Services: Containing Rogue Elephants*, ed. Hans Born and Marina Caparini. Aldershot: Ashgate.

CONTRIBUTORS

Holger Albrecht is associate professor of political science at the American University in Cairo and research fellow at Harvard University's Belfer Center for Science and International Affairs. He has also been a Jennings Randolph Senior Fellow at the United States Institute of Peace. His research interests include political-military relations, regime change, and political opposition in the Middle East and North Africa. He is the author of *Raging Against the Machine: Political Opposition Under Authoritarianism in Egypt* and the editor of *Contentious Politics in the Middle East.*

Risa A. Brooks is associate professor of political science at Marquette University. Her research focuses on issues related to civil-military relations, military effectiveness, and militant and terrorist organizations; she also has a regional interest in the Middle East. She is the author of *Shaping Strategy: The Civil-Military Politics of Strategic Assessment* and the editor (with Elizabeth Stanley) of *Creating Military Power: The Sources of Military Effectiveness* and has authored many articles in the field of international security.

Chérine Chams El-Dine is assistant professor of political science in the Faculty of Economics and Political Science at Cairo University. From September 2012 to January 2013, she was a research fellow at the German Institute for International and Security Affairs in Berlin. In 2011–2012, she was a lecturer in Middle Eastern politics at the Institute of Arab and Islamic Studies, University of Exeter. Her current research focuses on the resilience of authoritarianism and the democratization process in the Middle East, including political-business elite connections and civil-military relations, especially in Egypt and Iraq.

Virginie Collombier is research fellow at the European University Institute in Florence, where she coordinates a research project on social and political change in Egypt, Tunisia, and Libya. Her work focuses in particular on social transformations in post-Qaddafi Libya, where she has been conducting regular fieldwork since late 2012. Prior to this, she worked extensively on Egyptian politics and transformations within the regime before and after the 2011 revolution.

Aurel Croissant is professor of political science at the University of Heidelberg. His research interests include comparative politics, especially in East and Southeast Asia; theoretical and empirical research on democratization; civil-military relationships; terrorism; and political violence. He has published widely on issues of civil-military relations in autocracies, democratizing countries, and new democracies and is directing a multiyear research program on the military and politics in autocracies and democracies. He is coeditor of the journal *Democratization* and the author of *Military and Civilian Politics* (in German) and *Civilian Control and Democratization in Asia*.

Philippe Droz-Vincent is professor of political science and international relations at the University of Grenoble and Sciences-Po, Grenoble, France. He is the author of *The Middle East: Authoritarian Regimes and Stalled Societies* (in French) and *Dizziness of Power: The American Moment in the Middle East* (in French), along with numerous articles on civil-military relations in the Middle East.

Kevin Koehler received his doctorate from the European University Institute in Florence in 2013 and is currently assistant professor of political science at the American University in Cairo. He has been a research associate in the Department of War Studies, King's College, London. His research interests include political-military relations under autocracy, authoritarianism, and regime change as well as the reconfiguration of political regimes in the Middle East after the Arab Spring.

Fred H. Lawson is professor of government at Mills College. He is the author of *Bahrain: The Modernization of Autocracy* and *Global Security Watch: Syria* as well as other studies of governance and political-economic transformation in the contemporary Middle East and North Africa. From 2010 to 2012, he was president of the Syrian Studies Association.

Shana Marshall is associate director and research instructor at the Institute for Middle East Studies, George Washington University, and has held postdoctoral fellowships at the Crown Center for Middle East Studies, Brandeis University, and the Woodrow Wilson School of Public and International Affairs, Princeton University. Her research interests include the global arms trade, U.S. defense policy, and the political economy of military entrepreneurship in the Middle East. She is the author of several articles on regional militaries, including "Jordan's Military-Industrial Complex and the Middle East's New Model Army," *Middle East Report* (2013).

Dorothy Ohl is a doctoral candidate in political science at George Washington University, where her research focuses on military responses to domestic unrest. She has lived in Egypt, Jordan, and Kuwait as well as in Oman, where she conducted research supported by a Fulbright fellowship. Prior to her doctoral studies, she worked with Washington-based organizations to support economic and political reform in the Middle East.

David Pion-Berlin is professor of political science at the University of California, Riverside. He is a Latin Americanist widely known for his research and writings on civil-military relations, defense, security, political repression, and human rights. Among his publications are *Transforming Latin America: The International and Domestic Origins of Change*, coauthored with Craig Arceneaux; *Civil-Military Relations in Latin America: New Analytical Perspectives*; and *Through Corridors of Power: Institutions and Civil-Military Relations in Argentina*. His latest book is *Organización de la defensa y control civil de las fuerzas armadas en América Latina*, coedited with José Manuel Ugarte. Pion-Berlin's articles have appeared in *Comparative Politics*, *Comparative Political Studies*, the *Journal of Democracy*, the *Latin American Research Review*, and *Armed Forces and Society*.

Tobias Selge is a doctoral candidate and lecturer in comparative and Middle East politics in the Institute of Political Science at the University of Heidelberg. His research interests include civil-military relations, authoritarian regimes, and democratization studies as well as political Islam. His regional focus is the Middle East and North Africa. In his doctoral dissertation, he develops and tests a decision-theory model to explain military behavior during authoritarian regime crises.

Robert Springborg is professor (retired) in the Department of National Security Affairs at the Naval Postgraduate School in Monterey, California.

Previously he held the MBI Al Jaber Chair in Middle East Studies at the School of Oriental and African Studies in London, where he was also director of the London Middle East Institute. His publications include *Family Power and Politics in Egypt* (University of Pennsylvania Press, 1982), *Mubarak's Egypt: Fragmentation of the Political Order*, several editions of *Politics in the Middle East* (with James A. Bill), *Legislative Politics in the Arab World* (with Abdo I. Baaklini and Guilain P. Denoeux), and, with Clement M. Henry, *Globalization and the Politics of Development in the Middle East.*

INDEX